# Tabernacles of Clay

# TABERNACLES OF CLAY

*Sexuality and Gender in Modern Mormonism*

TAYLOR G. PETREY

THE UNIVERSITY OF NORTH CAROLINA PRESS

*Chapel Hill*

Set in Arno
by codeMantra, Inc.

Cover illustration: Rainbow colors © iStockPhoto/Sonya_illustration;
church © iStockPhoto/Mlenny

*Manufactured in the United States of America*

The University of North Carolina Press has been a member
of the Green Press Initiative since 2003.

LIBRARY OF CONGRESS CATALOGING-IN-PUBLICATION DATA
Names: Petrey, Taylor G., author.
Title: Tabernacles of clay : sexuality and gender in
modern Mormonism / Taylor G. Petrey.
Description: Chapel Hill : University of North Carolina Press, [2020] |
Includes bibliographical references and index.
Identifiers: LCCN 2019049798 | ISBN 9781469656212 (cloth : alk. paper) |
ISBN 9781469656229 (paperback : alk. paper) | ISBN 9781469656236 (ebook)
Subjects: LCSH: Church of Jesus Christ of Latter-day Saints—Doctrines—
History—20th century. | Church of Jesus Christ of Latter-day Saints—
Doctrines—History—21st century. | Gender identity—Religious
aspects—Church of Jesus Christ of Latter-day Saints. | Sexual orientation—
Religious aspects. | Mormon Church—United States—History—
20th century. | Mormon Church—Political activity—United States.
Classification: LCC BX8643.S49 P48 2020 | DDC 261.8/3570882893—dc23
LC record available at https://lccn.loc.gov/2019049798

*To Stacey Ford*

# Contents

# Acknowledgments

This project was both a detour in my career and an inevitable culmination of past events. I certainly did not start out my study of religion more than two decades ago with something like this in mind, though in hindsight it now feels like everything was leading in this direction. During my final years of graduate school working on gender in early Christianity, I began to reflect on what the implications of my research and studies would be for Mormonism. I started writing essays on philosophy of religion, Mormon theology, and gender theory in my early career. But when I went looking for a good history of Mormon concepts of gender and sexuality, I usually found a brief rehearsal of a handful of authoritative statements, and that was it. So, I had the idea that I needed to investigate more. I applied to the Women's Studies in Religion Program at Harvard University for my sabbatical to develop the idea. I cried when Ann Braude called to let me know my application had been accepted. I cried for joy, I am sure, but I think I also cried for fear. Now, I had to do it. No turning back.

The project started informed but unformed. I thought about charting the story from the beginning of Mormonism or maybe with polygamy. Perhaps the period after polygamy would be a crucial turning point in my analysis. Of course, all of these periods are important. I expect that future scholars will take them up in greater detail. But over the course of my research I became interested in a genealogy of contemporary beliefs that gender is an essential feature of one's identity.

What I found surprised me at first. It turned out that while Latter-day Saints have often expressed the values of gender and sexual essentialism, I started to see that this was a rhetorical effort to cover over a different ontology of gender and sexuality. Rather than seeing these categories as essential and fixed, Latter-day Saint leaders often talked about them as malleable and fluid—and showed that heterosexual desire and heteronormative roles are especially vulnerable to change. I needed to tell that story.

Researching and writing the book presented several challenges. My primary training used a different set of research skills. Learning to work in archives and to write illustrative narratives rather than close textual exegesis and managing an embarrassing richness of sources were all new experiences. Mastering a new field of scholarship on North American religion (and making new friends in the process) was one of the pleasures of the challenge. No doubt the project comes up short in many ways due to my own limitations, but I hope to have made a contribution to American religious studies, the history of sexuality, gender studies, and Mormon studies.

Among the issues that I need to address up front is the new style guide that the church put out in 2018 that declared that the term "Mormon" is no longer appropriate. Scholars and presses face a dilemma of either conforming to long-standing convention and widespread acceptance and recognition of the label or honoring the present wishes of the church's leadership to retire the term because of a preference for the full name of the church. In the end, I decided that "Mormon" is appropriate for my historical project because it was the term that the primary characters of the history accepted and touted for themselves. They were Mormons, and I chose to use their self-designation.

I was fortunate to work with several collections of archival materials, including those held in library archives at the Church History Library in Salt Lake City and in the Marriott Library Special Collections at the University of Utah. The librarians there and those at my home institution and at Harvard were incredibly helpful. I am also grateful to those who have made archives online of relevant source material, including Connell O'Donovan. Some of the documents that I rely on come from collections of documents that were not intended to be made public, including letters and memos between church leaders. In the end, I decided to make use of them because in all cases the documents are available to the public and have been discussed by media outlets and other historians.

The essential resources to get started and complete this project were provided by the Women's Studies in Religion Program at Harvard University and by Kalamazoo College. I owe debts of gratitude to many for listening to and reading my half-baked ideas, including those in my graduate seminar at Harvard Divinity School. I am especially grateful for the patience and guidance of my mentors and colleagues at the WSRP who taught me how to develop new skills, including Ann Braude, Catherine Brekus, Lynne Gerber, Rosalyn LaPier, Gwynn Kessler, and Chang Shen. Special thanks go to Tracy Wall for excellent administrative support and friendship. Claudia Bushman gave crucial support to get this project started. Many thanks are due others at Harvard who met to discuss my ideas or assisted me in my fellowship, including David Holland, Amy Hollywood, Mark Jordan, Karen King, and Laurel

Thatcher Ulrich. Numerous individuals read drafts or provided beneficial conversations or research material, including Seth Anderson, Matthew Bowman, Cary Crall, Michael Ferguson, Clyde Ford, Alexandra Griffin, Laurie Lee Hall, J. B. Haws, Joseph Hollist, Derek Knox, John Lyon, Tania Lyon, Sara Moslener, Connell O'Donovan, Mike Pope, Laura Portwood-Stacer, Gregory Prince, Joseph Stuart, Josh Weed, Heather White, Kendall Wilcox, and other friends who know who they are. I also thank the anonymous reviewers of the manuscript for their invaluable advice. In addition, I'd like to thank Becca Cain for her work copyediting the proofs and compiling the index, and all those at University of North Carolina Press for their close attention to every aspect of the book's production.

I wish to thank my beloved partner, Stacey Ford, who battled breast cancer and endured a long-distance relationship as I was researching and writing but who provided unfailing support, enthusiasm, and encouragement at every step of this process. Thank you for marrying me. Special thanks also go to my children, who bring me unending joy and pride.

*Tabernacles of Clay*

*Introduction*

# MODERN MORMONISM AND GENDER THEORY IN CONTEXT

*And now, if there are faults they are the mistakes of men.*

BOOK OF MORMON, title page

Like many other conservative religious groups, the leaders of the Church of Jesus Christ of Latter-day Saints (LDS/Mormon) have focused significant attention on cultural shifts of gender and sexuality in the period since World War II. As the church's leaders sought to police boundaries and assert their teachings publicly, they engaged in repeated clashes over social values with other interest groups and even with their own members. Their conservative teachings emerged in the context of larger social changes ushered in by the civil rights movement, the sexual revolution, feminism, and gay, lesbian, and trans rights movements. How did Mormon leaders respond to these changes, and how have they been shaped by them? What concerns have guided their views? This book argues that church leaders pitted themselves against these movements by offering competing theories of the nature of sexuality and sexual difference. These views were then communicated through preaching campaigns for sexual purity, gender roles, and marriage; the deployment of psychological approaches to "cure" homosexuality; and political activism against equal rights for women and same-sex marriage.

Latter-day Saints form a significant bloc in contemporary conservative Christianity in America, and their views about gender and sexuality warrant greater scholarly attention. Scholars have increasingly told the story of the broader American conservative response to the changing cultural dynamics ushered in by liberal social movements, yet Latter-day Saints are frequently left out of these historical accounts.[1] Mormonism is situated within this larger conservative family and developed its own views in tandem with conservative religious allies, but Mormonism's story is still a distinctive conservative articulation of gender and sexuality. Its unique theological resources, its independent scriptural and ecclesiastical authority, and its powerful centralized institution make for a different kind of engagement with gender and sexuality than that of other conservative Christian movements. For instance, biblical inerrancy and biblical literalism—two values important to evangelical and fundamentalist views on gender and sexuality—are only marginally important to Mormons.[2] These differences also mean that appeals to Christian theology or biblical hermeneutics serve little explanatory value in Mormon teaching. In spite of these differences, the Latter-day Saint tradition remains a profoundly useful example of a conservative religious response to shifting cultural values that can provide larger insight about religious engagement with change and the history of sexuality.

Rather than holding to a monolithic "traditional" view, Mormonism has been beset by competing theories of sexual difference over the past several decades. This book reveals a central tension that is threaded throughout this history—an insight that marks a distinctive contribution to the study of Mormonism, at the very least, and has larger implications for the study of religion in America, gender studies, and the history of sexuality. On the one hand, Mormon leaders have embraced the ideals of gender essentialism— the belief that there are fixed differences between male and female, which represent the natural and divine order of sexual difference. On the other hand, Mormon leaders have often taught that the differences between male and female are malleable and contingent, and so they must be guarded with strict social, ecclesiastical, and legal norms and sanctions. These theories are not timeless truths nor ahistorical doctrines that derive unmediated from Mormon texts or cosmology. Rather, they have emerged within a particular historical context in response to particular developments. Mormon leaders' claims about gender, race, romance, kinship, and sexuality are implicated in extra-theological historical and political trends that shape these ideas.

In order to explore these themes about sexual difference, this book looks at three areas of activity by LDS church officials in the modern period. One primary area of focus is public preaching and teaching, including sermons, manuals, and other literature about racial and gender purity, homosexuality, and marriage. There are extensive discussions of racial separatism, women's roles, and the Mormon concept of the "patriarchal order of marriage" in this period. LDS leaders warned their church members about the consequences of eroding the boundaries between male and female and black and white, especially in the earlier decades after World War II. They identified the possible threats to the purity of marriage as coming from a relaxation of both racial boundaries and gender roles.

Second, the book explores the history of new institutions and modes of knowledge to address concerns about gender, including homosexuality. Beginning in the middle of the twentieth century, the church launched new programs designed to strengthen patriarchal leadership in the home and devised spiritual or psychological treatments for "the homosexual." Mormonism responded to the cultural stimulus about this new concern of a weakening masculinity in American culture by mingling a psychological paradigm with religious frameworks for human behavior. In this period, Mormons developed an extensive apparatus for eliciting confessions, prescribing regimens of spiritual and physical practice, training leaders and counselors, enlisting families and friends to "support" the homosexual, and employing a cadre of professionals for their treatment.

Third, the church engaged in various sociopolitical interventions, including opposition to civil rights and the Equal Rights Amendment, and waged regional battles against same-sex marriage, such as California's Proposition 8. These countermovements to the feminist and sexual revolutions coalesced in the context of postwar American ideologies of gender and sexuality, especially within the so-called Religious Right. Mormons joined with other conservative Christians in these political campaigns to create and preserve "traditional" roles for women and negative social stigma and unequal citizenship for gays and lesbians. LDS church leaders opposed a U.S. constitutional amendment for equal rights for women and the decriminalization of "sodomy" and engaged in a multi-decade political battle to oppose same-sex marriage, including advocating for a U.S. constitutional amendment to enshrine heterosexual marriage. These political endeavors often enjoyed short-term success.

At this point, it is also useful to delimit the scope of this book, which is about Mormonism in the United States and treats only the Church of Jesus Christ of Latter-day Saints, leaving aside the smaller groups and rival branches of the movement. Though the church was expanding its borders geographically outside of the American West and the United States in the postwar period, its cultural roots and political interests remained primarily American. Further, this book focuses almost exclusively on the senior leaders of the church, who have been overwhelmingly older, male, and white

Americans. The choice of focus on the public activity of these particular leaders is in part because of the authority they wield to produce Mormonism's teachings.[3] These teachings are quoted in church publications, disseminated among members, and cited by other church leaders to define the direction that the church takes. They also have incredible longevity in these roles—often spanning multiple decades—granting them both a relative stability of vision and control of the direction of the church. Sociological, ethnographic, and anthropological studies, as well as those that focus on different centers of authority, such as Mormon scholars or popular teachers, could reveal a different history from the one I discuss here and competing interests. Further, a focus on these other groups could result in a different periodization for shifts in Mormon thought. I make occasional reference to these other groups, yet the teachings of senior male leaders represent widely shared views of their time, especially in aggregate. Their history is important to tell. With such limitations in mind, the story I offer is a heuristic one, a particular problem of sexual difference more than a comprehensive history of modern Mormonism per se, with all of its competing characters, narratives, and circumstances. This is the history of a discourse and how those ideas have been put into practice.

Some initial definitions of these leaders' titles are useful to orient readers who are unfamiliar with LDS ecclesiology. Within the senior-most ranks, there are committees (quorums) of church leaders with various responsibilities. The highest governing authority of the church is its president, who is also given the titles prophet, seer, and revelator. He comes into this role as the longest serving apostle, moving up the ranks as others pass away. After the president, two others (usually apostles) join him in the First Presidency, the highest governing body. The Quorum of the Twelve Apostles is the committee that carries out the direction of the First Presidency but also defines much of the way that the church uses its vast human and financial resources. The positions of president and apostle are the only ones with a lifetime appointment, and the apostles generally select a new colleague from a pool of other high-ranking leaders shortly after one has died. Below the apostles are various governing bodies of full-time paid church leaders known as the Seventy—though the affairs of the church are now vast enough that there are more than seventy men involved in this work in sub-quorums. Below them, church leadership positions are regionally bounded and staffed by unpaid appointees who serve for a period and are then replaced. There are some senior female leaders in the church who oversee the women's and children's organizations and report to the senior male leaders, but otherwise the general leadership is entirely male. All of these leadership positions are supported by a vast bureaucracy of professionals and experts in their respective fields.

## MORMONISM AND SEXUAL DIFFERENCE IN MODERNITY

The Church of Jesus Christ of Latter-day Saints has its roots in the nineteenth century under its founder, Joseph Smith Jr. (d. 1844), and his successor for the largest group of early followers, Brigham Young (d. 1877). After Smith's assassination at the hands of an anti-Mormon mob in Illinois, Young established a theocratic kingdom in the Utah Territory that became notorious for publicly practicing plural marriage. The main branch of the Utah church began to abandon the practice in 1890. The first half of the twentieth century then was marked by Mormonism's efforts to shed its polygamous heritage and assimilate into Progressive Era American culture.[4] Historian Thomas Alexander called this an "age of transition," as Mormonism redefined itself and sought after American respectability—if not the mainstream.[5] In a well-established pattern of modernity, Mormon efforts to earn respectability were manifest in the adoption of broader American sexual norms.[6]

Modern Mormonism—the focus of this book—refers to the Mormon confrontation and confluence with modernity and globalization after World War II. Modernity, as defined here, certainly stretches back to at least the Enlightenment in the eighteenth and nineteenth centuries. Mormonism emerged in this environment where premodernity and modernity intermingled. Still, Mormonism and modernity confronted one another afresh in the second half of the twentieth century. Scholars have increasingly treated this phase of Mormon history as a distinctive period.[7] Historians Gregory A. Prince and W. M. Robert Wright located "the rise of modern Mormonism" under the leadership of President David O. McKay (church president 1951–70).[8] There is no single date that marks this transition, and there was no particular moment of a decisive paradigm shift from one era to the next.[9] As a symbol of this transition, however, McKay was a charismatic, clean-shaven, and outwardly minded church president who quietly shed much of Mormonism's distinctive traditions and repackaged its message for a new global church. *Time* magazine wrote of him, "McKay was an affable new image of Mormonism to a world that had previously seen the Mormon leaders as dour, dark suited figures."[10] He reformed the church by redesigning its rituals, consolidating power in the male leadership, and redefining the message of Mormonism to be about neighborliness, strong families, and civic and social goodness.

Many of the defining features of contemporary Mormonism emerged in the mid-twentieth century. Mormon attendance at church meetings climbed from just 21 percent in 1921 to 36 percent in 1965, representing a revival of interest among church members that held steady for most of the next fifty years.[11] The church grew from converts as well. In 1947, the church reached a significant milestone when it claimed one million members of record worldwide. Membership numbers climbed to more than fifteen million globally up until the present.

Church teachings transformed as well to respond to new social conditions. Specifically, Mormonism was not shielded from the broader American scene of changing gender norms. Gender roles had been seriously disrupted during World War II. While millions of men were off fighting, women went to work in manufacturing, sought higher education for professions that had previously excluded them, and furthered the trends toward birth control and family planning that began in the Great Depression. These changes brought about greater regional and economic mobility for young women and the possibility of greater sexual freedom. Divorce became more common. Rates of marriage and childbirth tumbled. The social legitimacy of interracial marriage, homosexuality, birth control, and recreational sex increased in liberal regions.[12]

After the war, conservatives launched a postwar religious revival.[13] They believed gender relations would soon return to an imagined "tradition"—home and family life for women and steady income for male workers.[14] These messages about "what we're fighting for" pervaded film, advertising, and government, promising both freedom and domestic bliss. Men were promised a job and a supportive wife who would make them feel safe and would not question their outbursts or decisions. Women were promised a loving husband who would protect them and their children as he had done as a valiant soldier. The postwar period produced a vision of Americanness centered on an iconography of the home, family, and the new suburban consumerist lifestyle.[15] The GI Bill, tax reform, and propaganda commodified marriage and male leadership in the home as the key to emotional and material security.[16] Religious revivalists warned that national security was on the line as well if Americans did not live up to sexual standards.[17]

Mormons engaged these broader social changes and crafted their own conservative responses. McKay joined other religious and civic leaders in a religious reformation for a new American home after the war. In 1945, he taught, "The real source of security of our nation rests in the well ordered, properly conducted homes."[18] Since the end of polygamy, Mormons had turned away from dynastic kingdom building and toward a new emphasis on personal virtues and moral living. McKay oversaw reforms in the church that increasingly emphasized the importance of the patriarchal home as the divine model for household governance, such as the renewed Family Home Evening program. In responding to the various social ills that existed after the war, whether poverty, crime, or sexual deviance, Mormon leaders believed that stronger male leadership in the home was the basis of any solution. They emphasized distinctive LDS teachings on marriage ("sealing," in LDS parlance), an ordinance performed in LDS temples that linked families for time and eternity, bound in the patriarchal order by covenant.[19] The new Mormon ideology of family would become, in Lawrence Foster's terms, "more Victorian than the Victorians."[20]

Yet, Foster's framing of modern Mormonism as anachronistic or nostalgic for the nineteenth century in its articulation of gender and sexual norms does not do sufficient justice to the topic. Modern Mormons were not simply appealing to the past or rejecting the values of the sexual revolution and the counterculture of the 1960s. Rather, modern Mormon leaders began to speak about sexuality and gender in the modernist terms of psychological development, therapeutic values, and personal fulfillment. They promised health and happiness for those who conformed to strict gender norms and sexual restraint. This psychological turn in Mormonism is a distinctive feature of this period, mingling a broader therapeutic culture with scriptural and prophetic tradition. Modern Mormon views of gender and sexuality were products of the mid-twentieth century, even when they drew on and appealed to earlier periods.

This book sets off in a different direction from what has come before in the scholarship on Mormonism while building on these earlier studies. Previous scholarship on Mormonism and gender-related issues in the modern period has tended to represent one of three different approaches. In the first, scholars have treated Mormon views about gender and sexuality as a theory of essentialism—the belief that there are universal traits that make men and women fundamentally different from one another. This book will significantly challenge this paradigm, but it is easy to see why it has been so persuasive. In 1995, the church issued the brief authoritative statement "The Family: A Proclamation to the World." According to this document of Mormon orthodoxy, "gender is an essential characteristic of individual pre-mortal, mortal, and eternal identity and purpose." The use of the term "essential" supports the description of Mormonism's theory of gender as "essentialism." This binary division of male and female bodies and roles represents both a natural and divinely ordained system. Citing numerous historical examples, Terryl Givens describes a Mormon "doctrine of gender essentialism" and states that the teaching that "gender is eternal" is a "position that has never varied in Mormon theology."[21] I will argue that the record is far more complex, with Mormons advocating for a particular kind of gender and sexual malleability and fluidity (still rooted in heteronormativity) in this period alongside appeals to gender essentialism.

In the second approach, scholars have evaluated Mormon attitudes about gender and sexuality in this period as representative of the degree of Mormon assimilation or rejection of broader American culture. Armand Mauss and Gordon Shepherd and Gary Shepherd typify this sociological approach in their classic studies.[22] Mauss argues that Mormons have vacillated between trying to gain respectability through assimilation and trying to gain distinctiveness through separatism and retrenchment. He suggests that the Americanization of Mormonism in the "age of transition" began to reverse course in the second half of the twentieth century, a new period of retrenchment in Mormonism beginning around 1960 and peaking in the 1980s and 1990s. Mormons, he argues, ramped up the aspects that marked their values and identity as "peculiar" or distinctive, including focus on the Book of Mormon, temples, modern prophets and priesthood authority, and gender and the family.[23] Mauss's analysis frames Mormon liberalization as assimilation and conservatism as retrenchment. But Mormon conservatism is not isolationist or peculiar, especially with respect to its values about sexuality, gender, and family life in the second half of the twentieth century.[24] Sociologists Shepherd and Shepherd have offered a complementary theory about Mormon identity, noting "the LDS Church has continued to move toward conservative Protestantism."[25] Rather than seeing this as either assimilation or retrenchment, Shepherd and Shepherd call it "accommodation."[26] In this sense, Mormonism can both be distinctive from liberal churches and secular culture and share a great deal with the theological and political conservatism of evangelicals and Protestant fundamentalists. The degree of Mormon assimilation, retrenchment, or accommodation is not my primary question, but accommodation provides a useful lens for describing the particular ways that Mormons expressed conservative ideals about gender, sexuality, and family life in this period.

Women's, feminist, and gay and lesbian histories characterize the third major scholarly approach to gender-related issues. They seek to explain and evaluate asymmetrical power dynamics within Mormonism.[27] Women's histories have focused on the diminished roles for women in Mormon culture and the church over the course of the twentieth century and on the increased emphasis on motherhood.[28] While Mormon women once had greater opportunities for spiritual leadership, ritual life, and social activism, these were whittled away in the twentieth century. The women's organization the Relief Society—once a powerful force in the Progressive Era—was gutted of its authority and resources as it became a "companion organization to the priesthood." As historian Dave Hall notes, "Mormon women were left with few legitimate alternatives to the idealized and much touted domesticity of the postwar period."[29] Other scholars have chronicled the ways that women found meaning and agency in domestic roles.[30] Still others have discussed the greater level of women's personal autonomy and the rise of egalitarian marriages in Mormonism since the 1980s.[31] In all of these approaches, the guiding research question has hinged on identifying sites of agency (or lack thereof) in women's roles.[32]

Historians of same-sex intimacy and attitudes about homosexuality in the LDS context have similarly focused on analyses of power. In order to explain the negative attitudes toward and harsh treatment of those in same-sex relationships, these studies characterize modern LDS teachings as homophobic. Pioneers in this research like D. Michael Quinn and Connell O'Donovan charted a gloomy history from "relative tolerance" of same-sex intimacy in an earlier era to the rise of homophobia in contemporary LDS thought.[33] Quinn sets this homophobia in a broader postwar American context of Cold War hype. Other scholars note shifts in official LDS rhetoric in recent years that indicate greater "sympathy" toward homosexuality.[34] The most recent book in this vein is Gregory A. Prince's *Gay Rights and the Mormon Church: Intended Actions, Unintended Consequences*.[35] Especially in the case of Prince, these studies often argue from "the biological paradigm" of fixed and determined sexual identity.[36]

The separate treatment of "women" on the one hand and "gay and lesbian" sexuality on the other obscures a fundamental overlap between these two issues, not to mention the absence of attention to masculinity and males. Further, the focus on agency as the central analytic point has left Mormon concepts of gender and sexuality undertheorized. Alan Michael William's article "Mormon and Queer at the Crossroads" adduces, "The issue of homosexuality for the Church is, at its core, about gender." He continues by suggesting that the most important aspect of gender that same-sex relationships disrupt is the "ecclesiastical relationship between men and women" and ties it to the question of women's ordination to the priesthood—a practice currently prohibited in LDS teaching.[37]

Queer theory links the issue of gender and sexual difference to the issue of sexuality as related subjects of inquiry. Once a term of derision, scholars and activists have reclaimed "queer" as a mode of analysis and an identity that resists fixed categorization. While this approach traces its origins to feminist and gay and lesbian analysis—and holds its goals in affinity with those fields—queer theory takes as its subject something more fundamental, namely, the categories and distinctions between sexes, genders, sexualities, races, abilities, and so on.[38] This paradigm challenges the idea of the natural and self-evident and instead seeks to historicize and question claims about essential and stable identities by looking at where those boundaries wear thin. This method is the starting point for the present study. The supposed differences of sexes, genders, and races are historical and ideological, not natural and fixed. Poststructuralist queer approaches are attuned to the failure of categories; the fluidity of bodies, sexualities, and identities; and the genealogies of what is often taken for granted. This book builds on sociological approaches to gender, as well as on women's history and gay and lesbian history, but views these identity categories (and others) as the object of historical and theoretical inquiry. The modern genealogies of gender and sexuality must be analyzed together to produce the best explanation of Mormon approaches to these topics. This book then addresses a gap in the history of American sexuality by offering a detailed discussion of the interrelationship between gender and sexuality of a particular religious tradition.[39]

## THEORETICAL CONSIDERATIONS OF
## SEXUALITY AND SEXUAL DIFFERENCE

There are several reasons to bring Mormonism into conversation with queer theoretical approaches. One is that there is some theoretical confluence between queer theories of sexual subjectivity and conservative responses to homosexuality that rely on malleability, contestation, uncertainly, and fluidity. In one analysis, scholar Ludger H. Viefues-Bailey argues that conservative Christians do not see stability in heterosexual difference but "a drama of contestation over agency, aggression, power, and submission."[40] Conservative Christians worry about masculinity and femininity "in crisis."[41] This notion of an unstable sexuality and sexual difference overlaps with queer theory's anti-essentialist view. Putting conservative discourse about homosexuality into stark relief, scholar Lynne Gerber has noted, "There is something a little queer about the ex-gay movement." She points out that both queer theorists, like Judith Butler, and ex-gay advocates, like Exodus

International, are wary of "nature" as a source of gender essentialism and reject the homo/hetero binary as inadequate to describe human experience. Gerber does not suggest that these two movements are the same—they certainly have drastically different sexual ethics and political aims—but that the ex-gay movement is "queerish."[42] Tanya Erzen has similarly noted the overlap between queer theoretical accounts of sexuality and those in ex-gay and conversion ideologies.[43]

Queer theorists aren't the only ones noticing a similarity between their work and ex-gay approaches. Activists who teach about the possibility to "overcome" same-sex desires often cite queer theory's anti-essentialist views, especially with respect to sexual fluidity. In 2008, advocates for reparative therapy took note of University of Utah psychologist Lisa Diamond's book *Sexual Fluidity: Understanding Women's Love and Desire.*[44] Diamond's book tracks the relationships of women over the course of a decade and challenges the utility of sexual labels, concluding that desires are more fluid than fixed in actual practice. LDS scholar A. Dean Byrd was among those conservatives citing her work as evidence for the effectiveness of reparative therapy. At the time, he was the head of the ex-gay organization the National Association for Research and Therapy of Homosexuality (NARTH) and was former director of LDS Social Services, the church's counseling agency that provided, among other things, psychological treatment for same-sex attraction. Diamond publicly repudiated the misrepresentation of her work, but Byrd insisted, "NARTH's view is that people can adapt any way they want and there is freedom of choice. . . . If it says 'fluidity' it says 'fluidity.' How you interpret it is something else."[45] To an extent, Byrd's analysis was correct—how one interprets sexual fluidity is precisely the theoretical question at stake between queer and conservative approaches to sexual difference and sexuality. At the same time, his emphasis on voluntary adaptation and freedom describes a theory of sexual malleability more than sexual fluidity. These concepts are not unrelated—fluidity and malleability are sibling theories of sexual subjectivity that compete, like Jacob and Esau, for the birthright of psychoanalysis. While sexual fluidity attempts to describe the phenomenon of nonbinary sexual choice and identity in sociological and psychological terms, sexual malleability suggests that choice and intentional practices play a significant role in the formation of a sexual self.

Byrd's advocacy for sexual malleability is not just an anomaly in LDS teachings but strikes at the heart of what defines much of modern Mormonism. His view represents just one instance of how ideas about sexual malleability—and, as we will see, also gender fluidity and malleability—have been central to modern Mormon theories of sexual difference. When LDS church leaders talk about sexual and gender identity, these identities are not a question of essentialist ontology but of achievement. In this understanding, male and female identity is not secured or defined by the possession of a male or female body (or soul) alone but must be molded like clay to be socially legible as "male" or "female." Their advocacy for strong social, ecclesiastical, and legal norms guarding the gender boundary expresses anxiety about the possibility of blurring the lines between male and female. As Byrd put it in one of his books, heterosexuality must be encouraged in order for it to take.[46] Yet, this fluidity is not just a danger but also a tool. In this therapeutic approach, sexual fluidity is the solution for those wayward individuals to find their way back into heterosexuality or other approved gender norms with the proper help.

Queer theory certainly does not share these normative views, but it does help to explain the genealogy of sexual and gender fluidity, theories of malleability and self-fashioning, and a non-essentialist ontology of identity.[47] The canonical figures of Michel Foucault, Thomas Laqueur, Eve Sedgwick, and Judith Butler set some groundwork for explaining sexuality and gender in modernity. Siobhan B. Somerville is another who brought these insights to bear on modern notions of race—an idea to which I will return. These theorists have pointed out that modernity itself is characterized by a tension between competing approaches to human subjectivity. On one hand, Foucault charted the history of sexuality in modernity as gravitating toward fixed identities. His evaluation of the origins of homosexuality in the modern era remains influential: "Homosexuality appeared as one of the forms of sexuality when it was transposed from the practice of sodomy onto a kind of interior androgyny, a hermaphrodism of the soul. The sodomite had been a temporary aberration, the homosexual was now a species."[48] Foucault then suggested that modernity brought a paradigm shift in thinking about sexuality as a fixed aspect of human identity.

As Foucault had argued with respect to the modern origins of sexuality, Laqueur proposes that the notion of a fixed human "sex" was also a modern invention. "Sometime in the eighteenth century," he explains, "sex as we know it was invented. The reproductive organs went from being paradigmatic sites for displaying hierarchy . . . to being the foundation of incommensurable difference."[49] In this bold historical gloss, Laqueur submits that prior to the modern era, there was "one sex" that was manifest in hierarchical differences between men, who were warmer, harder, and dryer, and women, who were cooler, softer, and wetter. The premodern "one-sex" body was fungible and could experience slippage. The new scientific arguments that developed in modernity posited a "two-sex" model where men and women were not different in degree but in kind. In the "two-sex" model, there were essential characteristics that divided the sexes between male and female.

The modernity hypothesis then contended that there was a major paradigm shift toward fixed sexuality and sexual difference in the eighteenth and nineteenth centuries. However, the distinction between modern and premodern remains unsettled. Foucault's subsequent volumes in his *History of Sexuality* series trace a genealogy of sexuality as far back as classical Greece instead of remaining in the modern era, as originally planned. Further, the division between modern and premodern thinking about sexual difference in modernity was never a clean break from the past. Even Laqueur admits, "One-sex thinking flourished still. The play of difference never came to rest."[50] He sees Sigmund Freud, for instance, as an inheritor of both the Enlightenment "two-sex" model and the premodern "one-sex" model in his account of a singular psychological subjectivity. And not just Freud. In the 1930s, anthropologists, endocrinologists, and other psychologists challenged the "two-sex" theory of natural or inherent sexual differences by pointing to fluidity as the norm.[51]

Eve Sedgwick further complicates these claims about a break between modernity and premodernity in her account of modern sexuality. She also notes that fluidity persists in modernity. This view is revealed in numerous modern tropes about homosexuality—that young adults are susceptible to homosexual proselytism, that the homosexual is a developmental anomaly caused by weak fathers, or that same-sex relationships cause gender confusion among children. The ability of these tropes to communicate that homosexuality is a threat to a heterosexual order is only one of their social functions; they also suggest that the homosexual may still possess a heterosexuality beneath the layers of inappropriate desires and practices.[52] She therefore warns against a historical narrative that sees a single moment of transition from one paradigm to the other—a caution against Foucault's history. There is no Great Paradigm Shift but instead overlapping and incoherent options that exist side by side.[53]

Judith Butler complements these approaches to the instability of sexual and gender identity in a way that can explain the LDS deployment of these concepts of sexual instability. Her approach reveals how claims to gender essentialism are used to cover over a belief in the contingency and fragility of gender identity. In her book *Gender Trouble*, she suggests that gender is performative—imitative of a stylized ideal that does not ontologically exist.

She explains, "If gender attributes and acts, the various ways in which a body shows or produces its cultural signification, are performative, then there is no preexisting identity by which an act or attribute might be measured."[54] In other words, by looking for a foundation of essential differences in the attributes or acts of "men" and "women," one is perpetually looking into contingent historical and cultural representation of difference. She shows how this lack of anything essential about gender "constitutes a fluidity of identities that suggests an openness to resignification."[55] Gender, then, can be expressed only as an ideal that is always shifting. She argues that the structural possibility of transgression against the norm of gender reveals the way that any gender or sexual identity is always contingent—subject to change and failure because it is measured against a norm. The perpetual instability of gender requires its constant performance to imitate a norm and maintain the illusion of stability. Gender performativity is not the expression of an essence but a temporally bounded, tenuous gesture toward an approximation of an ideal.

Butler's repudiation of a gender theory of a "preexisting identity" leaps out for Mormon readers precisely because contemporary Mormon theories appeal to a preexistent gender to stabilize the apparent contingency of sexual difference. At the same time, her challenge to a stable identity exposes the very problem with which Mormon theories of gender contend: *If gender is essential and eternal, on what basis could it change?* Something else must seek to explain Mormon theories of gender and sexuality that accounts for the contingency of these practices and their vulnerability to fail to conform to normative regulations. Essentialism simply doesn't work as an explanatory theory of human behavior in Mormon teaching. This book challenges the view that modern Mormon leaders have consistently taught gender essentialism as the sole or even primary theory of sexual difference. Appeals to essentialism cover over the fear of sexual and gender fluidity.

The persistence and simultaneity of conflicting theories of gender and sexuality within modernity holds great explanatory value for the Mormon case. While these various accounts help to explain gender and sexuality in modernity as a social and historical norm, a recent treatment has lamented, "Religion, notably, has been left off this list of influential social institutions in making the modern sexual order."[56] There is an overlap—one that must be explained and contextualized—between Butler's performative theory and modern Mormon approaches to gender and sexuality. As the history of the rhetorical and practical efforts to enforce these norms reveals, sexual difference turns out to be more about what one does than what one is. My view is not that there is no essentialist binary in Mormon thought but that the supposedly fixed binary between male and female is not all that there is. The bulk of this book makes the case that in modern Mormonism, gender is a fluid concept that must be secured and produced with strong ecclesiastical, legal, and cultural norms. In Mormon evaluation, gender is perpetually liminal, never being finally accomplished. The effort to establish sexual difference as essential covers over the instability of the difference. This framework helps to make sense of this dimension of Mormon history.

Finally, this book attends to intersectional analysis of gender to note the intertwining and overlapping of different categories of identity. For instance, when queer theory is put into conversation with a history of race, some important convergences become evident. Siobhan B. Somerville notes parallel developments in the scientific invention of homosexuality and scientific racism at the end of the nineteenth century. Both modern discourses of race and sexuality coincided with new social and legal forces to clearly categorize people and to emphasize differences and hierarchy.[57] Even Foucault's formulation of the invention of the heterosexual as a "species" at the end of the nineteenth century shows the ways in which discourses about sex were facilitated by racializing discourses about species. The scientific discourses at the end of the nineteenth century proliferated and exploded as the "natural" way of understanding race and sexuality. Julian B. Carter has extended this analysis to show that whiteness and heterosexuality merged between 1880 and 1940 to define the "normal American."[58] Such ideas were reaching their crescendo in Mormonism at the time of World War II.

The goal here is not to suggest a *compatibility* between queer theory and Mormonism, however the normative ends of those two movements may be framed. Certainly, the social and political goals that derive from an account of gender and sexual fluidity and malleability diverge sharply between queer activists and Latter-day Saints. Rather, my goal is to provide an explanation for Mormon accounts of the nature of gender, sexuality, and race that rely heavily on concepts of fluidity and malleability—concepts that are best expressed by queer theorists. As a modern, or late-modern, articulation of an inherent instability of the social differences that are enmeshed in power, queer theorists have helped to sketch out a genealogy of the efforts to fix differences among apparent instability. Mormonism fits into this pattern of modernity.

## PLAN OF THE BOOK

Each chapter is organized around contested changes to LDS teachings on gender and sexuality during a specific period. Chapter 1 explores Mormon preaching about the porous boundaries between the races and sexes after World War II. Between 1945 and 1970, church leaders stressed the importance of a particular kind of marriage by defining it against competing cultural trends. They vigorously opposed interracial marriage and just as vigorously supported "patriarchal" marriage with strict division of gendered labor. These joint teachings were interconnected by ideologies about purity and boundaries—concerns that arose because the racial and sexual boundaries now appeared to be fluid and contingent. I situate these themes in a broader American context, showing how Mormon developments tracked closely with other conservative religious groups at the time but were expressed through distinctive Mormon teachings and texts.

The second chapter covers some of the same period as the first but traces the new Mormon use of psychological theories about gender acquisition and contingency. This chapter explores a key tension in this period between moral and psychological etiologies of homosexuality. LDS leaders used the concept of "the homosexual" for the first time in this era and classified it as a type of gender failure. When I refer to "the homosexual" and "homosexuality" here, I refer to the cultural forms these terms produced, linking gender and sexuality as composite categories of identity. This new classification also entailed that "the homosexual"—a distinctive subjectivity and newly constructed character—was in need not only of ecclesiastical censure but also of pastoral care, blending the moral and psychological discourses together into a new therapeutic orthodoxy. From 1970 until the 1990s, the pathological approach to homosexuality gave way to an effort to hire professional therapists and counselors to assist in the treatment of the homosexual. I discuss the LDS professionalization and psychologization of the therapeutics for homosexuality in the context of the rise of ex-gay movements in America in the 1970s.

Moving beyond preaching and psychology, chapter 3 deals with the political dimensions of Mormon worries about the erosion of sexual difference. Between 1970 and 1982, Mormon ideologies of sexual difference were transformed as Mormons joined forces with the Religious Right. I focus on the Mormon theorizing about sexual difference that occurred as the issue became politicized. In particular, I explore the arguments LDS leaders used against the Equal Rights Amendment and their support for anti-sodomy laws. Homosexuality and feminism were intertwining threats that would lead to a "unisex" society if they were not resisted. The opposition to the ERA also transformed Mormonism in other ways. I argue that it had the paradoxical effect of reintroducing language about egalitarian marriage back into Mormonism. This chapter then explores the tension between patriarchal Mormonism and a version of Mormonism that could accommodate "soft egalitarianism."

The fourth chapter brings together the preaching, political, and psychological features of Mormon worries about gender in the 1990s and beyond. Most importantly, in 1995 the church issued "The Family: A Proclamation to the World." This document consolidated its teachings about sexual difference, gender roles, and political action. The church became involved in anti-same-sex marriage politics but also relaxed about women's paid labor outside the home. While LDS church leaders alleviated their worries about gender roles, they transposed the weight of their concern about changing gender norms to same-sex marriage. These moves were not unrelated but jointly reordered LDS thought about gender and sexuality away from the patriarchal order to the heterosexual order. The heterosexual family finally replaced the patriarchal and racially segregated family of previous decades.

The final chapter moves into the more recent past but gives it some historical context. It outlines new developments in the early twenty-first century in Mormon preaching, politics, and therapeutic efforts. Mormons invented new doctrines about sexuality to accommodate gay and lesbian identities in this period by delaying the "cure" until the next life. They also began to back away from psychological approaches to homosexuality that had structured their thinking and institutions in previous decades. Eventually, Mormons shifted their political interests from "family values" of opposing same-sex marriage as a legal matter to "religious freedom" to oppose same-sex marriage as a matter of individual and institutional conscience. Despite these various shifts, Mormons continued to see gender as especially at risk in a changing society.

Mormonism has undoubtedly helped to shape the American sexual and gendered order not only for millions of its own followers but through its political influence beyond its chapel pews. The idea that appears self-evident to many observers, namely that Mormonism is essentially connected to heterosexuality in practice, ontology, and theology, turns out to have a specific history. Mormonism, as any religious tradition, draws its ideas about sexuality and sexual difference in part from its own tradition and in part from its cultural context. Further, Mormonism, as any religious tradition, has changed how it evaluates sexuality and gender difference over time. If the past is any indication of the future, Mormonism will continue to adapt to, reject, and accommodate social changes.

# Chapter One

# PURE MARRIAGE

In 1946 and 1947, the years immediately following World War II, apostle
Spencer W. Kimball (d. 1985) received two church assignments. Kimball had
been called as an apostle in 1943 and had held various responsibilities but had
not yet clearly found a niche within that role. That began to change when
in August 1946 he had a dream in which he saw himself among the Native
American tribes in Arizona and New Mexico. One month later, one of his
more senior colleagues tasked him to "look after the Indians." By October,
he was establishing connections between the church and the tribes.[1] This
assignment led Kimball to think about the relationships between races as a
central feature of his career, and had significant impacts on the direction of
the church in this period.

A few months after establishing connections with the "Indians," in early
1947 Kimball had another experience that would shape the rest of his career
in the church. After the death of one of the apostles who had handled these
issues before him, Kimball was asked to take over important pastoral counseling duties for those involved in sexual sins. He wrote in his journal that
senior apostle, "[J. Reuben] Clark called me to his office to suggest that they
would be sending to me more of the interviews and difficult cases."[2] His
biographers explain that "there began for him a disturbing flow of interviews
with Church members involved in fornication or adultery or homosexuality."[3] The interview and counseling sessions shaped how Kimball thought
about the destructive nature of sexual sin. He devoted himself not only to
preaching about repentance but to taking a preventive approach to sin with
strict moral guidelines. Part of that preventive approach included a focus on
the proper roles of men and women.

This chapter focuses on the interrelationships between race and gender roles in Mormon thought since 1945. Sexual purity will be deferred to

the next chapter. Kimball's dual focuses on racial relations and gender were rife with paradoxes as he worked through and evolved his own thinking on these topics. The connection between these two themes of race and gender roles (including sexuality), however, is not immediately obvious. The analysis in this chapter proceeds from the idea that both race and gender/ sexuality are contingent and culturally produced categories, not natural givens. As Siobhan B. Somerville has pointed out, the history of discourses about race as a category "must be understood as a crucial part of the history and representation of sexual formations, including lesbian and gay identity and compulsory heterosexuality in the United States."[4] The efforts to fix the differences between races and to enforce particular sexual configurations are related projects of modernity. I add to Somerville's analysis the importance of gender hierarchy in the discourses of race and sexuality.

Mormon teachings in this period expressed great anxiety about racial and gender purity. The coexisting conflicts over interracial marriage and gender roles were not historical accidents but intersected on the issue of boundary production and maintenance. Church leaders saw racial mixture as a fundamental threat to the existence of the LDS priesthood. They advanced doctrines of racial purity to enforce acceptable kinds of marriage. By "racial purity," I refer to teachings that race was a natural or divinely instituted category and that the different races should not procreate with one another. Concurrently, church leaders also believed relaxing gender norms would undermine the family and society. Church leaders taught that it was a duty to maintain "gender purity" by closely guarding how marriages were governed and what kinds of labor were permissible. The intense interests in policing the differences between the races and between sexes were related phenomena, and the eventual softening on these issues also followed a similar trajectory.

## INTERRACIAL MARRIAGE AND THE POLITICS OF SEGREGATION

From the mid-nineteenth century until 1978—when Kimball would receive a new revelation for the LDS church—race was a defining factor in Mormon teaching about sexual relations relating to who should marry whom. Several cultural and religious changes eventually brought an end to these teachings, but they were once deeply entrenched. The massive cultural and legal shifts in thinking about race after World War II preceded these eventual changes to Mormon doctrines. Americans in general were moving around for greater educational and economic opportunities and mingling with those of different races, religions, and regions to a greater extent than they had before. African Americans continued to migrate to northern cities for manufacturing jobs, creating new opportunities for contact and pressures for integration with white institutions. The war itself had brought greater racial interconnections. Black and white soldiers served side by side in many cases, and numbers of American soldiers serving in the Asian theater sought to marry Japanese women and bring them home. These cultural changes were followed by legal changes. The California Supreme Court struck down the state's ban on interracial marriage in *Perez v. Sharp* in 1948; many other states then revoked similar laws.[5] Over the next two decades, many Americans relaxed their opposition to interracial marriage.

Other Americans resisted this cultural transition toward greater racial integration because they believed it could undermine marriage. White southern Protestants (and many in the North and the West) rooted their social and legal arguments in biblical prohibitions of exogamy.[6] A 1948 pamphlet by J. David Simpson, a Presbyterian pastor, was titled *Non-segregation Means Eventual Inter-marriage*. He argued that there was "no doubt that God did not want the racial bounds separating the races broken down into hybrid races which will most certainly eventuate if all races move in and out among themselves with non-segregation and free social inter-mingling."[7] In 1954, Reverend G. T. Gillespie addressed the Synod of Mississippi of the Presbyterian Church of the United States, declaring that divine providence was behind the separation and segregation of the races and that the "chief reason for segregation is the desirability of preventing such intimacies as might lead to intermarriage and the amalgamation of the races."[8] The idea of racial mixing, "hybrid races," or "amalgamation" was at that time seen in moral terms and was believed to be able to biologically weaken white supremacy. In his review of the 1958 conviction of Mildred Delores Jeter and Richard Perry Loving for miscegenation, Virginia judge Leon M. Bazile concluded, "The Almighty God created the races white, black, yellow, malay, and red. . . . The fact that he separated the races shows that he did not intend for the races to mix."[9] The pro-segregation arguments hinged on the ideas that there were separate races, that this separation was ordained by God, and that intermingling the races would upset the natural and divine order in such a way as to eventually erase racial difference altogether. Such ideologies trace their lineage back at least to the period of American slavery.

In 1967, in *Loving vs. Virginia*, the U.S. Supreme Court unanimously ruled against Bazile's decision, concluding that antimiscegenation laws violated the Constitution.

Mormon leaders in the 1950s and 1960s, as much as any southerners, accepted this mythology as divine revelation. But they also had their own texts and traditions that supplemented these religious justifications for racial separation, not least their prohibition of black people to priesthood offices and participation in certain priesthood ordinances. Like their conservative religious peers, Mormons looked to the biblical stories of the sons of the patriarch Noah—Ham, Shem, and Japheth—for ideologies of race and racial difference. In Genesis, Noah cursed his grandson Canaan, son of Ham: "A servant of servants shall he be unto his brethren" (9:25, KJV). From this text, racist teachings justified the enslavement of Africans, whom many biblicists believed to be descendants of Canaan.[10] Others believed that Africans owed their descent to Cain, the first son of Adam who had been "cursed" with a "mark" for slaying his brother Abel (Gen. 4:11, 15). Such theories held that the descendants of these lineages were divinely cursed, while other lineages held God's favor. Further, Israelites were biblically enjoined to marry within their tribes, which many white Americans interpreted to prohibit interracial marriage.

To these stories, Mormonism's nineteenth-century founder, Joseph Smith, had added new scriptures that supported theories of racial difference and separation.[11] The Book of Mormon recounts how skin color differences were meant to prevent intermarriage. The Nephite peoples were "white, and exceedingly fair and delightsome," while the Lamanite peoples had been cursed with a "skin of blackness" so "they might not be enticing unto" the Nephites.[12] The text favorably compares the whiteness of the Nephites with that of European Americans.[13] Mormons commonly understood the Lamanites to be the ancestors of Native Americans, not Africans, but the text expressed the sentiment that difference in skin color should "not be enticing" in interrelationships. Smith also provided a miraculous translation of another scriptural text, the Book of Abraham, later canonized in the Pearl of Great Price. In that narrative, the biblical Ham, the cursed son of Noah, was specifically connected with the inhabitants of Egypt. Consequently, the first pharaoh, although a righteous man, was "of that lineage by which he could not have the right of Priesthood."[14] Though some black men were ordained to the priesthood under Joseph Smith's leadership, from Brigham Young until 1978 this text was interpreted to justify the exclusion of black men from ordination into the LDS priesthood orders and black men and women from temple rites, including "sealings," or "celestial marriage."[15]

Mormon leaders also put forward unique doctrines of racial separatism that affected how they thought about marriage. Many Mormons considered themselves to be descendants of the scattered tribes of ancient Israel. In 1863, president of the church Brigham Young warned, "If the white man who belongs to the chosen seed mixes his blood with the seed of Cain, the penalty, under the law of God, is death on the spot. This will always be so."[16] Such white-black relationships existed at the time among Mormons but provoked scandal. Indeed, Young's confrontation with several interracial marriages and extramarital sex between black Mormon men and white Mormon women deeply influenced his views that black men should not be ordained to the priesthood.[17] These views depended on ideas about racial purity and the danger of "mixing" through sexual exchange.

LDS teachings on race gained greater importance and clarification in the mid-twentieth century as leaders feared losing racial control amid the broader social trends toward racial equality and integration.[18] Like other segregationists after World War II, Mormon leaders publicly and privately expressed concern over interracial marriage, which prominent apostle J. Reuben Clark (d. 1961) called "a wicked virus" in 1946.[19] In 1949, after a series of exchanges over the course of a few years, a sociologist expressed surprise and frustration upon learning that there was a "fixed doctrine" about "the Negro" that codified LDS notions of white supremacy. The First Presidency wrote to him that the priesthood restriction was not a policy but rather a doctrine based on the conduct of spirits in the preexistence. The leaders elaborated that "social intercourse" between blacks and whites was "not welcome" because it would lead to intermarriage, "which the Lord has forbidden." The sociologist who was the recipient of the letter was not unfamiliar with Mormons; he had himself grown up in Utah, was a practicing Mormon, and had even published a book on Mormon life.[20] His lack of awareness about the doctrines on race suggested that church leaders had not emphasized the doctrines of racial separation in previous decades.

American attention to integration and civil rights also set the background to the renewed opposition to "race mixing" in LDS teaching. In 1954, the Supreme Court's decision in *Brown v. Board of Education* set in motion the controversial task of integrating public schools, though private businesses and neighborhoods remained places where it was legal and culturally acceptable to enforce segregation. Church president David O. McKay did not want to bring the church into the public debates about the issue, so he advised church leaders to "use our influence quietly" to oppose those civil rights that would lead to greater integration.[21] In the 1950s, J. Reuben Clark, by then McKay's First Counselor, authorized the use of LDS chapels to organize communities to "prevent negro settlement" and urged Belle Spafford (d. 1982), the president of the Relief Society—the LDS women's organization—to use her influence to prevent the National Council of Women from favoring "negro equality."[22]

While the efforts to work behind the scenes rather than in the public to oppose civil rights reflected some ambivalence, church leaders did not necessarily use their influence quietly. Several prominent officials publicly spoke in favor of segregation and antimiscegenation legislation. In their capacity as church leaders, they declared segregation to be the will of the Lord. They deployed the same theological arguments as southern segregationists, but they added special concerns about the effect that racial mixing would have on the ability of God's chosen people to be ordained to the LDS priesthood orders. Apostle Mark E. Petersen (d. 1984) publicly insisted that "the Lord segregated the Negro and who is man to change that segregation?"[23] Born in 1900, Petersen believed in divinely designed, hierarchical racial lineages. In his address at the church's flagship school, Brigham Young University (BYU), in 1954, just a few months after *Brown*, Petersen argued that socially mingling with "Negroes" should be resisted, just as mingling with sin should be resisted. He believed that "the Negro seeks absorption with the white race. He will not be satisfied until he achieves it by intermarriage."[24] For Petersen, LDS beliefs against ordaining black men to the priesthood sustained his segregationist fears. Invoking the Jim Crow legal blood quotient of "one drop" of "black blood" to establish ancestry, Petersen reflected segregationist racism. "If there is one drop of Negro blood in my children," he warned, "they receive the curse." After a few generations of acceptable intermarriage, "who could hold [the priesthood] in all America?"[25] Petersen's alarm about the diminished number of Americans who could be eligible for the LDS priesthood meant not only that opposition to interracial marriage was a matter of concern for members of the faith, but also that church leaders were invested in American culture and public policy that might affect the prospects for future converts.

Like other advocates of segregation, LDS leaders believed that segregation represented religious doctrine. Consequently, they believed that it was also socially just. Petersen complained that those who did not understand the LDS church's religious teachings were unfairly accusing it of bigotry. He insisted that one should behave with respect, generosity, and kindness toward "the Negro," including support for certain legal and social protections. Petersen explained the extent of his "generous" views: "I would be willing to let every Negro drive a Cadillac if they could afford it."[26] He believed his opinions on racial segregation were not only fair but even magnanimous, tolerant, and loving. By couching duties toward other races as encompassing only personal kindness and tolerance, church leaders like Petersen could overlook the structural inequities of racial segregation.

For LDS leaders, marriage was a key concern of the debates about integration. In the 1950s, they believed segregation was necessary to protect the institution of marriage. The First Presidency responded to one inquiry in 1954, "The Church is opposed on biological and other grounds, to intermarriage between whites and negroes, and . . . it discourages all social relationships and associations between the races, as among its members, that might lead to such marriages."[27] The scientific appeal to "biological grounds" to oppose interracial marriage helped to shore up the doctrinal arguments—though they were entirely unexplained. Scientific arguments would later become central to questions of gender hierarchy and homosexuality as well. The scientific racism that undergirded opposition to interracial marriage also supported white supremacy and was framed as rational and just.

Doctrinal arguments, however, often took center stage in LDS opposition to interracial marriage. Central among these was another unique Mormon idea, that racial lineages not only were ordained by God but were the result of an individual soul's choices made before the creation of the earth. In Mormon cosmology, human spirits lived before they were born into this world and participated in a "war in heaven" against those fallen from God's influence in this pre-mortal realm. Not all who participated in this war did so valiantly; such spirits were cursed and in their mortal life descended from Cain with black skin. President of the Quorum of the Twelve Apostles Joseph Fielding Smith (d. 1972) described a "flood" of letters from members inquiring about the church's "doctrine of segregation."[28] Born in 1876 as the grandson of Hyrum Smith, the brother of Mormonism's founder, Joseph Smith Jr., Joseph Fielding Smith was "Mormonism's most respected religious thinker" in this period.[29] In his fifteen-year column, serialized in his popular books *Answers to Gospel Questions*, Smith taught that the modern prohibition on interracial marriage had its basis in biblical narrative and Mormonism's revealed doctrines. Like Petersen, Smith insisted that he was in favor of full access to all social privileges but explained that because of their cowardly conduct in the preexistence, and because they descend from Cain, black men would not be able to receive the priesthood and therefore intermarriage was forbidden.

However, as one questioner pointed out, according to the Bible, Abraham, Joseph, and Moses all married Egyptian women. Joseph Fielding Smith countered that these "Egyptian wives" were actually Semitic, from the Hyksos peoples: "Abraham, Joseph, and Moses married women of their own race, and we need have no worry over our lineage, because we are of that same race."[30] Marriage and lineage were the driving factors of the LDS doctrine supporting segregation: "The doctrine of social equality and the common mingling of these races is said to be made for the purpose of eventually eliminating the Negro race by absorption through intermarriage." Only after Abel was to have his own posterity "on some other world" would the restrictions on the priesthood be lifted.[31] Present inequities for such souls were their just deserts for their shortcomings in the pre-mortal realm.

Bruce R. McConkie (d. 1985), Joseph Fielding Smith's son-in-law and at the time a president of the Seventy, shared these views on the divine origins of racial separation. In 1958, McConkie's encyclopedic *Mormon Doctrine* treated a number of doctrinal issues, including "Negro," "caste system," and others that taught that black people had been cursed in the preexistence and that their lineage was traced to the biblical anti-patriarchs Cain and Ham. He explained, "Caste systems have their root and origin in the gospel itself, and when they operate according to the divine decree, the resultant restrictions and *segregation* are right and proper and have the approval of the Lord. To illustrate; Cain, Ham, and the whole negro race have been cursed with a black skin, the mark of Cain, so they can be identified as a caste apart, a people with whom the other descendants of Adam should not intermarry."[32] According to "divine decree," American separation of the "negro race" was necessary to prevent intermarriage. LDS doctrines of race and marriage were inseparably connected.

Other church leaders in the 1960s continued to elaborate a mythology of divinely ordained racial difference that assigned different roles and places in society. In the 1950s and 1960s, apostle Alvin Dyer (d. 1977) had enormous influence over the church's missionary program.[33] In 1962, Dyer gave a talk to American LDS missionaries serving in Norway, asking them, "Why is it that you are white and not colored? . . . Is God such an unjust person that He would make you white and free and make a Negro cursed under the cursing of Cain that he could not hold the Priesthood of God?" In Dyer's view, the nations were divided between the "chosen" (descendants of Shem), the "Gentiles" (descendants of Japheth), and the "cursed" (descendent of Ham). Cursed spirits were born into "Negro bodies," so racial mixing would entail that one's descendants would be made up of those whom God had cursed in the pre-mortal existence. These teachings, while increasingly socially unacceptable in 1960s America, were further emphasized as essential to Mormonism. The prohibition of racial mixing and priesthood ordination, according to Dyer, "is not a matter of the declaration of a policy but of direct commandment from the Lord."[34] Dyer's talk was widely republished and distributed to LDS missionaries around the world.

Church leaders granted the doctrine preventing approval for interracial marriage the highest level of authority.[35] In 1961, President McKay explained, "We recommend negroes marry negroes, and that whites marry whites, and we cannot modify the statement. . . . We cannot change our attitude until we receive a revelation from the Lord directing otherwise."[36] McKay's belief that divine revelation prohibited interracial marriage—and that divine revelation was required to change it—indicated how fundamental and immutable he saw the doctrine of marriage as a system of racial purity. Though other conservative Christians also prohibited interracial marriage, LDS leaders taught that their theories of racial purity of marriage were not rooted merely in biblical interpretation or cultural prejudice but came from direct communication from God.

### INTERMARRIAGE AND THE LAMANITES

While the church was worrying about integration and interracial marriage between black and white people, it was also taking up anew a particular mission to socially integrate with Native Americans and Polynesians.[37] In the Utah context, Mormons had long relationships with particular tribes, including intermarriage, as a practice of racially "civilizing" these peoples.[38] Many Mormons considered the Native Americans to be descendants of the Lamanites described in the Book of Mormon. Though Lamanites were cursed with a "skin of blackness," the Book of Mormon also promises that they will be redeemed and become a "white and a delightsome" people.[39] For many Mormons in the 1950s, this prophecy could be accomplished through integration, which they welcomed—but not intermarriage. In 1954, the Relief Society's Social Services agency launched the Indian

Placement Program (IPP) that took Native children and placed them in white homes during the school year. This was part of a broader progressive cultural movement to "Americanize" Native peoples through integration and education.[40]

Apostle Spencer W. Kimball was a great proponent of the IPP and developed relationships with western tribes.[41] He chaired the church's Committee on Indian Relationships and held a strong belief in the fundamental equality between white and Native peoples. Kimball challenged prejudice against Natives and claimed that the greatest problem they face is "the white man."[42] He championed controversial integration programs, prophesied of the rise of the "Lamanite," and promoted Natives as church leaders.[43] He also taught that the "Lamanites" would experience a racial transformation along with their spiritual conversion.[44] In 1960, Kimball remarked on the successes of the IPP upon meeting a teenage convert who "was several shades lighter than her parents."[45] The promises of Lamanite whitening in the Book of Mormon seemed to him to be coming true. This young woman was proof of racial fluidity—a process that was embraced so long as the transition was a "darker" race becoming whiter.

However, Kimball believed there should be limits to integration between white and nonwhite Mormons. Though the "Lamanites" were technically equal to white members, he also worried about intermarriage as a destructive force for white communities. Within a few years of the launch of the IPP, Kimball learned that some had taken integration too far for his taste. In 1959, Kimball instructed caseworkers to develop more social programming for the Indian children "so they will be more inclined to socialize with and marry within their own race and not inter-marry with white people."[46] In a speech to church members, he warned, "When I said you must teach your people to overcome their prejudices and accept the Indians, I did not mean that you would encourage intermarriage. I mean that they should be brothers, to worship together and to work together and to play together; but we must discourage intermarriage, not because it is sin. I would like to make this very emphatic. A couple has not committed sin if an Indian boy and a white girl are married, or vice versa. . . . But it is not expedient."[47] Kimball's idea that interracial marriage was not "expedient" represented a tack on interracial marriage different from segregation. He emphasized that it was not a doctrine that white people and "Indians" should not marry, distinguishing his teaching from how McKay, Petersen, McConkie, and Smith had described the prohibition of intermarriage between blacks and whites as maintaining divinely ordained racial lineages. In the case of Native Americans, Kimball did not see this as the issue at all. He explained, "The interrace marriage problem is not one of inferiority or superiority. . . . It is a matter of backgrounds."[48] Kimball worried that interracial marriages between whites and Indians would be less stable and more likely to end in divorce. He transformed the theological concerns about racial lineages to a therapeutic cultural perspective on individual and familial happiness and stability. Kimball warned about the prejudices that white spouses and mixed-race children might face as obstacles to their success. However, his concern went only so far. Rather than teach against such prejudices, Kimball encouraged couples to maintain racial boundaries because of social prejudice.

The problems of racial integration and intermarriage cropped up in other church programs as well. The Church College of Hawaii and the Polynesian Cultural Center were established in Oahu in 1955 and 1963, respectively. For decades, Americans had sexualized Pacific Islanders as a sensual people who freely and seductively exposed their bodies. The church's educational presence on the island meant that white students and Polynesian students mingled together in academic, ecclesiastical, and social spaces. The relationships they formed created anxiety for school administrators, who cited Kimball's warnings against intermarriage to the students.[49] However, the apprehension about interracial marriage had more to do with maintaining white racial purity than with maintaining Polynesian ethnic distinctions. As former college president Owen J. Cook explained, "The Brethren were not concerned if a Tongan married a Maori or a Samoan married a Hawaiian. . . . Those types of marriages did not concern the Brethren, but the Caucasian did."[50]

## CIVIL RIGHTS CONTROVERSY

The church's teachings on segregation and its priesthood prohibition for black men attracted the attention of civil rights groups. This public pressure prompted the church to begin to adopt a more moderate position on integration. In 1963, the NAACP organized protests at Temple Square in Salt Lake City to shine a light on the segregation practices of LDS-owned businesses and on the church's policies about the exclusion of black men from the priesthood. The planned protests were averted when Sterling McMurrin, a liberal LDS scholar and U.S. commissioner of education in John F. Kennedy's administration, intervened. Apostle Hugh B. Brown (d. 1975) read a statement—authored by McMurrin—explaining that there was "no doctrine, belief, or practice that is intended to deny the enjoyment of full civil rights by any person regardless of race, color, or creed." The statement went further, asserting that denying civil rights was a "moral evil," and called upon "all men everywhere . . . to commit themselves to the establishment of full civil equality for all of God's children."[51] However, the statement, approved by President McKay, was in tension with the actions and policies of the church and its business and with the beliefs of many senior church officials.

Apostle Ezra Taft Benson (d. 1994) was one of the most vocal LDS opponents of the civil rights movement.[52] He was a former U.S. secretary of agriculture under President Dwight D. Eisenhower, but he also repeatedly publicly endorsed the radically conservative, anticommunist John Birch Society.[53] The group, founded by Robert Welch, was an extremist organization that built a loyal following spreading conspiracy theories about a communist takeover in the United States and infiltration of social and government organizations. Benson became a close friend of Welch's and spent much of his efforts as an apostle in the 1960s spreading conspiracy theories and preaching on Bircher themes, including opposition to racial integration and civil rights.[54]

Benson's Bircher activism brought him into close contact with leading southern segregationists. In 1968, he wanted to run for U.S. president with segregationist senator Strom Thurmond of South Carolina as his running mate but was soon asked to be the vice presidential candidate with segregationist George Wallace, governor of Alabama. Church president McKay ultimately rejected his request.[55] After repeatedly speaking about race and civil rights in General Conference—the semiannual meeting where church leaders preached to the entire church—Benson delivered one of his most direct speeches on race issues at a General Conference in 1967, drawing heavily from Birch Society publications.[56] Perhaps acting on false rumors of an intended armed assault on Temple Square, Benson landed a stinging rebuke of the civil rights movement.[57] Repeating themes central to much of his public preaching in LDS stake meetings—semiannual meetings where a single high-ranking church leader preaches to a region similar to a diocese— he asserted that the civil rights movement was a "Communist program for revolution in America" and warned of a potential "race war." He saw the riots in various metropolitan areas as a prelude to a conspiratorial communist takeover of the U.S. government. "Negroes," he explained, "are merely the unfortunate group that has been selected by professional Communist agitators to be used as the primary source of cannon fodder." These communists, he believed, were white men who were manipulating black populations by sowing discontent and encouraging them to ask for entitlement benefits.[58] Benson's belief that the civil rights movement was a secret front for a communist takeover of the United States never allowed him to take seriously the public issues of violence and racial injustice of segregation.

Other high-ranking church leaders were concerned and displeased with Benson's agitation, and he was even sent to Europe for two years after a particularly incendiary General Conference speech in October 1963 that warned against the enemy within the church, including potentially apostles.[59] Apostle Hugh Brown worked to oppose Benson's extreme views and his efforts to align the church with the John Birch Society. Brown wanted to accommodate the civil rights movement and even offer public support for its principles. But putting forward this position was a hard fight with his fellow apostles.[60] Yet a number of factors worked to lift up Brown's more moderate position and downplay Benson's influence at this time. When Michigan governor George Romney, who was LDS, ran for president at the end of the 1960s, the press put the church's racial teachings under significant scrutiny, and church leaders turned to the rhetoric first offered in the 1963 speech authored by McMurrin and read by Brown.[61] On December 15, 1969, McKay's First Presidency issued another statement expressing its support for civil rights, its sympathy with oppressed peoples because of a history of oppression of Mormons, and "love, compassion, and the deepest appreciation for the rich talents, endowments, and the earnest strivings of our Negro brothers and sisters." However, these views distinguished between what was appropriate for civil law and what was a matter of religious duty. Church leaders also provided an explanation that their doctrines need not be consistent with civil law and that they had no choice but to follow the revelations that excluded black people from the priesthood—their talents and endowments and earnest strivings could still not be fully accepted in the church.[62]

Church leaders in the 1960s slowly backed away from their previous opposition to racial integration in other ways as well. This included attitudes about interracial marriage. In 1963, the Utah legislature overturned the state's antimiscegenation statute, making it the second-to-last state in the West to do so, before Wyoming in 1965.[63] But these legal and social accommodations did little to affect the cause of racial equality within the church—even if church leaders could now support racial equality and even intermarriage in civil law. While the church could prove itself flexible on the legality and social acceptability of marriages that it deemed doctrinally forbidden, it remained steadfast in its internal opposition to forms of marriage that violated its doctrines of racial segregation. Civil marriages did not have the same soteriological stakes as ecclesiastical marriages performed in LDS temples, and Mormons came to accept a distinction between church and state on this matter. Despite their earlier fears that interracial marriages would destabilize society and threaten the future of the LDS priesthood, by the end of the 1960s church leaders were content to apply these teachings only to Mormon marriages. This would prove a resilient formula—from initial resistance to accommodation to social change—in future clashes with society on marriage practices.

## HOUSEHOLD GOVERNMENT, ECONOMIC ROLES, AND EGALITARIANISM

In addition to racial purity, in the postwar period church leaders adopted a companion purity ideology fueled by much of the same reasoning. Like racial difference, they regarded sexual difference as divinely ordained. Like racial difference, sexual difference was also at risk of dissolution amid the cultural changes of the era. Like racial difference, church leaders believed sexual difference was hierarchical. And like racial difference, church leaders believed that sexual difference was necessary to protect the proper transmission and exercise of the priesthood. The possibility of a blurring or mixing of the categories of male and female inspired church leaders to emphasize a prophylactic boundary—a division of roles, dress, and comportment between men and women, masculinity and femininity. Sexual difference was not a natural given but a highly contingent feature of human existence that must be guarded by strict norms. As many church leaders had once opposed the civil rights movement's goals of full integration of black people into white society, these same church officials also opposed feminism's goals of providing equal opportunities to integrate women in men's spheres—and were more resistant to changes on this matter than they had been to changes on church doctrines on race.

Church teachings on gender purity emerged as American ideals about gender relations transformed during World War II. Family and home life had been topics for preaching in the past, but statistical research shows that LDS preaching about the home dramatically increased after the war.[64] During the war, women had gone to work and enjoyed financial and personal autonomy. But Americans still idealized male labor and female domesticity and sought to enshrine these values in public policy.[65] The 1950s was publicly depicted as a "golden age" of these values, often symbolized by the television show *Leave It to Beaver*, which featured an idealized white suburban family with clearly defined roles and morality. Conservative Christians capitalized on this period of national renewal by spreading their own doctrines of moral strength as a form of patriotism and religious duty. Fundamentalists and evangelicals launched young adult organizations that focused on dancing, socializing, and wholesome activities that would protect chastity and lead to marriage.[66] They taught about separate spheres for men and women, presenting nineteenth-century Victorian gender ideologies as immutable biblical truth.[67]

At the same time, the 1950s were actually a period of fierce struggle to shape a new American identity in the early Cold War. Conservatives adopted a confrontational approach to the changing family dynamics of divorce, birth control, and greater autonomy for women. "The normal Christian home," wrote evangelical scholar Charles Ryrie in 1952, "consists of husband, wife, and children each with his or her own particular place and responsibility." The wife is "obedient *in all things*. . . . Although Christianity as no other religion gives freedom to women, in the Christian home this freedom is distinctly regulated."[68] Ryrie's rhetoric connected key themes about the ideologies of gender that were consolidated in this period. Household governance became an important topic for preaching, with heavy emphasis on women's roles. Not only were women supposed to submit to their husbands, but such submission was called freedom. Women's domesticity became a tenet of conservatism's new revival of Victorian patriarchy.

After World War II, Mormon leaders joined in these conservative calls for a new American home founded on male hierarchy. Mormon teachings about the importance of "patriarchy" were a significant legacy of its nineteenth-century teachings on polygamy.[69] However, Mormons were not simply repackaging their own nineteenth-century ideologies of domestic life. They were rather uncomfortable with their polygamous heritage and rarely used it to justify the new postwar emphasis on male hierarchy and authority. Mormons had formally abandoned polygamy, or what they called plural marriage, in 1890 in order to save the church from federal prosecution. Unfortunately, they had never really lived down their forebears' reputation in the broader American consciousness. It did not help that fundamentalist Mormons—schismatic groups and individuals who rejected the church's teachings on monogamy—continued to exist and even thrive in remote parts of Utah, Idaho, Arizona, Canada, and Mexico. These groups frequently captured the public imagination and the attention of law enforcement. On July 26, 1953, state authorities raided the polygamous colony in Short Creek, Arizona, to "rescue" the women and children from the horrors of "white slavery."[70] The episode received national attention, including major articles in *Time* and *Newsweek* magazines, generating some sympathetic press for the polygamists. The LDS church's newspaper was not so sympathetic; the *Deseret News* ran an editorial commending the raid and expressing hope that "the unfortunate activities at Short Creek will be cleaned up once and for all."[71] The new Mormon patriarchy would not abide the old Mormon polygamy.

Many LDS church members were embarrassed by the continued existence of polygamous rivals that negatively impacted mainstream-LDS desires for respectability. After the raid, apostle Mark E. Petersen instructed local church leaders in southern Utah to excommunicate polygamists in their boundaries.[72] But public conversation about the topic remained muted. Historian Martha Sontag Bradley notes, "After 1950, Church leaders rarely mentioned the subject of plural marriage. . . . Avoiding the subject rather than dealing with the questions it presented was one way to prevent confusion among the members or difficulties with the doctrine."[73] The new Mormon family was to be strictly monogamous and well ordered. Church leaders mostly ignored the polygamous past—though polygamy for men in the afterlife continued in the practice of sealing multiple women to one man, so long as he was married in this life to only one woman at a time.

Women's roles and polygamous groups were not the only issues to receive greater scrutiny in this period; male roles and comportment received significant attention as well. Church leaders taught that a spiritual life was necessary for a correct masculinity, a muscular Mormonism—one that was situated between feminine weakness and overaggressive manliness.[74] Sexual virtue was especially important in these ideals of manhood, as distinguished from its secular stereotype. McKay promised that "chastity strengthens manhood" and provided "virility."[75] Apostle Stephen L. Richards (d. 1959) taught, "There are some who may regard the acknowledgment of spiritual power as a stigma of weakness, . . . incompatible with strength of manhood and self-determination. That was in large measure the doctrine of Hitler and is today the philosophy of Communism. I hope there are not many who adopt such a philosophy of life."[76] Pairing feminine spirituality with masculine strength, church leaders believed that proper gender performances were a bulwark against rival ideologies, especially fascism and communism. A balanced manhood—both strong and spiritual—had been the greatest defense against Nazism, and now the Soviets.

Sexual difference was established through practice and acceptance of boundaries, especially for men, who, it was feared, might become too effeminate if their wives led in the home. Indeed, the failure of patriarchal leadership in the home was among the greatest threats to manhood. Church leaders made the well-ordered home the primary concern over the next several decades, invoking what they called the "patriarchal order of marriage" as the divine model for household governance. LDS leaders looked to the Bible to define these normative family relations. There, they saw a benevolent patriarchy as the system of home governance, which included the submission of wives to their husbands' authority as well as a responsibility of husbands to rule justly. The 1950 Mormon best seller (republished numerous times) *A Marvelous Work and a Wonder* by apostle LeGrand Richards quoted approvingly Ephesians 5:22: "Wives, submit yourselves unto your own husbands, as unto the Lord." He explained that in the order of the family, "the husband is the head of the wife."[77] This deutero-Pauline passage was a staple in LDS preaching on the family as a patriarchal institution. In 1954, apostle Stephen L. Richards taught that after its witness of God and Jesus Christ, "perhaps the greatest contribution emanating from the holy Bible is its historical and doctrinal support for the unity of the family in the patriarchal order."[78] The commandment for wives to submit was often repeated during this period in General Conference, far more than had been done before.[79]

The patriarchal order of marriage not only was about male leadership in the home but also entailed that women stay away from paid labor. Quoting 1 Peter 3:1, "Ye wives, be in subjection to your own husbands," Bruce R. McConkie's *Mormon Doctrine* explained in 1958, "Woman's primary place is in the home, where she is to rear children and abide by the righteous counsel of her husband."[80] In 1963, Spencer W. Kimball delivered a General Conference talk with a simple message titled "Keep Mothers in the Home."[81] For church leaders in this period, gender purity was not just hierarchical but also required segregated economic roles to preserve the differences between men and women.

LDS officials did not believe that a husband and father's rule over his family was an unchecked authority. Citing an important passage from the LDS scriptural canon Doctrine and Covenants, church leaders warned men against "unrighteous dominion" (121:39). Rulership and leadership should be based on virtue, not strength. Still, they defended submission of wives except in the case of requiring unrighteousness. In 1958, apostle Stephen L. Richards further explained the deutero-Pauline teachings of spousal hierarchy: "When properly interpreted and applied I do not see how good women should take exception to it."[82] He conceded that "some husbands and fathers have made it difficult for respect to be maintained for them," yet he believed that even in these circumstances "to abandon the principle and thus remove from fathers the responsibility of maintaining virtue and goodness among their children would certainly avail nothing."[83] A man's right to rule his family supposedly created incentives for him to use that power justly, and for some church leaders he deserved this right even when he fell short of worthiness. Others were less sure. Apostle Hugh B. Brown taught Ephesians 5:22 in General Conference, but he was quick to offer a qualification: "This requirement of the wives to submit to their husbands presupposes righteousness on the husbands[' part]."[84] But if a husband was "righteous," a wife's duty was to submit to him.

Church leaders were not the only ones pushing for patriarchal leadership. LDS women also were actively involved in emergent antifeminist thought, pushing back against notions of equality and greater access to opportunities for women. In 1965, Helen B. Andelin, a Latter-day Saint and graduate of BYU's home economics program, began selling her book *Fascinating Womanhood* out of her garage. (The book has since sold millions of copies.)[85] In response to those women who were discontent with their postwar domestic roles and who had informed Betty Friedan's 1963 feminist jeremiad against "housewifery" in *The Feminine Mystique*, Andelin believed that happiness could not be found in feminism but in connecting with one's "feminine nature." Her self-improvement program was not based on women's "liberation" but on just the opposite.[86] In her writings and workshops, she taught women how to have a happy marriage and to enjoy housewife duties by cultivating feminine "dependency" and "childlikeness." She suggested that there was a binary between male and female that must be strictly guarded. Her advice to wives included, "Don't act, look, or think like men"; "Don't be efficient in men's affairs, such as leadership, making major decisions, providing a living, etc."; and, "Revere your husband and honor his right to rule you and his children."[87] These views set up a boundary and hierarchy that would preserve female difference from males. Andelin's reputation and success spread far beyond her Mormon background but seemed clearly rooted in her view of LDS ideals for womanhood.[88] Many LDS women were attracted to the message, though it did get some pushback. Andelin had a falling out with the General Presidency of the Relief Society—the highest governing body of the LDS women's organization—which did not embrace her views.[89] Andelin's worry that women might become too much like men, and vice versa, expressed a belief in the fragility of sexual difference.

Male church leaders instituted several programs to ensure that the proper household patriarchal order would be carried out—and that gender roles would be maintained. In 1960, apostle Harold B. Lee (d. 1973) was placed in charge of the Priesthood Correlation Committee. Lee was a shrewd organizational manager who was responsible for some of the most important LDS reforms of the twentieth century. He was born in 1899 in a rural environment but moved to Salt Lake City as a young man and made his way in government. During the Great Depression, the church recognized his organizational expertise and appointed him director of the Church Welfare Program in 1932, a program that earned national praise.[90] Less than a decade later, he was appointed an apostle.

The Correlation Committee under Lee's charge carried massive authority to usher in a new era of Mormon teaching and to centralize church finances, administrative power, and decision making.[91] In the 1960s, Correlation leadership slowly weakened the Relief Society, stripping it of its budget, its independent publications, and its active Social Services agency. A goal of this movement was to diminish women's authority in the church in deference to the male priesthood. According to Lee, "The whole effort of correlation is to strengthen the home and to give aid to the home in its problems."[92] One of his employees wrote even more pointedly, "The whole tone of Priesthood Correlation seems to be the establishment of the divine Patriarchal Order."[93] The Correlation movement was dedicated to patriarchal leadership in the church and in the home, under the guidance of the "Priesthood."

Priesthood Correlation domesticated religion by making it a key feature of the ideal home life. This entailed that male authority in the home also displace female autonomy in women's sphere of influence. Correlation introduced two major innovations for male home management—the Home Teaching program in 1963 and Family Home Evening in 1964. Home Teaching expanded the earlier "ward teaching" program to assign male members to visit with other members and offer teaching and instruction in their homes to the entire family—and occasionally investigate church members suspected of serious sins.[94] This provided a mode of surveillance over the families of the congregation and ensured that churchly messages were communicated in the home. Home Teaching, Lee explained, "is to help the parents with home problems in their efforts to teach their families the fundamentals of parental responsibility."[95] It also added a proxy father/husband figure in the home where male leadership was absent or weak. The male home teacher was expected to make regular visits, provide priesthood blessings, and deliver spiritual teachings to the assigned household.

The Family Home Evening program encouraged parents to set aside an evening for family prayer, hymns, spiritual and moral instruction, parental interviews of children, and shared entertainment activities. The program was new, though Lee grounded it in precedent. Citing a 1915 letter advising a "family home evening," Lee acknowledged that little had actually been done about it over the previous fifty years. In fact, the practice had never been mentioned before in General Conference.[96] The new program, by contrast, received massive institutional support. The church provided the *Family Home Evening Manual* (1965) to every family.[97] In 1966, congregations were encouraged to set aside a night for Family Home Evening. By 1970, the church instituted Monday night as the designated time for Family Home Evening and prohibited scheduling other church activities during that time.[98]

Male leadership was a central aspect of these new initiatives. To accompany the new Family Home Evening program, the church issued a weekly curriculum for the adult men in 1965 and provided trainings for bishops and home teachers on these topics.[99] The manual was a departure from previous priesthood manuals, which had been dedicated to teaching scripture, theology, and history.[100] The new priesthood manual made the doctrine of the home and family the focus. The manual included lessons titled "The Family and the Patriarchal Order," "The Priesthood Holder Is a Patriarch in His Home," and "The Priesthood Holder Is a Partner with His Heavenly Father in Teaching the Gospel." These lessons emphasized the exclusive duties of the patriarch/father to lead and teach in his home and to guide those under his care to follow church teachings. These lessons contrasted the ideal role of the father with autocratic forms of the patriarchal family. As the manual instructed, "The Lord intended the priesthood holder to be more a blessing to his family than a ruler over them." This would include the requirement for a man to develop a "partnership" with his wife. The partnership was nevertheless hierarchical—the husband was the "head" of the household, and the wife was the "heart."[101] This oft-repeated division of labor between a heart and a head was built on stereotypes of male rationality and female sentimentality.

Apostle Spencer W. Kimball was a strong advocate of these new programs as a mechanism for instituting proper male leadership in the home. In a 1965 sermon, he taught, "In the great Home Teaching Program and Family

Home Evenings, the responsibilities lie first and properly on the head of the father. The wife will assist. What true father would shirk this great privilege? What father would shift the planning, organizing, conducting [of] such family programs? What dutiful father would evade this teaching, opportunity, and responsibility?" These programs also institutionalized the submission of wives. Quoting the relevant New Testament passages on submission of wives, Kimball noted, "Certainly no sane woman would hesitate to give submission to her own really righteous husband in everything. We are sometimes shocked to see the wife take over the leadership, naming the one to pray, the place to be, the things to do."[102] The notion of male responsibility and female submission was reinforced across church programs. As an example, in *A Blue Ribbon Affair*, part of the 1969 Parent and Youth Night program, one female character explains, "I'm glad I'm a girl. Boys have to make so many decisions."[103] Church instruction warned against "diminished" responsibilities for men if women took over too much control in the home.[104]

The Relief Society curriculum underwent similar changes over the course of the 1960s to redefine women's roles. Prior to these changes, the manuals included nine "Work Meeting" lessons a year, written by professional home economics scholars on budgeting, service, and nutrition. Coinciding with Correlation and the new doctrinal emphasis on the home, in 1966, BYU English professor Celestia Taylor took over writing the lessons. Now called "Homemaking," Taylor wrote until Correlation eliminated the *Relief Society Magazine* in 1970. The change in name from "Work Meeting" to "Homemaking" signaled a change in female duties, narrowing the scope of work to housework. Taylor's lessons also marked a shift in tone. Historian Kate Holbrook notes that Taylor "contributed to a romanticization of home life and even expanded the boundaries of housework to include women's physical presentation."[105] Women were encouraged to exercise, watch their speech, develop a "pleasing personality," and be attentive to their looks.[106] In emphasizing women's work as homemaking and their duties to please their husbands, these curricular changes designated an increasingly narrow scope of women's place in society and the church.

## SEXUAL DIFFERENCE AND
## THEOLOGICAL ANTHROPOLOGY

As noted above, LDS leaders sought to explain and justify racial segregation and hierarchy by referencing events in a pre-mortal state. Similarly, these leaders looked to a time before the creation and after death for clues about sexual difference in this life. They appealed to distinctive aspects of Mormon cosmology—including a pre-mortal and post-mortal existence—to provide a foundation for sexual hierarchy in ways that resembled their assessment of racial hierarchy. Rather than appealing to an absolute, essential, and eternal form of sexual difference, Mormon leaders in the postwar period actually saw the pre-mortal and post-mortal periods as extensions of the gender fluidity and malleability of the mortal phase of human existence. That is, Mormons in this era were more likely to see sexual difference as the result of intentionally chosen gendered practices than as an unalterable nature of human identity. The perpetual liminality of sexual difference in Mormon theological anthropology was manifest in the way Mormons talked about the origins and destiny of gender in the grand sweep of the cosmos.

For many Mormon leaders, the pre-mortal existence explained gendered features and conditions of mortal life. As with racial difference, the disparity in opportunity, success, and God's favor reflected just rewards and punishment for choices that human spirits had made before they were born. Yet, the acquisition of sexual difference was not caused by a "war in heaven" or a rift between good and evil in the primordial sphere. Sexual difference was established before that. These Mormon leaders taught that human spirits were sexually dimorphic—whatever that might entail—but this cosmology of gender was far more complex in LDS theology. Before a spirit existed as a spiritual son or daughter of Heavenly Parents, there was a prior stage of existence; an individual existed first as "intelligence."[107] The doctrine of intelligence as an eternal being pointed to some aspect of humanness that preceded spiritual birth, some aspect that was more fundamental to one's identity than being gendered offspring of divinity.

The idea that the original being, the intelligence, was ungendered received some attention in Mormon thought in the postwar period. All the LDS creation accounts depict a certain moment when the divine beings "made male and female."[108] LDS thinkers described a moment of "spirit birth" as the time when gender was applied to uncreated intelligences. By portraying gender as a created and contingent feature of human identity, some church teachers used the idea of the primal agency to think about the choice an intelligence made to become male or female. In a 1967 book, BYU religious education professor Hyrum L. Andrus described the "two stages" of pre-mortal life and the transition from intelligence to spirit. Intelligences are without form: "Nowhere in scripture or in any authoritative source is the central primal life of man said to be 'an intelligence' that existed as a living entity in the form and stature of man."[109] That is, intelligences were a pre-anthropomorphic—and pre-gendered—state of existence. By 1972, another BYU religious education professor, Rodney Turner, offered the idea that gender is not an eternal characteristic, nor did God arbitrarily assign spirits to one gender or the other. Invoking Mormon ideas of agency, Turner taught that God did not coerce anyone in the moment of creation to being male or female. Instead, he proposed that pre-mortal agency and proclivities influenced which spirits became males and females: "The principle of agency must have played a part in anything God did. . . . The arbitrary assignment of sex would have rendered him particularly vulnerable to criticism."[110] A human's choice to be male or female was an ancient one that went back much further than mortal birth but was nevertheless a distinct moment of personal autonomy for a pre-mortal intelligence, not assigned by God.[111]

In a 1965 General Conference address, an assistant to the Quorum of the Twelve Apostles, William J. Critchlow Jr. (d. 1968), considered Turner's theory that one's gender identity was the result of a pre-mortal choice. In an explanation for why women did not hold the LDS priesthood, Critchlow hypothesized that in the preexistence some chose "mother's love" and others chose "priesthood authority." He listed the various gifts and virtues of wives and mothers that would have influenced their choice to become women.

> Did women by their own first choice choose to be partners
> with God in his creative processes? Faced with an alternative—
> partnership or priesthood—did you, Sister, pass up priesthood? . . .
> Did women by their own free choice choose to be the family
> heart rather than the family head? . . . Now, Sister, faced with the
> alternative family head or family heart, did you turn down the head?
> Faced again with a choice between mother's love or priesthood
> authority, did you pass up authority? . . . Now, which in this list of
> womanly virtues might possibly have influenced your choice—if
> and when, of course, you had a choice?[112]

Critchlow proposed various considerations that "influenced you to be woman rather than man," listing the roles and responsibilities of women for their husbands and children. He saw in the result a conscious choice to be male or female.[113]

Priesthood ordination became a crucial marker of both gender and racial differences, rewarding "choices" individuals had made as spiritual beings before their birth. Leaders and teachers advanced a theory of a gender-choice in the preexistence to explain and justify the hierarchy between men and women, just as they appealed to choices in the preexistence to explain and justify white hierarchy over black people. Both women and black men had "passed up" the priesthood and now occupied a different role in the mortal sphere. Critchlow and Turner suggested that prior to the choice to be male or female, a pre-gendered spirit may have certain proclivities that might push someone in one direction or the other. But like race, gender was ultimately chosen, not assigned. Mormon teachings about agency were put to use to explain and maintain social and ecclesiastical boundaries and con-stitutively create differences. But one critic of Turner's book noted, "If sex was voluntarily acquired at any point in pre-mortal life, then it should not completely shape mortal existence. Women should be people first."[114] Mak-ing sexual difference a choice did not necessarily make it more important; it suggested that there was something else more fundamental—humanness preceded sexual difference.

Not all Mormon leaders and teachers agreed with Critchlow's and Turn-er's position. In Bruce R. McConkie's 1958 *Mormon Doctrine*, intelligence is the state *after* spirit birth, not before.[115] But one leader from an earlier gener-ation, James Talmage (d. 1933), had written an important piece in 1914 called "The Eternity of Sex" that would play an important role in these debates over the nature of sexual difference.[116] In his brief essay, he affirmed, "Children of God have comprised male and female from the beginning. Man is man and woman is woman, fundamentally, unchangeably, eternally." Rather than seeing sexual difference as contingent or mutable, Talmage was an early pro-ponent of fixed, eternal differences. For Talmage, these differences were also hierarchical. In the preexistent state, he insisted, human spirits were either male or female. In the mortal sphere, "the body takes form as male or female according to the sex of the spirit whose appointment it is to tenant that body as a tabernacle formed of the elements of the earth." But Talmage's essay left many things undefined that had opened up the space for his successors to approach sexual difference in the preexistence differently. For instance, he did not deal with the period of existence prior to a spiritual creation as intel-ligence. Furthermore, citing the creation accounts ("male and female created he them"), he assigned to God the choice of who was male or female as a fea-ture of a spiritual creation. How could one both assert that God created male and female at a specific moment in time and hold that sexual difference was eternal and unchanging? Critchlow, Turner, and others were trying to solve two problems with Talmage's essentialist view. First, how can one account for the scriptural and theological point that male and female were the products of a moment in creation? Second, there was a problem of theodicy that Talmage introduced—if God created male and female difference, is not he also the source of a potentially unjust hierarchy? The anti-essentialists pointed to human agency as the solution to both problems.

The doctrine of a pre-mortal choice seemed to enjoy some currency in LDS teaching until it was officially rebutted in 1983. Apostle Gordon B. Hinckley (d. 2008) reintroduced Talmage's view. Hinckley taught, "I know of no doctrine which states that we made a choice when we came to earth as to whether we wished to be male or female. That choice was made by our Father in Heaven in his infinite wisdom."[117] Refuting Critchlow's worry that removing individual choice from divine gender assignment would make God "vulnerable to criticism," Hinckley's version of the preexistence pushed the problem into a different corner. Gender may not have been a choice of the individual spirit, but it was nevertheless someone's choice. If God chose the gender for any given individual, it was not an essential, uncreated element. The idea of a non-gendered "primal element" common to all human beings rendered sexual difference a secondary, contingent feature of what it meant to be human.

### NEITHER MALE NOR FEMALE AFTER DEATH

Many midcentury LDS leaders believed not only that being either male or female was a contingent feature of human identity but also that it was possible to be neither male nor female at all. Joseph Fielding Smith addressed the question of the eschatological future of sexual difference in his popular column. In 1963, a church member noted that according to church teachings, only those in the highest level of the celestial kingdom would remain married. (Mormons distinguish between a tripartite heaven—celestial, terrestrial, and telestial "kingdoms"—rather than a binary division between heaven and hell.)[118] A dispute had arisen in the member's Sunday School class. The problem, as the member noted, was that if sexual difference persisted eternally, then there would be lots of unmarried males and females in the lower kingdoms. The question proposed a delicious dilemma for Mormon literalism: "What will prevent them from living together outside the marriage covenant?" In other words, wouldn't all of these unmarried males and females have *illicit* sex in the afterlife? The seriousness of the person's question was built around Mormon ideas of a material heaven, but one that was also supposed to restrict sexual access exclusively to married persons in the highest heaven. Could not resurrected beings simply have sexual intercourse as unmarried persons? Wouldn't this be especially likely given their unrighteous position to begin with, having failed to reach the highest kingdom? How will sexual access be restricted for those unrighteous bodies?

Smith's answer was important because it tackled the problem from the member's assumption about gender. He started out by assuring the member that God had thought about this potential problem and had addressed it. Both males and females will indeed be judged and sent to the other kingdoms together. Smith explained, however, that "there will be differences in the bodies of the inhabitants of the several kingdoms." As evidence, he cited nineteenth-century Mormon theologian Orson Pratt's idea of "some physical peculiarity" that marked the bodies in the lower kingdoms from those in the celestial realm. From this, Smith concluded that there will be a physical difference in the resurrected inhabitants outside of celestial glory that prevents them from both the "privileges" of reproduction and sexual intercourse. What is the particular physical marker? Smith explained: "Is not the sectarian world justified in their doctrine generally proclaimed, that after the resurrection there will be neither male or female sex? It is a logical conclusion for them to reach and is apparently in full harmony with what the Lord has revealed regarding the kingdoms into which evidently the vast majority of mankind is likely to go."[119] Alluding to Galatians 3:28 that there is "neither male nor female . . . in Christ," Smith argued that other churches were largely correct in their rejection of a sexed afterlife. The idea that there would be some other sex, a neuter being that is neither man nor woman, as the norm for the vast majority of those in the afterlife made binary gender the exception for resurrected beings, not the rule.

Smith had thought through this issue before and taught it consistently in his ministry. In his 1954 book, *Doctrines of Salvation*, he made a similar statement about sexual difference as a privilege in the afterlife. He argued that those who do not dwell in the highest kingdom will lose the power of procreation just as they lose their marriages and families. Their bodies will be marked and will function differently. He explained, "Some of the functions in the celestial body will not appear in the terrestrial body, neither in the telestial body, and the power of procreation will be removed. I take it that men and women will, in these kingdoms, be just what the so-called Christian world expects us all to be—neither man nor woman, merely immortal beings having received the resurrection."[120] Since the functions of non-celestial bodies do not include reproduction and sexual intercourse, the form of these bodies will necessarily be different as well. There would be three sexes, man, woman, and immortal being—an undifferentiated human. His teaching suggested that sexual difference was a contingent, situational experience that makes sense only if there is something besides sexual dimorphism.

Joseph Fielding Smith's doctrines on the ontology of sexual difference help to frame what was at stake in postwar LDS teachings about gender. They represented sexual difference as a contingent feature of human existence, a "privilege" for those who advanced and who could maintain this feature in the face of a possible loss. In this sense, sexual difference was always the result of a set of individual choices—whether in the preexistence or in the mortal sphere. Sexual difference would persist only if one chose to follow the practices associated with one's gender. This influential strand of Mormon thought suggested that the primal element of human beings was essentially ungendered, and Mormon soteriology suggested that sexual difference was a crucial feature only of exalted individuals. To be without gender was to occupy a lower state of existence. Social forces that threatened to weaken sexual difference were then soteriologically dangerous because they pushed humans toward being "neither male nor female," which meant further away from divine favor. Mormon theology thus helped to establish the idea not only that sexual difference was contingent, fluid, and malleable but that idealized forms of sexual difference marked some bodies as more righteous than others. In a proleptic theology, proper performance of maleness and femaleness in this life would ensure their preservation in the next life. But sexual difference could be erased, returning once again to a lower form of existence before sexual difference was established, moving down the ladder of created order.

## INTERRACIAL MARRIAGE AND 1978

While teachings on sexual difference were being worked out, at the beginning of the 1970s church leaders were still ensnared in the sedimentation of racial purity doctrines about cursed and blessed lineages. Church leaders had navigated the controversies about civil rights in the 1960s with a mixed record, having ultimately offered their support, to the chagrin of apostle Ezra Taft Benson, at least. But, the racial policies within the church continued to attract negative attention. Black men were still barred from being ordained to the priesthood, and black men and women were consequently excluded from saving rituals performed in LDS temples. Any person considered to have "one drop" of "Negro" blood was similarly excluded by the blood quotient. The church faced negative public backlash for its belief that those with African ancestry were under a "curse." Protesters disrupted BYU athletic events, and black and white players on opposing teams refused to play against BYU. Invoking ideas of religious freedom, BYU president Ernest Wilkinson proactively sought to instill an ethic of tolerance for the church's teachings about racial purity.[121]

The church's racial policy continued to have important implications for the legitimacy of interracial marriage. In the 1970s, LDS church leaders began to put forward therapeutic arguments against interracial marriage that appeared more credible than talk about cursed lineages. Spencer W. Kimball had already begun to offer these arguments in the context of Native American–white marriages in the 1950s, teaching that mixed-race marriages were not expedient and were more likely to fail. There remained, however, the special case of black-white marriages and the barring of the priesthood and temple rituals for the children of such marriages. In 1976, he taught in a BYU devotional, "We recommend that people marry those who are of the same racial background generally, and of somewhat the same economic and social and educational background (some of those are not an absolute necessity, but preferred), and above all, the same religious background, without question."[122] Kimball continued to press an argument against interracial marriage based on expedience rather than on doctrine, grounding his teaching in the newer language of marital advice rather than in earlier doctrines of racial segregation. He put race into the same category as economic, social, and educational "background." Some church leaders framed the opposition to interracial marriage as "counsel"—a demotion from the status of doctrine that leaders in the 1950s and 1960s taught.[123]

When Kimball took over leadership of the church at the end of 1973, Time predicted, "The new president is not likely to change Mormon views on the family or race."[124] Such predictions were partially inaccurate. The policy barring black men from the priesthood and black men and women from temple participation had been the subject of much private dispute among church leaders since the 1950s.[125] Many of the senior apostles believed that only a revelation could end the racial doctrines. Kimball spent many hours in the Salt Lake Temple in prayer on the matter.[126] When he received a revelation on June 1, 1978, he announced, "All worthy male members of the Church may be ordained to the priesthood without regard for race or color."[127] The revelation created the possibility for a renewed American respectability for the church and opened new doors to international proselytism.

The new revelation gave full fellowship to black members but did not address a change in church teachings against interracial marriage. Kimball continued to believe it was not expedient for members to marry someone with a different racial identity. Appearing alongside the announcement of the new revelation, the church's official newspaper, *Church News*, printed a statement titled "Interracial Marriage Discouraged" in the June 17, 1978, edition. The practice was not prohibited, but social and cultural opposition policed the boundaries of interracial dating and marriage even after any doctrinal reasons had been eliminated. While earlier teachings had been rooted in ideas of divinely appointed racial hierarchies of chosen and cursed races, the newer teaching drew on Kimball's reasoning that interracial marriages were less stable.

The 1978 revelation did little to address the status of earlier church teachings about race, racial hierarchy, and even the nature of the ban itself. While most Mormons accepted the new revelation, many could not reconcile the change in doctrine with past statements of church leaders. In August 1978, just a few months after the revelation was announced, apostle Bruce R. McConkie answered the LDS detractors of the new revelation at a BYU symposium:

> There are statements in our literature by the early brethren which we have interpreted to mean that the Negroes would not receive the priesthood in mortality. I have said the same things, and people write me letters and say, "You said such and such, and how is it now that we do such and such?" And all I can say to that is that it is time disbelieving people repented and got in line and believed in a living, modern prophet. Forget everything that I have said, or what President Brigham Young or President George Q. Cannon or whomsoever has said in days past that is contrary to the present revelation. We spoke with a limited understanding and without the light and knowledge that now has come into the world. . . . They don't matter any more. . . . It doesn't make a particle of difference what anybody ever said about the Negro matter before the first day of June of this year.[128]

McConkie's speech emphasized "present revelation" as the foundation for doctrinal change. At the same time, confusion persisted among the Saints about the nature of the change. The prohibition on the priesthood had been lifted, but what was the status of the doctrines surrounding this practice, such as racial hierarchy or pre-mortal sins of spirits who came into "Negro" bodies? Was the original policy based in revelation, or cultural prejudice? For many, the new revelation flatly contradicted past authoritative teachings on racial purity and lacked convincing precedent. Forgetting did nothing to explain the past teachings. The persistence of advice against interracial marriage only added to the confusion. No clear answer emerged.

### RACE, MARRIAGE, AND THE NEW COLOR-BLIND TEACHINGS

The remainder of this chapter provides a historical coda to the question of race, which serves as an example of how LDS leaders managed the transition away from doctrines they once took as immutable. After 1978, church leaders basically stopped talking about race for nearly thirty years.[129] They generally believed that Spencer W. Kimball's revelation spoke for itself and did not require further elaboration.[130] However, the teachings against interracial marriage persisted. Kimball's 1976 recommendation in his BYU devotional was often taught in BYU marriage classes and republished in instruction manuals for teenagers and young adults (as recently as 2011). However, no other senior church leader publicly taught against interracial marriage in the interim. In preaching, racial mixing no longer appeared as a threat to the family. As church leaders stopped emphasizing racial difference as an essential and defining feature of human identity, they leaned more heavily on sexual difference. Human beings could be defined as simply male or female without also racializing those differences. The gradual shift toward a "color-blind" theology rested on a new universal difference between male and female that transcended formerly fixed racial boundaries.

In March 2006, Helen Whitney, famed documentary filmmaker, asked apostle Jeffrey R. Holland about the "lingering folklore" regarding why black men were excluded from the priesthood. Holland's response was candid and revealing. Specifically, Holland referenced the "folklore" that "there were decisions made in the premortal councils where someone had not been as decisive in their loyalty to a Gospel plan." As Hinckley had done with theories of pre-mortal choice for sexual difference, Holland was unsympathetic to this view of pre-mortal choice for racial difference. "But I think that's the part that must never be taught until anybody knows a lot more than I know," he added. Holland was making a historical claim that no one knew why black men were excluded from the priesthood and black women from the temple. "We just don't know, in the historical context of the time, why it was practiced. . . . That's my principal [concern], is that we don't perpetuate explanations about things we don't know." At the same time, Holland admitted that earlier apostles had indeed perpetuated such explanations. He lamented in a rare critical admission, "I have to concede to my earlier colleagues. . . . They, I'm sure, in their own way, were doing the best they knew to give shape to [the policy], to give context for it, to give even history to it. All I can say is however well intended the explanations were, I think almost all of them were inadequate and/or wrong. It probably would have been advantageous to say nothing. . . . At the very least, there should be no effort to perpetuate those efforts to explain why that doctrine existed."[131] Holland's statement that earlier apostles had been "wrong" was limited to the doctrinal explanations that had been given for the racial exclusions, not the exclusion itself. But it showed a willingness to abandon past doctrines, particularly by the "newer and younger" apostles. However, the persistence of racist teachings in the church nearly three decades after the change in practice revealed a deeper problem.

Holland's interview was closely correlated with another important development in LDS racial teachings. After decades of LDS leaders' silence on racial issues, Gordon B. Hinckley, by this time president of the church, delivered an important address in the 2006 General Conference against racism. Hinckley's leadership had been transformative and even progressive on women's issues compared with that of his predecessors, and he brought some of that progressive spirit to issues of race. He made racism a topic of moral concern for the first time in LDS preaching since the public statements on civil rights in the 1960s. Hinckley lamented that "racial strife still lifts its ugly head. I am advised that even right here among us there is some of this. I cannot understand how it can be. It seemed to me that we all rejoiced in the 1978 revelation given [to] President Kimball." He warned, "No man who makes disparaging remarks concerning those of another race can consider himself a true disciple of Christ. Nor can he consider himself to be in harmony with the teachings of the Church of Christ."[132] Hinckley's remarks fell short of a clarification on the status on prior church teachings about racial purity and hierarchy, and they did not address the question of interracial marriage. Nevertheless, they represented a major, official condemnation of racism. A few years later, a church spokesman added that "the church has no policy against interracial marriage."[133] The clarification stated the obvious at that point. There had been no policy against it since 1978, but the statement did not address whether the church still advised against interracial marriage.

There were no other major speeches on race after 2006, but the lingering scars of the doctrines prior to 1978 still marked the church by reputation and created confusion about the status of those teachings. In the satirical 2011 Broadway musical *The Book of Mormon*, the main character Elder Price sings, "I believe that in 1978 God changed his mind about black people!" The tongue-in-cheek declaration captured the lingering theological predicament. Had the church leaders' teachings on racial purity, interracial marriage, and cursed lineages been revealed and supported by God? Did saying that "we don't know" why the practice had been in place imply that it was God's will, however inscrutable?

By the 2010s, the church began to make more efforts to address the racism of previous teachings and the lingering cultural attitudes. Some of these issues arose in the context of Mitt Romney's 2008 and 2012 presidential bids, which brought renewed public attention to the church's history on race. In an uncomfortable 2012 interview with the *Washington Post*, BYU professor of religious education Randy Bott explained his understanding of LDS teachings on racial lineage—that black people were descended from Cain and Ham and that the mark on Cain was "the flat nose and black skin." He expressed the idea that black people were not mature enough before 1978 and that the LDS priesthood and temple restriction was "the greatest blessing God could give them."[134] For Bott, it seems, Elder Price's declaration seemed to ring true. LDS church headquarters was not pleased with Bott's reiteration of doctrines of racial lineages—though many like it circulated in the absence of any official repudiation of the ban. LDS Public Affairs issued an unprecedented statement condemning the popular teacher: "The positions attributed to BYU professor Randy Bott in a recent Washington Post article absolutely do not represent the teachings and doctrines of The Church of Jesus Christ of Latter-day Saints."[135] Bott was reprimanded but not fired.[136]

Many members of the church remained unsatisfied that a prominent BYU professor could still be repeating racist doctrines in the classroom and to reporters in 2012. The long silence on the issue of race had not resolved the outstanding questions nor clarified how church members were to interpret the teachings of past leaders. Condemnations of racism notwithstanding, the problems remained. Without a specific repudiation of the earlier teachings on racial hierarchy or curses, these ideas continued to be taught in church settings and at church colleges and universities.

In 2012 and 2013, the church issued two new documents on race.[137] One was an extensive historical discussion of the church's teachings. Importantly, the document spoke about the status of these prior teachings: "Today, the Church disavows the theories advanced in the past that black skin is a sign of divine disfavor or curse, or that it reflects unrighteous actions in a premortal life; that mixed-race marriages are a sin; or that blacks or people of any other race or ethnicity are inferior in any way to anyone else. Church leaders today unequivocally condemn all racism, past and present, in any form."[138] This disavowal echoed McConkie's 1978 instruction to "forget" what he and other church leaders had said about race and the priesthood, but the new statement expanded it to cover interracial marriage—which the 1978 teachings had not overturned. And yet even here, there is no repudiation of counsel against mixed-race marriage, just a declaration that it is not a sin.

Still, the church was displaying new signs of openness. An indication that the church culture had changed attitudes against interracial marriage came in the official "I'm A Mormon" advertising campaign launched in 2011.[139] Several interracial couples and their children were featured in the promotional videos.[140] The campaign attempted to highlight the racial diversity of Mormonism as well as the broad kinds of people who were Mormon in the early twenty-first century. One of the "I'm a Mormon" videos featured Mia Love, who was at the time the mayor of Saratoga Springs, a small town in Utah.[141] Born in 1975 to Haitian immigrants, Love grew up Catholic but converted to Mormonism in 1998, having first met her husband while he was serving as an LDS missionary in New England. The two married shortly after he completed his service and lived in heavily white communities in Utah. Getting involved in her new community, Love eventually found a place in local politics. A few years later, she would rocket to national fame when she was elected as the first black Republican woman to the U.S. Congress, serving from 2014 to 2018. Not long after her successful election campaign, the LDS-owned *Deseret News* ran a flattering profile about her white husband, "Mr. (Mia) Love: The Man behind the Congresswoman."[142] The profile reflected some of the lingering male-centered biases of the culture; there were no similar profiles of the wives of male elected representatives. Jason Love held a senior position at a small software company, but the story wasn't about his accomplishments. The Loves' "mixed-marriage" was a bit of a curiosity in this conservative Mormon region. The *Deseret News* painted a positive picture of their family and home life, despite being an interracial relationship where the wife and mother worked outside the home—and outside the state—in a demanding and high-profile public career.

What was the new doctrine of marriage that could accommodate this change? Interracial couples and working wives with small children at home were now earning positive press in Mormon media outlets. The idea of abandoning racial purity doctrines goes only so far to explain the shift. The old doctrines had to be replaced with something else. The answer lay in a new theory of humanness that deracialized people. At the fortieth anniversary celebration of Kimball's revelation, the new church president Russell M. Nelson articulated this view: "Differences in culture, language, gender, race, and nationality fade into insignificance as the faithful enter the covenant path and come unto our beloved Redeemer." He continued, "Only the comprehension of the true Fatherhood of God can bring full appreciation of the true brotherhood of men and the true sisterhood of women."[143] Instead of race, the primary difference in humanity was sexual difference—and this sexual difference was no longer tied to a strict division of roles. In the decades when interracial marriage was prohibited, marriage was between a man and a woman, qualified by their compatible racial identities. As heterosexuality became the exclusive feature of an authorized marriage, race fell away as a defining norm for who could marry whom. Mormon marriage doctrine was no longer tied to the doctrines of racial purity that structured which men and women could marry; now, it was tied to heterosexuality. Similarly, sexual difference was attached less to gender roles and more to biological sex. Race was becoming more fluid by abandoning lineage doctrines, and sexual difference more fixed by focusing on bodies, not roles.

The evolving doctrines against racial and gender mixing that came into full flower in the 1950s and 1960s were never fully erased as they transformed in the 1990s and into the next century. However, older doctrines against racial mixing and doctrines of white supremacy were increasingly and explicitly rejected by church authorities.[144] But doctrines about gender roles, and the worries about gender fluidity, morphed into new concerns and spawned new forms of power. In its most pointed form, homosexuality became the ultimate threat of gender fluidity and its most prevalent expression. As church leaders relaxed their teachings on racial difference and hierarchy, they increased their attention to sexual difference as a defining aspect of human identity—especially as it was manifest in sexuality. The following chapter explores that theme.

# Chapter Two

# SODOM AND CUMORAH

In 1975, then church president Spencer W. Kimball asked Victor L. Brown Jr. to write a series of reports on the causes of "deviant" sexual activities and to present his findings to senior church leaders. Brown, a trained psychologist and director of LDS Social Services, spent a year preparing his remarks. When he delivered the report in 1976, Brown laid out his theory: sexual sins were "symptoms" whose "causes" lay at a deeper level. This deeper level could be located in the foundations created in parental interaction in homes. The report began by quoting 1 Timothy 3:5: "For if a man know not how to rule his own house, how shall he take care of the church of God?" Brown argued that the masculine father was the crucial figure in the family and the key to preventing problems in children, from minor emotional fragility to sexual deviance—especially homosexuality. He was concerned that fathers were neglecting their duty and were prone to falter in their responsibilities: "The weakest link in the temple ordinance chain is the man—the priesthood holder." Meanwhile, "women are, by nature, more responsive to goodness than men."[1] He concluded, "The root problem, therefore, is the failure, not of mothers—but of fathers, to magnify their calling."[2] Delinquent male leadership and sexual deviance were inextricably linked.

The impetus for the presentation was just as important as the conclusions. Something new was happening with Brown's presence and influence. This chapter follows a competing set of ideologies for thinking about same-sex relationships from the 1950s to the 1970s, from moral causes and cures to psychological causes and cures.[3] This period shows that church leaders were increasingly turning to the discourse of science to vindicate their teachings on sexual morality, specifically tying (male) homosexuality to failed masculinity and weakened patriarchy. But masculinity was more than just a set of practices—it was also a psychological phenomenon.

The psychological lens on homosexuality was not necessarily a natural outcome of moral crusades. Church leaders arrived at a therapeutic Mormonism in the mid-1970s after a great deal of ambivalence. As noted at the outset of chapter 1, Kimball's early concern about homosexuality—a descriptive term of significant contestation, as we shall see—arose in part after his assignment to counsel members of the church involved in sexual sin. The way in which he and his colleagues in senior leadership positions in the church approached this topic deserves specific treatment. While the previous chapter looked at the anxiety about porous boundaries of racial and gender fluidity, this chapter examines the invention of (male) homosexuality during this same transformative period as another site of instability and mutable identities. In addition to the supposedly natural and divinely sanctioned binaries between black and white and male and female discussed in chapter 1, church leaders adopted another dichotomy between normal and deviant.

Among the many changes to LDS teachings that took place during this period, church leaders adopted a religio-psychological framework that viewed sexuality in broadly Freudian, psychoanalytic terms. In this view, sexuality and object attachment were not innate but developed in early childhood and adolescence.[4] In addition, this framework increasingly defined sexuality in terms of gender, such that the proper performance of maleness and femaleness was deeply connected to heterosexuality—both explaining its presence and providing a path to rectifying any deviations. That is, while gender instability was a source of significant anxiety in the evaluation of gender roles and paid labor, the fact of its instability also meant that one's gender and sexuality could be manipulated and reformed. This shift put increasing burdens on parents and the family as the institution that would instill heterosexuality in young people. The psychological discourse thus brought new expertise and power to bear while privileging the family as the most important instrument in preventing homosexuality.

Queer theorists similarly trace the genealogy of their notions of gender fluidity to a psychoanalytic framework that sees human subjectivity as produced rather than given.[5] They too reject biologically deterministic and binary accounts of sexuality, challenging the homo/hetero dichotomy as insufficient and constrictive, and point out that the overlap between heterosexuality and homosexuality is a site for rethinking these categories altogether. However, these theories look for critical strategies and resources for subversion in these psychoanalytic accounts.

In contrast, Mormon theories of human subjectivity in this period positively embraced this fluidity to both explain the possibility of nonheterosexual desires and chart a path of cure for those who had been lost. Gender fluidity was not something to be avoided entirely but something that could be strategically harnessed to heal the homosexual. This chapter then contributes to the history of sexuality by showing how the psychological category of "homosexuality" was merged with a religious worldview. Conservative religious communities, like Mormon leaders, rejected modernist ideas of essentialism and put the fluidity and malleability of identity to use.

## HOMOSEXUAL PANIC IN MIDCENTURY

The grafting of psychological theories of homosexuality onto LDS notions of sin needs to be set in two broader contexts. First, there was in general a newly formed interest in a category of "homosexuality" after World War II in American culture.[6] The first half of the twentieth century provides mostly a profound silence of LDS discourse on the sins of sodomy, homosexuality, or other cognates.[7] The same relative absence also characterizes Protestant sermons, commentaries, and literature.[8] However, the lack of ecclesiastical attention in sermons does not mean the possibility and practice of same-sex intercourse was unknown among the Saints;[9] rather, this awareness was widespread and dates to the earliest days of the church. For example, charges of exchanging positions of rank in the Nauvoo Legion for sexual favors from men were made against the disgraced John C. Bennett, second in the church at the time only to Joseph Smith.[10] And in official preaching, nineteenth-century apostle George Q. Cannon mentioned "the crime against nature" on occasion.[11] He even declared that such sexual acts were caused by the "false tradition" of monogamous marriage![12] In the October 1897 General Conference, in the context of the well-publicized British trial of Oscar Wilde, Cannon suggested that the cure for sodomy would be the destruction of all such practitioners in one generation, preventing its spread through contagion.[13] Cannon presupposed all were at risk of sodomy. He was also among the last to speak publicly on this topic for decades. Even though LDS historians have documented numerous queer relationships among prominent Mormons in the early twentieth century,[14] there was virtually no public teaching on same-sex sexual relationships in the church. The birth of LDS attention to what was becoming known as "homosexuality" belongs to the period after World War II.

This is unsurprising. Historians of American sexuality have noted that the period after World War II marked a transition in sensibilities toward same-sex sexual relationships.[15] Gay and lesbian communities had sprouted in cities in the 1920s and 1930s, but the war years and subsequent decades facilitated new contacts. Urbanization, migration, and the war itself had created more opportunities for encounters and greater organization of gay subcultures.[16] But such subcultures were not the only place for same-sex intimacy. In 1948, Alfred Kinsey's monumental report, *Sexual Behavior in the Human Male*, demonstrated the ubiquity of sexual contact between men: over one-third of all males had participated in postadolescent same-sex sexual exchange. The dry, scientific study was a sensation. It eventually sold a quarter million copies and spent twenty-seven weeks on the *New York Times* best-seller list. The revelations contained in the study shocked traditional sensibilities, even while it revealed the hypocrisies of those sexual standards. For Kinsey at least, the pervasiveness of same-sex relations rendered them morally banal.

Kinsey's report also contained information about pre- and extramarital opposite-sex sexual practices, which had similarly become quite common. But the relative tolerance toward this kind of deviance did not always spill over. Historians John D'Emilio and Estelle B. Freedman have noted that "with the more permissive attitudes of sexual liberalism toward most forms of heterosexual expression went an effort to label homosexual behavior as deviant."[17] This new sexual deviant was both common and exotic. In 1950, the U.S. Senate commissioned a report on the government employment of "homosexuals and other perverts." Legislators worried deeply about the contagious character of this condition and noted, "These perverts will frequently attempt to entice normal individuals to engage in perverted practices.... One homosexual can pollute a government office."[18] Numerous individuals were dismissed, barred from federal employment, and labeled national security risks. The prevailing theory here was that homosexuality was a contagious practice that put "normal" people at great risk.

In addition, psychiatric treatment of sexual deviance was increasingly a well-established field in its own right. Sexologists, psychoanalysts, and psychologists were pioneering classifications, etiologies, and treatments in the first half of the twentieth century. In the postwar era, the rising attention to homosexuality led to a greater prevalence of psychiatric evaluation and treatment for this "condition."[19] The moral scare of the 1950s authorized police to harass gay men and women with impunity and to enforce sodomy laws. Beginning in the 1950s, Utah courts sentenced convicted "sexual deviants" to psychiatric care.[20] Psychiatrists joined police to regulate homosexuals and other sexual deviants. These new forms of power operated not by means of punishment and condemnation (at least not only by these means) but by means of rehabilitation, care, and regimens to change desires and behaviors.

The homosexual menace emerged as a veritable social panic, and other institutions rallied to the cause.[21] For instance, the American Psychiatric Association listed homosexuality as a sociopathic personality disturbance in its first edition of the *Diagnostic and Statistical Manual of Mental Disorders* in 1952.[23] Rather than accepting Kinsey's assessment of homosexuality as banality, many treated the ubiquity of same-sex sexual encounters and relationships as an urgent moral crisis. Similarly, historian Mark Jordan notes that it was not until the 1950s, in the wake of the Kinsey report, that American churches started to discuss same-sex desire with any amount of frequency or depth.[22] When they did, he argues, they adopted the psychological and sexological language about "the homosexual" produced at the turn of the twentieth century in scientific literature and the new concern in psychological literature.

The adoption of the category "the homosexual" by churches marked the shift from thinking about the act of sodomy to considering a whole new range of disciplinary mechanisms for social and psychological sins. Here, I follow the usage of "the homosexual" as a rhetorical construction, an imagined subject rather than a stable, clearly defined, ahistorical identity. As Michel Foucault pointed out, the term "sodomy" had generally described a set of acts, while the term "homosexual" was increasingly being used to describe a person's identity. The implication of this historicizing perspective is not that people have not always engaged in same-sex sexual encounters and relationships across cultures but that the label "homosexual" is a distinctive concept of the modern West—a new way of thinking about people that produced, rather than reflected, a new identity. Others, like Mark Jordan, have significantly nuanced this transition from acts to identity as an overstatement of the historical record. These perspectives show at minimum a conflict over the new kinds of identity embedded in the concept of a discrete "homosexual."[24] Kinsey had proposed the use of the term "homosexual" as an adjective to describe responses and acts, and he questioned the idea that homosexuals were a distinct type of person. Other homophile activists, however, framed homosexuality as an oppressed minority class, similar to the status of race, in need of protection and outlets for cultural, political, and spiritual community.[25]

Psychology was not the only discourse that gave voice to the midcentury panic about these sexual practices. In a sociosexual theory of culture, conservatives warned that immorality threatened national health and survival and that the pervasiveness of homosexual acts signaled a state of social decline.[26] The Mormon anxiety about racial, gender, and sexual boundaries was deeply connected to broader American postwar concerns about the status of the new American global power. The religious revival during this period reclaimed themes of moral purity as a key to national survival.

The Cold War ideology of American supremacy was then deeply connected to an idea that America was a safeguard in the world in a battle between good and evil. Protestant fundamentalist and evangelical preachers gave voice to many of these concerns. Billy Graham rose to prominence in the 1950s by preaching on the topic of sexual temptation and the need for moral purity among American youth. Warning that moral decay would lead to national collapse and give strength to Soviet Communism, Graham framed the sexual decisions of young people as a question of a national security. He explained, "America is truly the last bulwark of Christian civilization. . . . If you would be a true patriot, then become a Christian. . . . America cannot survive, she cannot fulfill her divine purpose, she cannot carry out her God-appointed mission without the spiritual emphasis which was hers from the outset."[27] Sexual purity and the sanctity of the patriarchal family were at the center of his concern for America's strength.[28]

Graham and other Christian fundamentalists and nationalists did not invent the narrative of immorality and civilizational decline on their own. They drew on a number of intellectual resources that purported to explain civilizational strength and weakness through the lens of sexual restraint or permissiveness. The theme was found in Edward Gibbon's late eighteenth-century classical study, *The History of the Decline and Fall of the Roman Empire*, which enjoyed a renewed interest in the Cold War period. Gibbon had actually criticized religion's role in the fall of Rome but also indicated that moral lapses contributed to its degeneration. LDS apostle Marion G. Romney (d. 1988) cited Gibbon's claim that "the undermining of the dignity and sanctity of the home" was the first thing to erode civilizational strength. Romney concluded that the Home Teaching and Family Home Evening programs were not only for the members of the church but for the strength of Western civilization itself.[29]

This narrative plotline was amplified by a number of twentieth-century anthropologists, historians, and cultural critics. J. D. Unwin, Will Durant, Pitirim Sorokin, Arnold J. Toynbee, and others contributed to providing an intellectual support system for conservative Christians.[30] Midcentury Mormons were not immune to this trend in conservatism to situate sexual morality and family life as the bedrock of civilization. In their sermons, they often taught that American strength was dependent upon the spiritual vitality of its people, especially in the bedroom and the home. Church president David O. McKay frequently made this point: "Infidelity and sexual immorality are two principal evils that threaten to weaken and to wreck present-day civilization."[31] But this was not all; gender roles were also vital to this project of civilizational preservation: "The more woman becomes like man, the less he will respect her; civilization weakens as man's estimate of woman lessens."[32] McKay cited the common sources for the story of civilizational decline. First publishing in the 1930s, J. D. Unwin, a British anthropologist at Cambridge, was an important figure for Christian preaching in the 1960s.[33] He purported to study eighty civilizations over four thousand years and concluded, in McKay's summary, "that a society either chooses sexual promiscuity and decline, or sexual discipline and creative energy."[34] Unwin's theory that sexual restraint produced cultural productivity was loosely based on the Freudian notion of psychological sublimation, that displacement of sexual aims would redirect such energy into other human achievements.

Apostle Ezra Taft Benson was particularly fond of theories of civilizational decline. He taught in 1947, "The family is a divine institution established by our Heavenly Father. It is basic to civilization and particularly to Christian civilization."[35] Benson was influenced by the popular histories of Will Durant, especially his volume on the fall of Rome: "[Durant] lists the major causes why this great civilization fell apart. I wonder if there is anything in what he says for us to take note of today. As I read this volume I was caused to reflect on the similarity of conditions and practices then and now. . . . They had to do with the limitation of families, the deferment and avoidance of marriage, the refusal of men and women to shoulder the great responsibilities."[36] He told an apocalyptic story about America's decline: "I do not believe the greatest threat to our future is from bombs or guided missiles. I do not think our civilization will die that way. I think it will die when we no longer care, when the spiritual forces that make us wish to be right and noble die in the hearts of men, when we disregard the importance of law and order. If American freedom is lost, if America is destroyed, if our blood-bought freedom is surrendered, it will be because of Americans."[37] This fear-based approach to the role of sexual purity, gender roles, and familial stability supported Mormon worries about homosexuality as a particularly depraved threat to civilization itself.

## PASTORAL COUNSELING

The second significant context that needs to be laid out in order to explain how LDS leaders merged psychology with their approach to homosexuality is the sociosexual response to homosexuality, which was distinctive in its deployment of new forms of power. The changes introduced in this period took part in a broader arc in the way American churches redefined religious authority and leadership over the course of the twentieth century. E. Brooks Holifield's assessment of the history of pastoral care in America notes that religious leaders in that century redefined their roles with congregants, moving "from salvation to self-realization."[38] This self-help model came to dominate the way that pastoral care was conceived in early twentieth-century America. Among these influences, eclectic New Thought movements focused on the power of the mind and preached on the control of thought as the key to health, happiness, and wealth.[39]

These adaptations of therapy to theology shared the modernist values of scientific progress, naturalism, and the reinterpretation of Christianity in light of historical and scientific knowledge. At Harvard Divinity School, Richard Cabot pioneered new requirements for ministers to receive training in counseling, just as physicians would receive. Other Protestants applied the therapeutic sciences to the treatment of particular social problems, proclaiming the new gospel of mental hygiene. Harry Emerson Fosdick was among the most famous examples of the convergence of medicine and morality. A giant of modernist Protestant theology and the Social Gospel, his best-selling book *On Being a Real Person* (1943) merged psychology and psychiatry together in a hybrid of theological therapy. The book set out the beginnings of a mainstream idea of religious and pastoral counseling, launching journals and new professional training for ministers, and left in its wake a series of religiously based self-help books.[40] Fosdick emphasized choice, responsibility, self-control, and the possibility of real change and improvement as characteristics of the Christian gospel.

The boom in psychology and psychiatry after World War II set the stage for the combination of scientific and religious oversight of the homosexual.

What had previously been counted as "sins," including crime, intemperance, violence, and sexual delinquency, were transformed into "illnesses" with religio-psychological diagnoses and cures. These two systems of knowledge increasingly overlapped and were integrated in American Protestant—and LDS—contexts. The confluence of the invention of "the homosexual" as a distinctive pathological and medical case and the psychologization of religion in the twentieth century produced a new kind of response. As Heather White explains, "The religious, medical, and legal stigmas against homosexuality that so preoccupied Americans of the postwar era were not the archaic remains of a religious past. Rather, they reflected the surfacing of a new synthesis, which knitted together disease theories and religious teaching into an emergent therapeutic orthodoxy."[41] The blend of social liberalization, greater visibility and organization of homophile groups, and the conservative response to homosexuality as a pathological condition sat at the heart of social tensions on this issue.

Mormons were no exception when it came to propagating the self-help gospel and the synergy of religious and popular psychological principles. In the 1930s, the Relief Society ran a series of articles advocating the best of the "mental hygiene" movement.[42] Pastoral figures like Fosdick were well known to Mormon leaders, who had quoted his works regularly and approvingly in General Conference sermons since the 1920s. His emphasis on agency, change, and an optimism in human potential resonated with Mormonism's progressive sensibilities from the first half of the twentieth century. In the 1960s, church leaders still quoted Fosdick's *On Being a Real Person* and other works many times in their public sermons.[43] Self-improvement and mind cures were promulgated by senior church leaders and structured the new moral discourse, pastoral ethic, and doctrines of human agency and potential.

Similarly, Norman Vincent Peale was an important popularizer of this approach. A pastor who rocketed to national fame and advised U.S. presidents, Peale's 1952 best seller, *The Power of Positive Thinking*, taught through anecdote that holding an optimistic attitude could enable an individual to accomplish great things. He encouraged readers to use visualization and self-affirmation to achieve success and overcome difficulties in life. His later book *Sex, Sin, and Self-Control* (1966) drew on these same principles about controlling one's thoughts. Self-discipline was not a constraint but a key to individual freedom. These popular psychological principles were repurposed to affirm traditional Christian values in the idiom of therapeutic virtues. Peale made an impression on LDS authorities in the 1960s, who cited his work frequently as well.[44] He even sought a blessing from Spencer W. Kimball in 1975.[45]

LDS adoption and adaptation of counseling sessions to "treat" the sinner with mind cures coincided with broader shifts in LDS pastoral practices. Mormon practices of confession, for instance, corresponded to the gradual ascendency of pastoral counseling as the primary response to sin. Public confession, especially when the act had been publicly known, had been the dominant Mormon model until the middle of the twentieth century, finally being eliminated in 1976.[46] Confession of serious transgressions gradually transformed from a public act in a congregation to a private act in a bishop's office. This new spiritual technology connected a Catholic model of confession with the inquisitorial model of Mormon bishops' juridical authority. Bishops had originally dealt with temporal matters, leaving spiritual matters to high priests. Beginning in 1913, the church put forward a new model of the bishop as a spiritual leader. In addition to hearing confessions and providing judgments for informal church discipline or holding a "bishop's court," bishops took on pastoral care as a new responsibility.[47] These models gradually took ascendancy over the course of this century.

### THE INVENTION OF HOMOSEXUALITY AND ITS CURE

The shift in pastoral and psychological care set up the transition to a new Mormon response to same-sex intimacy. This shift was made possible by a new categorization of same-sex dynamics, as Latter-day Saints transitioned from the moral and legal category of sodomy to the religio-psychological and medical discourse of homosexuality in this period.[48] Mormons in the nineteenth and early twentieth centuries had not condoned same-sex sexual activity but had treated it less harshly than other sexual sins. A regional history of Utah reveals a thriving subculture for same-sex encounters in the 1930s, 1940s, and 1950s.[49] These kinds of encounters were common enough that even high-ranking church leaders engaged in them. In 1946, the church's presiding patriarch, Joseph F. Smith (d. 1964; not to be confused with the earlier church president of the same name), took a young male lover who had just returned from service in the navy. The young man's father outed Smith to church authorities when he discovered the relationship. As a consequence, Smith was released from his church duties and moved in exile to Hawaii on the pretense of his back injuries—but was not excommunicated.[50]

In contrast, when church leaders discovered a sexual affair of apostle Richard R. Lyman (d. 1963) with his elderly mistress in this same period, they publicly announced his excommunication for violating "the Christian law of chastity."[51]

In subsequent decades, church leaders adopted increasingly alarmist positions about the harms of same-sex intercourse and relationships. This was a change. Historian D. Michael Quinn traces a transition in LDS leaders' attitudes toward homosexuality in these midcentury decades, arguing that during the 1950s the church moved from "relative tolerance" to "homophobia" and strident opposition.[52] But "homophobia"—itself a pathological diagnosis—goes only so far as an explanation for changing church attitudes about same-sex intimacy. For instance, church leaders were also concerned with race and gender mixing, but their fears about these forms of mixing manifested in different ways. What animated Mormon approaches to homosexuality was the concoction of new forms of pastoral and psychological power that framed homosexuality as a particularly insidious form of gender failure.

In 1947, Spencer W. Kimball was assigned to work with people involved in sexual transgressions, including those who had engaged in same-sex erotic relationships and encounters.[53] In spite of well-known instances—such as Patriarch Joseph F. Smith's case—there was initially little public discussion about same-sex intimacies by church leaders. In fact, the first mention of the phenomenon came in 1952, when apostle J. Reuben Clark became the first senior authority of the church to use the words "homosexual" and "homosexuality" in a public speech—the same year that the American Psychiatric Association first listed homosexuality as a sociopathic personality disturbance. Clark complained of this "softer name" for the sins of Sodom and Gomorrah.[54] We can thus date the invention of "the homosexual" in Mormon thought to 1952.

In spite of these early rumblings, church leaders still gave little public attention to the topic of homosexuality for most of the 1950s. Clark mentioned "that filthy crime of homosexuality" in a laundry list of sins in a 1954 speech to the men of the church.[55] Yet, there was no mention of the practice in the official instruction handbook for church leaders. The 1956 instruction manual *Handling the Transgressor* outlined the procedures for church discipline of various sexual sins yet made no mention of same-sex erotic activity.[56] Apostle Bruce R. McConkie's encyclopedic 1958 *Mormon Doctrine* also offered little discussion of the topic. Both the entries on "homosexuality" and "sodomy" pointed to the more general entry on "sex immorality." In that brief entry, same-sex sexual relationships remained a primarily legal concern—he lamented the lack of capital punishment for sexual crimes as evidence of society's "apostasy." McConkie provided no discussion of causes or cures of homosexuality, nor did he advise any kind of pastoral, let alone professional, care. There was no suggestion that sexual sins of any type should receive therapeutic or pastoral attention outside of punishment.[57]

By the late 1950s, however, church leaders increasingly worried that homosexuality was a growing problem in need of a solution. There were likely a number of reasons why, including the national scare about the practice. But there may have been specific reasons that pushed LDS church leaders to speak out against it more frequently than they had previously and to "straighten" Mormonism's public image. In 1959, the best-selling book *Advise and Consent* depicted a Mormon U.S. senator as a clandestine homosexual.[58] The book won the Pulitzer Prize for fiction and was adapted into a film, though the film version never mentioned Mormonism directly.

That same year, President McKay assigned apostle Mark E. Petersen to join with Kimball to develop a scripturally based solution to "homosexual problems."[59] They counseled individuals but also began to define new church policies to address the matter. These were largely disciplinary and aimed to create social and ecclesiastical pressures to discourage the practice. In 1962, Kimball and Petersen instructed BYU not to admit any student about whom "we have convincing evidence is a homosexual."[60]

This policy may have come at the request of BYU president Ernest Wilkinson. In 1959, he had launched a new surveillance program on students suspected of homosexuality. Wilkinson had massively increased his authority over students and faculty in purity campaigns to protect the campus from unwanted ideas and practices. He requested permission from senior church leaders to send questionnaires to bishops asking for the names of students who had confessed in ecclesiastical interviews to "immorality of anything of that kind." He proposed to BYU's Executive Committee that the university suspend any student who was not "really repentant" for their acts.[61] By tying educational status and the prospects of a future profession to morality standards, BYU had more leverage over its students than church leaders did to enforce these rules. These worries took hold across church leadership. In 1960, Clark had written in his diary that there was a "serious 'homo' situation at B.Y.U."[62]

Church leaders were also concerned about BYU students primarily because they saw homosexuality as a problem for young men. In January

1965, Kimball spoke to the BYU student body and explained, "I cannot imagine that this university would ever enroll a pervert knowingly, an unrepentant one. I cannot imagine this university ever tolerating on its campus one day or one week any adulterer or fornicator or pervert, [who was] unrepentant."[63] "Pervert" was his preferred term for gay men and women. Near the end of that year, Wilkinson believed that the problem was still growing at BYU, and he also decided to address the campus about the matter: "If any of you have this tendency and have not completely abandoned it, may I suggest that you leave the university immediately after this assembly. . . . We do not want others on this campus to be contaminated by your presence."[64] Wilkinson promised to refund the tuition of any homosexual who confessed it to be the reason for leaving. By 1967, he was finally allowed to institute his plan to have bishops inform the Standards Office about students who had confessed in ecclesiastical interviews. That year, the Standards Office met with seventy-two students "suspected of homosexual activity."[65] Students were pressured to report the names of others as part of efforts to rid the school of homosexuals in 1968.[66] In addition to sanctions at BYU, Kimball taught in 1964 that excommunication should be the punishment for same-sex relationships, though the transgression still did not appear in any instruction manual for church leaders.[67] "Homosexuality" was formally added to the list of excommunicable offenses in the church in 1968.[68]

There was certainly some continuity between sodomy and homosexuality as conceptual categories. Both imagined that same-sex intimacy was primarily about sexual gratification rather than a drive to create relationships. But the new discourse of homosexuality really constituted a revolution for Mormon moral discourse. The epistemic shift that enabled the transition from the "sin of Sodom and Gomorrah" to "homosexuality" created an occasion for new forms of knowledge and new forms of power. The homosexual was a pathological case and was consequently deserving of heightened concern and new techniques for surveillance, punishment, and ultimately rehabilitation.

It is worth noting at this point that in the 1950s and 1960s, church leaders regularly spoke of "homosexuality" and "homosexuals" without qualification. While they resisted the essentialism of these terms, they fully accepted the medical pathology behind them. Homosexuality was a perversion, an illness, and unnatural—but could also be healed. However, as the term "homosexual" was increasingly associated with a fixed identity and immutable nature, church leaders later became hesitant to adopt it. But in the 1950s and 1960s, the term still implied sexual malleability for church leaders. Not only could the homosexual be cured and return to "normal," but the contagious effects of homosexuality could also corrupt the "normal" person. Wilkinson's worry about the "contamination" of homosexuality reflected his belief that the practice could be enticing to anyone. The theory that dominated this panic was based on the perpetual, universal risks of homosexual contagion and the perpetual opportunities for a return to heterosexuality for the repentant.

## MASCULINITY AND SELF-MASTERY IN EARLY CAUSES AND CURES

Just as the category of (male) homosexuality was being developed, the prospects of its prevention and cure were taking shape in teachings about masculinity and "self-mastery." As part of his assigned duties to find a solution to homosexuality in the 1950s, Spencer W. Kimball eventually produced new literature targeting homosexuals, developed new pastoral techniques and spiritual practices that would promise a cure, and established institutions that would produce knowledge about these topics. Kimball's paradigm for pastoral care had been deeply influenced by positive thinking movements, from New Thought to the teachings of Norman Vincent Peale and other self-help ideologies, which taught that self-discipline of the mind was key to success in life. For instance, Kimball frequently quoted and recommended self-help guru James Allen's 1903 best seller, *As a Man Thinketh,* in his accounts of sin and repentance, believing that the mind could be controlled and shaped to overcome sin.[69] Kimball's books, speeches, and pamphlets drew on notions of homosexuality as mental illness that could be cured by the will. The homosexual had transformed from being an occasional deviant to being mentally inflicted and in need of a therapeutic cure. Kimball spearheaded the adaptation of pastoral therapy—rooted in a gospel of self-help—as a solution to homosexuality.

In these years, LDS leaders like Kimball had an uneasy relationship with the rise of professional psychologists. The psychologists of the day often challenged or replaced ecclesiastical authority and questioned the premises of self-help ideologies. LDS leaders perceived professional psychology and psychotherapy (not its Protestant therapeutic manifestation) as naturalistic at best and immoral at worst. While earlier generations of modernist Mormon leaders, such as James E. Talmage, B. H. Roberts, and others, had been open to accommodating science, by midcentury many Mormon leaders were openly hostile to secular knowledge.[70] For instance, McConkie's *Mormon Doctrine* held strongly anti-evolutionary and anti-scientific views—the entry under "psychiatry" pointed readers to the entry on "church of the devil." McConkie admitted there may be some benefits, "but in practice, in many instances, it is in effect a form of apostate religion."[71] He gave the specific example of a psychiatrist who might attempt to persuade some that their guilt for masturbation should be readjusted because masturbation is "not an evil." Instead of professional mental health workers, he prescribed working with church leaders to "gain the mental and spiritual peace that overcomes mental disorders."[72] McConkie situated ecclesiastical counseling over and against the psychiatrist's couch, seeing the latter as a diabolical version of the former. At the same time, his framing revealed that he considered church authorities to be engaged in similar therapeutic work, offering a superior product.

Despite these hostile attitudes, some LDS individuals pursued careers in psychology as part of the postwar boom in that field. For instance, BYU began offering clinical psychology courses in 1941 and established a counseling center in 1946, collaborating with local church leadership. By 1958, BYU offered a PhD in clinical psychology.[73] Many Latter-day Saints were influenced by these modernist cultural movements and were undeterred by the anti-psychological teachings of prominent LDS leaders.

In the 1960s, LDS leaders seemed a little more open to collaboration with professional psychologists to accomplish shared goals. Softening his earlier skepticism of psychology, Kimball began to appropriate LDS professionals in his assignment to find a solution to "homosexual problems." At their invitation, perhaps in early 1964, Kimball addressed a group of LDS psychiatrists on various sexual maladies, including masturbation, petting, and fornication. These were the well-known situations and somewhat routine, but the psychiatrists were especially eager to receive counsel on a different class of sexual deviants: "peeping toms, exhibitionists, homosexuals, and perverts in other areas."[74] This speech in its original form is now lost, but Kimball gave a very similar speech a few months later. On July 10, 1964, Kimball enlisted the help of the Church Educational System teachers of the youth and young adults to help with the "counseling problem." Kimball drew extensively from his speech to the psychiatrists.

The speech was significant as a historical marker. It was the earliest instruction to deal so thoroughly with pastoral approaches to homosexuality and offered some insights into the pathologizing framework that Kimball was using. He explained to the teachers that they could assist bishops in providing the "cure" and encouraged them to prevent homosexuality "as you indoctrinate in the preventive spiritual medicine."[75] With the talk of sickness, cures, prevention, spiritual medication, and treatment and the comparison of bishops to physicians, Kimball fully accepted the epistemology of medicine in his approach to homosexuality. The homosexual was a pathological subject, and church leaders could administer a cure with pastoral care.

Kimball's devotion to finding a cure for homosexuality framed his advice to church teachers and psychologists. His confidence in a cure was pitted against the growing claims that homosexuality was immutable and part of a fixed identity. In perspective, his opposition to sexual essentialism was a mainstream idea at the time. Again and again, Irving Bieber's research comes up as highly influential on LDS views on homosexuality during this period. Bieber's landmark study in 1962 had classified homosexuality as a pathology and suggested the psychiatric outlines of a cure.[76] His ideas were reported in the popular press as well. In February 1965, *Time* magazine ran a short article on this research titled "Homosexuality Can Be Cured," reflecting the common belief.[77] Kimball relied on such popularized scientific ideas to form his own views. Citing the June 5, 1964, article "Therapeutic Hope for Homosexuals" from the newsletter *Medical World News*, which summarized Bieber's findings, Kimball insisted that homosexuality could be cured by the strength of the patient's desire to change. He advised LDS psychologists and church educators, "The cure for this malady lies in self mastery which is the fundamental basis of the whole gospel program."[78] Kimball boldly attested, "We know such a disease is curable."[79] Homosexuality was a disease, and the mind could cure it.

Masculine self-mastery was an important concept for Kimball in describing both the causes and cures of homosexuality, revealing the ways that homosexuality was asymmetrically gendered as a male issue. He reported that the practice may be as prevalent among women as it is among men but referred almost exclusively to the male offender. "Men who have come dejected," he explained, "have gone out later ... ready to manfully take their part in society and even in the Church on an approved cured basis."[80] Quoting extensively from Allen's *As a Man Thinketh*, Kimball questioned the masculinity of someone who could not master himself. But the primary advice for the cure was not focused on gender reconstruction per se—there was no attention to bodily comportment, interests in sports or mechanics, or the relationship with one's father. Rather, the treatment consisted of "constructive activity so full of good works there is no time nor thought for evil."[81] The failure of masculinity was in lack of self-control, not object choice or gender performance. These ideas would later develop into full reconstructions of masculine comportment.

Kimball still insisted that ecclesiastical authority outranked competing treatments. His speech to LDS psychologists in 1964 was evidence that he was providing them with instruction, not seeking their advice. After a series of arrests of men charged with homosexual activity in northern Utah, Kimball recounted that the church had assigned a bishop to produce a rehabilitation program. Kimball explained, "Our helper bishop and our program of rehabilitation are known now to the police, the courts and the judges who refer many cases directly. When cases come to us, we usually interview the person then refer him to our special assistant. In many cases, the offenders have been referred to him by judges on a probation basis."[82] As the church collaborated with the state to treat and cure homosexuals, Kimball emphasized that the methods of this anonymous bishop were not those of trained psychiatrists or social workers: "His methods of helping in the cures might not pass a state board of professional examiners, but they seem to pass well with the offenders and with the Lord for there have been numerous cures."[83] Regardless of what professional psychologists might conclude, Kimball believed that the added dimension of the spiritual power of LDS church leaders changed the likelihood of successful outcomes of treatment favorably.

Kimball's sincerity matched his severity. He advocated "a soft approach of helpfulness, not condemnation" of the homosexual.[84] Kimball was the first LDS leader to employ the phrase "he hates the sin, but loves the sinner" as a standard for LDS pastoral counselors.[85] He himself spent hours counseling people in their homes and in his, recovering people from bars and casinos, and exchanging countless letters with people from around the country. Kimball was confident in the successes of his teachings. Between 1961 and 1969, Kimball and Petersen reported that they had counseled over one thousand individuals.[86] In 1968, Kimball reported to McKay, "We have lost some who did not cooperate and were belligerent and went to the large cities to hide, but I feel there are many happy people today because of the work that Brother Petersen and I have done through the years."[87] Kimball believed that these counseling sessions would persuade these individuals to adopt heterosexual practices and achieve the therapeutic outcome of happiness.

The promotion of the pastoral care model in LDS practice drew on the broader Protestant adaptation of psychological models while also expressing contempt for the competing authority of the secular psychologists.[88] This contempt obscured just how much of the language, frameworks, and methods of psychology the church was adopting. The therapeutic turn in church counseling was seen as a complement to traditional modes of piety and kept the church's approach to sin relevant in a time saturated with popular psychological perspectives. The combination of religion and therapy brought together powerful narratives of change and transformation, putting forward an optimistic view of humanity built on the mutability of sexual and gendered subjectivity. Self-transformation was salvation—and sex was at the center of this new regulatory ideal.

Kimball's confidence in a cure also meant that he believed homosexuality could be prevented. The language of self-mastery resonated with Kimball's overall theory of human agency and positive thinking. In a 1965 speech to BYU students titled "Love vs. Lust," Kimball addressed some of the issues he had raised to psychologists and church educators the year before. He lamented that "this unholy transgression seems to be rapidly growing." But he promised that homosexuality "is overcomable and forgivable, but again, only upon a deep and abiding repentance which means total abandonment and complete transformation of thought and act." Those who say that God made them "that way" are rationalizing and excusing their sins, he insisted.[89] Essentialism meant that people couldn't change, but Kimball believed that the problem both was growing in society and could also be diminished—sexuality was mutable.[90]

Masturbation took on special significance, as Victorian-era theories that masturbation caused mental insanity were repurposed in the era of homosexual panic.[91] Kimball warned the BYU students, "Sometimes masturbation is the introduction to the more serious sins of exhibitionism and the gross sin of homosexuality."[92] As a result of this etiology, Kimball strictly counseled against masturbation.[93] In this view, homosexuality had a clear cause and could happen to anyone who was not exercising self-mastery.

With his decades of counseling people involved in sexual sin, Kimball wanted to put together a useful treatise on repentance and forgiveness.[94] In 1967 Kimball completed his manuscript and by 1969 had published his pastoral magnum opus, *The Miracle of Forgiveness*. With all of its hopefulness about the possibility of repentance, Kimball represented same-sex relationships in the darkest terms—"revolting," "detestable," "ugly," "repugnant," and so on. While his earlier public statements had been harsh with a dose of pastoral empathy, Kimball's rhetoric in this book was vitriolic. Referring to the "crime against nature" and "sin of the ages," he placed same-sex intimacy just below murder in the hierarchy of sins.[95] The chapter on homosexuality began with a condemnation of masturbation. While not equivalent in seriousness, Kimball warned that masturbation "too often leads to grievous sin, even to that sin against nature, homosexuality."[96] Kimball's emphasis on "nature" was based on the scriptural citation of Romans 1:26–27, in which Paul makes an apparent allusion to men and women exchanging their "natural" inclinations for intercourse with members of the same sex. Nature could be corrupted and contravened. Nature, it turned out, was not a fixed foundation but one that was highly vulnerable to change. Kimball warned that "those who would claim that the homosexual is a third sex and that there is nothing wrong in those associations can hardly believe in God or his scriptures."[97] The notion of a "third sex" arose first as a nineteenth-century medical theory about inborn homosexuality, and one that 1960s and 1970s activists for and against homosexuality still argued over.[98] But the term implied too much fixity for Kimball. Nature could only be dimorphic and heterosexual, or else it was unnatural.

In *The Miracle of Forgiveness*, Kimball depicted same-sex intimacy as both an ancient scourge and a modern phenomenon gaining popularity. In so doing, he invoked the myth that sexual immorality, especially homosexuality, was always associated with civilizational decline. Mormons were engaging not only a pathological view of homosexuality but a sociology of homosexuality that taught that society was at risk with changes to socio-sexual norms. This view hinged on the ideas that homosexuality was contagious and also led to even more serious degeneracy: "Sin in sex practices tends to have a 'snowballing' effect. As the restraints fall away, Satan incites the carnal man to ever-deepening degeneracy in his search for excitement until in many instances he is lost to any former considerations of decency. Thus it is that through the ages, perhaps as an extension of homosexual practices, men and women have sunk even to seeking sexual satisfactions with animals."[99] The trajectory of sexual degeneracy ran from the acceptance of masturbation, to homosexuality, and ultimately to bestiality. Citing Leviticus 20, Kimball noted that homosexuality and bestiality both were deserving of the death penalty and that "regrettably," "the law is less severe now," as was the community's attitude. The weakened sanctions themselves could be disastrous: "All this is done in the open, to the detriment alike of impressionable minds, susceptible urges, and our national decency."[100] Kimball's invocation of "impressionable" and "susceptible" features of human beings expressed his belief in the fundamental fragility of heterosexuality.

Despite this fragility, Kimball believed that redemption was manifest in overcoming one's susceptibilities. When Kimball published *The Miracle of Forgiveness* in 1969, he believed that his outlined steps toward repentance from sexual sins would equip individuals and ecclesiastical leaders with everything they would need. He provided a path to a cure based on confession, strict obedience to the commandments, and a determined will to never return to sin. There was little by way of appeal to divine grace or supernatural transformation as the means for being cured. In all of this, Kimball depicted a state of sin as a state of internal torment. He concluded the book by promising that "those who heed the call … can be partakers of the miracle of forgiveness. God will wipe away from their eyes the tears of anguish, and remorse, and consternation, and fear, and guilt. Dry eyes will replace the wet ones, and smiles of satisfaction will replace the worried, anxious look."[101] Kimball's account of sin was completely psychologized. Sin's primary victim was the practitioner who was overwhelmed by guilt, anxiety, fear, and worry. For Kimball, sin was the cause of internal mental anguish and righteousness the solution for internal peace.

### THERAPEUTIC MINISTRY

Kimball's various speeches in the 1960s and in *The Miracle of Forgiveness* discussing pastoral counseling foreshadowed a massive investment in discourse about homosexuality. In *The Miracle of Forgiveness*, Kimball touted the "Church Program for Assistance," a bootstrap effort that consisted of two senior leaders (Kimball himself and Petersen) and a handful of bishops and stake presidents (a stake president was a leader of approximately five thousand church members and overseer of multiple congregations).[102] This program was, however, on the cusp of a dramatic change that expanded its scope and the number of agents involved.

In this context, Mormon leaders entered the 1970s with a series of new tools for addressing homosexuality among LDS membership. On March 19, 1970, the First Presidency sent a letter to all regional leaders—stake and mission presidents—expressing "concern" about "the apparent increase in homosexuality." The highest governing body encouraged local leaders to "be alert to this menace in your own area and see to it that you and your bishops keep the matter in mind when interviewing people." The letter referred to homosexuals as "unfortunate" and "unhappy" and encouraged "sympathetic treatment" and "kind persuasion." "They can also be assured," the letter explained, "that in spite of all they may have heard from other sources, they can overcome and return to total normal, happy living."[103] The letter anticipated new resources to assist local LDS leaders in guiding the homosexual back to "normal."

The initial pastoral offerings were based on self-help teachings. Kimball's general attention to sin in *The Miracle of Forgiveness* turned to a laser-like focus on the most grievous sin of homosexuality. Shortly after the March 1970 letter, the church published its first pamphlet on homosexuality prescribing a cure through pastoral therapy. Authored by Kimball and Petersen, *Hope for Transgressors* advised church leaders for the first time how to respond to homosexual activity among their members beyond ecclesiastical sanction. This pamphlet marked the beginning of a new literature to assist church leaders and those seeking to change, for homosexuality was a distinctive case from other sins. In this pastoral framework, the publication advocated kindness coupled with discipline. It explained to the church leader "your responsibility to assist any such person to recover himself and become normal again. . . . [He] can often be helped to a total cure by a kindly Church official who understands."[104] Ecclesiastical leaders continued to be the primary locus of authority for addressing and curing homosexuality, and the pamphlet for church leaders emphatically declared that bishops were more prepared than therapists to offer treatment: "Even though you may not be a trained social worker, psychiatrist nor psychologist, you have a power that no such specialist could ever have from his training only."[105] It insisted that "homosexuality CAN be cured."[106]

The *Hope for Transgressors* publication advised making sure that repentant individuals practiced heteronormative values and gender roles. It warned, "Some homosexuals become effeminate and some lesbians become masculine in the dress, voice and mannerisms."[107] These were affectations that could be overcome with training. As a regimen for cure, the pamphlet gave several pieces of practical advice for the homosexual male. First, he should abandon those with whom he is involved. In so doing, *Hope for Transgressors* resisted acknowledging that homosexuality was not exclusively about sex. "Many perverts will claim," it explained, "to have great 'love' for some with whom they have been involved."[108] Such claims were simply dismissed and minimized so that the sexual element of the relationship could take priority as its defining feature. Second, the sinner should get rid of all reading material related to homosexuality and focus on the scriptures. Third, the pamphlet advised prayer, and fourth, rigorous supervision through mandatory confession: "He should make a confidential report to you every few days at first and occasionally for a long time until he feels secure."[109] Finally, "when you feel he is ready, he should be encouraged to date and gradually move his life toward the normal." The goal was to leverage the ability to "move their romantic interests" so that they could be "normal," namely, heterosexual.[110] Those who practiced other kinds of sexual, romantic, and committed relationships were deviant. The language of normalcy and deviancy from psychological discourse provided the structure for this new approach. Church leaders came to believe that the proper response to sickness was not just reprobation but care.

Despite having adopted much of the language of psychology, at the outset of the 1970s church leaders like Kimball were still suspicious of secular psychologists. Kimball perceived professionals as normalizing homosexuality, as they had done with masturbation. In the 1971 pamphlet *New Horizons for Homosexuals* (retitled in 1978 as *A Letter to a Friend*), Kimball warned, "Even if your partner in sin should be a psychiatrist, a medical man, a psychologist, and if he teaches that these immoralities are harmless, he is either deceived or a vicious deceiver. Shun him."[111] He assured that "the bishop has power and resources far beyond secular training" in providing a cure.[112] Arguing against the idea that homosexuality was natural and normal, Kimball promised, "Let us assure you that you are not permanently trapped in this unholy practice if you will exert yourself. Though it's like an octopus with numerous tentacles to drag you to your tragedy, the sin is curable and you may totally recover from its tentacles."[113] The seeming intractability of homosexual desire was evidence of its pernicious danger. These beliefs allowed Mormons to contrast themselves with an outside "secular" world that was hostile to God and morality.

LDS leaders maintained that the combination of human agency and divine support could bring about change for the homosexual, regardless of homosexuality's origins. Kimball had an optimistic take on human nature and potential, with a boundless conception of agency as a human power to accomplish great things. The idea that certain desires were not chosen challenged an uncompromising faith Mormons held in human freedom and the power of humans to shape themselves. Mormons had long ago rejected Calvinist Christianity, including the idea of a natural depravity, and substituted it with an idea of almost limitless human potential and the capacity to do good. The gay rights argument based on sexual essentialism—that people were unable to change their sexual orientation—looked to these Mormon leaders

*Sodom and Cumorah*

like either a justification for sinful behavior or a limited view of human potential and freedom. Homosexuality may be a part of the fallen world, but it was not an irredeemable part of anyone's nature.

## THE APA, CHRISTIAN THERAPY, AND
## FOCUS ON THE FAMILY

At the same time as these developments toward pastoral treatment were being established in the church, the ground was shifting quickly beneath Mormons' feet in the broader culture—and may help explain a bifurcated response to psychology in the 1970s by Spencer W. Kimball. Already in the late 1950s, psychologists like Evelyn Hooker had begun to challenge the view that homosexuality was a pathology.[114] Gay liberation activists appealed to nature to explain their desires. Since at least the Stonewall riots in New York City in 1969, activists in urban areas began to organize for legal and social changes that would allow them to "come out." These activists disrupted the meetings of the American Psychiatric Association (APA) in 1970 and 1972 to challenge the classification of homosexuality as abnormal and pathological. Their efforts paid off. Professional opinion was shifting as the research and experience increasingly invalidated pathologization.[115] In 1973, the APA removed homosexuality from its list of mental disorders for good. After scores of studies, there was no compelling evidence that homosexuality was a pathology; rather, it was only a deviation from conventional norms.[116]

The APA's break from pathologizing homosexuality set off alarm bells in conservative American Christianity, which felt that the secular intellectual establishment was turning its back on traditional morality. When mainstream psychological organizations moved away from pathologizing homosexuality and treating it therapeutically, conservative religious groups embraced the abandoned scientific paradigm. They rallied around psychoanalytic theories that homosexuality was a maladjustment from childhood and new behaviorist techniques for reparative therapy—a psychological umbrella term for a variety of methods designed to change same-sex desires to heterosexual ones. Irving Bieber's 1962 study and Charles Socarides's 1969 study depended upon Sigmund Freud's Oedipal theory to classify homosexuality as a pathology.[117] The attraction of these disputed scientific claims for many conservative Christians was that they challenged gay rights activists who appealed to an immutable, innate sexual identity. The gay rights movement was modeling itself on the successes of the civil rights movement by invoking a quasi-ethnic identity. Conservatives resisted with a scientific discourse that homosexuality was not a fixed feature but a contingent and fluid aberration that could (and should) be repaired.

A handful of psychologists defected from the APA's changes, including Bieber and Socarides.[118] But James Dobson in particular began to exemplify a new Christian psychology, positioning it as both complementary and oppositional to mainstream scholarship, especially with respect to sexual morality and homosexuality. Dobson sought to ground conservative Christian teachings on sexuality, gender roles, and reproduction in therapeutic and psychological science. In 1977 he founded his nonprofit ministry, Focus on the Family, which sponsored books, pamphlets, speaking engagements, and a national radio broadcast. He came to prominence as he bucked the psychological establishment on the proper way to raise children. Dobson's *Dare to Discipline* (1970) challenged permissive parenting, favoring parental (and patriarchal) authority. He believed poor parenting was the cause of the excesses of the 1960s, including the sexual revolution, drug use, and political and social unrest.[119] He added the authority of an "expert" to support Christian objections to these activities as sin and was the most prominent example of evangelicals adopting psychological theories.

The growth of Dobson's Christian psychology of "the family" laid special emphasis on parenting, gender roles, and sexuality. Indeed, these foci were deeply intertwined. Parents were supposed to perform their assigned "complementary" gender roles to model for children masculine aggression and feminine softness and nurturing. He saw gender roles and sexual difference as "natural" but at the same time explained that children needed to be socialized into their gender roles. If men or women were not following their assigned roles, they could confuse the gender of their children. Homosexuality, then, was the result of a child's inability to transfer his or her infantile homosociality to an adolescent heterosexuality.[120] Women who usurped male authority in the home or workplace threatened the development of masculinity. Feminism and homosexuality, as well as fathers who shirked their duties, all contributed to the psychological and spiritual disordering of children that would manifest in aberrant sexuality. Dobson's worldview was rooted in Freudian theories of psychosexual development not only to diagnose but also to cure homosexuality.

In this period, other conservative Christians founded numerous "ex-gay" ministries—organizations that treated homosexuality based on psychological

*Sodom and Cumorah*

principles. This represented a hope in science to vindicate anti-homosexual teaching. The earliest known dedicated ex-gay ministry was founded in 1973 by Frank Worthen, which sprang up the same year the APA de-pathologized homosexuality, in order to provide a Christian alternative to secular psychiatry.[121] Called "Love in Action," Worthen's San Francisco Bay Area group sought to rescue young gay men. Exodus International, the most famous "ex-gay" organization, was founded in 1976, though it was built on networks of earlier local ministries like Love in Action.[122] In 1978, Anita Bryant Ministries launched in order "to help homosexuals who want to be delivered from that kind of lifestyle." Many others would follow. These approaches combined therapy, psychoanalysis, and science with biblical prohibitions of same-sex intercourse. As a cure to homosexual desires, they prescribed practices of Christian piety, such as prayer, scripture study, and worship; mechanisms of supervision and surveillance; and a required reordering of social contacts and fellowship. These approaches resulted in residential programs modeled on those treating addiction, as well as self-help booklets for those who worked alone. Latter-day Saints would both imitate these developments and closely work with them in later forms.

### THE EMERGENCE OF PROFESSIONALIZATION

Mormons were at the forefront of the movement to establish therapeutic ministries to cure homosexuality, though this history has been invisible in accounts of the movement in part because Mormons were acting largely independently in these earlier years. Though nothing like a Mormon version of Focus on the Family or Love in Action appeared, by offering professionalized treatment for homosexuality LDS leaders made use of psychology that was in line with these developments in fundamentalist and evangelical Christianity. Interest in this kind of treatment was coming not only from professional Mormon psychologists but also from local LDS leaders charged with pastoral duties. In the early 1970s, bishops and stake presidents were clamoring for greater support from the church as they were tasked with treating homosexuality. A group of five stake presidents wrote to church leaders to ask for more resources.[123] Whether directly or indirectly, the answer to the stake presidents' request for support in treating homosexuality involved a complete reorganization of the kinds of pastoral and professional therapy the church had previously provided. Some of these transitions were already underway behind the scenes.

In 1969, the Priesthood Correlation Committee put the Relief Society's social service efforts under the control of the male leaders of the church. When Victor L. Brown Jr. became director of this agency in 1971, it was then assigned to his father, Victor L. Brown Sr., among others, who was then a counselor in the presiding bishopric.[124] For legal liability reasons, LDS Social Services was created as a separate corporate entity in 1973, but church authorities continued to direct its activities. LDS Social Services employed a host of professional therapists to deal with all kinds of issues such as addiction, abuse, and other mental health issues—including homosexuality. The same year that the APA de-pathologized homosexuality and Frank Worthen founded his ex-gay ministry, LDS officials were launching their own version of professionalized care for the homosexual. This built on programs that Kimball had been running for nearly a decade already.

Professional treatment offered alternative theories about the psycho-developmental causes and cures of homosexuality, downplaying moral explanations about masturbation and bad habits. Gender roles took on special importance. In 1971, Brown Sr. explained, "The Lord defined some very basic differences between men and women. He gave the male what we call masculine traits and the female feminine traits. He did not intend either of the sexes to adopt the other's traits but, rather, that men should look and act like men and that women should look and act like women. When these differences are ignored, an unwholesome relationship develops, which, if not checked, can lead to the reprehensible, tragic sin of homosexuality. In other words, we have a responsibility as priesthood bearers to be examples of true manhood."[125] For Brown Sr., the performance of maleness was the solution to developing the traits of "true manhood" for the male homosexual. His belief that looking and acting like the wrong gender would lead to homosexuality was based on a notion of inversion, or gender instability.

Victor Brown Jr. was a trained psychologist and BYU instructor who would go on to sponsor aversion therapy and to advocate for reparative therapy. He was influenced by Freudian theories of the subconscious and depth psychology. Brown believed that homosexuality had deeper emotional causes—which was why pastoral counseling and individual repentance did not always work. Consequently, deeper problems required deeper solutions. Under his direction, LDS Social Services published a packet of information and instructions for employees and church leaders. *Homosexuality: Welfare Services Packet 1* (1973) provided information on church discipline for homosexual behavior and discussed the psycho-developmental nature of homosexuality.[126] The manual also described homosexual activity as "devilish," a "degenerate practice," and "vile behavior" and gave leaders the tools to counter the "rationalizations" of their congregants to "expose the lies and deceptions surrounding homosexual behavior."[127] The manual insisted that "the gospel makes the issue clear." It attested, "Homosexuality is a sin, is learned behavior (not inborn), and can be stopped."[128]

According to this new guidebook, the primary tools for change were confession and treatment of emotional or social problems that caused aberrant gendered behavior. Bishops and other leaders were instructed to routinely question those seeking temple recommends—permission slips that allowed adults to participate in the most sacred LDS rites—and youth about their sexual involvement with members of the same sex.[129] Further, it authorized church leaders "to make special confidential inquiries into suspected behavior . . . to offer evidence concerning the accusation."[130] It stipulated that the repentant person must divulge others who were involved in homosexual activity and that church leaders should not reveal their sources when accusing members.[131] Church leaders were instructed in numerous subsequent letters throughout the 1970s that they must inquire about homosexual activity as part of the screening for prospective missionaries and in other interviews.[132]

Because of Kimball's belief in the close connection between masturbation and homosexuality, LDS Social Services assessed that there was a need to offer some clarification. Masturbation, the manual explained, "is not homosexuality when practiced alone. When one person masturbates another, it *is* a homosexual act."[133] Nevertheless, it advised, "Never touch the intimate parts of your body except during normal toilet processes," "never stay in the bath more than five or six minutes," and "dress yourself for the night so securely that you cannot easily touch your vital parts, and so that it would be difficult and time consuming for you to remove those clothes."[134] LDS Social Services frequently distributed suggestions for how to stop masturbation in these years, repeating many of the instructions from the masturbation panic of the Victorian period. These included practical suggestions such as "take cool brief showers," "keep your bladder empty," "reduce the amount of spices and condiments in your food," and "wear pajamas that are difficult to open"; in addition, "in very severe cases it may be necessary to tie a hand to the bed frame with a tie in order that the habit of masturbating in a semi-sleep condition may be broken."[135]

Masculinity was defined far more broadly than self-mastery in this new psychological approach. Gender normativity was an important tool for ferreting out who may be involved in homosexuality and for providing a cure.

When seeking to identify suspected homosexuals, the *Welfare Services Packet* explained, "among the more reliable signs are excessive involvement with members of the same sex by those who are physically mature, who do not date, and who lack interest in marriage."[136] With respect to boys who have "rounded hips, slightly enlarged breasts, or feminine voices" and girls who have "narrow hips," it suggested that the chemical imbalances that cause these mixed physical characteristics do not necessarily cause homosexuality but that the reactions to these differences may cause the emotional problems that lead to homosexuality.[137] The appeal to supposedly biological explanations for the failure of some bodies to conform to gender norms did not become an occasion to rethink the naturalness of nonheterosexuality. Rather, since sexuality was thought to be primarily social and psychological, it could therefore be adapted and morphed. Church leaders were advised to provide "social support" that included learning "what a heterosexual life is and what a manly priesthood leader and father does."[138] The instruction of a proper masculinity included learning the "heterosexual or 'straight' way of life." Similarly, the "lesbian . . . needs to learn feminine behavior."[139] Church leaders were to assist with "personal refinement." This included dealing with low self-esteem: "Other [homosexuals] may be overweight or might have a skin problem." Helping resolve these issues would give the homosexual the necessary self-respect to become "normal."[140] From self-mastery to self-respect, the pathologized homosexual had become the psychologized homosexual.

The 1973 manual put forward a model of a cooperative relationship between church leaders and professional psychologists. This was the beginning of a new formal relationship between LDS leaders and professional therapists—but these relationships had some constraints. Professionals should be involved only "if they understand and support gospel truth concerning proper behavior. Because the world does not view homosexuality as the Church does, i.e. as a sin, counsel received from 'worldly' counselors could be very confusing to a Latter-day Saint."[141] The LDS version of an ex-gay ministry in the 1970s invested resources to develop a network of "approved therapists" to supplement pastoral leaders' efforts. The new resources demarcated the lines of authority between the ecclesiastical leaders and the professional counselors it employed. The 1974 *Welfare Services Handbook,* a guidebook of general instructions about how to utilize this new agency, provided further instruction and clarification for local church leaders: "The bishop and Melchizedek Priesthood quorum and group leaders are the Lord's ecclesiastical leaders. They cannot and must not abdicate their responsibility to any agency. Social services agencies are established to be a resource to the ecclesiastical leaders. There is no substitute for the inspired counsel and priesthood blessing by the bishop or quorum or group leader."[142] Ecclesiastical leaders retained their place in the hierarchy relative to the professional counselors. The risks of therapists providing contrary counsel was neutralized by creating a cohort of church-employed professionals who could ensure their "harmony" with church teachings.[143] But the overlap in their efforts also pointed to the fundamentally therapeutic paradigm for LDS pastoral counseling.

Even though the lines of authority put professional counselors in a supportive role, their expert knowledge and paradigms gained greater hegemony in this period. The conservative therapeutic paradigm declared that the cause of homosexuality was not personal sin and habits like masturbation but a failure of the family and blurring of sexual difference. The new psychodevelopmental theory of homosexuality in LDS culture framed it less as a sin and more as a response to certain emotional deficits. *Homosexuality: Welfare Services Packet 1* explained, "Many active Latter-day Saints involved in homosexuality are seeking the same companionship and emotional intimacy that others seek. They are usually unable to find it and are thus lonely and insecure. This leads them toward homosexuality."[144] In this view, the homosexual was attracted to the same sex because of emotional needs, not sexual ones. It posited that these emotional needs were fundamentally normal, only misdirected. The psychological homosexual was not a wanton sinner but a disturbed individual who required emotional healing. The psychological evaluation was an inversion of Kimball's paradigm, which saw emotional damage as the result, not the cause, of homosexuality.

## AMCAP AND THE VALUES INSTITUTE

LDS psychologists in private practice and those employed by the church developed other institutions to address the growing concern about how to treat homosexuality. By 1975, LDS psychologists and counselors organized the Association for Mormon Counselors and Psychiatrists (AMCAP).[145] The organization directly addressed growing LDS concern about homosexuality since the APA had changed its assessment. The inaugural theme of the 1975 AMCAP meeting was "Current Issues Facing Mormon Counselors and Psychotherapists." Two of the three presentations focused on counseling issues of homosexuality—one dealing with church settings and the other with private practice.[146] Victor Brown Jr.'s deputy in LDS Social Services,

Robert L. Blattner, presented a pathologized depiction of the homosexual and advised controlling masturbation as the key to thwarting homosexual fantasy.[147] The overlaps in personnel between LDS Social Services, scholars, and private practitioners ensured shared knowledge about homosexuality and close professional and personal relationships. Latter-day Saint professionals who specialized in anti-homosexuality scholarship offered training for the staff of LDS Social Services. These interrelationships made certain that official LDS teachings were widely disseminated from seemingly different centers of authority.

AMCAP saw the early 1970s as a turning point for LDS attitudes about professional psychology. An editorial in the first issue of its journal proclaimed, "The day is past that we as AMCAP members need lower our eyes, dig our toes in the sand and apologize for our respective professions."[148] Though LDS Social Services had adopted psychology and therapy as a major aspect of its work a few years before, AMCAP continued to emphasize the compatibility of LDS teachings with psychological theories and treatments. Various high-ranking church officials spoke at the inaugural conference, praising the work of psychologists in "healing the soul."[149] Carlfred Broderick, a nationally prominent family therapist, was the keynote speaker at the initial meeting and spoke openly of the hostility between church leaders and professionals as "not without cause." Nevertheless, he argued, "there is a whole new wave of counseling styles and techniques that are eminently consistent with Gospel principles."[150] The journal's publication guidelines emphasized the standards of the church as the most important. The counselors earned the trust of the church leaders by holding closely to church teachings. A new day had dawned for efforts to professionalize the psychologization of Mormonism—but these efforts also Mormonized psychology.

The tectonic shift that brought psycho-developmental theories of homosexuality into prominence marked the beginnings of a new understanding that placed the family at the center of the battle. Outside of stuffy manuals, journals, and academic conferences, these theories were making their way into mainstream LDS venues. In 1975 Brown presented in the *Ensign*—the church's official magazine—a psycho-developmental theory of malformed sexual desires, stating, "Parents need to know that lack of proper affection in the home can result in unnatural behavior in their children such as homosexuality." Parents were instructed to inculcate proper masculinity and femininity in their children, "to learn how to be men or women in Zion."[151]

This view won a number of disciples among senior LDS officials. In General Conference, J. Richard Clarke taught in 1977, "Many of these problems would be alleviated if parents would spend more time teaching and rearing their children. . . . A clinical researcher who, after studying 850 individual cases, stated: 'Homosexuality would not occur where there is a normal, loving father-and-son relationship.'"[152] The quote seems to be a paraphrase of Irving Bieber's work.[153] The rhetoric of a breakdown of family values explained the apparent rise in the practice of homosexuality. The psycho-developmental theory posited a fragile heterosexuality and fragile masculinity. If masculinity was taught to male children, homosexuality would not exist. Such a view placed the responsibility for defending against gender fluidity in the hands of parents.

Women's leadership in the home was particularly problematic for the development of a proper masculinity. When Brown presented his report on the psychological causes of homosexuality to the senior leadership of the church in 1976, discussed in the opening of this chapter, he laid out the case for the church's push for the patriarchal order. The report criticized the amount of time fathers spent away from their children in LDS culture, lamenting that strong women's leadership in LDS children's and youth education entailed "absence or disinterest of fathers in ways which contribute to unique LDS homosexuality and other sexual perversions."[154] The report warned against "modern, democratic principles of child-rearing, which run counter to the revealed authoritative, patriarchal presiding pattern."[155] If the patriarchal role of the father was weakened, it "plants seeds of . . . grave sin."[156] The report cited studies, including those produced at BYU, concluding that the lack of a loving, involved father or a good father-son relationship was a cause of homosexuality. The threat of homosexuality became a justification for fathers not only to spend more time with their children but especially to adopt an authoritative patriarchal role in the home. Believing that prevention was worth more than a cure, Brown recommended that the church spend time in 1977 emphasizing the "patriarchal order."[157] Equality for women would result in increasing male homosexuality.

Brown's report in 1976 to the senior church leaders was a follow-up to one he had delivered a year earlier on sexual misbehavior. But LDS Social Services was not equipped to produce scientific research that would counter the de-pathologization of homosexuality in the APA. Brown believed such research was necessary to convince his secular psychologist colleagues. He argued that patriarchy was a solution to homosexuality, but he soon suggested another project as well—the creation of a research institute on human behavior at BYU. Paid for by Welfare Services, the parent organization to LDS Social Services, this institute would study sexual behavior as a psychological question and seek secular evidence to support church teachings. The president of BYU, Dallin H. Oaks, explained, "The objective of the project was to prepare a manuscript along the lines outlined by Victor Brown Jr. in his oral presentation, which would set forth significant empirical evidence in support of the Church's position on homosexuality. The Church would fund the project. The resulting book was to be published by a press having nothing to do with the Church in order to magnify its acceptability in the scholarly community and among non-Mormons."[158] Church leaders aspired to make contributions to the anti-homosexuality movement far beyond the boundaries of the church itself.

The mission of the newly created Institute for Studies in Values and Human Behavior, also called the Values Institute, was to produce empirical scholarship to validate LDS leaders' teachings that homosexuality could be cured. It brought together existing resources and forged new collaborations to present a scholarly foundation for anti-homosexuality. Among the existing resources was research on aversion therapies, conducted by BYU's psychology professors, beginning in the mid-1960s. Dr. Eugene Thorne performed these therapies into the 1970s.[159] The institute brought under its umbrella this experimentation with different reparative and aversion therapies. Thorne's doctoral student Ford McBride completed a dissertation in 1976, "Effect of Visual Stimuli in Electric Aversion Therapy," which paired pornographic images with an electric shock to induce aversion for homosexual stimuli. Aversion therapy was a branch of behavioralist psychology that thought to train human subjects with rewards and punishments. These aversion treatments dated back to 1935 as an alternative to criminal punishment and had some mainstream acceptance into the 1960s.[160] The BYU Standards Office referred uncooperative gay students for such therapies administered by BYU researchers.[161] Blattner, a special assistant to the LDS commissioner on personal welfare, spoke approvingly of this research, asserting that "most people coming to us can be helped" by "aversion therapy, relaxation or desensitization."[162] By the 1970s, these efforts had fallen out of favor in mainstream circles as "abusive," ineffective, and unnecessary once homosexuality had been depathologized.[163] (The practice seems to have continued at least until the late-1980s at BYU).[164]

Ultimately, the Values Institute failed to reach its goals of empirical research to validate church teachings. By late 1979, Oaks admitted, "Our objective to present the evidence in this manner with maximum effect cannot be achieved."[165] The institute was closed soon after. Brown did publish his related research in 1981 in *Human Intimacy: Illusion and Reality*, but the book was not issued by a press that would magnify its scholarly impact as originally planned.[166] Nevertheless, LDS church headquarters distributed a copy of the book to every bishop and stake president.[167] While not dealing extensively with homosexuality in the book, Brown argued against masturbation, criticized American sexual values as selfish, and advocated for a view of human relationships that was less focused on sexuality and more on "intimacy." The book did not receive attention outside LDS circles, and even LDS psychologists expressed criticism, especially for Brown's downplaying of the importance of sexual intimacy.[168] One reviewer complained, "Reality always comes down on the side of traditional Mormon values, while every other point of view ends up being illusion. It seems as if the conclusions precede the analysis."[169] Not all professional LDS psychologists believed that its Mormonized manifestation was necessarily correct.

### GAY MORMONS AND REVERSE DISCOURSE

Resistance to LDS teachings on sexuality and relationships was most clearly seen in 1977 when BYU undergraduate student Cloy Jenkins published a scathing fifty-seven-page manifesto, later titled *Prologue: An Examination of the Mormon Attitude toward Homosexuality*.[170] The treatise was written in the form of a letter to his psychology professor, Dr. Reed Payne (the document was first called "The Payne Papers"). Payne was a member of the Values Institute, which had been working on psychological research opposing homosexuality. His spring 1977 introductory psychology course at BYU featured a lecture describing homosexuality as a pathology. Jenkins, along with the help of BYU instructor Lee Williams, put together an anonymous response designed for a wide readership (they revealed their identities later). Gay men were starting to speak back after almost a decade of church-produced anti-homosexuality literature.

The booklet recounts Jenkins's own history as a gay man who wanted to change his desires as a teenager and then sought treatment from professional counselors, a behavioral therapist, and two psychologists at BYU and beyond. But nothing changed. His research investigations took him in a different direction. Quoting extensively from scholarly sources, he argued that homosexuality was not a conscious choice and criticized the psychological research from earlier generations for its lack of rigor, objectivity, and methodology. Jenkins relayed his own personal experiences and those of his friends alongside a well-researched scholarly refutation of specific LDS psychologists, President Kimball, and other church leaders. He was especially critical of the shock therapy treatments conducted by Ford McBride, noting that one of the supposed "star cases" of McBride's research was now in love with a man. Further, Jenkins contested "the emphatic and persistent urging of General Authorities" that a heterosexual experience in marriage would be a "cure" for a young homosexual male. He argued that the sexual stereotypes about gay men misperceive homosexuality as essentially sexual when, in reality, "homosexuality is no less of a complex interplay of emotions, affections, identity, needs, aspirations and sexuality than is heterosexuality." It is the moralists, he pointed out, that contend that relationships are all about sex instead of love. He took on the scriptural claims one by one to show their limitations. Finally, Jenkins predicted, "As the homosexual becomes less and less willing to submit to this damaging influence, and the rest of the world comes to realize the plight of the Mormon homosexual, the Church stands to face a very serious and embarrassing blow to its integrity."[171] The first of its kind, the manifesto was a comprehensive intellectual challenge.

The "Payne Papers" circulated widely among church members, BYU faculty and administrators, and church leaders. It was soon published as a small pamphlet as *Prologue* and distributed through a contact in the church office headquarters to all General Authorities.[172] The gay publication in Salt Lake City, *The Open Door*, began to serialize the letter beginning September 1, 1977. By February 2, 1978, the national gay magazine *The Advocate* announced the publication of the letters in its pages.[173]

At BYU, several top administrators met to discuss the "Payne Papers" and craft a reply to what they called "the rather sophisticated pro-homosexuality platform."[174] A few of the leaders at the Values Institute wrote up their rejoinders to the pamphlet. In one case, copies of a response were recalled because they were seen as an "embarrassment," according to one source. A second attempt, this time by Victor Brown Jr., was never approved for release.[175] The competing uses of psychological theories between LDS psychologists and LDS gay activists drove a wedge in Mormon therapeutic orthodoxy.

Jenkins's writing took place in a larger context of scholarly and activist work to reconcile homosexual identity with Christianity. In the scholarly realm, popular gay-friendly church histories such as Derrick Sherwin Bailey's 1955 work, *Homosexuality and the Western Christian Tradition*, sought to challenge traditional assumptions about Christianity's relationship to homosexuality through internal critique.[176] (Jenkins quoted this work in *Prologue*.) A few years later, John Boswell's landmark 1980 book, *Christianity, Social Tolerance, and Homosexuality*, would influence gay and lesbian Christians in reconciling their identities with their faith.[177]

Religious gay and lesbian organizations also first appeared in the 1970s. These organizations took on several names, including Dignity (for Catholics), Integrity (for Lutherans), and Affirmation (for Methodists). LDS gay and lesbian activists formed Affirmation: Gay Mormons United in 1977 (soon changed to Affirmation: Gay and Lesbian Mormons). The activists in Affirmation sought to provide a social, psychological, and spiritual home for gay and lesbian current and former members of the church. Chapters were organized first in Salt Lake City, Los Angeles, and Denver.[178] Over the next few years the group sputtered but soon became more focused as new leaders emerged.[179] Its 1982 charter affirmed that "homosexuality and homosexual relationships can be consistent with the gospel of Jesus Christ." Its purpose was to "work for the understanding and acceptance of gays and lesbians as full, equal, and worthy persons within the Church of Jesus Christ of Latter-day Saints and society; and to help them realize and affirm self worth."[180] Organizers ran ads in *The Advocate* to find new members, held an annual conference, and distributed a newsletter, and each chapter held meetings at least once a month. A new voice emerged, crying out from the wilderness.

## THE PERSISTENCE OF MORALISTIC CURES
## AND THE DANGER OF LANGUAGE

Despite official sponsorship, scientific and psycho-developmental theories of homosexuality still faced some skepticism among the highest-ranking church leaders in the 1970s. They worried that psycho-developmental theories displaced responsibility from the individual and undermined agency. These leaders continued to advance moral explanations on the causes of homosexuality to accompany psychological ideas that childhood had been a sexually formative stage. Apostle Boyd K. Packer was a key figure who held this view. Packer had been called at age forty-five to the role of apostle in 1970. He had served in World War II and then held a career in the Church Educational System before being admitted to the upper ranks of church leaders in 1961. Packer became one of the most vocal church leaders on homosexuality beginning in the 1970s until his death in 2015. His speeches on gender and sexuality in the late 1970s were deeply influenced by Spencer

W. Kimball, who by then was the president of the church. Like Kimball, Packer adopted pathological language about homosexuality, speculating on its causes and promising a total cure, but remained skeptical about psychological etiologies.

Packer did agree with the emergent compatibility of psychology with the church on some issues—that homosexuality was caused in childhood and was a failure of gender norms. But he still believed that the emotional conditions were the result of bad habits, not the other way around. In the male-only session of General Conference on October 2, 1976, Packer delivered a talk titled "To Young Men Only." The speech was widely distributed for decades afterward in ecclesiastical counseling sessions.[181] After instructing young men to vigorously control their bodies and their thoughts, Packer warned the audience of an indelicate subject: "There are some circumstances in which young men may be tempted to handle one another, to have contact with one another physically in unusual ways. . . . Sometimes this begins in a moment of idle foolishness, when boys are just playing around. . . . Such practices, however tempting, are perversion. When a young man is finding his way into manhood, such experiences can misdirect his normal desires and pervert him not only physically but emotionally and spiritually as well."[182] He warned against recruitment into such practices and praised a missionary who assaulted his companion who had made a sexual advance. "I am not recommending that course to you, but I am not omitting it," he warned as the audience laughed. "You must protect yourself."[183] Packer refuted the idea of a natural homosexuality, explaining, "No one is locked into that kind of life. . . . There is no mismatching of bodies and spirits. Boys are to become men—masculine, manly men—ultimately to become husbands and fathers. No one is predestined to a perverted use of these powers."[184] Conflating homosexuality with contemporary ideas about transsexuality, Packer insisted that a male homosexual was not a female spirit trapped in a man's body. Nor was it a condition that afflicted only a minority of people. His rejection of sexual essentialism suggested homosexuality was a universal risk. Packer's view of the causes of male homosexuality was not connected to parental failure but rather to an instability of sexual desires on the way to manhood that could be awakened by masturbation. This fragile moment required extra caution, up to and including physical violence to "protect" oneself against it.

Packer addressed homosexuality again a few years later. Kimball had asked him to speak on the subject at BYU not long after the Values Institute's responses to the "Payne Papers" were shuttered.[185] Titled "To the One,"

Packer's March 5, 1978, speech also became a widely distributed pamphlet in LDS pastoral counseling sessions. He took a harsh tone, describing same-sex "immorality" as "dangerous" and "spiritually destructive." But Packer's speech marked the beginning of a new LDS discomfort with the language around homosexuality and its limitations.[186] Packer began to believe that language itself could be constitutive of identity. At the outset, he explained, "To introduce [the subject] I must use a word. I will use it one time only. Please notice that I use it as an adjective, not as a noun. I reject it as a noun. I speak to those few, those very few, who may be subject to homosexual temptation. I repeat, I accept that word as an adjective to describe a temporary condition. I reject it as a noun naming a permanent one."[187] He gave voice to a worry that other church leaders had begun to express as well. In a 1975 letter from the First Presidency to local church leaders advised, "Leaders should be careful not to label people as homosexuals because this both discourages and tends to make the matter seem beyond solving."[188]

Packer's linguistic argument dominated the next few decades and began a new era of renaming and reclassifying "the homosexual," as later chapters will show. At the heart of this linguistic move was a philosophical one— sexuality was too fluid to be fixed in a rigid term like "homosexual." This conception of the performativity of language, the contagion of words, and the desires to control what may be uttered and how it may be phrased resisted an essentialist notion that "homosexual" was a referential term. As Judith Butler has commented on speech, "The specific performativity attributed to homosexual utterance is not simply that the utterance performs the sexuality of which it speaks, but that it transmits sexuality through speech: the utterance is figured as a site of contagion."[189] Sexuality could be constituted by language, not just by the state of the individual psyche or the repetition of bad habits. Packer introduced a new taboo on the term "homosexual," especially as a referent to an identity, in a recognition that sexuality, masculinity, and maleness were contingent upon the various performances that made them possible. But he also saw this term as performative—it did something in its utterance to shape identity.

Packer's speech was also a rebuke of psychological theories, even while it was imbued with the pathologizing framework of homosexuality. He explained, "The cause of this condition . . . is an essential step in developing a cure."[190] He again traced its causes to "innocent" adolescent sex play: "Now it is not all that unusual for a boy or a girl, in a moment of childish play with someone of the same gender, to enter into some mischief that should remain essentially innocent and meaningless and should be forgotten. And two young men or two young women, motivated by some attraction or respond-ing to a desire for affection—any kind of affection—sometimes are drawn almost innocently into unnatural behavior."[191] Invoking theories of gender inversion, Packer rooted these desires for same-sex intimacy in desires for greater identification with one's prescribed gender: "It is normal for a male to want to become more masculine, or for a female to want to become more feminine. But one cannot increase masculinity or femininity by deviant physical contact with one of his own gender. There are many variations of this disorder, some of them very difficult to identify and all of them difficult to understand. When one projects himself in some confused role-playing way with those of the same gender in an effort to become more masculine or more feminine, something flips over and precisely the opposite results."[192]

Packer's theory was that in the acquisition of gender identity through adolescent sex play, it is possible to inadvertently acquire the "opposite" gender by trying too hard to be the prescribed gender. An inversion, or con-fusion, of gender can occur—a "disorder" in psychological parlance. He con-tinued, "Because the body cannot change, the emotional part may struggle to transform itself into the opposite gender."[193] A failure to properly identify, bodily and emotionally, with one's proper gender had eternal consequences: "If an individual becomes trapped somewhere between masculinity and fem-ininity, he can be captive of the adversary and under the threat of losing his potential godhood."[194] As Joseph Fielding Smith and others had taught in the prior decades, performing sexual difference was essential to exaltation to the highest levels of the celestial kingdom, a process that divinized the individual. Failure to perform as either male or female in the proper way risked satanic captivity. For Packer, there was no future healing of the emotions in the next life, only the eternal consequences for failure to achieve one's assigned gender. Gender was not reducible to bodies but was what one did and how one felt about oneself.

Packer objected to any "physical" or perhaps biological causes of such gender confusion. "The next obvious place to look," he explained, "is the emotional or psychological part of our nature. Here we come closer." How-ever, he admitted, psychiatric treatment had not yet found a remedy and "they have some very convincing evidence" that "there really is not much that can be done about it."[195] Packer, however, was unconvinced by this secular conclusion. "But where do we turn when the physical and the emo-tional treatments are only partly successful?" he asked rhetorically. "To Latter-day Saints the answer ought to be obvious. We turn to the spiritual nature."[196] He believed that medical science could not treat homosexuality because it did not have the tools to research or address a "spiritual disorder." He mused,

> Have you explored the possibility that the cause, when found, will turn out to be a very typical form of selfishness—selfishness in a very subtle form? Now—and understand this—I do not think for a minute that the form of selfishness at the root of perversion is a conscious one, at least not to begin with. I am sure it is quite the opposite. Selfishness can attach itself to an individual without his being aware that he is afflicted with it. It can become imbedded so deeply and disguised so artfully as to be almost indistinguishable.[197]

Invoking the unconscious, Packer believed that selfishness could be essentially invisible and only manifest itself in errant desires. Nevertheless, recognizing this spiritual infirmity was the key to a cure for homosexuality: "When one has the humility to admit that a spiritual disorder is tied to perversion and that selfishness rests at the root of it, already the way is open to the treatment of the condition. . . . It is very possible to cure it by treating selfishness."[198]

Packer admitted that there was no "spiritual shock treatment" that could provide a cure. He remained skeptical of professional psychologists: "Overcoming moral temptation is a very private battle, an internal battle. There are many around you who want to help and who can help—parents, branch president, bishop, for a few a marriage partner. And after that, if necessary, there are counselors and professionals to help you. But do not start with them."[199] He instructed any who experienced these desires to "suppress them" and pointed to the societal ills that appeared when people stopped suppressing their desires.[200]

From 1970 to 1980, a decade after local church leaders requested greater support for their new counseling aims in curing homosexuality, their requests had been answered many times over. Kimball had published two pamphlets and Packer one pamphlet to be used in counseling sessions. LDS Social Services had published two manuals of information and enlisted the support of professional counselors. Therapists in private practice and those employed by the church collaborated and shared research for treatment. And a research institute had been established at BYU for the purpose of addressing homosexuality. Over the course of the 1970s, both psychological and moralistic perspectives on homosexuality were fully mainstreamed into LDS thought. A new discourse was born. The homosexual was now firmly a subject of both pastoral and psychological care. Church leaders deployed the concept of sexual malleability to explain how someone could become homosexual to begin with and also to offer a plan for that person to embrace heterosexuality.

## ENLISTING PARENTS IN PREVENTING HOMOSEXUALITY

In the 1980s, LDS leaders continued to invest in efforts to support psycho-developmental treatments for homosexuality and pastoral and professional counseling. These proliferated into the home. In 1981, the church published a new internal document for LDS Social Services therapists, *Understanding and Changing Homosexual Orientation Problems*, replacing the various therapeutic guides of the 1970s for professional counselors.[201] This manual specifically cited Victor Brown Jr. and the Institute for Studies in Values and Human Behavior, revealing how their work was influential. The emphasis in the title on "changing homosexual orientation" reflected the new goals of treatment. This document cited Bieber, Socarides, and others and stratified different kinds of homosexuality. This ranking of mild, moderate, and severe "symptoms" of a "homosexual orientation problem" prescribed different therapies depending on the difficulties of the case. There were also different stages of homosexuality, beginning with "confusion" about gender roles, "filling the void" through masturbatory fantasy and mutual masturbation, "sexual identity crisis" wherein "he" feels he must choose between two competing identities, and finally a "resolution" when "he" makes the choice.[202]

Despite the language of choice to describe these orientations, the psycho-developmental diagnosis was clear: "Homosexual orientation problems . . . are often a reflection of poor interpersonal relationships with parents, siblings, and peers."[203] Gender roles were particularly important: "The homosexually oriented man knows he is male but does not fully understand how a masculine male is supposed to think and act."[204] This document ignored the moralistic explanations, such as masturbation, or spiritual explanations, such as selfishness, and fully advocated psycho-developmental theories on the etiology of homosexuality. The homosexual was more of a victim than a sinner. More serious cases warranted therapeutic practices like empathy training, physical fitness programs, systematic desensitization, emotional meter, bibliotherapy, stop-thought technique, and others.[205] The possibility of a cure then placed the responsibility to achieve it back on the victim—he was ultimately responsible for his own actions.

These same teachings were disseminated to local church leaders as well. In 1981, the church published a new booklet simply titled *Homosexuality*. A digest of the longer *Understanding and Changing*, which was directed at professional therapists, the booklet *Homosexuality* advised church leaders that "homosexual behavior is learned and can be overcome." It continued, "To believe that immoral behavior is inborn or hereditary is to deny that men have agency to choose between sin and righteousness."[206] But the manual then encouraged local church leaders to adopt therapeutic approaches similar to those used by professionals. They were instructed to assess the categories of homosexual behavior and rank them on the severity of the issue. More serious cases were to be referred to professionals, but church leaders could work with others who had "emotional problems." Church leaders were directed to inquire about the causes of the behavior, including family background, poor social skills, and lack of understanding of "gospel truths." They should invite the repentant individual to set spiritual (fasting and prayer), social (dating), physical (exercise, nutrition, and grooming), self-discipline (control thoughts), and emotional (building self-esteem) goals. Eliminating masturbation received special attention.[207]

Psycho-developmental theories rooted the causes of homosexuality in the family and gender roles, which led to new disciplinary techniques as preventive measures.[208] An article in the *Ensign* taught, "We need to teach our children plainly that homosexuality is a perversion of the Lord's designated roles of men and women."[209] The home was a sanctum of proper values. The idea that vulnerable children were under attack from an immoral world helped to frame the family as the primary place to protect them. In addition to ecclesiastical leaders and therapists, parents were enlisted in the support, discipline, and surveillance of the homosexual. Kimball's teaching that masturbation may lead to homosexuality was now included in the training for parents.[210] The home became a parallel institution to the church to instill gender roles—and to warn about their fragility.

The focus on the home as the primary site for gender instruction was animated by a philosophy of gender as learned, not innate. As an aid for ensuring the proper acquisition of gender, the church published a manual titled *A Parent's Guide* (1985). This fifty-two-page book gave parents instructions on how to educate their children about "physical intimacies and to prepare them to follow the Lord's plan in expressing their own intimacy."[211] This was the most comprehensive introduction to the psycho-developmental idea of an acquired gender and sexual identity that the church ever produced for its general membership. It advised that parents should teach a child "a sense of happiness and security in being a boy or a girl" and instructed parents to follow and model gendered divisions of labor in a patriarchal household.[212] Parents should teach gender roles by example. It suggested that from birth until age three, "a child becomes aware of gender." From this young age, parents are to begin to teach that, "depending on their gender, their goals are to become effective fathers or mothers."[213] The book stressed that gender is not just about being male or female but also about performing, identifying, and feeling good about this identity: "It is in this early stage of life, as the roles of male and female are acquired, that the foundation of sexual health is laid or sexual distress begins. . . . Consistent parenting helps children accept themselves and their gender identity during these years."[214] Within this framework, the idea that gender identity was only tenuously acquired in the right circumstances explained gender and sexual fluidity.

The next developmental stage takes place between four and eleven years. This is an "interlude" of gender and sexual development, and the primary parental responsibility is to "refine" gender roles and identities. In this period, "each child is learning how to be male or female."[215] These differences focus on "divinely mandated roles special to the respective sexes." Gender was what one did more than what one's body might indicate. Rather than being biologically natural, this guidebook depicted gender as an acquired characteristic expressed primarily through assigned roles. Children should be taught that "they will grow and be happy by accepting these roles."[216] Invoking Mormon cosmological ideas like the preexistence, the book explained, "We covenanted to accept and magnify, with increasing responsibility, the various roles of eternal life. We agreed to go beyond being brothers and sisters to the sacred mortal roles of daughters and sons, wives and husbands, and mothers and fathers. These roles are eternal and are ordained of God. They are not subject to revision by social scientists, by legislation, or by personal decision."[217] Among these divinely decreed roles, "mothers work along with daughters to bake bread, sew, and plan family menus and budgets . . . sing, play musical instruments, compose music, write poems, and develop artistic talents." In contrast, "fathers work with sons in repairing things around the house, maintaining the yard or car, and planning the budget . . . hike or play ball or engage in other mutually satisfying activities."[218] These stereotypical roles were depicted as unchanging but at the same time confined to mortal experience. Baking bread, sewing, doing yard work, and budgeting were roles that could be expressed only in the mortal sphere, with no accounting as to why they were divinely ordained or what they had to do with eternal life.

*Sodom and Cumorah*

Within the psycho-developmental paradigm, these binary roles of mothers and fathers turned out to be highly fungible. In this schema, the most important thing was the *symbolic* division of gender roles. These approaches to gender posed a problem for families where a parent may have died, or for divorced families, or in other situations where one parent was regularly absent. Would this mean that the children of such families were doomed to gender failure? According to *A Parent's Guide*, "In cases where a parent is missing . . . it is crucial that a substitute give enough example of the missing gender behavior, including approval and love."[219] The idea of a "substitute" who could fill in for the "missing gender behavior" relied on the theory that the roles needed to be modeled rather than on the idea that they were innate or natural. It also suggested that the father and mother figures were interchangeable with others who could step in in their stead. The adoption of these theories in official church documents represented the compatibilist impulse of bridging theories of neo-Freudian childhood development with LDS notions of sexual difference. The resources for accomplishing this were not in the scriptures or in moral rhetoric but in a religio-psychological hybrid of heteronormativity.

These teachings became deeply rooted in professional LDS psychological circles as well. Throughout the 1980s, LDS researchers in private practice continued the work of establishing a counter-science to the acceptance of homosexuality by deploying these psycho-developmental theories. LDS therapists Thomas Pritt and Ann Pritt adopted prominent ex-gay researcher Elizabeth Moberly's etiology of homosexuality as unmet needs caused by childhood trauma and detachment from a same-sex parent. Moberly's *Homosexuality: A New Christian Ethic* (1983) quickly became a classic in ex-gay ministries and provided the foundation for much of the contemporaneous conservative etiologies and therapies for homosexuality.[220] In their 1987 article in the *AMCAP Journal*, Pritt and Pritt, following Moberly, explained that childhood trauma "sets in motion the dynamics which eventually result in estrangement from his sex-role."[221] Such approaches continued to offer near-exclusive attention to men. Pritt and Pritt wrote that the "sex-role" of male homosexuals was disrupted when "during their childhood they had not felt competent or happy and successful in many of those sports and rough-and-tumble bonding activities that preadolescent boys commonly enjoy together."[222] What follows is masturbation and "addiction" into sexual deviation. The pathological language of "role dysphoria," "gender dysphoria," and "role-appropriate wholeness and worth" described a maladjustment in male development. Further, it framed homosexuality as a conflation of sex and love. As part of treatment, according to Pritt and Pritt, the homosexual should learn to develop fulfilling, nonsexual relationships with members of the same sex, which would resolve the emotional deficit. The homosexual should "look and act more like heterosexual men" or "engag[e] in sports."[223] Pritt and Pritt affirmed that "as the heterosexual child within matures, the individual will take care of his own responsiveness."[224] Masculinity entailed heterosexuality, hence the idea that homosexuality was a type of acquired gender dysphoria. This approach sought to wrap conforming desires, gender, and sexual practices into a single bundle of what they called a therapeutic belief in a "true, inner heterogender."[225] Deviations from this heterogender were pathological missteps. Gender performances were the key to unlocking the "true" interior gender.

### MIXED-SEX MARRIAGE AS A CURE

Besides sports and same-sex bonding, LDS leaders and psychologists often taught that mixed-sex marriage was among the various practices that would ensure the acquisition of a "heterogender." In the 1960s and 1970s, Spencer W. Kimball had taught that marriage was the ultimate goal of the repentance process and rehabilitation. Homosexuality could be completely overcome, and once a young man felt ready, then he should marry.[226] Cloy Jenkins's *Prologue* had attested that the teaching was ubiquitous in pastoral counseling sessions, including from the highest ranking church authorities. For such leaders, male-female marriage was the fulfillment of the created order. Some LDS bishops and counselors reportedly encouraged homosexual men to marry women well into the early decades of the twenty-first century.[227]

The role of marriage in the cure for homosexuality began to be controversial in this period. LDS author Carol Lynn Pearson told her own story of having followed this counsel. She recounted how her husband left her after he came out as gay and subsequently contracted HIV, which developed into AIDS. She took care of him as he died of AIDS-related causes and told the story in her nationally best-selling memoir, *Goodbye, I Love You* (1986). Pearson's book drew media attention to the LDS teachings about gay men marrying straight women. In 1986, apostle Dallin H. Oaks denied having any knowledge of church leaders advising marriage to men as a cure for homosexuality.[228] In the following year, however, apostle Gordon B. Hinckley offered further clarification to LDS therapists, counselors, and leaders: "Marriage should not be viewed as a therapeutic step to solve problems such as homosexual inclinations or practices." He added that marriage was still a goal but should be pursued only once homosexual inclinations were "overcome with a firm and fixed determination never to slip to such practices again."[229] Here, the language of determination of the individual remained central to the therapeutic response and framing of homosexuality. This statement suggested that marriage was for those committed not to practice homosexuality, even if their inclinations had not been overcome.

The LDS community of professional psychologists was open to these clarifications about marriage as a therapeutic practice.[230] The 1987 meeting of AMCAP was devoted exclusively to homosexuality. Rather than give a high-ranking church official the opportunity to present the keynote address, as had been the group's custom, Pearson was invited to share her story and insight. The conference even opened up to positions that challenged the therapeutic cure theory that had dominated the conference since its founding. At the conference, gay individuals and representatives of the LDS gay and lesbian group Affirmation presented their views. Other gay-identified Mormons who condemned "the gay lifestyle" also presented their stories. Some LDS psychiatrists following mainstream psychological consensus, including Jan Stout, did not "feel that sexual orientation is a treatable disorder." Thomas Pritt and Ann Pritt disagreed, touting the successes of psychotherapy and reparative therapy.[231] Some members of AMCAP resigned or wrote letters in protest of the fact that other organization members accepted homosexuality as non-pathological.[232] The internal dispute of the professional therapists foreshadowed coming shifts in church teachings that would manifest decades later—perhaps homosexuality could not be "cured" after all.

### TRANS ISSUES AND HOMOSEXUALITY

Trans issues further illustrated the way that gender identity was intimately intertwined with sexuality for LDS leadership in this period. When Boyd K. Packer had warned that some individuals who had physical contact with their same gender might "flip" to identify with the "opposite" gender, he was drawing on psychological notions of gender inversion. The "transsexual"— another contested category construction—lurked in the background of LDS discussion about gender and sexuality as church leaders grappled with the competing ideas about gender essentialism and gender fluidity in this era.

LDS leaders dealt with it by linking trans people to homosexuality as a way of condemning them both.

From the 1950s until the 1980s, there was an emergent discourse about trans issues in popular culture and among LDS leaders. In the 1950s, doctors performed some of the first "transsexual" surgeries, which were widely reported. In 1952, American Christine Jorgensen underwent surgical and hormonal treatment in Europe and became the most written about topic in the media in 1953.[233] She was not the first to undergo such treatments, but her transformation from soldier to beauty was a captivating story of the progress of science and the malleability of the human subject. Trans issues piqued American curiosities about nonnormative identities.

The advent of the possibility of surgical transformation—accomplished by the advances in surgical skill and technology developed during World War II—changed the nature of the conversations about trans issues. Like homosexuality, the category of the "transsexual" first arose in psychological contexts. Psychotherapists and physicians were drawn to people they saw as in need of evaluation and care. They developed pathological and medical constructs to make sense of this phenomenon and offer "treatments." Unlike the reactionary elements against homosexuality, these new medical opinions framed transsexuality as a condition that should be addressed with surgery instead of therapy. This theory held that gender was not a biological or morphological category but a psychological one. The body was mutable, but the interior gender was fixed. It was better to mold the body to "match" the interior gender than to mold the interior psychology to "match" the body. In now-outmoded terminology, trans individuals and their advocates spoke of a mismatch between the gender of the soul and the sex of the body.

These theories were also closely linked to the discourse about gender that had defined the concept of homosexuality. Because homosexuality was classed as "gender inversion," it was easy to conflate with trans identities, as well as other practices such as drag. This new medical ideology still defined the "normal" as the heterosexual and then attempted to fix the deviations in various ways, including surgical intervention. Gender inversion and even the idea of a "third sex" helped explain the experiences and lives of many who did not conform to heterosexual cultural orthodoxy.[234] But, the trans person was supposed to conform to heterosexual norms after the transition by behaving and presenting in clearly masculine or feminine ways and being sexually interested in the former gender, as the case warranted. From the mid-1960s to the late 1970s, American university-based research into trans issues supported those transitioning but also was concerned with reestablishing heteronormativity through the medicalization and psychologization of the phenomenon. As Susan Stryker explains, "Access to transsexual medical services became entangled with a socially conservative attempt to maintain traditional gender configurations in which changing sex was grudgingly permitted for the few seeking to do so, to the extent that the practice did not trouble the gender binary for the many."[235] These individuals were rendered as "exceptions" to the rule of binary heteronormativity, and the efforts to remedy their situation stipulated that they submit to traditional gender expectations in the form of medical intervention.

A string of remarks on gender transitions by LDS leaders in the 1970s was part of a larger conservative backlash against the changes to gender norms in this period. The LDS warnings against feminism and homosexuality gave leaders a context for opposing trans issues as well. There was at least one reported instance in which a trans person was baptized, endowed, and sealed in an LDS temple to her male partner, but midlevel church leaders contested granting permission for the ceremony.[236] For the senior leaders Packer and Kimball, the trans individual was an extreme case of gender inversion and the final result of an extended homosexual practice. If the homosexual was someone who failed to identify with his or her proper gender, then the transsexual was even more so the outcome of this failure. In his speeches in the late 1970s, as noted earlier, Packer had instructed that "there is no mismatching of bodies and spirits. Boys are to become men—masculine, manly men—ultimately to become husbands and fathers."[237] In these cases, LDS leaders looked to bodies, not to souls or psychological states, to mediate the conflicted ideologies about gender. But they insisted that bodies alone were not enough to secure gender or sexual difference. It was the coordination of body and soul in emotion and identity that ultimately established gender.

Kimball agreed. In these early debates about trans identity, he insisted that spirits must correspond to bodies because of divine providence. In 1974 he had taught, "God made man in his own image, male and female made he them [Gen 1:27]. With relatively few accidents of nature, we are born male or female. The Lord knew best. Certainly, men and women who would change their sex status will answer to their Maker."[238] Kimball's apparent reference to intersex individuals as "accidents of nature" was an unfortunate dehumanizing turn of phrase. But his acknowledgment that there was no universal gender binary in nature did not trouble his views that such a binary was still socially binding—and theologically expedient. And the connection between transsexuality and homosexuality was emphasized when other church leaders during this time period cited Kimball: "The promoters of homosexuality say they were born that way, but I do not believe this is true. There are no female spirits trapped in male bodies and vice versa. He who made them made them male and female."[239] Homosexuality was a form of transsexuality and vice versa.

While in the minds of LDS leaders in this period, transsexuality and homosexuality overlapped as a seamless phenomenon, the trans and gay liberation movements were often fractured from one another. In particular, they approached the use of medical and psychological expertise differently. This split, and other tensions between trans individuals and gays and lesbians in the 1970s, often left trans people outside of the cultural coalitions seeking social change.[240] While gay and lesbian activists worked to de-pathologize homosexuality, some trans activists actually sought the protection and support that came from medical oversight—including legitimacy and insurance coverage for expensive treatments and procedures. By 1980, gender identity disorder was added to the psychological establishment's *Diagnostic and Statistical Manual of Mental Disorders* for the first time, the first revision of the handbook since the 1973 edition de-pathologized homosexuality. Unfortunately, the classification of gender identity disorder as a medical condition did not result in insurance coverage for treatments in the 1980s. Health plans still categorized them as "elective" and "cosmetic."[241] While the scientific discourse was increasingly willing to distinguish between sexuality and gender identity, the conflation between transsexuality and homosexuality continued to be a powerful ideology governing how trans people were categorized.

The possibility of surgical change was particularly troubling to LDS leaders who saw these transitions in moralistic terms, not as merely medical or psychological conditions. In 1980, under Kimball's direction of the church, the *General Handbook of Instructions* addressed the issue for the first time: "Members who have undergone transsexual operations must be excommunicated."[242] Those who had transitioned before joining the church could be baptized but faced permanent restrictions on their membership. Ecclesiastical disciplinary action was also to be meted out to any doctors who performed such procedures. These new sanctions were limited to medical intervention. As the 1980 guidelines explained, "Any disciplinary action is deferred until the individual has made a decision whether to undergo the operation."[243] The 1983 revision softened the requirement from a mandatory excommunication, indicating the procedure "ordinarily justifies excommunication."[244]

These policies did not explicitly preclude nonsurgical transitions, but the social pressures against trans identities in LDS communities did not make such practices welcome. In the 1989 update to these policies, the disciplinary

*Sodom and Cumorah*

action against doctors was dropped, but the procedure was now classified as an "elective transsexual operation."[245] The addition of the adjective "elective" functioned to further delegitimize transitioning as a choice that could then be classified as sinful. Choice and self-determination remained guiding ideas that framed how LDS leaders thought about nonnormative identities.

─────────────────────────────────

In addition to the hierarchical relationships between black and white and male and female, LDS leaders latched onto another binary hierarchy after World War II: normal and deviant. When applied to same-sex sexual and romantic relationships, this new framework created an epistemic regime. LDS leaders developed new forms of power and knowledge to address this apparently growing phenomenon, including pastoral techniques, research institutes, scientific studies, pamphlets, manuals for ecclesiastical leaders and parents, and church agencies that hired psychologists to aid in treatment. While various kinds of sexual sins were forbidden in church teachings—from masturbation, to necking and petting, and up to fornication and adultery—only same-sex intimacy took on this categorization as deviance. It was a special case, deserving of special consideration. As part of this conceptual framework, the figure of the homosexual was invented in Mormon thought in the 1950s, was thoroughly pathologized in the 1960s, and was psychologically treated in the 1970s and beyond. These methods were mingled together with moral preaching campaigns based on self-help ideologies that emphasized personal choice and the power of the determined will.

The coexistence of moralistic and psychological theories, and their convergence in pastoral and professional care, characterized Mormon treatment of homosexuality in the 1970s and 1980s. These two frameworks were able to work together because they actually shared some foundational principles. First, both argued that homosexuality was best understood as a failure of a proper understanding of gender norms. Second, both believed that heterosexuality was the "normal" condition of human beings and that homosexuality was a deviation. Combining these two positions, a mentally and spiritually healthy person identified with his or her socially prescribed gender, which included having sexual desires for the opposite sex. Third, both the psychological and moral understandings of homosexuality reduced same-sex relationships to a matter of sexual desires and acts. The homosexual may not be essentially tied to homosexuality, but homosexuality was essentially tied to sex. Finally, both had resisted an essentialist understanding of a homosexual identity. In the fight against essentialist understandings of sexuality, LDS leaders had to accept fluid and malleable accounts of sexual difference, opting for a number of competing etiologies that focused on parental failures, bad habits, learned behavior, and choice. But "choice" alone is an insufficient description. Rather, this chapter has suggested that a more complex moral etiology alongside psychological explanations created a picture of a vulnerable and malleable sexual subjectivity in modern Mormon assessments of homosexuality. Mormons believed that anyone could become a homosexual and anyone could become a heterosexual. Rather than seeing sexual and gender fluidity in exclusively negative terms, LDS solutions to homosexuality leveraged this belief in malleability as both the cause of the condition and as the basis of a cure.

It is here worth restating that homosexuality was a largely gendered term in Mormonism, as were its many variants and euphemisms. Homosexuality was conceived of as a problem for men, a result of their abundant sexuality, overflowing imaginations, and misplaced attachments and, importantly, a failure of their masculinity. The therapeutic approach to homosexuality, then, was asymmetrically gendered along these lines. There were a handful of references and admissions that women may engage in same-sex relationships too, but the constructed homosexual was almost always a male who must be rescued to return to his masculinity. The homosexual was to regain himself, exercise self-mastery, resolve his problems with his father, and ultimately fulfill his male duties as a husband and father. This approach was not so much about cultivating heterosexual desire but about becoming a man through masculine comportment. Homosexuality was more than a particular sexual sin; it was a sin against gender norms by exposing the fragility of gender itself. The control of gender and the control of sexuality were inseparably linked.

The LDS appropriation of psychology as a framework for thinking about homosexuality was one way that the church grappled with the changing landscape of modernity. Such an outlook was part of a larger trend that historian Eric Swedin has called "the psychologization of the LDS community."[246] Far from being a way that LDS people distinguished themselves from "the world," LDS therapeutic and psychological approaches to homosexuality closely tracked with non-LDS developments. Pursuing a compatibilist approach, LDS leaders increasingly adopted the view that homosexuality was not just a sin but a mental/emotional disorder that distinguished it from other sexual sins. Its causes had to be diagnosed and prevented and its cures researched and implemented. Long after this view was abandoned by mainstream professionals, LDS leaders continued to accept this model as the driving force explaining homosexuality, offering an alternative etiology and promising a cure. This powerful view was sustained by the creation of new institutions of knowledge whose purpose was to counter secularism by using the tools and discourses of secular psychological research. But this psychological approach was constrained by traditional Mormon views as well, predetermining the conclusions in many cases.

In the traditional history of sexuality, heterosexuality and homosexuality jointly emerged as fixed identities in modernity. Queer theorists have objected to this modernist characterization of sexuality, historicizing and relativizing these categories and embracing fluidity, ambiguity, and performativity instead. But Mormonism does not fit neatly into this traditional history of sexuality. Instead, Mormon leaders also sought for relativity, ambiguity, and especially malleability to explain the fragility of heterosexual desires. The prescribed cure for gender failure was to perform heterosexuality and heteronormative gender roles—especially those that supported the "patriarchal order"—until they took root in the individual. But these leaders also came to believe that accomplishing the goal of getting people to make the preferred choice would require more than pastoral and psychological intervention. Politics was next.

# Chapter Three

# POLITICS AND THE
# PATRIARCHAL ORDER

In November 1974, Catholic antifeminist activist Phyllis Schlafly booked a flight to Salt Lake City and secured a meeting with the newly appointed General President of the Relief Society, Barbara Bradshaw Smith (d. 2010).[1] Smith had just been sustained in her new role over the church's global women's organization one month before the meeting. Schlafly was looking for new recruits in her battle against the Equal Rights Amendment, a proposed federal amendment that would ensure that men and women were treated equally by the law. At the time, Schlafly's efforts to oppose the ERA seemed like a long-shot political strategy—it had the support of mainstream Republicans and Democrats and was steamrolling through the states. Mormons at the time also seemed unlikely to get involved—they rarely spoke on political matters and had not attempted to mass-mobilize their membership on specific political issues since Prohibition. Even more speculative was the idea that Mormons and Catholics would work side by side, since neither had a strong ecumenical record. Schlafly, however, was determined to build a broad coalition of conservative voices and to activate religious outsiders who did not think in political terms. In their meeting, Smith expressed some skepticism at first but warmed to the idea of getting the LDS church involved in the fight to oppose the ERA. After all, if the church taught that gender was at risk from changing sexual and cultural norms in secular society, shouldn't its leaders act to protect it in the public sphere?

The meeting with Schlafly proved consequential. It marked an official beginning of the Mormon affiliation with the rising movement known as the Religious Right—a broad coalition of conservatives who felt alienated from the mainstream Republican Party and sought to make their voices heard through political action. Mormons had flirted around the edges of anti–civil rights activism in the 1950s and 1960s, but their leaders felt called in the 1970s on various fronts in the battle against feminism and homosexuality. In addition to preaching and a therapeutic outreach, Mormon leaders took on a political strategy that protected the church's members and a broader culture from a sociology of gender fluidity. By focusing on the possibility that gender norms could change and positing that as a source of danger and a cause for fear rather than liberation, LDS political activism in the 1970s framed gender and sexuality as the province of government regulation.

Mormons did not exit this battle against the ERA in the same way that they entered. The politicization of Mormon teachings about gender left an unexpected mark on church teachings. The history of LDS political activism needs to be told from both the inside out and the outside in—how Mormon teachings influenced Mormons' political actions and also how this political engagement shaped Mormon teachings. While most approaches to LDS politics discuss how Mormon doctrines inspired LDS activists' efforts, this chapter also traces how LDS political activism redefined Mormon teachings. Specifically, Mormon antifeminist teachings and activism came to express moderate feminist ideals in the course of LDS activists' political efforts. Emulating the rhetoric of segregationist political doctrines on race, at least some Mormons began to argue that male-female difference was not hierarchical but rather a "separate but equal" complementary difference. While opposing equal rights, Mormons nevertheless came to accept male-female equality as an ideal, however imperfectly. This tension, between the patriarchal order and soft egalitarianism, shot through this period as Mormon leaders struggled to articulate a doctrine for women in a changing era. This included significant transitions in how church leaders talked about the sexual relationship between husbands and wives and women's paid labor outside the home.

## FROM EQUAL RIGHTS TO THE RELIGIOUS RIGHT

Like the 1950s, the 1970s marked another major resurgence of sexual moralism in the United States. After the social changes in the 1960s, conservative Americans in the 1970s were expressing concern over the "breakdown" of the family. This was a complicated time of deepening divisions between Americans with competing visions of morality and justice. The sense of moral and political crisis in the 1970s drew on much of the same concerns of the 1950s—that the fabric of society was vulnerable to collapse without a strong sense of order.[2] The terms of that order had changed, of course, as racial separation receded in importance in the renewed conservative movement.

Commenting on the new rights of interracial couples to marry, President Richard Nixon said in 1970 that he could understand it. When asked if he could allow same-sex couples the same rights, he cautioned, "I can't go that far," adding, "that's the year 2000."[3]

Similarly, Christian fundamentalists and evangelicals shifted away from the politics of race, segregation, and opposition to interracial marriage as the expected causes of social decay. There were exceptions, such as the policies of Bob Jones University, "white flight" to the suburbs, and the private Christian school movement ("segregation academies") in the late 1960s that were a reaction against public school desegregation.[4] But even the segregationist origins of some of these schools soon conceded to the victories of the civil rights movement.[5] By the mid-1970s, many evangelicals had publicly pivoted to the politics of gender as a primary danger to society. The politically organized Religious Right—consisting of fundamentalists, evangelicals, conservative Catholics, and Mormons—reshaped the political map in part by placing "family values" at the center of not only their preaching but also their political agenda.[6] This movement invoked a nostalgia for an imaginary stable time—a time of conservatism, prosperity, and social harmony.[7]

The gender politics of family values were expressions of deep concern about the structure of society itself. For many conservative Christians, the image of the woman with "equal rights" as a feminist and perhaps a lesbian raised the possibility that women might reject their natural and divinely ordained roles in the patriarchal order. As scholar Ludger Viefhues-Bailey puts it, these ideas helped to delineate conservative Christian heterosexual relationships as "structured by a hierarchy of submission."[8] In the Mormon context, that much may be true as well. Many Mormons were deeply committed to what they called "the patriarchal order," with its clearly defined roles and hierarchical structuring of society, church, and family. This belief was entrenched in the church's Priesthood Correlation reforms in the 1950s through the 1970s, as the previous chapters showed. It then also informed LDS leaders' political opposition to equal rights for women and for gays and lesbians.

The family values framework sought to unite different denominations and mask disagreements on other matters under a common "Christian" banner. The movement was intentionally inclusive of a wide coalition of disparate traditions—Baptists, Methodists, Presbyterians, and others. These Protestant groups then collaborated with Catholics, bridging a former chasm between them. Their political success depended on overlooking theological and denominational dividing lines. Led by preachers and activists such as Phyllis Schlafly, Pat Robertson, James Robison, Billy Graham, Jerry Falwell, Tim LaHaye, and others, conservatives galvanized around an alleged threat to American prosperity and identity. They believed the liberal social movements seeking to expand freedoms for women, gays, and lesbians were instances of social decay and the result of failure of fathers and mothers in the home. The malleability of the phrase "family values" also allowed for different interpretations of its meaning. Conservatives defined family values in various overlapping but distinctive ways: the family should have stronger affective bonds, men should lead in the home, women should devote their time primarily to child care rather than work outside the home, sex should be restricted to the marital unit, homosexuality should be not only socially unacceptable but illegal, contraceptives and abortion were morally suspect, and families should practice "self-reliance" rather than receive government services. As historian Janice Irvine described this period, "The nascent Christian Right recognized the mobilizing power of sexuality."[9]

One of the first major rallying points for the emergent Religious Right was to oppose the Equal Rights Amendment. Gender issues took center stage in a conservative resurgence against the liberal social values of mainstream Republicans. The ERA had been part of the progressive agenda since the 1920s but had finally picked up enough steam to pass both houses of Congress in 1972. Its ultimate passage seemed inevitable at the time. There were Democratic majorities in both houses of Congress, and the Republican president Nixon immediately endorsed the amendment after it was passed. Women's rights were not yet a partisan political issue but enjoyed broad public support. Mainstream conservatives, still bruising from their losses on civil rights in the prior decade, were eager to prove their bona fides on the right side of social justice. The ERA was sent to the states requiring a two-thirds majority for authorization and quickly passed in twenty-two state legislatures in the first year.

Despite its broad political support, the idea of women's equality in and out of the home was still controversial in some quarters. For many conservative religious groups, hierarchy and strictly defined gender roles were influential norms that could inspire political action.[10] In 1972, Catholic activist Phyllis Schlafly founded her organization STOP ERA. Schlafly first came to national prominence as an anticommunist in the 1950s. She once again drew national attention as part of the unpopular 1964 presidential campaign of Barry Goldwater, who had run on the idea that "extremism in the defense of liberty is no vice." In support of his candidacy, Schlafly distributed her self-published book, *A Choice, Not an Echo*, that denounced "liberal" Republicans.[11] When she wrote in 1972 "What's Wrong with 'Equal Rights' for Women?," she already had a track record of conservative mobilizing and a vision for a more conservative movement to redefine Republican politics.[12]

Aggressive while assuming a hyperfeminine persona, Schlafly instantly became an icon of the antifeminist women's movement and launched a nationwide speaking and organizing tour.[13] The family—specifically restrictive in its definition—was an important wedge in her rhetoric. In her pamphlet against the ERA, she argued that there was a fundamental difference between men and women: "Women have babies and men don't." From this, she argued that different social duties for men and women followed: "If you don't like this fundamental difference, you will have to take up your complaint with God because He created us this way." Schlafly claimed that the ERA was not really about equal pay and more vocational and educational opportunities but was actually a "deadly poison" far more insidious in its true goals. She asserted that "women's lib" was a "total assault" on American women. "Why should we trade in our special privileges and honored status for the alleged advantage of working in an office or assembly line? Most women would rather cuddle a baby than a typewriter or factory machine."[14] Contrasting the warm ideals of domestic life with the harsh technocratic world of paid labor, Schlafly coded these two realms as feminine and masculine respectively.

Schlafly's opposition to the ERA rejected the feminist premise that patriarchy was oppressive to women. Her argument was audacious in its account of the status of women. Schlafly took the view that "of all the classes of people who ever lived, the American woman is the most privileged. We have the most rights and rewards, and the fewest duties."[15] Instead of inequality, Schlafly stated that American women enjoyed "special privileges"—most importantly financial support from husbands that kept them out of the dreary and insecure world of the labor force. She warned that these privileges would be erased by the ERA. Schlafly's argument contrasted an idealized domestic arrangement with a dystopian world for women if they were treated like men. The family itself was inconsistent with a world where women were equal because it would bring women down from their lofty position in society. Her rhetoric was persuasive to many because it captured the pro-ERA arguments by redefining equality. Rather than seeing women as oppressed and excluded from power, antifeminists like Schlafly took the view that women were actually highly empowered and privileged in a society that rejected "equal rights." Equality was a demotion.

Mormons were well positioned to join the politicization of the family in the 1970s. They had been eager participants in the postwar religious revival focused on the patriarchal home, and such values remained central to Mormon identity throughout this period. Many LDS women were attracted to this message and sought to counter feminism with a message of submission. They promised not only greater stability in the home and society but greater happiness for women than "women's liberation" could offer. As discussed in an earlier chapter, Helen B. Andelin's *Fascinating Womanhood* bred imitators and attracted proselytes. In the late 1960s in her local ward building in Arizona, Jacquie Davison had enrolled in a "Fascinating Womanhood" workshop led by Andelin and was inspired to start an organization to bring these ideas into the political sphere. Two years before Phyllis Schlafly's STOP ERA, Davison founded the Happiness of Womanhood organization. It not only was dedicated to defeating the ERA but also opposed abortion, pornography, and homosexuality. The organization spread in Mormon-dominated areas of Utah, Arizona, and California, gaining ten thousand members in all fifty states by 1973. Davison saw in Andelin's message a necessary turn to politics to sustain the patriarchal order.[16]

LDS church leaders continued previous warnings that gender segregation was necessary to prevent dangerous gender fluidity. Motherhood, to the exclusion of paid labor, was a special concern. Harold B. Lee, the conservative reformer of the Priesthood Correlation program, became president of the church from 1970 to 1973. In 1970, Correlation shut down the fifty-year-old *Relief Society Magazine*, and with it any independent venue for women and women's leadership to write and publish according to their own editorial priorities. Lee's stance on gender issues defined the church's message. In 1972, he published an article in the new church magazine the *Ensign* titled "Maintain Your Place as a Woman." Lee taught, "To be what God intended you to be as a woman depends on the way you think, believe, live, dress, and conduct yourselves as true examples of Latter-day Saint womanhood, examples of that for which you were created and made." Womanhood was vulnerable to dissolution if it was not practiced. Among these practices, encouraged by Lee, were starting families without delay and having as many children as women were able. Lee warned of divine retribution for those who did not comply and blessings for those who did. If a married woman must work outside the home, she "should not neglect the cares and duties in the home." He reprised the teachings about the patriarchal order of the family, explaining that "the wife is to obey the law of her husband only as he obeys the laws of God. . . . The good wife commandeth her husband in any equal matter by constantly obeying him." Lee admonished that spousal submission and clear roles maintained boundaries between men and women. He believed that any weakening of these boundaries, even in seemingly trivial matters, might incur greater occurrences of lesbianism. "For a woman to adopt the mode of a man's dress," Lee warned, "is to encourage the wave of sexual perversion, when men adopt women's tendencies and women become mannish in their desires."[17] Feminism and lesbianism were paired phenomena. Women should "maintain their place" against the cultural tides that undermined hierarchical sexual difference and ensured heterosexual desires.

Other church leaders in this period published similar antifeminist articles that defined women as essentially mothers. Like Lee, they warned especially against working women as a site of gender instability. Apostle Thomas S. Monson (d. 2018) complained in an article titled "The Women's Liberation Movement: Liberation or Deception?" that some women were demanding "free abortion, free childcare, and equal employment." Monson believed that these women were abandoning their divinely ordered responsibilities. He emphasized that "every woman is endowed by God with distinctive characteristics, gifts, and talents, in order that she may fulfill a specific mission in the eternal plan," namely, motherhood.[18] Another senior church leader warned, "One of the greatest tragedies of our day is the confusion of minds of some which would cause mothers to go to work in the marketplace."[19] Another apostle explained that women's liberation and the sexual revolution are "Satan's way of destroying women, the home, and the family."[20] Working women not only were unfaithful and disobedient and at risk of lesbianism but also advanced satanic purposes.

These ideas were not entirely out of sync with broader American sentiments. While feminists were fiercely battling notions of hierarchical marriage and restrictions on women's work, in 1970 the vast majority of American women under forty-five still believed that the ideal home life consisted of a wife who stayed at home.[21] Antifeminist sentiment was not simply a top-down phenomenon but a grassroots reaction to changing social norms as well.

In between the hierarchy and the grass roots, LDS scholars and enthusiasts increasingly began to publish their own thoughts on scripture, Mormon history, and doctrine to reinforce antifeminist views in these years. The College of Religious Education at BYU employed many such religious experts, including Rodney Turner, a popular lecturer and writer who had

*Politics and the Patriarchal Order*

earned a doctorate of education from the University of Southern California. Turner's 1972 book, *Woman and the Priesthood*, was published by the church's commercial press and spoke to the feeling that marriage norms were under attack in secular society. Turner's book-length apologetic for patriarchy, coupled with his status at BYU and representation in the church-owned press, sheds some light on where many LDS conservatives were in this period. He laid special blame upon feminists as the cause of the problem for the family. Turner warned against marriage "between peers," which emphasized the "virtual equality of the sexes" and behaved as a 50/50 "partnership." "Being a two-headed affair," he explained, "the modern marriage is, in actuality, headless. . . . It is pure democracy."[22] These were not compliments. Turner argued that women's "essential milieu is the home rather than the world at large." He worried, "No woman can fully identify with the work-a-day world of men and escape unmarked."[23] Gender, according to Turner, is spatially defined—the entire space outside of the home is the "masculine world." Men, by spending too much time indoors in the modern world, also risked feminization. Turner diagnosed the modern problem with gender as one where "the two sexes are breaking away from their natural moorings and drifting toward each other." This androgyny, or "uni-sex society," was the result of a view of the equality of the sexes.[24] The appeal to a "natural" order that was produced by social norms highlighted the philosophical conflict about gender throughout this period. Gender was both natural and constructed.

Like many LDS leaders in this period, Turner also interpreted the Adam and Eve story as a divine authorization of patriarchy.[25] He saw Eve's partaking of the fruit as naive transgression, not a noble act: "She was, for all her physical maturity, like a little girl who, lacking experience, succumbs to the blandishments of a would-be molester. Hers was not the knowing, sophisticated sin of a worldly person. It was more the seduction of an innocent, trusting child. Note that the stated reasons for her disobedience reflect her feminine nature: the fruit was good for food (tasty), pleasant to the eyes (beautiful), and would make her wise (curiosity). Doubtless, the last rationalization was the deciding factor—feminine curiosity being what it is."[26] Invoking powerful stereotypes about "feminine nature," Turner compared Eve to a sexually vulnerable child and explained her choice as the consequence of her inferior virtues. In contrast, "Adam, having greater understanding, was impervious to such appeals. He was not beguiled; he partook 'that man might be.'"[27] Quoting church leaders such as Brigham Young and others, Turner believed that Adam dutifully sacrificed himself because of Eve's inferior understanding. Because of the fall, the hierarchy of male over female was officially introduced, and the male became the mediator between God and woman.[28] In this instance, Turner's interpretation saw the postlapsarian condition of hierarchy as the ideal, "feminine curiosity being what it is."

Like Lee, Turner's worry about gender fluidity was inseparably connected to his promotion of male hierarchy. To reassert the difference between male and female, Turner advocated a benevolent patriarchy rooted in a spiritual union of shared commitment to the practice of church teachings. He offered several examples to justify the hierarchy of husband over wife. "The true order of marriage," he explained, "is patriarchal in design. The husband leads because he is the living embodiment of that priesthood which governs all things." Continuing, he explained, "There is no more reason for a woman in Israel to chafe under this commandment than it is for a child to resist the guidance of loving parents."[29] The duty of the woman to submit was a part of her social position. He wrote, "As long as a woman is under her father's roof she owes him her chief loyalty. When she marries, that loyalty passes to her husband."[30] The comparison of the woman to the child undergirded Turner's belief that there was a natural order to patriarchy. A woman's humility in submitting even to a husband who was "less gifted or less knowledgeable" was a virtue.[31] In another analogy, he explained that the father's "position in the home is similar to that of a bishop over a ward, a president over a stake, the prophet over the Church or God over the universe."[32] The comparison of a father's authority to God's authority was meant to imply a benevolent patriarchy, not a license for abuse.[33] But patriarchy was the order of things.

Church teachings on gender purity in this period reflected the importance of bounded roles. They maintained that there were two options for a gendered society, either separate roles in hierarchical order or a unisex society that erased male and female difference. Accordingly, they defined male and female as a set of performances. A man leads and a woman assists. A woman who leads risks becoming a lesbian and mannish, and a man who fails to lead risks feminization and homosexuality. The discourse of gender in this period advanced essentialist theories of fixed difference but were actually dependent upon a theory of gender fluidity and malleability. Sexual difference could be maintained only by cultural and legal norms.

## PATRIARCHY AND THE EQUAL RIGHTS AMENDMENT

Mormonism's patriarchal teachings informed how Latter-day Saints engaged with the emerging Religious Right. Months after Schlafly launched her STOP ERA campaign, two new LDS officials took key leadership positions. At the end of 1973, Spencer W. Kimball became the president of the church, replacing Lee, who died unexpectedly after just nineteen months in that office. And in late 1974, Barbara Bradshaw Smith became president of the Relief Society. Her predecessor, Belle S. Spafford, had run the organization for thirty years and also served as the president of the National Council of Women, the nonsectarian women's advocacy organization founded by Francis Willard, Susan B. Anthony, and other important nineteenth-century feminists. Spafford's leading role in the church and her national profile were big shoes to fill. Smith, a mother of seven, had never been employed outside the home, but she had served in prominent church positions before. She was about to intervene in the direction of the church in a decisive and long-lasting way.

Senior church leaders began to explore the possibility of formal opposition to the ERA in the early 1970s. They were intrigued by Schlafly's STOP ERA coalition, tentatively at first. Even Spafford had publicly stated to a small group of New York businessmen in the summer of 1974 that she did not support the ERA, but her remarks received little attention.[34] In November 1974, Schlafly secured the aforementioned meeting with the new General Relief Society president. In the encounter, Smith explained, "I didn't think the Church would take a stand against the ERA, because they only took a stand against moral issues." Schlafly, recognizing the opening, responded that she "felt that the ERA was one of the greatest moral issues of our day and that it would be very destructive to the family." The response persuaded Smith to investigate the issue more. "After that particular experience," she recalled, "I felt maybe we needed to do something more about it." She scheduled a meeting with apostle Thomas S. Monson, who indicated that "he felt the Church would want to take some action, because they too felt that it would be a very destructive thing for the morals of the community and the family."[35] The twin arguments— that the ERA would damage "morals" and "the family"—motivated church leaders to take a stand. This also signaled an important turn as gender issues became external political fodder for the church, not just a matter of internal preaching. Smith's initial observation that she did not believe the church would get involved revealed that gender had not yet become a political force for church leaders. Indeed, President Kimball declined to comment on the ERA in January 1975—just a few months after Smith and Schlafly's meeting—because it was a "political" issue.[36] That was about to change.

Schlafly's influence on Smith extended to being a role model as well. She showed that women could become the leading spokespeople of anti-feminist political activism. When Smith proposed the idea of getting the church involved, the apostles "felt it was appropriate for me as the leader of the women of the Church to announce my stand against the Equal Rights Amendment."[37] Acting quickly, they arranged a large audience for her at the University of Utah on December 13, 1974. Smith's speech was measured and cautious, even as it closely followed some of Schlafly's points. The ERA, she argued, would be a "step backward."[38] She enumerated the concrete reasons that women were dissatisfied, including unequal pay, a lack of a voice in public decision-making, guilt over failure to conform to stereotyped roles, lack of access to credit, and other instances of discrimination and inequality. Smith conceded that all of these were genuine problems but concluded that the Equal Rights Amendment was not the solution. She believed that it carried with it some potential risks: "It would nullify all of the laws covering the gamut of domestic relations and probably take away the financial liability of the father to support the wife and the children[,] . . . military conscription would be a mandate . . . ," and so on. For supporters of the ERA, these ideas had little legal credibility, but fears proved powerful.[39]

Smith's worry that the ERA would erode sexual difference, morality, and the family was effective precisely because it was a broadside attack. Many Mormon women had supported the ERA. Smith spoke to this group to convince them that she shared their concerns, including a desire for at least some reforms, but that there was danger in the ERA.[40] Her position also marked a rhetorical stance that some male church leaders would imitate. They too would express sympathy for the reasons that people might want to support the ERA but also propose alternatives that offered fewer potential risks, as they saw them. Rather than simply condemning equal rights or dismissing the concerns that inspired the proposed amendment, Smith charted a middle path by claiming the side of women's equality and also opposing the ERA. Mormons like Smith did not just turn away from feminism; they also made it their own. They adopted new language about equality between men and women and spoke about equality in their own religious idiom. Unmitigated patriarchy was not the only option for a political Mormonism.

At the same time, Smith and others taught that the ERA would bring about destructive changes to sexual differences and gender roles. They often charged that it was vague in its scope and application, that it would fail to accomplish what it intended, and that it would have far-reaching unintended effects. The problem ultimately boiled down to a single philosophical issue. As Smith explained, "We would find ourselves locked into a system that did not provide for the emotional, physical, or biological differences between the sexes. . . . It would be unlikely that any of those differences could be accommodated."[41] For Smith, the ERA would entail a society without any meaningful sexual difference because such differences were either produced or undermined by the "system." The supposedly fixed emotional, physical, and even biological differences would be erased by the law.

Even though President Kimball had declined to comment publicly on the ERA a few weeks after Smith's speech, one week later, on January 11, 1975, just before the Utah legislature was opening the session that would vote on the amendment, the LDS *Church News* issued an editorial that called the ERA "not only imperfect, but dangerous." The strong language was not ambiguous or measured. It too adopted the argument that gender was at risk of dissolution under this amendment. The editorial warned it would lead to a "unisex" law.[42] With equality under the law, creation itself could be undone by the weakening of strict division of gender roles. The unsigned editorial, along with Smith's speech, had an immediate effect of signaling to church members that they too should oppose the ERA. In November 1974, when Schlafly first approached Smith, 63 percent of Mormons supported the ERA. After Smith's speech and the church's editorial, by February 1975 that support tumbled to 31 percent. The amendment was defeated in the Utah legislature on February 18, 1975.[43]

With such success, by 1976 LDS church leaders decided to flex their political muscles to oppose the ERA on the national stage. They issued statements against it and ultimately organized church membership in a coordinated attack across several states.[44] As historian Martha Sontag Bradley interprets this shift, "It slowly became apparent that Barbara B. Smith, though the highest-ranking woman in the church, did not have sufficient authority to maintain a united front among Mormon women."[45] The First Presidency, under the direction of Kimball, now took the lead. This period was one of the low points (among many) for LDS women's leadership and authority.[46] While LDS men organized such efforts, LDS women were the primary actors on the ground.[47] The male leaders brought greater organization and disciplinary approaches to the early national political strategy, creating their own anti-ERA organizations and directing members into them. These groups were instructed to appear as "grassroots" collections of "concerned citizens" and not to reveal backing from the LDS church.[48] These battles played out for the next six years, state by state.

The ERA was not only about women's roles but also about a whole system that favored heterosexuality. Nor was the ERA fight the only political action on gender and sexuality the church undertook in the 1970s. The connection between the ERA and anti-homosexuality politics is frequently under-recognized.[49] As Phyllis Schlafly had become the face of national antifeminist politics, Anita Bryant became a symbol of anti-homosexual conservative politics in this period. She had been well known as a beauty queen and advertising spokeswoman, but she quickly rose again to fame as a Christian mother who worried about those whom she depicted as homosexual predators in Dade County, Florida. Unlike the Catholic Schlafly, Bryant was an evangelical. She embodied an ideal female role in conservative religion, being outspoken in defense of the anti-homosexual gospel but also projecting conservative feminine ideals. She contrasted Christian purity with homosexual perversion, pedophilia, degradation, and the supposed existential threat it posed to the nation. Her message of "Save Our Children" and her status as a conservative mother resonated widely and mobilized the Religious Right. Replaying the anticommunist tactics from the McCarthy era, she painted a picture of a vast "militant" homosexual network whose agenda was to undermine America's churches and political institutions and to recruit more homosexuals from America's precarious youth.[50] Her belief in sexual malleability—that heterosexuals could be converted to homosexuality and vice versa—structured her worldview of a contest between right and wrong.

LDS leaders similarly believed in the grave social threat of homosexuality and increasingly thought of a political solution. They drew on religio-sociological ideas that U.S. strength was connected to the moral purity of its people and on the popular socio-sexual mythology that civilizations fell when they became sexually lax. In 1970, Spencer W. Kimball and Mark Petersen warned, "It is obvious that the world would be doomed by homosexuality for it can never produce a child. And without a continuing army of spirits coming to the earth to be embodied, the race would die out in one generation. . . . Proper marriage and family life is the only thing to save this confused world and if men waste their seed . . . certainly the race will disappear."[51] In 1971, Kimball declared that homosexuality "means waste of power, an end to the family and to the civilization. One generation of it would depopulate the world."[52] Homosexuality weakened men and wasted their reproductive potential because it was a non-procreative sexual exchange.

*Politics and the Patriarchal Order*

It was also, apparently, extremely alluring. The idea that permitting homosexuality would bring about civilizational destruction within one generation not only inflamed the fears of its danger but also suggested that it was a legitimately attractive option that was prevented only by social and legal norms against it. Absent those sanctioning norms, homosexuality could have a universal appeal. This warranted political action.

The fears about sexual fluidity were closely intertwined to the theories of gender fluidity and "unisex" persons.[53] One would certainly lead to the other, which explained why church leaders fought against both with equal vigor. For Kimball, homosexuality was the ultimate result of a theory of gender similarity. It could be countered only by strict divisions between male and female. In 1974, he taught, "Every form of homosexuality is sin. . . . Some people are ignorant or vicious and apparently attempting to destroy the concept of masculinity and femininity. More and more girls dress, groom, and act like men. More and more men dress, groom, and act like women. The high purposes of life are damaged and destroyed by the growing unisex theory."[54] The emphasis on sexual difference extended to clothing, actions, and grooming. The "unisex theory" of humanity, he believed, posed a great risk of trapping human beings in persistent gender liminality, not least of all leading to homosexuality. Laws that prevented the collapse of sexual difference were crucial in this battle of theories. Kimball's statement reveals how the idea of the "unisex" individual was a code for homosexuality in much of the anti-ERA rhetoric. It also confirmed Thomas Laqueur's observation that the one-sex theory "did not die" at the end of the seventeenth century; rather, "it lives today in many guises."[55]

Church leaders viewed the notion of a breakdown of gender differences as a direct cause of homosexuality and saw women's equality as complicit in this outcome. In October 1978, the First Presidency reaffirmed its earlier opposition to the ERA. The amendment, the leaders warned, would lead to "encouragement of those who seek a unisex society, an increase in the practice of homosexual and lesbian activities, and other concepts which could alter the natural, God-given relationship of men and women."[56] Homosexuality was the political cost of gender equality. In March 1980, church leaders included a twenty-three-page insert in the *Ensign* that stated that the ERA would lead to "same-sex lesbian and homosexual marriages." The marriages themselves would be "immoral," but worse, they would give "legal sanction to the rearing of children in such homes."[57] LDS objection to same-sex marriage at this time reflected a broader social fear that homosexuals were threatening to children. Linking women's rights, which had broad public support, to gay and lesbian rights, which had much softer public support, damaged the ERA by playing on these prejudices. Further, it was not just same-sex sexual activity that was condemned but same-sex kinship and families. The conflation of same-sex families with immoral sexual activity proved an enduring argument in later political campaigns.

Church leaders translated their moral concerns into political positions about homosexuality. They had long supported harsh anti-sodomy legislation. Dating back to 1965, in his first public address to discuss homosexuality, Kimball had warned, "Toleration for sin is terrifying."[58] This view was the result of his belief that sexual immorality was just below murder in the hierarchy of sins. In the published version of this talk, he continued, "This heinous homosexual sin is of the ages. Many cities and civilizations have gone out of existence because of it. . . . In Exodus, the law required death for the culprit who had sex play with animals, the deviate who committed incest, or the depraved one who had homosexual or other vicious practices."[59] Responding to the wave of states decriminalizing sodomy, Kimball complained that "some governments and some churches and numerous corrupted individuals have tried to reduce such [homosexual] behavior from criminal offense to personal privilege."[60] He repeated the worry in an address in 1974.[61]

These issues became more urgent by the following year. In California, the Consenting Adults Bill proposed to decriminalize same-sex intercourse in that state. Opponents organized a referendum to keep the anti-sodomy laws in place. LDS church officials directed local LDS leaders in California to "give every support to the referendum" but didn't give further organizational backing.[62] Senior LDS leaders continued to publicly preach in favor of anti-sodomy laws during the fight. Homosexuality not only was psychologically depraved and socially toxic but should be criminal because of its threat to civilization as a whole. In October 1977 Kimball again warned against legalizing the "sin of the ages" of Sodom and Gomorrah: "We do not hesitate to tell the world that the cure for these evils is not in surrender."[63] For Kimball, anti-sodomy laws protected against civilizational destruction.

Mark Petersen, Kimball's close colleague in combating homosexuality, similarly worried about its decriminalization. In late-1970s, Petersen wrote in the *Church News* in support of anti-sodomy laws, saying in one editorial that, "The persistent drive to make homosexuality an 'accepted' and legal way of life should disgust every thinking person."[64] Petersen railed against homosexuality as "repulsive and disgusting" and "severely condemned by the Almighty God."[65] Between 1977 and 1979, Petersen would write six editorials—unsigned—on the subject, imploring legislators and "every thinking person" to consider homosexuality a grave crime.[66] The editorials specifically praised Anita Bryant's political operations.

The LDS church did not get directly involved in Bryant's campaign to keep gay men and women from teaching in public schools. However, Bryant was invited to Utah as part of her national campaign in June 1977. President Kimball and Relief Society president Barbara B. Smith hailed Bryant's arrival to Utah and praised her anti-homosexuality teachings.[67] Politically, though, there wasn't much to do in LDS spheres of political influence. Sodomy was already outlawed in Utah, and in June 1977, the Utah State House of Representatives overwhelmingly voted to make same-sex marriage illegal.[68] Whatever the reason, the church did relatively little to organize its members as it was doing to organize against the ERA.[69] Preventing the ERA, it seemed, was enough to prevent homosexuality.

The interrelated approaches of a psychological and political opposition to homosexuality were aimed at stigmatizing it as deviant. The introduction of these new ways to respond to homosexuality in the 1970s underscored just how seriously LDS church leaders took the new problem. At the same time, it revealed that the invention of new ways of thinking about homosexuality in this period were drawn almost entirely from outside of the LDS tradition. While Mormons were borrowing a pathologizing language about homosexuality from the fringes of psychology, they were also borrowing a political discourse of fear from the emergent Religious Right.

## SOFT EGALITARIANISM AND THE
## EQUAL RIGHTS AMENDMENT

It is easy to see how the patriarchal teachings of so many LDS leaders led them to oppose social and legal changes that would grant women and sexual minorities more autonomy and legal protection. What is less easy to see is how their opposition to the ERA refined and transformed Mormon patriarchy. Paradoxically, some church leaders began to adopt a more egalitarian doctrine of marriage just as the church was opposing the Equal Rights Amendment. Their support for patriarchy had always qualified it as a benevolent institution, but increasingly this benevolence was giving way to egalitarianism as its ultimate expression. This campaign molded LDS official discourse to embrace the dueling teachings of husbands presiding in the home and the equality of husband and wife.

Sometimes, this new egalitarian rhetoric was deployed strategically to oppose equal rights. Recalling the defense of racial segregation, church leaders emphasized the importance of divinely established gender roles but also insisted on equality in that difference. The First Presidency issued a statement at the end of 1976 opposing the ERA, arguing that the amendment threatened the traditional family and that it would thwart sexual difference. Men and women were "equally important before the Lord, but with differences biologically, emotionally, and in other ways." The claim that men and women were equally important to God and biologically different was really a non sequitur in terms of the legal questions. But it capitalized on the strategy of nullifying the need for the ERA by invoking a "separate but equal" doctrine. Despite the appeals to fixed biological and divinely created differences, equal treatment in the law introduced the possibility for a perpetual liminality of sexual difference. Women were especially vulnerable to such a relaxation of boundaries. Church leaders announced, "We fear it will even stifle many God-given feminine instincts."[70]

The language of difference and equality woven together in this period blunted some of the language about hierarchy and introduced a lasting wedge in Mormon doctrines about gender. In a 1976 interview for the *Ensign*, Barbara B. Smith began to put forward a more egalitarian notion of marriage: "All that the Brethren have taught me says that we have a companion relationship—not inferior or subordinate, but companion, side-by-side." She did admit that the "priesthood presides" but suggested that the cooperative relationship did not require women's submission.[71] The message was full of contradictions. Her appeal to male authority to support her teachings and her claim that men presided in the relationship undermined her assertion that women were not subordinate to their husbands. Still, statements like this charted new doctrinal ground for a soft egalitarianism in Mormon homes—companionate patriarchy.

The new teachings about women's equality undermined the teachings about women's subordination. Just a few years before the church's announcement to join the anti-ERA movement, Rodney Turner—quoting numerous church leaders to substantiate his interpretation—had written that the fall of Adam and Eve was both caused by and justification for women's inferior status. Adam was to "rule over" Eve ever after. But this doctrine would not work for a new kind of companionate patriarchy. Rather than seeing male self-sacrifice and noble leadership as the moral of the story, LDS leaders

*Politics and the Patriarchal Order*

reshaped their representation of Eve to take on these roles. But male church leaders had to work hard against the text to put a positive spin on the paradigmatic woman, long maligned in LDS thought. In 1976, President Kimball introduced a new framework for this text:

> The Lord said to the woman: " . . . in sorrow thou shalt bring forth children." I wonder if those who translated the Bible might have used the term *distress* instead of sorrow. It would mean much the same, except I think there is great gladness in most Latter-day Saint homes when there is to be a child there. As He concludes this statement he says, "and thy desire shall be to thy husband, and he shall rule over thee" [Gen. 3:16]. I have a question about the word *rule*. It gives the wrong impression. I would prefer to use the word *preside* because that's what he does. A righteous husband presides over his wife and family.[72]

Kimball saw himself as simply offering another interpretation of these terms, but this change to the text reversed its meaning in one case and softened it in another. He suggested that children do not bring sorrow but joy and that husbands do not rule but "preside." Notably, Kimball did nothing to alter the curse of opposite-sex desire. Feminist Mormons, however, were pleased with the progress. One commenter noted that Kimball's drastic changes implied "a major step toward more egalitarian relationships."[73] Presiding was still a form of benevolent rule, but as he said, it gives a better impression. Kimball's changes to the text of Genesis were not justified based on close linguistic analysis but only on Kimball's own sense that the text was not quite right. It was a good example of the situational freedom LDS leaders could use when interpreting scripture.

Not all LDS church leaders were accepting of soft egalitarian possibilities within marriage. The idea introduced a lasting struggle between patriarchal and egalitarian impulses among the highest-ranking church leaders. This was, after all, only the beginning of a transition. In the anti-ERA campaign, many church leaders still linked the importance of sexual difference to hierarchical gender roles. They saw hierarchy as the essence of difference. In 1977, apostle Boyd K. Packer traveled to Pocatello, Idaho, to a gathering of various opponents of the ERA. In his remarks, he warned, "The more strident supporters [of the ERA] will view it, no doubt, as symbolic support for antifamily and unisex values."[74] These arguments were based on a rhetorical production of the masculine woman or feminine male to conjure a backwards "unisex" world. He emphasized difference in the character of what makes a man and a woman: "These differences make women, in basic needs, literally opposite from men. A man, for instance, needs to feel protective, and yes, dominant, if you will, in leading his family. A woman needs to feel protected, in the bearing of children and in the nurturing of them."[75] For Packer, both roles and feelings defined what it meant to be a man or a woman. A man felt he was a man and a woman felt she was a woman, and they expressed those feelings by performing assigned roles. But this binary required legal and social norms to ensure its existence. He explained, "I am for protecting the rights of a woman to be a woman, a feminine, female woman; a wife and a mother. I am for protecting the rights of a man to be a man, a masculine, male man; a husband and a father. . . . I am for recognizing the inherent God-given differences between men and women."[76] The ERA, he insisted, was not an extension of rights but an attack on the rights to be a man or a woman. Invoking essentialist theories of difference, Packer identified "inherent" characteristics that were also fragile enough to need legislation to both protect and create them. He warned that without protection of masculinity and femininity, the very categories of man and woman were at risk of collapsing into a dreaded "unisex." Hierarchical gender roles were the antidote—husband/wife, father/mother, masculine/feminine.

Other church leaders emphasized the importance of hierarchical gender roles as the defining feature of what it meant to be a man or a woman. Ezra Taft Benson emerged as a crucial figure in articulating this view.[77] He transformed his earlier opposition to civil rights into antifeminism (he never spoke about race publicly again after 1971). His 1974 book, *God, Family, Country: Our Three Great Loyalties,* put forward a conservative political vision based on traditional gender roles, opposition to welfare, and promotion of free markets.[78] At the end of the 1970s, he increasingly emphasized the economic roles for men and women and the hierarchy of those roles. Gender replaced his focus on race, but the segregationist impulse to maintain purity animated both concerns. Benson's teachings in a 1979 BYU address captured the idea of segregated roles: "It is divinely ordained what a woman should do, but a man must seek out his work. The divine work of women involves companionship, homemaking, and motherhood. . . . Brethren, it is your role to be the leader in the home. While the wife may be considered the heart of the home, you are the head. You are the provider, and it takes the edge off your manliness when you have the mother of your children also be a provider."[79] For Benson, masculinity was explicitly tied to male headship in the home, not only as decision maker but as economic provider. To have a wife who worked outside the home would indicate that a husband was unmanly.

For Benson, the system of gender purity was symbolized most potently in the economic segregation of paid labor for men and unpaid labor for women.

Benson focused his primary concern on the roles of women.[80] In 1981, still in the context of the anti-ERA campaign, Benson warned in his address "The Honored Place of Woman" that "beguiling voices in the world cry out for 'alternative life-styles' for women. They maintain that some women are better suited for careers than for marriage and motherhood. . . . They also say it is wise to limit your family so you can have more time for personal goals and self-fulfillment." He warned women not to pursue education and work outside the home "for an unforeseen eventuality." He read from women's letters to him saying how much they enjoyed being a housewife—and he cautioned against the "experts" that told a different story. He encouraged mothers to hold regular Family Home Evenings "under your husband's direction." This language of hierarchy described a wife as subordinate partner: "Support, encourage, and strengthen your husband in his responsibility as patriarch in the home. You are partners with him. A woman's role in a man's life is to lift him, to help him uphold lofty standards, and to prepare through righteous living to be his queen for all eternity."[81] Women had a place—to serve their husbands—but Benson branded it a place of honor.

There was a central tension in LDS rhetoric on this matter that existed side by side with little comment. As Barbara B. Smith had first modeled, some argued that the ERA was not the right method to accomplish equal rights, not that equal rights themselves were problematic. When Rex E. Lee, the church's legal counsel, dean of BYU's law school, and U.S. solicitor general under President Reagan from 1981 to 1985, published his popular book *A Lawyer Looks at the Equal Rights Amendment* in 1980, he argued that current laws could protect women's rights and that a constitutional amendment would have unintended consequences.[82] As LDS leaders honed their argument against the ERA, at least some increasingly adopted the language of equal rights and recognized a need for legal reform but believed that the ERA was the incorrect instrument.

LDS women found a place in the reigning patriarchy by helping to define the new soft egalitarianism of companionate patriarchy, following the lead of Smith. In one case, Maurine Ward (later Maurine Proctor), a popular author with a graduate degree in education from Harvard, took on the ERA and feminism. Her 1981 book, *From Adam's Rib to Women's Lib: A Mormon Looks at the Women's Movement*, argued that women are "equal" to men but also "different" from them.[83] Ward believed in an equality within a benevolent patriarchy: "Making the husband the head of the house does not mean that there is any primacy to his wishes or desires over his family."[84] She contended that priesthood acted as a "sacred restraint" to abusive patriarchy.[85] This soft egalitarianism had found a foothold in Mormon teaching.

The soft egalitarian message—with all its contradictions between men presiding and being side by side with their wives—resonated with apostle Gordon B. Hinckley. Hinckley had been on the newly organized Special Affairs Committee in 1974 when Smith approached them about speaking out against the ERA. Hinckley helped arrange her public remarks at the University of Utah and was one of the primary organizers of the anti-ERA campaign from 1974 until 1982. But Hinckley seems to have been a moderate in comparison with his peers, adopting the soft egalitarianism that had emerged in the anti-ERA period. In a 1983 address, on the heels of defeating the ERA, Hinckley offered a more egalitarian message than the patriarchal headship teachings of many of his male colleagues: "Under the gospel plan marriage is a companionship, with equality between the partners. We walk side by side with respect, appreciation, and love one for another. There can be nothing of inferiority or superiority between the husband and wife in the plan of the Lord."[86] Hinckley's talk reprised some of the same language as Smith's, denouncing inferiority and superiority and offering a metaphor of a "side by side" journey of husband and wife.

These competing teachings of patriarchal marriage and a budding view of a companionate, egalitarian marriage were not entirely new. This tension was a manifestation of long-standing battles in gender politics. Indeed, early Mormon feminists at the turn of the twentieth century had also expounded on a vision of egalitarian marriage.[87] Newly resurgent Mormon feminists in the 1970s were hoping for more egalitarian marriage relationships as well, and some appealed to the paradoxical independence of their polygamous forebears as prototypes.[88] But these messages had been out of favor among senior male church leadership since the revival of the cult of domesticity and motherhood expressed in the doctrines of the patriarchal order of marriage in the 1950s. Cracks were appearing in the uniformity of these teachings among the highest church leaders under the pressure of a cultural shift.

Other historians of gender relations in Mormonism have also traced the introduction of alternatives to male-headship doctrines to the 1970s, specifically with Barbara B. Smith.[89] But it is important to situate these changes in the context of LDS anti-ERA activism. Opposing equal rights for women had the effect of moderating the patriarchal basis of that opposition. It is certainly fair to say that these new doctrines of soft egalitarianism could provide cover for anti-egalitarian positions—the moderated Mormon patriarchy was a more effective political stance. But, this view alone is ultimately too cynical.

Mormons did not just oppose feminism; they were influenced by it in their own way and were willing to change their doctrines to accommodate social and demographic changes on gender roles. Mormon leaders were making their own nascent feminist discoveries that marital hierarchy may not be appropriate in a more modern age.

In hindsight, there remains a genuine question about whether this emerging change in LDS teachings was more rhetorical than actual—whether framing women's and men's separate roles as equal provided any concrete changes to women's strictures that excluded them from paid labor or even decision-making in the home, let alone in the church. Likewise, one could ask whether the rhetoric of the patriarchal marriage had any practical implications that were not complicated by the lived experiences and power dynamics of such marriages. These are important sociological questions, but the focus here is the rhetorical shift itself. For some Mormon leaders at this time, the pressing questions about women's roles meant that sexual difference need not be hierarchical to be meaningful. Heterosexuality might not rest only on hierarchy but perhaps could accommodate equality, or something approximating that, between spouses.

## MORMON FEMINISTS REBORN

Not all LDS women were satisfied with these small gestures in a culture that remained overwhelmingly patriarchal.[90] Other religious feminists in this era lobbied for full egalitarianism not only in the home but in their churches as well.[91] As these religious feminists were speaking out, Mormon feminists emerged in the 1960s and 1970s and found themselves in some tension with LDS male leaders on religious issues—even when they were faithfully petitioning for compatibility between feminism and Mormonism.[92] Progressive Mormon women often went after the low-hanging fruit of classical patriarchy. Claudia Bushman's book review of Rodney Turner's *Woman and the Priesthood* lamented that "its confident tone and scholarly trappings will convince some readers that he speaks the truth." Nevertheless, she dismissed it as "one man's opinion."[93] Bushman was part of an emergent body of LDS women organizing and engaging with feminism.[94] In Boston and Cambridge, Massachusetts, a group of such women had begun to meet, read, and discuss feminist ideas in the early 1970s. They eventually established their own publication, modeling it on the late nineteenth- and early twentieth-century Mormon women's magazine *The Woman's Exponent*, which had featured many progressive voices on women's rights. Their inaugural issue of *Exponent II* in 1974 announced their "dual platforms of Mormonism and Feminism."[95] From this group emerged numerous influential historians who looked to the past for stories of women and led an (ongoing) organization that sponsored retreats and study groups and supported women scholars and activists.

Mormon feminists were not always sure how to position themselves in relationship to the church. The "dual platforms of Mormonism and Feminism" were not always easy to stand on simultaneously. Ecclesiastical patriarchy was particularly challenging. For much of the twentieth century, women's ordination movements had been active in most mainline Protestant denominations and in Catholic churches. These churches were issuing statements in opposition to or embracing the change, especially in the 1960s to 1990s. Mainline Lutherans began to ordain women in 1970. By 1976, the American Episcopal Church likewise voted to ordain women, and the Reformed Church in America followed suit in 1979. Mormon women were not untouched by these calls for change and pressed for them within their own community. Among some, it was not just a set of practices that were at issue, but Mormon theology itself had developed in such ways as to diminish the status and importance of women and their contributions. As other Christian feminist theologians were calling for women's ordination and a rethinking of the privileged maleness of God, some Mormon feminists turned their critical attention to these issues as well.

Some early attempts to address this topic came in the form of direct questions to church leaders. In a 1965 General Conference address, an assistant to the Quorum of the Twelve Apostles, William J. Critchlow Jr., reported that he received a woman's letter who had asked why women were excluded from LDS priesthood ordination. His answer to this questioner was that women chose to "pass up authority" in the preexistence and instead embraced "womanly virtues" like motherhood.[96] Contrasting motherhood and priesthood (rather than motherhood and fatherhood), Critchlow suggested that there were separate roles that limited women's authority to the home and gave men authority over the church.[97] The issue seemed settled to LDS leaders. The strict segregation of gender roles precluded the possibility that Mormon women might obtain priesthood ordination, just as it excluded black men at the time. These were divine decrees that emanated from choices human spirits had made in the pre-mortal existence.

When black men were finally allowed to be ordained to the LDS priesthood after Spencer W. Kimball's 1978 revelation, the change in LDS doctrines raised the question of whether the ordination of women might eventually follow. If such fundamental teachings on racial lineages were open to revision,

*Politics and the Patriarchal Order*

why not teachings on women? A few months after the 1978 revelation, a *Time* magazine reporter asked Kimball about the likelihood of women's ordination. His terse reply was "impossible."[98] Kimball's statement was representative of broad Mormon opinion. While LDS doctrines about race had been under serious internal scrutiny since the 1950s, doctrines about gender purity and gender role segregation were hardly challenged at all by the all-male leaders. Neither was there yet a concerted effort on the part of LDS women to organize or petition for women's ordination and little external pressure to change. The emerging Mormon feminists in the 1970s complained mostly about the diminution of women's authority and autonomy in the wake of the Priesthood Correlation movement, in the home and in the church.[99] Women's ordination was a fringe issue on their agenda.

The 1970s were tough for Mormon feminists, as many sought accommodations with the church yet found themselves increasingly in tension with the church during the anti-ERA years. While many Mormon feminists were able to adapt themselves to the strictures of the church and work for incremental change, others took more critical and oppositional positions on the church's public policy positions and internal culture and teachings. The politicization of Mormonism to oppose women's equality then also resulted in sustained public dissent from within the church. A growing body of men and women pressed for more ambitious reforms.

On that end of the spectrum, Sonia Johnson, self-proclaimed Mormon "housewife to heretic," founded the grassroots "Mormons for ERA." She began to write and teach that Mormonism was compatible with egalitarian feminism, citing nineteenth-century Mormon feminists as an example, and to publicly challenge the LDS male leadership's opposition to the ERA. As Johnson faced official pushback concerning her position, she became more critical of Mormonism. She began to believe that the church was perhaps irredeemably in conflict with feminist values. In 1979, she lamented that, "saturated as it is with anti-female bias that is patriarchy's very definition and reason for being, the Mormon Church can legitimately be termed 'The Last Unmitigated Western Patriarchy.'" In a blistering complaint about the hostility church leaders demonstrated toward Mormon feminists, Johnson suggested that this patriarchy would no longer go "unchallenged" and that the "death rattle of the patriarchy" could be heard.[100] Citing this speech, LDS leaders excommunicated Johnson on December 1, 1979, for having "spoken evil of the Lord's anointed."[101]

Other women saw an upending of this ecclesiastical patriarchy as a necessary solution to the receding autonomy of women in the 1970s. Mormon feminist Nadine Hansen was also a member of the Mormons for ERA and was among the first to break the taboo on openly advocating for Mormon women's priesthood ordination. Challenging Kimball's assessment that women's ordination was "impossible" in Mormonism, her 1981 essay "Women and the Priesthood" appealed to biblical precedent and Mormon history and theology to call for a change to this practice.[102] While BYU religious education professor Rodney Turner had argued for a distinct hierarchy of men over women as the core of the church's message, less than decade later Hansen articulated a vision of equality and inclusion as the essence of LDS scriptural teachings and destiny. Citing the precedent of Kimball's 1978 revelation that expanded the borders of who could be ordained to the priesthood, Hansen expressed hope in a gender-egalitarian future in which men and women shared the "blessings and burdens" of the priesthood together.

Mormon feminists also scrutinized LDS theological teachings about God. The concept of a female deity was finding resonance with other religious feminists in the 1970s and 1980s. In 1973, Mary Daly's blockbuster feminist theological tome, *Beyond God the Father*, critiqued androcentric depictions of deity. She explained, "If God is male, then male is God."[103] Feminist thinkers were increasingly pointing out the effects of the exclusion of women from the representation of the divine. Merlin Stone's 1976 best seller *When God Was a Woman* charted a history of the suppression of women through a suppression of a female deity.[104] By 1984, Luce Irigaray would articulate her religious feminist view: "As long as woman lacks a divine made in her image she cannot establish her subjectivity or achieve a goal on her own."[105] Though their ideas had some distinctive features relative to other feminists, Mormon women were participants in the broader religious feminist turn to a divine feminine. The idea dated back at least to Joseph Smith's early followers and began to have some prominence in the early Utah period.[106] After falling out of popular discussion, Heavenly Mother was making a comeback in Mormon feminist circles. In 1978, LDS poet Margaret Rampton Munk wrote about her longing for an absent Heavenly Mother, comparing it to her adopted daughter's longing for her "other mother."[107] Mormon feminists felt that the undervaluing of a Heavenly Mother represented their own diminished status within Mormonism.

But male Mormon leaders had not ignored the existence of a Heavenly Mother entirely. In April 1978, the same year Munk's poem was published, Kimball had publicly praised "the restrained, queenly elegance of our Heavenly Mother" and bore witness to "her influence on us as individuals." But it was not just about acknowledging her existence. The way she was represented was contested. Kimball deployed the figure of the Heavenly Mother as a prototype of a particular kind of woman, "the ultimate in maternal modesty."[108] His speech seemed to intervene in the budding conversations about the divine woman. Rather than seeing her as a symbol of increased freedom and expanded roles for women, Kimball sought to frame her as the symbol of the obedient woman who followed her righteous husband's lead. For Kimball, the Heavenly Mother's "restrained" and "maternal" place reinforced the ideals of patriarchal rule rather than equality for women.

For LDS feminists, Kimball's depiction of a Heavenly Mother seemed not only insufficient but even demeaning. In the fall of 1980, Mormon feminist Linda P. Wilcox published an article in the relatively new independent Mormon magazine *Sunstone.* Wilcox's now classic essay "The Mormon Concept of a Mother in Heaven" attempted to resurrect a notion of a divine feminine from the patriarchal discourse that had dominated recent LDS culture. She described the Mother as "shadowy and elusive" in "Mormon consciousness." In Wilcox's description, "she exists, apparently, but has not been very evident in Mormon meetings or writings, and little if any 'theology' has been developed to elucidate her nature and characterize our relationship to her."[109] Wilcox traced the history of the teachings and examined different phases of LDS thought about a divine woman. For the 1960s and 1970s, she noted only a handful of official mentions that a Heavenly Mother even existed. Recent church leaders like Kimball had created an image of a Heavenly Mother that promoted the purpose of women to be "basically baby factories" and "to provide an aesthetically pleasing environment with sights and sounds of unimaginable glory to welcome her children home."[110] In contrast to these depictions, Wilcox described grassroots Mormon women who were turning to a Heavenly Mother in their devotional life. They were pushing for a version of a Heavenly Mother "who is a full partner and co-creator with the Father (of something other than babies)."[111]

### SEXUAL RELATIONSHIPS WITHIN MARRIAGE

While the feminist efforts toward women's ordination and a renewed interest in a Heavenly Mother were stunted, church leaders were making some accommodations to long-standing issues that affected both women and men in order to create more egalitarian marriages. The effects of the changes in favor of soft egalitarianism altered the way that LDS leaders thought about marriage and consequently also altered how they thought about sexual morality. Specifically, they began to seriously examine the theory of sexuality as about reproduction as opposed to the theory of sexuality about spousal bonding—at least for mixed-sex married couples. These debates preceded significant changes in the way the church talked about birth control and consensual sexual practices within marriage.

Changes on birth control were slow to appear. Birth control had been a matter of massive public debate since the beginning of the twentieth century. When monogamy became the only outlet for creating progeny at the turn of the twentieth century, male Mormon leaders taught that their wives should not limit their output.[112] In his earlier years, David O. McKay had declared that sex for pleasure alone put "the marriage relationship on a level with the panderer and the courtesan. They befoul the pure fountains of life with the slime of indulgence and sensuality."[113] Besides these moral evaluations favoring a procreationist ethic, church leaders also repeated late nineteenth- and early twentieth-century teachings that birth control was hazardous to women's health and damaged sexual pleasure and the quality of the marriage.[114] By the 1940s, church leaders had taught that women's primary duties were in the unpaid and supportive labor of housewife and mother. Giving birth to many children was a sacred duty and responsibility of women specifically.[115]

New contraceptive methods became available in the 1960s, and the public conversation began to shift dramatically in favor, with many Protestants even embracing its use as a Christian obligation.[116] The budding secular feminist movement was also gaining ground on this issue.[117] As birth control received greater acceptance in broader society, initially church leaders began to be more explicit and urgent in their opposition. In 1965, church president Joseph Fielding Smith warned that those who used birth control "may be denied the glorious celestial kingdom"—which also meant, in his view, a loss of sexual difference and the ability to procreate at all.[118] In 1969, the First Presidency sent a letter defining the church's official position, explaining, "It is contrary to the teachings of the Church artificially to curtail or prevent the birth of children. We believe that those who practice birth control will reap disappointment by and by." The letter acknowledged that in the case of the mother's "health and strength" a couple might need to curtail their childbearing and advised "self-control."[119] Joseph Fielding Smith taught that unborn spirits were a missionary opportunity; the faithful could bring them into Mormon families rather than leave them "to take bodies in the families of the wicked."[120] The Mormon zeal for missionary work in the period after World War II was gendered for men to preach to the world and women to give bodies to spirits in their own community as a form of missionary service.[121]

These teachings were not strictly practiced by Mormons. Even in the 1970s, use of birth control among Mormons was high—fully two-thirds of Mormon women graduates of BYU ages twenty-four to forty-eight reported using some form of contraceptives in 1970.[122] The widespread practice precipitated some important LDS shifts in teaching. Church leaders began to consider the prohibition on birth control to be a relativized commandment, softening the strident opposition of previous church president Joseph Fielding Smith. Using the notions of soft egalitarianism in marriage, church leaders began to teach that birth control was a decision best left to the couple. Apostle Hinckley explained the change in the *General Handbook of Instructions* in 1983:

> The Lord has told us to multiply and replenish the earth [Gen 1:28] that we might have joy in our posterity, and there is no greater joy than the joy that comes of happy children in good families. But he did not designate the number, nor has the Church. That is a sacred matter left to the couple and the Lord. The official statement of the Church includes this language: "Husbands must be considerate of their wives, who have the greater responsibility not only of bearing children but of caring for them through childhood, and should help them conserve their health and strength."[123]

This new teaching abandoned the threats to personal salvation for those who used birth control and made family planning a personal decision about sexual pleasure and emotional health. This was a decision "left to the couple." But traces of the patriarchal order haunted these new teachings. When quoting the official statement, husbands, specifically, were asked to be "considerate" of their wives in making decisions about family planning.

This change in doctrine on birth control qualified the imperative to multiply and replenish in two ways. First, the status of women's physical and emotional health subsequently outweighed the importance of procreation. The church statement on birth control cited Genesis 1:28 but noted, "Husband and wife are encouraged to pray and counsel together as they plan their families. Issues to consider include the physical and mental health of the mother and father and their capacity to provide the basic necessities of life for their children. Decisions about birth control and the consequences of those decisions rest solely with each married couple." This change gave women greater autonomy in family planning and changed the calculus in decisions about family size. Second, church leaders expanded the purpose of a sexual encounter between husband and wife to include bonding. They now taught that sexual encounters need not all be procreative but were "also a means of expressing love and strengthening emotional and spiritual ties between husband and wife."[124]

The addition of "emotion" as a category for thinking about sexuality represented a theological counterweight to the previously unconditional requirement of procreation. This marked a major departure in the interpretation of what it meant to "multiply and replenish"—there is no caveat in Genesis 1:28 and no emotional dimension to reproduction or sexuality there. Essentially, the relativization of the injunction to "multiply and replenish" was an extratextual limitation on reproduction that defined sexuality as irreducible to reproductive encounters. Sex could also be about creating a companionate relationship.

These changes in instruction on birth control were closely connected to other kinds of changes to LDS teachings on nonreproductive sexual exchanges between spouses. At first, LDS leaders opted for more restrictive and invasive regulations on spousal sex. In the 1970s, church leaders began to modify the questions of worthiness for those seeking to worship in LDS temples—part of the campaign to investigate homosexual practices among church members. By 1978, LDS officials issued new questions for local church leaders to ask in these interviews but now also included a statement on sex that was to be read at the outset of each interview: "Our Heavenly Father is very displeased when any of his children engage in impure, unholy, and unnatural sex acts." The statement further indicated that anyone guilty of such acts could not be admitted to the temple.[125] Naturally, the ambiguity about what constituted such practices led to varying interpretations. What kinds of sex were unnatural? What was impure? What was unholy? Was this referring to homosexual, premarital, and extramarital sexual encounters, or were there certain classes of sexual acts that inherently fit these definitions?

The ambiguity was too much. Within a few years, church leaders issued explicit guidelines to refine these new questions. On January 5, 1982, Kimball's First Presidency sent a letter to local leaders responsible for conducting "worthiness" interviews for church members seeking to attend and worship at LDS temples and those seeking to become missionaries. The letter announced a new policy for interview techniques and questions and explained that church leaders should inquire what the prospective missionary thought "moral cleanliness" might mean. If not mentioned in the answer, the leader should explain that homosexual acts were considered impure practices. At this point, the interviewee "should be reminded again that he is being interviewed by a representative of the Lord, and the Lord knows what he is doing and how he is living."[126] The campaign to ferret out homosexuality was brought to young prospective male missionaries with increasing precision.

Yet, homosexuality was not the only target, either. The new guidelines also established acceptable sexual practices between spouses. Kimball was bringing his moral reform to the marriage bed as well. The letter offered further instruction for couples and clarified what was meant by the reference to certain forbidden sex acts that displeased the Lord. It advised that married persons should have restraints on the kinds of sexual practices they engage in if they are to be worthy to worship in the temple. The January 1982 letter explained that "the First Presidency has interpreted oral sex as constituting an unnatural, impure, or unholy practice."[127] Married couples were advised to cease such a practice if they were to be worthy to enter the temple. On another occasion, Kimball explained, "If it is unnatural, you just don't do it. That is all, and all the family life should be kept clean and worthy and on a very high plane. There are some people who have said that behind the bedroom doors anything goes. That is not true and the Lord would not condone it."[128] The classification of oral sex between heterosexual spouses as "unnatural" put it into the same category as homosexuality. But the objection to oral sex between married persons was not only that it was not reproductive—oral sex may be engaged in as foreplay to reproductive sexual encounters—but also that it was "impure" and "unholy."

The letter sparked widespread controversy. Local church leaders began to ask married couples about their sexual practices, specifically whether they practiced oral sex, in their annual "worthiness" interviews. Members and local leaders were not happy.[129] It was invasive and embarrassing for all involved. By October 15, 1982, the First Presidency issued a follow-up letter and reversed course. Since January, the governing leaders explained, "we have received a number of letters from members of the Church which indicate clearly that some local leaders have been delving into private, sensitive matters beyond the scope of what is appropriate." The clarification did not change the status of oral sex but advised further discretion in the interview process. It explained to local leaders, "You should never inquire into personal, intimate matters involving marital relations.... If in the course of such interviews a member asks questions about the propriety of specific conduct, you should not pursue the matter but should merely suggest that if the member has enough anxiety about the propriety of the conduct to ask about it, the best course would be to discontinue it."[130] The clarification traded on an impossible ambiguity. On one hand, oral sex was deemed to be explicitly forbidden and disqualifying for entering the temple. On the other hand, church leaders were forbidden from asking about it explicitly and also prevented from explicitly forbidding it. Kimball's instructions here also invoked the idea of "anxiety" about sexual acts, even those within marriage, as evidence that they were immoral.

Controversy over oral sex within marriage faded with the passing of Kimball in the mid-1980s. The compromise was a "don't ask, don't tell" approach to oral sex between married couples. In 1985, the statement explaining the seriousness of "impure, unholy, and unnatural sex acts" was fully eliminated from the temple recommend questions.[131] From then on, the stance of the church on oral sex followed the precedent on birth control. It was not encouraged but no longer officially forbidden, either. Sex between spouses did not need to be exclusively reproductive but could also build intimacy and love. In 1990, Hinckley issued a warning to abusive patriarchs in the home, including those who "demand offensive intimate relations." But he insisted that there would not be official questions from bishops on this matter. Instead, he instructed, "You must judge within your heart whether you are guilty of any practice that is unholy, impure, or in any way evil before the Lord."[132] Within certain boundaries, LDS teachings on sexual immorality relaxed to allow personal conscience to be the guide between married mixed-sex couples. All kinds of sex could be for pleasure between spouses, as long as both felt comfortable with it.

## "COME HOME"

Not only were Mormon women using birth control and engaging in oral sex in spite of official prohibitions in the 1970s, they were also working outside the home. In the 1980s, American women and mothers continued to work outside the home in increasing numbers. There were fewer sole male-breadwinner families, and many women raised their children mostly alone. Whether for economic necessity or personal need and fulfillment, women made up almost half the Utah workforce and worked at nearly the identical rates as women throughout the United States.[133] Birth rates in Utah spiked during the 1970s while falling throughout the United States more generally, but beginning in 1980 the birth rates in Utah slipped back down and only slightly outpaced the national average.[134] Rather than making accommodations as they had done with other issues in the early 1980s, women's paid labor remained a controversial subject for church leaders. This, at least, seemed to LDS leaders to remain a crucial firewall against crumbling sexual differences. For them, motherhood was at risk.

Ezra Taft Benson—John Birch Society sympathizer and civil rights opponent turned antifeminist—succeeded Spencer W. Kimball as president of the church in 1985. Benson targeted working women as the special subjects of censure in his battle to prevent sexual difference from collapsing. In his controversial 1987 address "To the Mothers in Zion," Benson taught, "God established that fathers are to preside in the home. . . . But a mother's role is also God-ordained. Mothers are to conceive, to nourish, to love, and to train. So declare the revelations."[135] This divine division of roles—with fathers presiding and providing and mothers nurturing and nourishing—admonished women to have many children and not work outside the home except in cases of serious necessity. While feminists were pointing to marriage as a system designed to oppress women, conservatives like Benson saw it as a system to protect them from losing their gender identity. Pleading with women to "come home" from work, Benson outlined the specific role and duties of women, including "cooking meals, washing dishes, [and] making beds for one's precious husband and children."[136] Women's spiritual contributions were defined in terms of housekeeping. These mundane tasks were given sacred weight. Benson advocated patriarchal families and economically dependent women as a means to preserving gender purity. He believed that when women entered the business world, they became "aggressive and competitive." He did not doubt their skills and potential but insisted that they would become too masculine if they worked, diminishing their "godly attributes."[137]

In a companion talk a few months later, Benson delivered the address "To the Fathers in Israel."[138] Just as femininity required economic dependence, masculinity required providing for a wife and children. "An able-bodied husband," Benson explained, "is expected to be the breadwinner." Citing the deutero-Pauline proof texts, he laid out the principles of this benevolent patriarchy that should not use force or coercion. He advised husbands to love their wives and show them kindness: "Help with the dishes, change diapers, get up with a crying child in the night, and leave the television or newspaper to help with dinner." (Help with making beds was not included on the list.) For Benson, the father's leadership was on display both inside and outside the home. He explained, "Mothers play an important role as the heart of the home, but this in no way lessens the equally important role fathers should play, as head of the home, in nurturing, training, and loving their children. . . . You must help create a home where the Spirit of the Lord can abide. Your place is to give direction to all family life."[139] While the mother's nature was limited to the home, the father actually held significant domestic responsibilities as well. There were not two independent spheres; the husband also presided over the wife's domestic domain.

The 1980s witnessed sustained shifts toward new doctrines of family governmentality and the division of labor. Despite Benson's influence, LDS teachings on patriarchal ideology continued to move to soft egalitarianism within and beyond the domestic sphere. Church publications adopted the language of soft egalitarianism between husband and wife more frequently in this era. A 1988 column in the *Ensign* stated, "All important deliberations and decisions within the family should involve the husband and wife equally. . . . The couple should discuss their differences, candidly consider the pros and cons, then make a decision both can live with."[140] While continuing to insist that the father presided, such joint decision-making increasingly became the model. A 1989 *Ensign* article explained that the husband and wife were a "partnership" and that a "husband should not make decrees. Rather, he should work with his wife until a joint decision palatable to both is developed."[141] These articles revealed the continued need to temper strong notions of patriarchal authority in the home. Just as church leaders were comfortable with conflicting discourses about homosexuality, the psychological and the moral, so too would they tolerate conflicting discourses about women's equality, the patriarchal and egalitarian.[142]

One church authority in particular subtly worked to offer a different perspective from Benson's by promoting egalitarian marriage and accommodation to women's changing roles in society and the workforce. Gordon B. Hinckley gave an address the year after Benson's controversial talk "To the Mothers in Zion." He expressed, "I am greatly concerned over what may be happening with the young women of the Church." His concern was that women were being devalued. In contrast to Benson, Hinckley offered a positive view of women's work outside the home: "Strong and able women today fill responsible posts in industry, government, education, and the professions." He specifically cited the example of British prime minister Margaret Thatcher on women's positive contributions in all areas of society. He also gave an affirmative view of women's education: "Do we encourage education? By all means. Every young woman ought to be encouraged to refine her skills and increase her abilities, to broaden her knowledge and strengthen

*Politics and the Patriarchal Order*

her capacity."[143] Hinckley downplayed the problem with women's work and emphasized spousal partnership rather than hierarchy in the home. His views would eventually shape how the church approached these issues in the coming decades. Egalitarianism was creeping further into Mormon teachings about gender.

---

In this period, Mormonism's doctrines on gender and sexuality were in significant flux as they grappled with the challenges posed by 1970s egalitarian feminism. One idea that emerged in this period had a lasting influence— sexual difference depended on the state and other social conditions to sustain a sexual order. The dystopian vision of a "unisex" society that would eventually erase the differences between male and female inspired LDS opposition to any hint that women and men might be treated the same. In this perspective, official LDS opposition emerged in response to a changing world, drawing a distinction between its values and what it saw as a secular sexual and gender revolution.

At the same time, while Mormonism was by no means enthusiastic about feminist values and clearly opposed them by exercising new political power on the national stage, these values still left their mark on Mormon teachings. Mormons did not simply reject social change but accommodated and adapted to it. These official doctrinal and policy changes mostly lagged behind changes in LDS practice and demographic preferences on the ground. But a few Mormon leaders paved the way to relax the strict hierarchy of male over female, increase marital sexual privacy and choice, tolerate the use of birth control, and express some support for women's paid labor, at least rhetorically. Some leaders started to embrace soft egalitarianism and complementarianism as viable alternative doctrines to the formerly hierarchical doctrines of Mormonism's post–World War II revival of the patriarchal order of marriage. But in this period there was not simply a liberalization of Mormon teachings but a transformation of those teachings from the patriarchal order of marriage to the heterosexual order of marriage. A new kind of individual and familial subjectivity was on the rise, and it came into sharp relief in the 1990s.

## Chapter Four

# PROCLAIMING THE NEW
# HETEROSEXUAL FAMILY

In the 1990s, LDS church leaders significantly revised their teachings on heterosexuality, renewing confrontation with a perceived threat about growing social acceptance of homosexuality. One moment defined how the church would see itself, its members, and its doctrines in this new battlefront. At the General Relief Society Meeting in the Salt Lake Tabernacle on September 23, 1995, President Gordon B. Hinckley stood and read a 605-word document, "The Family: A Proclamation to the World."[1] Hinckley, then eighty-four years old, had just ascended to the church presidency in March, following the death of his feeble predecessor Howard W. Hunter, who had served a mere nine months in the role. The short document became a sensation in subsequent years—a doctrinal foundation that branded the message and identity of the church itself. Faithful church members framed and hung the message on their walls and pasted copies into their scriptures. Eventually, BYU would develop a required class based on the text. Church leaders had issued only a handful of proclamations, mostly in the nineteenth century.[2] The 1995 proclamation on the family was different from all those that had come before—and no other proclamation has been issued since. It became simply *the* Proclamation, in common parlance.

The Proclamation codified church teachings about gender roles, parenting, heterosexual marriage, and public policy. It reflected the embrace of politics as a means of furthering the church's vision for society. The family was given an explicitly political goal in the text: "We call upon responsible citizens and officers of government everywhere to promote those measures designed to maintain and strengthen the family as the fundamental unit of society." Failure to heed this warning would result in dire consequences: "We warn that the disintegration of the family will bring upon individuals, communities, and nations the calamities foretold by ancient and modern prophets." Invoking the socio-sexual myth of civilizational decline, the Proclamation taught that the modern heterosexual family was a part of the created order and brought peace and stability to the nation and the world.

This chapter is about how LDS leaders were thinking about gender roles in the 1990s to define their political and psychological agendas, both leading up to the Proclamation and in its aftermath. But this was also a time that LDS teachings about gender roles were in significant flux. LDS leaders backed away from strong prohibitions against women's work and demoted those teachings to optional counsel. Church leaders altered the terms of proper heterosexual performance to accommodate practices once deemed essential to the bulwark of sexual difference itself. The competing ideologies of patriarchal and egalitarian marriages continued to wrestle for dominance. Yet, this conflict seemed less important now—the category of heterosexuality could accommodate these changes to earlier ideals. Heterosexuality ascended over patriarchy as the defining Mormon doctrine of marriage and family.

### THE PROCLAMATION AND GENDER ROLES

Mormon ideas of gender roles continued to move toward the soft egalitarianism that had budded up in the 1970s and 1980s alongside the patriarchal order of marriage. Rather than commit to a transition from one model to the other, however, church leaders instead embraced both positions simultaneously and attempted to reconcile them. The Proclamation had claimed that "gender" was "eternal," invoking some of the same concepts laid out by James E. Talmage in a 1914 article titled "The Eternity of Sex."[3] Talmage argued that "sex" defined pre-mortal, mortal, and post-mortal life. Anthropologists and feminists at the time of his writing did not yet distinguish between an idea of fixed bodily "sex" as male and female and culturally contingent "gender" as masculine and feminine. At the time of the Proclamation, though, such a distinction was common parlance. The Proclamation's adaptation of Talmage to speak about "gender" as "eternal" challenged the idea that gender behavior and roles might be mutable.

Gender roles were central to the message of the Proclamation, not biological sex. The eternal "purpose" of men is to "preside," "provide," and give "protection," and the eternal purpose of women is to "nurture." Masculinity and femininity were defined as these performed roles. It prescribed that in ideal circumstances the father should work and the mother should be home with the children. At the same time, it taught that couples should be "equal partners" in parenting—but it limited equality to that sphere alone. The document perfectly captured the new emphases in the 1990s of a softened patriarchal family with egalitarian impulses as the ideal Mormon family. In the Proclamation, there was no discussion of doctrines of submission of wives, nor was there any discussion of race as an important factor for the family. Such doctrines were quietly abandoned. The Proclamation cemented the new Mormon teachings about family that began at the end of the 1970s, adapting modest feminist notions of equality to be compatible with patriarchal authority in soft egalitarianism.

The teachings in the Proclamation that there are eternal "purposes" to each gender was deeply connected to the idea of separate roles for men and women rather than inherent or natural features. Church leaders often expressed gender roles in the most mundane of tasks, though it was unclear how these roles translated to pre-mortal and post-mortal identity. Boyd K. Packer had joked just a few years before the Proclamation that "Grandpas don't bake pies." He added, "Some roles are best suited to the masculine nature and others to the feminine nature. Both the scriptures and the patterns of nature place man as the protector, the provider." By associating femininity with domestic tasks like cooking and baking and masculinity with working outside the home, Packer mapped twentieth-century divisions of labor onto "nature." But these also expressed an eternal schema. He taught, "The different roles of man and woman are set forth in exalted celestial declarations."[4] He believed that "the most devastating effect" of World War II—presumably after the Holocaust, atomic bombs, and millions killed—"was on the family" because women had to work outside the home during that time.[5] That revivalist, postwar idealized family still captivated the leaders who came of age in that era. But it also revealed that masculinity and femininity were not only "set forth" but also cultivated in the everyday practices associated with those traits. A few years later, Packer warned, "Be careful lest you unknowingly foster influences and activities which tend to erase the masculine and feminine differences nature has established.... There is a distinct masculine nature and a distinct feminine nature essential to the foundation of the home and the family. Whatever disturbs or weakens or tends to erase that difference erodes the family and reduces the probability of happiness for all concerned."[6] Sexual difference was fragile. Whether in the Proclamation or other preaching, when the church leaders appealed to nature and essentialism, they were making normative claims about what ought to be, not descriptive claims about an ontology of sexual difference.

*Proclaiming the New Heterosexual Family*

Other church leaders were more open to the shifting culture of gender roles, especially around women's labor. Referencing Ezra Taft Benson's controversial 1987 address "To the Mothers in Zion," in 1996 President Hinckley again subtly countered its message as he had done before.

> Some years ago President Benson delivered a message to the women of the Church. He encouraged them to leave their employment and give their individual time to their children. I sustain the position which he took. Nevertheless, I recognize, as he recognized, that there are some women (it has become very many in fact) who have to work to provide for the needs of their families. To you I say, do the very best you can. I hope that if you are employed full-time you are doing it to ensure that basic needs are met and not simply to indulge a taste for an elaborate home, fancy cars, and other luxuries.[7]

Though he reiterated Benson's basic idea that women should not work, he acknowledged that "very many" women could not meet this ideal and expressed his support for them.

Hinckley's blessing to working women helped to destigmatize the choice to work that by that point most LDS women had already made. However, he still believed that it was only economic necessity that would justify a woman working outside of the home. Hinckley was wary of the consumerist impulses that he believed were driving dual-earning families and undermining the patriarchal order. While acknowledging these changes, Hinckley also sought to preserve some continuity with the ideals of the teachings of past leaders. To young women, he taught, "Your first objective should be a happy marriage, sealed in the temple of the Lord, and followed by the rearing of a good family. Education can better equip you for the realization of those ideals."[8] Hinckley acknowledged that the world had changed and that church leaders' teachings about women's work and education should change as well. He seemed to have grasped these demographic shifts, explaining, "I urge each of you young women to get all of the schooling you can get. You will need it for the world into which you will move. . . . The world is changing, and it is so very important that we equip ourselves to move with that change. . . . No other generation in all of history has offered women so many opportunities."[9] These opportunities clearly extended beyond the path of the exclusive homemaker. For Hinckley, at least, women working outside the home no longer posed the threat to gender purity that earlier leaders had taught.

Heterosexuality was beginning to overshadow patriarchy as the fundamental feature of LDS teachings on marriage.

At the same time, many church leaders continued to embrace the older model of family governmentality, citing the Proclamation's claim about fathers "presiding." Patriarchal marriage wasn't dead yet. In a 2004 General Conference address, apostle L. Tom Perry (d. 2015) reiterated, "The father is the head of the family." For Perry, patriarchal leadership consisted of leading worship in the home, blessing and performing ordinances, teaching the family, and providing financially. Perry approvingly quoted the patriarchal teachings from Benson's "To the Mothers in Zion" talk and cited LDS president Joseph F. Smith's 1902 instructions on the patriarchal family, "The Rights of Fatherhood." From that document, Perry reiterated, "The patriarchal order is of divine origin and will continue throughout time and eternity"; "no other authority is paramount" to that of the father in the home. The husband's role was as "leader" and the wife's as "companion." At the same time, Perry undercut this argument with an egalitarian view: "There is not a president or a vice president in a family. The couple works together for the good of the family."[10] Perry's talk did little to work out the contradiction, letting both statements stand. The incoherence of the soft egalitarian and patriarchal governmentality had become the official rhetorical position.

Scholar Caroline Kline calls these conflicting discourses in turn-of-the-century Mormonism "a simultaneous resistance and accommodation to egalitarian ideals."[11] The competing values of patriarchal marriage and egalitarian marriage continued to mark LDS teachings on family governmentality, and women were still tasked with the primary responsibilities of child-rearing and housework. However, church leaders' embrace of the possible equality between spouses did not dramatically disrupt prior LDS doctrines about gender purity. Mormons adapted feminist language to their own ends, deploying a definition of marriage that was no longer dependent on hierarchy—even if that hierarchy remained implicitly and explicitly in place. But this tension could coexist precisely because a new kind of marriage relationship externalized the threat to sexual difference. Same-sex marriages were the true disruption to gender roles, while mixed-sex relationships could accommodate a variety of egalitarian and patriarchal forms. The discourse of heterosexuality could take on the ideals of gender purity while maintaining some ambivalences about male headship and strict gender roles. The Proclamation had brought together these conflicting ideals, which worked in a productive tension to accommodate both change and continuity.

What precipitated the need for a proclamation on the family? This was not just about addressing internal changes; the 1995 document was specifically addressed to "the world." The groundwork for the political ambitions expressed in the Proclamation had been laid in the decades prior to its release. This document about gender roles was a consolidation of a broader message about society itself. After the pursuit of anti-sodomy laws and opposition to the ERA in the 1970s and early 1980s, church leaders did not completely abandon political ambitions on gender and sexuality issues. Behind the scenes, LDS officials were still trying to think about how to strategically affect legislation concerning homosexuality and how to pick their battles wisely. In the summer of 1984, just a few months after being called as an apostle, Dallin H. Oaks authored an internal memorandum for his colleagues titled "Principles to Govern Possible Public Statement on Legislation Affecting Rights of Homosexuals."[12] Prior to his call to the role of apostle, Oaks had been a prominent lawyer and justice on the Utah Supreme Court and the president of Brigham Young University. Oaks had taken a lead on gender and sexuality issues before. In the 1970s, Oaks oversaw the Values Institute's anti-homosexuality research at BYU. He himself published an article in defense of anti-sodomy laws in this same period.[13] As an apostle, he brought his legal expertise and familiarity with political and psychological anti-homosexuality ideologies to bear on proposing a new direction for the church. His memo set a political strategy that defined how church leaders would chart their course for the next three decades.

Oaks's recommendations in the memorandum came shortly after the church's success against the ERA. But in that context, American liberals and conservatives were increasingly getting involved in the politics of gay rights. The Democratic Party's platform that national election year supported anti-discrimination laws for gays and lesbians in the workplace, in the armed forces, and in immigration law. In contrast, in 1984 Catholic Charities spoke out against an antidiscrimination bill in New York City that would have protected sexual orientation.[14] Other religious groups were deciding the issue of homosexuality's place in society differently. The Unitarian Universalist Association became the first major American religious group to approve of same-sex marriages in 1984.

Oaks's memorandum noted these cultural trends and outlined a future legal and political strategy. Expecting the issues of gay rights to continue to be a national political topic, Oaks wanted to be judicious and proactive rather than reactive. This involved greater discipline and changing course on previous policy advice from the 1970s. Reversing the public positions of his predecessor Mark E. Petersen's editorials in the *Church News*, Oaks argued that the church should generally not get involved in matters relating to anti-sodomy laws or antidiscrimination legislation, "reserving its influence for more important matters."[15] He even favored antidiscrimination legislation with the "well-reasoned exceptions" of jobs that engage with youth.[16] There was, he claimed, a demonstrable need to "protect youth from homosexual proselyting."[17]

With the worry about the spread of homosexuality through proselytism, Oaks's beliefs about sexual fluidity and masculine vulnerability informed his political proposals. At the same time, Oaks attempted to lay out a politically expedient and democratically pluralistic framework for accommodating competing interests. Taking some positions that were more open than those taken by church leaders in the prior decade—including his own—Oaks maintained that the church should be politically concerned only with same-sex marriage. He admonished, "The interests at stake in the proposed legalization of so-called homosexual marriages are sufficient to justify a formal Church position and significant efforts in opposition."[18] Oaks offered four justifications for making same-sex marriage a critical issue requiring political activity: (1) the church speaks in defense of the family, (2) marriage is for the purpose of procreation, (3) marriage is a time-honored institution that is greater than cohabitation of people of the same sex, and (4) "one generation of homosexual 'marriages' would depopulate a nation, and, if sufficiently widespread, would extinguish its people. Our marriage laws should not abet national suicide."[19] All were essentially based on the theory of the spread of homosexuality as the result of social "approval" of same-sex marriage. Pluralism and mutual respect had its limits because homosexuality was ultimately an existential threat. All of these arguments hinged on the idea that same-sex marriages would be a direct trade-off for mixed-sex marriages—perhaps even more alluring. The fight over the limits of marriage was a fight for the number of heterosexual marriages. Sexual fluidity informed the politics against same-sex marriage, even if other accommodations toward homosexuality could be tolerated. Religious freedom was not yet a concern.

It is unknown how Oaks's memorandum was received by his new colleagues. However, it seems to have been influential. As events played out over the next decade and beyond, Oaks's strategy seems to have informed much of what transpired, including the momentous issuance of the Proclamation on the family. But this memo, which was meant for internal deliberation, reveals more than a blueprint for the future. It shows church leaders, especially new ones, willing to reconsider some of the political and social teachings from earlier LDS officials. It also shows deliberate and strategic thinking about how and whether the church should use its authority to weigh in on political matters. Finally, it shows that church leaders considered homosexuality to be a political problem and that they hoped to use state power to ensure their teachings were protected against a massive shift in attitudes. So long as the state allowed only mixed-sex marriage, society itself would prefer heterosexuality, Oaks reasoned. Absent a preference in the law, society itself could prefer homosexuality.

## THE POLITICS OF PROCLAIMING THE FAMILY

The 1995 Proclamation arose out of the political concerns about efforts to normalize same-sex relationships. Rather than locate this document in a distinctively LDS genre of "proclamation," it is instructive to note that the "The Family: A Proclamation to the World" belongs to a similar genre of such texts produced by churches and organizations of the Religious Right. In the 1980s and 1990s, various organs of this coalition issued similar documents to promote heterosexual marriage and binary gender roles. Because so little is known about the production of the LDS document, it is impossible to identify what resources were consulted in crafting the genre and form of the statement. Nevertheless, the Proclamation shared a number of features with these other documents, like verbal formulas, topics, and structure. The groups that produced these statements were also well known to LDS church leaders. For instance, in 1988 Jerry Falwell's Moral Majority, Phyllis Schlafly's Eagle Forum, James Dobson's Family Research Council, and other institutions of the Religious Right jointly released a policy document titled "Family Manifesto."[20] This document explained that "marriage is a covenant of divine origin." On gender roles, it affirmed, "We proclaim that male and female were established by the Creator in their diversity, with equal dignity and complementary value . . . and [that male and female] extends to psychological traits which set natural constraints on gender roles. . . . The role of the male is most effectively that of provider, and the role of the female one of nurturer." The document's teachings on gender emphasized not only biological difference but also social and psychological difference, which naturalized roles for men outside the home and roles for women inside the home. The manifesto promoted procreation and outlined its views of the rights of children. It further called on society to enact specific proposals that would ensure that marriage is "protected by government in public policy."[21]

Other organizations released similar documents in this era. In 1989, the evangelical Center for Biblical Manhood and Womanhood released the "Danvers Statement" in a paid advertisement in *Christianity Today*. This document taught that there were "distinctions in masculine and feminine roles" that included "the husband's loving, humble headship" and "the wife's intelligent, willing submission." At the same time, it affirmed that these roles are "equally high in value and dignity." The statement was opposed to interpretations of Christian teaching that favored egalitarianism at home and in the church. It concluded by asserting, "We are convinced that a denial or neglect of these principles will lead to increasingly destructive consequences in our families, our churches, and the culture at large."[22] The conclusion pointed to the broader political ambitions regarding the family that the Religious Right harbored.

By the mid-1990s, these ambitions were bearing fruit on a number of different fronts. In May 1995, the Christian Coalition introduced Pat Robertson and Ralph Reed's legislative goals in the "Contract with the American Family," a supplement to Newt Gingrich's 1994 "Contract with America," part of his congressional campaign to institute conservative economic policy.[23] Focusing mostly on reshaping America's public education, Robertson and Reed's vision of strengthening the family was an expression of Christian nationalism. In Reed's words, "We have no intention of doing to this Congress what the feminists, unions and the gay lobby did to Bill Clinton when he took office."[24] Feminism and homosexuality were still the declared enemies. A renewed revival of "the family" was underway.

At least one other major document like the Proclamation came out of this period. In 1998, the Southern Baptist Convention adopted Article XVIII on "The Family" as a part of the Baptist Faith and Message. The document was similar to the others of this genre. It outlined the teachings on the family that were the most central, including lifelong, heterosexual, monogamous marriage; the relationships of husbands and wives; and the duties of and toward children. On gender roles, the document affirmed, "A wife is to submit herself graciously to the servant leadership of her husband." At the same time, the text also stated that since both male and female were created in the image of God, a wife "is equal to" her husband. Her duties of submission entail respecting and helping him and nurturing their children. His duties are to love, provide, protect, and lead the family.[25] This document, as the others before, held many resonances with the LDS Proclamation in terms of the outlook and topics, specific language and biblical interpretation of creation, and tensions about hierarchy and equality between spouses.

TROUBLE IN PARADISE

In the LDS case, there was also a more specific action that framed Mormons' approach to the new politics of the family. On May 5, 1993, the Hawaii Supreme Court ruled that prohibiting same-sex marriages amounted to sex discrimination unless the state could find a compelling reason to bar such unions. Dallin H. Oaks's long-awaited strategy was called into action—and the decade-long silence on the politics of homosexuality had built some political capital. When the church first entered the political arena on same-sex marriage in the 1990s, Donald Hallstrom, the regional representative in the Oahu Hawaii North Region, later explained, "The Church has not attempted to oppose basic civil rights for homosexuals or any other group. This is not our work nor our focus."[26] Marriage was the issue, and the church had saved its energies for that battle.

The Hawaii Supreme Court decision put church leaders on high alert. Just a few weeks later, on May 18, 1993, apostle Boyd K. Packer warned that gay and lesbian rights activists made up one of the three "dangers" for the church, along with feminists and intellectuals.[27] Church leaders portrayed themselves and the church as under siege by people seeking equal rights. Another apostle, Russell M. Nelson, spoke at the 1993 Parliament of World Religions in September of that year. Nelson had worked as a globally recognized expert in cardiovascular research and surgery, having been a part of the team that developed the first open-heart surgery techniques. Nelson had also served as the personal physician for Spencer W. Kimball and performed his open-heart surgery in 1972. Kimball later called him as an apostle in 1984 at the same time as Oaks. Nelson's speech at the parliament exhibited some of his personality and interests. He openly sought collaboration with other religious groups. Urging such cooperation, he explained, "We are under obligation to take a strong stand on moral issues in order to preserve a wholesome and ethical environment. As religious leaders, our participation in the political process may be needed to protect precious religious liberty."[28] Without mentioning same-sex marriage directly, Nelson indicated the need for religious communities to work together in the political realm to support a "wholesome" environment. This was in line with what Oaks had expressed in his 1984 internal memorandum. But Nelson saw the issue as more acute—religious liberty was also under attack in a zero-sum game with same-sex marriage rights.

A few months later, LDS church leaders were making more specific pleas to their members to counter gay and lesbian marriage rights. In February 1994, the First Presidency issued a letter to be read in LDS congregations urging "members to appeal to legislators, judges and other government officials to preserve the purposes and sanctity of marriage between a man and a woman." The letter explained the seriousness of the request: "The principles of the gospel and the sacred responsibilities given us require that The Church of Jesus Christ of Latter-day Saints oppose any efforts to give legal authorization to marriages between persons of the same gender."[29] Church leaders saw themselves as having political responsibilities to promote "principles of the gospel" in the law.

A year after the First Presidency's political appeal, Utah legislators moved to pass a bill that prevented the state from recognizing same-sex marriages from other states.[30] The first legislation of its kind, the Utah example quickly spread. Other states began legislation to ban same-sex marriages and to refuse to recognize such marriages performed in other states.[31] These measures had broad bipartisan support. At the federal level, in 1996 President William J. Clinton's administration signed the Defense of Marriage Act, which denied federal recognition of same-sex marriages performed in any state and affirmed the right of states to not recognize such marriages from other states.[32] All of this had been sparked by a Hawaii Supreme Court decision that had not yet come into effect.

The church's political mobilization against same-sex marriage alarmed gay and lesbian Latter-day Saints. In a newspaper interview in March 1994, Marty Baudet, the executive director of Affirmation, a gay and lesbian Mormon support group, said, "I predict society will acknowledge gay rights and, 20 years down the road, the church will find itself out of step once again [as in the case of LDS racial restrictions] and trying not to look bad."[33] Baudet's prediction, which was off by one year in its accuracy, was based on the idea that social change would vindicate the position of those seeking gay rights, including marriage. Church leaders did not necessarily disagree, but they sought to stave off this change for as long as possible. They too believed that society was moving toward greater acceptance and tolerance of homosexuality but thought this indicated decline, not progress. Conservatives and progressives read the meaning of social change differently.

*Proclaiming the New Heterosexual Family*

Church leaders closely followed the case in Hawaii and actively tried to get involved.[34] The court had given the state the opportunity to come up with a compelling reason to prohibit same-sex marriages before granting them. However, the LDS church faced a number of setbacks in its efforts to influence the final outcome of the case. In February 1995, the church petitioned the Circuit Court of Hawaii to become a party on the side of the state to oppose same-sex marriage.[35] The church argued that if same-sex marriage was legalized, the state could revoke its license to perform marriages and the church could be subject to discrimination lawsuits for refusing to perform such marriages. The arguments were rejected by the circuit and supreme courts, which noted that no one was required to perform any marriage and that freedom of religion prevented the church from having to perform same-sex marriages.[36] The church's request was denied. Religious liberty arguments against same-sex marriage were not legally persuasive in Hawaii's courts, but they would continue to be mobilized in church rhetoric.

In a second legal setback, LDS representatives were excluded from a decision-making body to counsel the governor on how to respond to the court. The legislature had originally mandated two LDS representatives, along with two Catholic representatives, to sit on the eleven-member Hawaii Governor's Commission on Sexual Orientation and the Law. The commission had been organized to respond to the same-sex marriage decision from the prior year, as the court had asked for evidence of compelling reasons to oppose same-sex marriage, and the LDS representatives and others on the commission were tasked with developing the state's response to the court's decision. But in September 1995, the Hawaii Supreme Court disbanded the commission as a violation of the separation of church and state.[37] (A new seven-member commission was formed that ultimately recommended the legalization of same-sex marriage.)[38]

After being locked out of the legal case on two fronts, LDS warnings became increasingly emphatic. A few weeks after the court prohibited the LDS representatives from shaping the state response to same-sex marriage, Gordon B. Hinckley delivered the Proclamation, making a blanket appeal to citizens, legislators, and the courts in dire terms. That same month, apostle James E. Faust (d. 2007) warned that "alternatives to the legal and loving marriage between a man and a woman are helping to unravel the fabric of human society. I am sure this is pleasing to the devil. . . . If practiced by all adults, these lifestyle would mean the end of the human family."[39] Echoing the private comments of Dallin H. Oaks from a decade before about civilizational "suicide" if same-sex marriage were permitted, Faust sounded the alarm about sexual fluidity. Same-sex marriage might become so popular that it could spread universally among adults. For LDS leaders, this was not about minority rights but about the universal risks such social legitimization posed.

Turning to a new strategy, LDS officials began to collaborate with Catholic leaders in the self-described "grassroots" organization called Hawaii's Future Today (HFT) to lobby and influence public opinion.[40] The details of this organizing were made public after an employee of the Salt Lake City–based Church History Library leaked the documents to a prominent gay rights activist in 2009.[41] The documents were widely reported on in the press and available on numerous websites. In these documents, Hinckley had specifically requested that a lobbying organization be set up in Hawaii that would not bring attention to the church.[42] Loren Dunn of the Seventy reported that after the initial organization had been created, "we have distanced the Church from the coalition itself but still have input where necessary through our local source."[43] Using back channels "almost every day," Dunn reassured senior church leaders that "the ideas are introduced but the Church is not visible."[44] LDS church funds were "used in an area of coalition activity that does not have to be reported."[45] On financing, Dunn noted, "as expected, the majority needs to come from us."[46] After the HFT was founded, the First Presidency issued a letter announcing support for the organization that was read in Sunday church meetings in Hawaii.[47] The church's representatives helped select the coalition's leadership and organize media campaigns, fund-raising, tax and donation strategy, and letter-writing campaigns to discredit the reconstituted Commission on Sexual Orientation and the Law report that favored same-sex marriage.[48] As a lobbying organization, the HFT proved quite effective. Within just a year, Dunn noted that the coalition "turned legislators out of office and affected the leadership of the State Senate."[49]

The HFT organization lobbied officials and attempted to sway public opinion against same-sex marriage. But these opponents of same-sex marriage homed in on their primary strategy—a state constitutional amendment to counter the court's decision, which was seemingly unpersuaded by the legal arguments to oppose same-sex marriage. In 1998, the Hawaii ballot finally included a proposed state constitutional amendment that defined marriage as only between a man and a woman. After having organized the lobbying group HFT, the coalition called Save Traditional Marriage '98 was formed around the ballot measure and supported by HFT finances, local fund-raising, and fund-raising events in Utah.[50]

*Proclaiming the New Heterosexual Family*

Meanwhile, a similar constitutional measure popped up in Alaska. Like in Hawaii, two males had applied for a marriage license but were declined. Alaska's supreme court ruled that the state must grant the license unless it could come up with a compelling reason not to. The Alaska legislature immediately proposed a state constitutional amendment to address the matter. The measure was publicly supported by the Alaska Family Coalition, a group similar to the HFT, and the Catholic Bishops of Alaska. Though not on-the-ground organizers in Alaska, LDS church officials donated cash directly to the campaign efforts—$600,000 in Hawaii and $500,000 in Alaska.[51]

These donations earned praise for the LDS church from many other groups and churches who opposed same-sex marriage.[52] From the church's perspective, one of the real benefits of this political organizing was that it provided the occasion to collaborate and solidify relationships with other groups of the Religious Right that favored "family values." The coalition building in Hawaii and Alaska had been mostly with Catholics. Initially, evangelicals had been suspicious of collaboration with the Mormons. Following the strategy in Alaska of offering big money in the final days of a state election, the church offered $600,000 to the evangelicals leading the campaign against same-sex marriage in Nebraska in 2000. They rejected the offer.[53]

### CALIFORNIA'S PROP 22

Loren Dunn, president of the North America West Area, which included both Hawaii and California, organized the efforts in Hawaii and began thinking about California as the next stage for political involvement.[54] These efforts were not just aimed at mobilizing Mormons. Due to the successes in Hawaii, the church's Public Affairs Committee asked Dunn in 1997 to meet with a Catholic bishop in California to start a similar public referendum modeled on the HFT coalition, with an eye toward the 1998 election.[55] In response, Dunn noted that the church would not have to provide as much of the funding in California as it had in Hawaii, because many other religious and Republican leaders had already gotten involved on the issue. He and other LDS representatives initiated meetings with the Catholic Bishops Conference in California, which accepted the invitation to join with the Mormon effort.[56]

Ultimately, California's Defense of Marriage Initiative, Proposition 22, also known as the Knight Initiative, made it onto the ballot for the March 2000 election. The initiative was entirely preventive as no court case or legislation had brought the issue to California voters, in contrast to the Hawaii and Alaska cases. Nevertheless, LDS involvement in California's Prop 22 was extensive.[57] The wording of the Prop 22 referendum was vetted by BYU law professor Lynn Wardle and two members of the Quorum of the Seventy, Marlin K. Jensen and David E. Sorenson, indicating the close ties between the Catholic legislative sponsors and Latter-day Saints.[58]

LDS leadership publicly asked church members to fund the campaign by donations. In May 1999, the church began sending communications to its California congregations, urging members to "do all you can by donating your means and time to assure a successful vote." The Area Authorities sent a letter to stake presidents at the "request of the First Presidency" instructing local church leaders to engage in fund-raising activities for the Defense of Marriage Committee and to "begin with more affluent members, suggesting an appropriate contribution."[59] The letter also explained that the church would keep an accounting of donors with a form asking about the donor's stake and ward and would make that list available to stake presidents so the local leaders would be directly aware of who had donated and how much.[60] The church's ecclesiastical leaders could quickly be mobilized as campaign fund-raisers.

Besides raising money, church leaders activated volunteers for the campaign. Stake presidents were issued packets with instructions for their specific congregations for volunteering as precinct walkers, including voter lists, handouts, and guidelines for speaking about Prop 22.[61] Wards and stakes assigned "Knight Coordinators," who were responsible for organizing the precinct walk volunteers. The campaign recruited BYU students, among others, to intern and offered in exchange "a semester's worth of credit living and working in California from January through March, 2000."[62] LDS youth organizations distributed lawn signs, and LDS Institute directors—leaders of the para-ecclesial educational organization for young adults—instructed students to register and then vote for Prop 22. Local LDS leaders announced the efforts in church meetings and organized phone banking meetings for adults and youth.[63]

As it had done during the battle against the ERA, church leaders justified their political activation because same-sex marriage was a "moral" issue. At the October 1999 General Conference, Hinckley thanked those who were "contributing . . . time and talents in a cause that in some quarters may not be politically correct but which nevertheless lies at the heart of the Lord's eternal plan for His children." He continued, "Some portray legalization of so-called same-sex marriage as a civil right, [but] this is not a matter of civil rights; it is a matter of morality. . . . Nevertheless . . . our opposition to legalize

*Proclaiming the New Heterosexual Family*

same-sex marriage should never be interpreted as justification for hatred, intolerance, or abuse of those who profess homosexual tendencies."[64] LDS leaders rejected the claims that marriage was a civil right. At the same time, they emphasized that it was not hatred that inspired them to depict same-sex marriage as in opposition to divine will; it was LDS doctrines about protecting sexual difference. Just as some leaders in earlier generations had framed racial hierarchy and opposition to civil rights as an expression of divine will, church leaders in this period relinquished responsibility and agency by asserting that they were following a divine command. Instead of a divinely ordained racial lineage, though, the doctrine's essential feature was now heterosexuality.

Prop 22 passed with 61 percent support from California voters in the spring of 2000. Like Hawaii and Alaska, California was another political victory for the church and strengthened the church's relationships with its Catholic collaborators. But these gains came at certain costs. Many members of the church expressed disapproval of the efforts to get involved in the politics of same-sex marriage.[65] Some had objected in Hawaii and Alaska, but the efforts in California touched many more Mormons because of the large numbers in the state. In response, apostle M. Russell Ballard emphasized, "In the Lord's Church there is no such thing as a loyal opposition." He warned, "False prophets and false teachers are also those who attempt to change the God-given and scripturally based doctrines that protect the sanctity of marriage, the divine nature of the family, and the essential doctrine of personal morality. They advocate a redefinition of morality to justify fornication, adultery, and homosexual relationships. Some openly champion the legalization of so-called same-gender marriages."[66] Church leadership stressed the need for obedience to their teachings. Mormons were taught that as an act of obedience they should not only vote in favor of Prop 22 but also actively contribute time, means, and talents to the cause. Supporting ballot measures became a natural extension of the duty to follow church leaders.

These calls for obedience and acceptance of LDS teachings about the goals of same-sex marriage advocates were too much to bear for some. In the context of Prop 22, three suicides of gay Mormons made news. Stuart Matis took his own life on the steps of an LDS chapel in Los Altos, California, on February 25, 2000, just a few weeks before the Prop 22 vote.[67] Matis rejected the characterization of same-sex marriage as a sexual liberation movement that was distinctive from heterosexual marriage in its structure and impulse. He implored his coreligionists, "We have the same needs as you. We desire to love and be loved. We desire to live our lives with happiness. We are not a threat to you or your families. We are your sons, daughters, brothers, sisters, neighbors, co-workers and friends, and most importantly, we are all children of God."[68] Matis's suicide set off a tragic chain reaction. A few weeks later, on March 9, 2000, days after Prop 22 passed, another gay Mormon, D. J. Thompson, took his own life, citing in his note, "It is unfortunate that the lives of good people such as Stuart Matis, Matthew Shepherd [sic, a gay man murdered in 1998], and many others go unnoticed. I see Proposition 22 as a last straw in my life-long battle to see peace in the world I live in."[69] Clay Whitmer, a friend of Matis's, took his life on March 20, 2000.[70]

The Proclamation was hugely successful in mobilizing Mormons against same-sex marriage, but it also took a large toll on the mental health of many gay and lesbian Mormons (at the least). For Latter-day Saints, the political calculation not only was about this issue but also was deeply intertwined with gender and the family. At the same time, it was based on theories that gender and sexuality were vulnerable because of their inherent fluidity and that society, laws, and individual circumstances could shape one's sexual preferences. The political efforts to thwart the acceptance of same-sex marriage, and the preaching on men's and women's roles, remained integrally connected to LDS psychological efforts to cure homosexuality.

## REPARATIVE THERAPY AND INBORN FEELINGS

The Proclamation did not mention homosexuality directly, and it did not reference psychological treatments, but the perspective that gender roles must be maintained was a shared feature of the normative political and preaching goals of the document and the conservative psychological theories church leaders were promoting in this period. These political and psychological activities also reveal the complex and intertwined relationships that church leaders were developing with other anti-homosexuality Christians. In addition, LDS leaders forged connections with psychological researchers outside the faith who would support their views. In the 1990s, religious conservatives persevered in their quest against the normalization of homosexuality in the psychological establishment. Nearly twenty years after the American Psychiatric Association's decision to remove homosexuality from its list of disorders, a small group of researchers continued to work to delegitimize same-sex relationships as psychologically abnormal. In 1992, these efforts took on renewed seriousness when Benjamin Kaufman, Charles Socarides, and Joseph Nicolosi founded the National Association for Research and Therapy of Homosexuality (NARTH), which revived the

*Proclaiming the New Heterosexual Family*

discredited scholarly arguments of the 1950s and 1960s that saw homosexuality as a pathology and taught that it could, and should, be cured with proper treatment.[71] These activists pushed for the possibility and benefits of sexual orientation change therapies, sometimes called conversion or reparative therapy. NARTH's research and advocacy agenda was based on the mutability of sexual orientation, saw same-sex attraction as a psycho-developmental adaptation to gender failures, and focused on helping those with "unwanted homosexual attractions."[72] The group facilitated "ethical, clinically licensed sexual orientation change therapy" and argued that there was no "reliable" evidence that it harmed people. The American Psychological Association criticized these methods.[73] Still, this counter-scientific authority lent credence to religious opposition to homosexuality. Though NARTH was not affiliated with any specific religious organization, it kept close ties with many evangelical ex-gay ministries, especially Exodus International.

In the 1990s, LDS church leaders were also committed to the practices of reparative therapy and worked closely with other groups that shared this approach. This treatment emphasized that human will was responsible for homosexual actions and desires and that with the proper treatment, both could conform to heterosexual norms. The First Presidency sent a letter to local church leaders in 1991 explaining this approach: "There is a distinction between immoral thoughts and feelings and participating in either immoral heterosexual or any homosexual behavior." Both immoral thoughts and immoral actions were condemned as sinful, but "such thoughts and feelings, regardless of their causes, can and should be overcome." The 1991 letter's caveat, "regardless of their causes," expressed ambivalence about the competing theories of causation of homosexuality. Nevertheless, the cure still hinged on a doctrine of sexual mutability based on gender roles. The letter explained, "A correct understanding of the divinely appointed roles of men and women will fortify all against sinful practices." The prescription for accomplishing heteronormative sexual and gender expressions was faith, repentance, and "persistent effort" to achieve gender norms.[74] Eternal gender entailed heterosexuality.

The LDS cure for homosexuality focused on the complete transformation of desires into heterosexually appropriate thoughts and feelings. In 1992, the church produced a document for ecclesiastical leaders titled *Understanding and Helping Those Who Have Homosexual Problems*.[75] The booklet updated the 1981 handbook for LDS Social Services, *Understanding and Changing Homosexual Orientation Problems*. The revision in the title, from "changing" to "helping," reflected a minor alteration in goals. However, this document was largely consistent with previous LDS therapeutic appropriations of ex-gay teachings—including the pathologizing language of homosexuality. While citing ambivalence about the causes, *Understanding and Helping* maintained that "[homosexual] thoughts and feelings should be overcome." Change should include both thoughts and actions: "In order to change homosexual behavior, a person must understand the seriousness of the transgression, feel deeply repentant, and have a firm commitment to change. These same elements will help a person overcome thoughts and feelings, which, although less serious, lead to deviant behavior." It continued, "Members of the church are commanded to control their sexual thoughts and desires."[76] The New Thought movement lived on in the self-help ideology of reparative therapy.

*Understanding and Helping* provided numerous techniques to aid ecclesiastical leaders in their pastoral counseling role to facilitate change. The leader should listen compassionately and teach the confessor to exercise self-mastery over thoughts, to overcome deviant practices, to develop appropriate relationships, and to enlist the help of family and friends. In addition, the manual referred repentant individuals to seek "professional assistance" from "qualified therapists who understand and honor gospel principles."[77] At the root of these problems were not merely misplaced emotional needs but also an incorrect understanding of "divinely appointed roles of men and women." Masculine and feminine performances would ensure heterosexual outcomes. Consistent with previous teachings about the vulnerability of children, the manual advised that "a secure family environment helps children develop healthy sexual attitudes."[78] Deviant sexuality could be prevented in the well-ordered home.

Language remained an important battleground against sexual essentialism. LDS leaders also adopted the language coming from the ex-gay movement to describe homosexuality in this era. In the early 1990s, church leaders still hadn't settled on a serious alternative to "homosexuality" as a term, even if they had rejected it as a noun, as Boyd K. Packer had advised in 1978. In 1992, Packer still rejected sexual essentialism associated with the existing labels. He believed that homosexuality was not manifest in "nature," pointing out (incorrectly) that "animals do not pair up with their own gender to satisfy their mating instincts."[79] Because same-sex desires and relationships were depicted as outside of nature, LDS documents spoke of those who experience "homosexual problems" rather than attributing any fixed identity to the individual. The concern for the constitutive power of words framed how LDS leaders used language. As the 1992 *Understanding and Helping* advised, "Be careful not to label the person as 'homosexual' or 'gay.' Such labels can undermine the person's belief that change is possible and may communicate the mistaken notion that a man or a woman is born with homosexual identity that cannot be changed. It is more appropriate to speak of homosexual thoughts, feelings, and behavior."[80] Such use of labels could successfully stigmatize the desires without stigmatizing the person. The booklet encouraged people to believe that their desires were fluid and subject to change.

Church leaders sent mixed messages about how to treat gays and lesbians throughout this decade. They continued to emphasize the importance of condemning the sin but loving the sinner. What exactly this meant was difficult to define. According to *Understanding and Helping*, church leaders were instructed to express love for the person having "homosexual problems." At the same time, the rhetoric continued to depict gays and lesbians as hostile and worthy of condemnation. In 1993, the year after *Understanding and Helping* was published, Packer set off controversy by describing a growing threat to the church: "The dangers I speak of come from the gay-lesbian movement, the feminist movement (both of which are relatively new), and the ever-present challenge from the so-called scholars or intellectuals. Our local leaders must deal with all three of them with ever-increasing frequency." There was a danger of being too loving toward gays and lesbians, which would imply that one condoned or even accepted them. He warned the audience neither to "sympathize with" nor "comfort them" in their struggles with the church because such actions could undermine faith in church leaders.[81]

Packer saw homosexuality as deeply insidious. A few years earlier, he had compared homosexual intercourse to grave crimes, including incest and "the molesting of little children of either gender."[82] The trope of the homosexual and the pedophile framed both as equivalent sexual sins, which justified their harsh treatment. Some years later, Packer described the love that members of the church should have toward gays and lesbians as a "*tough* love." "We must teach and we must warn," he explained.[83] Love should by no means include supporting an individual in his or her choices to form same-sex relationships. For some leaders, these teachings meant that sanctions could be put on family and friends for being too sympathetic. In 1995, Dallin H. Oaks issued a warning to LDS members that "[ecclesiastical] discipline can be given for encouraging sin by others."[84] These ideas rested on the hope for the transformation of sexual desires and threatened church members who did not accept this theory.

Consistent with the advice in *Understanding and Helping*, LDS leaders continued to sponsor the joint approach of reparative therapy alongside pastoral counseling as the method of curing homosexual thoughts and behavior.

In 1993, psychologists reviewing the state of the field explained, "The Church has supported efforts of the LDS Social Services and other consulting professionals to research the issues and to offer a reparative therapy approach which assumes that homosexual behavior can be changed."[85] A. Dean Byrd and Mark D. Chamberlain studied clients from LDS therapists in private practice and from those who were employed by LDS Social Services who were "specializing in the treatment of individuals dealing with issues of homosexuality."[86] LDS therapists referred clients to the ex-gay literature canon, such as writings by Jeff Konrad and Elizabeth Moberly.[87] In the 1990s, Byrd directed the training for treatment of homosexuality for LDS Social Services and touted therapeutic successes to LDS and non-LDS audiences. Byrd was closely affiliated with conservative Christian ex-gay treatment advocates, as well as NARTH, where he eventually served as president in 2008. In his 1993 survey with Chamberlain, they noted that the research subjects were also participating in group therapy sessions and some were attending "a Salt Lake area Saturday Morning sports therapy program."[88] Imitating other ex-gay ministries, LDS therapists believed sports would instill the proper masculine socialization and gender comportment that would lead to heterosexual desires.[89] These psychological and therapeutic views that had been abandoned by mainstream science continued to provide a foundation for heteronormative values for gender and sexuality.

## "YOU DON'T HAVE TO BE GAY"

Church leaders and the church's professional therapists were developing relationships not only with ex-gay institutions and reparative therapy methods but also with new activist organizations in this period. In 1989, a group of eleven men in Salt Lake City founded Evergreen, a semi-independent organization for Latter-day Saints seeking group and reparative therapy. The idea quickly spread, and new chapters were founded around the United States. Pastoral counseling and LDS Social Services seemed insufficient for these individuals, who sought new forms of treatment.

Though it was open to men and women, Evergreen focused primarily on men. The 1990 flyer announcing its inaugural conference in Salt Lake City boldly declared, "YOU DON'T HAVE TO BE GAY: Developing a Healthy Male Identity." The conference promised to "cover new and previously overlooked thinking about the origins of homosexuality" and to "explore the stages of growth out of homosexuality into a healthy male identity."[90] For Evergreen activists, homosexuality was a problem of gender identity for men.

*Proclaiming the New Heterosexual Family*

Men were at the center. It wasn't until 1998 that the first Evergreen group for "female strugglers" was formed. By the end of the 1990s, there were thirty-six groups for men, eight for friends and family, and only two for women.[91]

Evergreen was the principal LDS-affiliated organization dedicated to people with "unwanted" homosexual attractions, a rival to Affirmation, the gay- and lesbian-affirming Mormon group that was founded in the late 1970s. As an organization, Evergreen functioned as a referral service claiming to have the "world's largest database" of reparative therapists, in addition to its own support groups. It also provided direct training to therapists through its subsidiary organization, the Center for the Study of Gender-Affirmative Therapy, founded in 2001. Evergreen provided knowledge resources in the form of newsletters, books, articles, and pamphlets to LDS members around the world, selling more than 25,000 materials over a period of twenty years. It helped authors publish their books and facilitated publications in magazines.[92] In 1998, LDS reparative therapist David Matheson cowrote the *Evergreen Workbook for Men*.[93] Matheson himself said that he had "experienced attraction to other men, but learned to control it and lead a straight life."[94] Matheson's theory about "gender wholeness" as the cure to homosexuality was promoted at Evergreen conferences, and he served as the organization's executive director.

Evergreen never embraced the "ex-gay" label for itself but shared the same approach, rhetoric, and promises as other ex-gay organizations. At its first conference in 1990, it advertised "two leaders of the ex-gay movement," Joe Dallas of the evangelical group New Creations and Jeff Konrad, author of *You Don't Have to Be Gay* (1987). In subsequent years, the biggest names in reparative therapy were invited guests. Joseph Nicolosi from NARTH and representatives from Frank Worthen's Love in Action all presented at the annual conferences. At these meetings, ex-gay leaders interacted with LDS reparative therapists and high-ranking LDS church officials. Evergreen hosted the annual NARTH conference in Salt Lake City in 2003. Exodus International also had close ties with Evergreen. Numerous Exodus officials spoke at its conferences over the years, including Alan Chambers, the president of Exodus International. Other ex-gay and conservative organizations, such as Jews Offering New Alternatives for Healing (JONAH), Focus on the Family, and Courage, all collaborated with Evergreen.[95] Non-Mormon reparative therapist advocates continued to have influence in LDS circles during this decade. In 2006, Neil Whitehead, author of the Christian book *My Genes Made Me Do It*, delivered a "fireside" for Evergreen and provided training for LDS Family Services.[96]

Through Evergreen, private practice counselors advertised their services for LDS clients and published their own literature on this topic. Matheson's book *Becoming a Whole Man: Principles and Archetypes* (2013) drew on his experience working in Evergreen. He was trained under Nicolosi, who advocated gender identity deficit theories of homosexuality. Matheson subscribed to these ideas and cofounded "Journey into Manhood" weekend retreats.[97] These retreats came under some scrutiny when undercover journalist Ted Cox published an exposé about the weekends. Cox alleged that he participated in a series of "homoerotic exercises," like healing and touch sessions, gym class and showering reenactments, and attempts to heal the "Father Wound."[98] Other prominent LDS reparative therapists included Jeffrey W. Robinson, who also worked closely with Evergreen. Robinson's approach was outlined on his website "The Guard Rail." He explained, "I have often told my clients that the only real difference between them and me is that they can remember how to be sexually attracted to other men and I can't."[99] In this psycho-developmental approach, same-sex attractions were natural but also must be outgrown. Robinson, who completed his BYU dissertation on this topic, worked with Evergreen and in private practice from this approach.

The LDS church itself also maintained direct ties and affiliation with Evergreen. In 2009, Evergreen produced a twenty-year history that chronicled these extensive relationships. Emeritus General Authorities always served on its board of trustees, as did members of BYU faculty. The board met regularly with Area Presidencies and other high-ranking church leaders. LDS Social Services cooperated closely with Evergreen to create and support meeting groups. Evergreen held its events in church meetinghouses, organized church-sponsored "fireside" events, and promoted sessions at BYU Women's Conferences, and General Authorities provided keynote addresses at Evergreen's conferences. Evergreen leaders held training sessions for local priesthood and Relief Society leaders around the United States, claiming to have educated nearly twelve thousand church leaders, and also provided training for therapists in AMCAP. It also collaborated with the church when bringing out speakers from the ex-gay movement. None of these collaborations would have been possible without approval at the highest levels of church leaders. A. Dean Byrd, who had designed the church's reparative therapy approaches while working at LDS Social Services, acted as liaison between Evergreen and church leaders. Byrd was an active promoter of ideas of sexual fluidity and saw heterosexuality as a viable option for people dedicated to treatment. This close relationship helped to keep Evergreen under indirect management of church authorities, who could withdraw support if Evergreen leaders acted contrary to the church leaders' views.[100]

Through the 1990s and the first decade of the 2000s, the reparative therapy efforts sponsored by the church's LDS Social Services, private practitioners, and affiliate organizations like Evergreen defied mainstream psychological acceptance of homosexuality as non-pathological. The church and these organizations worked closely with the broader ex-gay movement, including its most important representatives, to give legitimacy to sexual orientation change efforts. The twin belief that homosexuality could and should be changed through therapeutic efforts was not, however, an exclusively psychological view; it rested on a sociology of sexuality as well. Individual treatment was nothing without a culture that also promoted heterosexual values. And the fight against same-sex marriage continued to be the most important for maintaining hetero-supremacy.

### THE ROAD TO PROP 8

When Prop 22 passed in 2000 prohibiting same-sex marriage in California, it escalated a national fight that would last for the next fifteen years. The stakes were high as activists on both sides pressed their case. The decisive victories for traditional marriage in every state ballot measure, along with the extension of Defense of Marriage Act laws in many states and at the federal level, showed that conservatives were in control of popular sentiment on the issue. Though most Democrats at the time also publicly opposed same-sex marriage, the issue became a central feature of the Republican social agenda in the first part of the twenty-first century and revived the flagging Religious Right, helping divert attention from the troubled war in Iraq. The question of same-sex marriage was by then a defining issue in the culture wars and would drive conservatives to the polls in national and state elections for the next several years.

Advocates of same-sex marriage were not ready to retreat in the face of overwhelming defeats. They continued to press for a legal strategy to win in the courts, imitating successful civil rights battles against segregation and antimiscegenation laws. Though Vermont already had legalized civil unions, the first state to cross the line into same-sex marriage was Massachusetts on November 18, 2003 (the decision did not take effect until May 2004). Still, just a few weeks after the highly publicized Massachusetts ruling, President Hinckley took time during his Christmas devotional to repeat the importance of heterosexual marriage. He explained that "the family" was "under attack." He warned of the "sinful practices" of Sodom and Gomorrah as the example of what happens when the "traditional family" falls apart—"when there was no repentance, it was [God's] withering hand that destroyed them."[101] The apocalyptic warnings about punishments that were awaiting civilizations that accepted same-sex marriage reprised the threats outlined in the 1995 Proclamation.

The dramatic message against same-sex marriage was not just directed internally to church members. Church leaders continued coalition building with other conservative religious groups to oppose same-sex marriage. A few months after the Massachusetts ruling, on February 28, 2004, the church hosted a conference in its Washington, D.C., Temple Visitors Center for the anti-gay interfaith group Family Action Council International, "Defending Marriage and the Family: By Faith and by Reason." Sheri Dew, former member of the General Presidency of the Relief Society and CEO of the church's publication company, Deseret Book, was the main LDS representative. She likened the situation of opposing same-sex marriage to the imperative to oppose Nazism. She demurred, "At first it may seem a bit extreme to imply a comparison between the atrocities of Hitler and what is happening in terms of contemporary threats against the family—but maybe not."[102] The irony of associating advocates of same-sex marriage with the Nazis, when homosexuals had been targeted by the Nazis, was not lost on Dew's critics.[103]

LDS member Mitt Romney was the governor of Massachusetts at the time the same-sex marriage ruling was handed down in his state. Romney vigorously opposed the court's decision and launched an opposition strategy to suspend the ruling and find other ways to circumvent it.[104] Additionally, the First Presidency sent a letter to congregations in Massachusetts reiterating LDS doctrine on the family and inviting members to write to their local legislators to express their opinion on the matter. Yet nothing really came of these efforts. Romney's attempts to block the law or limit it failed, and LDS members did not formally organize to oppose same-sex marriage in the state.

The issue was not yet over. In the 2004 election cycle, many states put forward anti-same-sex-marriage ballot measures. Church leaders did not repeat the organizational strategies they had employed in Hawaii and California, nor did they repeat the donation offers they had made in Hawaii, Alaska, and Nebraska. Rather, the church simply endorsed these political efforts and expressed unqualified opposition to civil unions, domestic partnerships, and other compromise measures that would grant "legal status on any other sexual relationship" beside mixed-sex marriage.[105] The LDS church was certainly not alone in its efforts. A revived Religious Right turned to the national sphere, hoping to roll back same-sex marriage in liberal states as well. A proposal to pass a U.S. constitutional amendment defining marriage as only "between one man and one woman" was put onto the 2004 Republican Party national platform.[106]

These efforts continued after the 2004 election cycle. On April 25, 2006, apostle Russell M. Nelson joined the conservative Religious Coalition on Marriage, which advocated for a federal marriage amendment.[107] The signatories to the "Letter from America's Religious Leaders in Defense of Marriage" included evangelical luminaries such as James Dobson, Ted Haggard, and Richard Land; numerous Catholic cardinals and archbishops; Greek Orthodox archbishop Demetrios; and a few rabbis. The organization's website offered links to "social scientific arguments" against same-sex marriage, pamphlets that could be printed and passed out in congregations, and "sample sermons" from numerous conservative denominations.[108]

With all the electoral successes, the national temperature seemed definitively to reject same-sex marriage. At this point, opponents of same-sex marriage had more than a decade of experience with a perfect victory rate when the issue was put to a popular vote. Yet following the court decision in Massachusetts, advocates for same-sex marriage continued to use state courts as a primary method for advancing their cause. In 2007 and 2008, the California Supreme Court heard a number of cases, consolidated as the *In re Marriage Cases*, and decided that same-sex marriage was protected under California's constitution—overturning Prop 22. The stage was set.

LAST STAND

The California decision immediately mobilized opponents. As in Hawaii and other states, the only solution to the court's decision seemed to be a state constitutional amendment. Opponents of the court's decision drafted California's Proposition 8, which would establish a state constitutional amendment restating Prop 22, "Only marriage between a man and a woman is valid or recognized in California." But the legal stakes were relatively minimal in a change in the law. Since January 1, 2005, California-registered "domestic partners" held "the same rights, protections, and benefits, and shall be subject to the same responsibilities, obligations, and duties under law, whether they derive from statutes, administrative regulations, court rules, government policies, common law, or any other provisions or sources of law, as are granted to and imposed upon spouses."[109] But the courts ruled that the domestic partnership law amounted to treating people differently based on sexual orientation because it still limited the term "marriage" to mixed-sex couples. Proposition 8 did not seek to overturn the domestic partnership law or challenge the legal benefits of same-sex couples but was worded so as to reserve the term "marriage" for mixed-sex couples alone.

While all the public signals over the previous decade had made it clear where the church stood on the issue, LDS leadership appeared to have entered the Prop 8 campaign rather late. From publicly available information, Catholic donors had funded the initial efforts to gather signatures to put Prop 8 on the ballot in the spring of 2008.[110] In May 2008, LDS leaders were the last religious group to join the coalition formally, somewhat reluctant to take on as large a public role as they had in 2000.[111] Catholic archbishop George H. Niederauer of San Francisco, who had previously served as the bishop of Salt Lake City, extended the invitation.[112]

LDS leadership was not, however, entirely absent from the scene prior to formally joining the coalition. Local LDS Public Affairs representative Mark Jansson sat on the committee that developed the initiative, and LDS political operative Gary Lawrence consulted for the committee.[113] The National Organization for Marriage was the primary political entity involved in the California theater, performing a similar function as Hawaii's Future Today had a decade earlier. Matthew S. Holland, son of apostle Jeffrey R. Holland, was one of the founding members of the organization in 2007 and served on its board through the campaign season until 2009.[114]

LDS leaders made their intentions known to members in California through a letter read in church meetings on June 29, 2008. The letter was almost identical to the one sent in 1999 regarding Prop 22, in both cases asking members to donate "means and time" and for their "best efforts" to aid the passage of the initiative.[115] The opening strategy too was almost identical. On the instruction from Area Authorities, stake presidents and bishops made individual requests for direct campaign contributions through appointments and mail, sometimes for specific donation amounts. Members of the Quorum of the Seventy made targeted calls to high-net-worth Mormons, specifically asking them to donate $25,000 each.[116] Stakes and wards called or assigned individuals to help organize the fund-raising and campaigning efforts. The church itself made some in-kind donations totaling just under $200,000.[117]

LDS organizational efforts were in complete sync with the "Yes on 8" campaign. The church set up an "Ecclesiastical Arm" to focus on Mormons and a "Grassroots Arm" to concentrate on non-Mormon involvement.[118] The ecclesiastical endeavors ensured that the membership was "taught the doctrine" in LDS meetings and received all messages from the leadership.

*Proclaiming the New Heterosexual Family*

The grassroots organizing of the "Protect Marriage" coalition was led by two Mormons, Glen Greener and Gary Lawrence, who leveraged LDS membership to staff the coalition, in full cooperation with LDS leadership at all levels. These men organized LDS members at the stake and regional level to select and train zip code supervisors, who organized precinct walks and distributed signs.[119] (Catholics undertook similar grassroots organizational efforts.)[120]

Mormon worries about gender and sexual fluidity informed their support for Prop 8. They offered political arguments that same-sex marriage posed a threat to children's sexual vulnerability and to religious people and institutions. One of the most influential pieces of literature produced in support of Prop 8 was the anonymously authored "Six Consequences If Prop 8 Fails." The document, later revealed to be written by LDS organizer Gary Lawrence, went viral in Mormon social media and in popular outlets. The document claimed that "children will be taught that marriage is a relation between any two adults" and that this would cause clashes with parents' rights. It further asserted that churches and ministers would be sued, religious adoption agencies and schools would be shut down or lose tax exemption, and that same-sex marriage "will cost you money" because of these lawsuits. Morris Thurston, a liberal-leaning Mormon, wrote an influential response to these "consequences" calling them "untrue or misleading."[121] Still, the exaggerated idea that same-sex marriage threatened children's morality and perhaps even churches themselves stoked fears that Prop 8 was a contest between righteous religion and wicked gay people.

The church itself was particularly concerned with the effect of same-sex marriage on children. As part of this campaign, the church published a politico-theological statement on August 13, 2008, called "The Divine Institution of Marriage." This document reflected a changing sentiment in the wake of legal same-sex marriage and domestic partnership in various states, softening its previous statement in 2004 that objected to any "legal status" for nonheterosexual couples. The 2008 essay explained that church teachings now had "no objection" to a number of spousal rights, such as those "regarding hospitalization and medical care, fair housing and employment rights, or probate rights, so long as these do not infringe on the integrity of the family or the constitutional rights of churches and their adherents to administer and practice their religion free from government interference."[122] It stopped short, however, of adoptions for gay couples or individuals, arguing that these families posed risks to the best interests of children. Opposing same-sex marriage, it declared, "is the only course of safety for the Church and for the nation."[123] The powerful mythology of civilizational decline lived on.

What were the specific dangers and scenarios for such a catastrophe? The document explained, "The Church's opposition to same-sex marriage derives from its doctrine and teachings, as well as from its concern about the consequences of same-sex marriage on religious freedom, society, families, and children."[124] This position paper mixed legal analysis, socio-sexual theories of civilizational decline, and theological argumentation to explain how the church thought about marriage and sexuality and why the church decided to get politically involved. It warned that same-sex marriage "marks a fundamental change in the institution of marriage in ways that are contrary to God's purposes for His children and detrimental to the long-term interests of society."[125] The stakes were existential.

Gender was at the core of the theological and social-scientific justification for opposing same-sex marriage. "The Divine Institution of Marriage" depicted gender as fragile and fluid and suggested that social norms were the only thing that produced legitimate gender outcomes. Children were especially vulnerable to its insidious effects. Specifically, the document contended that same-sex marriage was a threat to children in the public education system. Updating Anita Bryant's homophobic arguments about the dangers of predatory recruitment in schools, the new argument warned that the idea of same-sex marriage itself was destabilizing to young people's vulnerable sexuality. In this view, children would be "forced" to learn that same-sex marriages exist, and schools would no longer be allowed to teach that only heterosexual relationships are morally superior. The text explained, "When marriage is undermined by gender confusion and by distortions of its God-given meaning, the rising generation of children and youth will find it increasingly difficult to develop their natural identity as a man or a woman."[126] Gender identity—a psychological category—was presumed to be properly heterosexual. But culture trumped nature in the acquisition of gender identity, especially for young people's psycho-development. Heterosexual families were described as the "optimal environment" for children to learn these values. The children of same-sex couples would be in particular danger of losing gender: "Traditional marriage . . . increases the likelihood that [children] will be able to form a clear gender identity, with sexuality closely linked to both love and procreation. By contrast, the legalization of same-sex marriage likely will erode the social identity, gender development, and moral character of children. Is it really wise for society to pursue such a radical experiment without considering its long-term consequences for children?"[127] The argument here was that the formation and acquisition of "gender identity" and "moral character" of children was superior in heterosexual marriage. In this view, same-sex marriage failed to properly inculcate necessary gender norms because it was already itself a failure of such norms. Children were at risk, not through direct predatory recruitment, but through the inherent failures of the gender of their parents, who would pass on such "gender confusion."

The social-scientific research the document cited was about single mothers but was put to use against two-parent same-sex families. The actual research cited in the document did not discuss same-sex families.[128] No evidence could be put forward to justify the claim that same-sex marriage weakened the institution of marriage for mixed-sex couples or that teaching children about same-sex marriage would make them less likely to marry. The document suggested that in the "long term" this would be the case, but the scenario was not particularly clear even then. Only the fear of gender and sexual fluidity and the risk of homosexual contagion explained the church's concerns. In the church's view, legitimized same-sex marriage might prove too powerful an attraction for young people.

In opposition to same-sex marriage, church leaders were defensive when their opponents called for pluralism, tolerance, and mutual respect between religious groups and same-sex families. Church leaders wanted to blunt these arguments and were adamant that all people were worthy of love and that they should be engaged respectfully. But these leaders were highly skeptical of social tolerance that would weaken the legal preference for heterosexuality. "The Divine Institution of Marriage" made an extended case against "tolerance" of same-sex kinship. It rejected the pluralistic claims that tolerance means "acceptance of wrongful behavior" and maintained that "today's politically palatable definition [of tolerance] insists that unless one accepts the sin he does not tolerate the sinner."[129] It staked out the limits of tolerance in a pluralistic society; tolerance required love, but not abandoning political standards or public policy choices. Making moral arguments against same-sex marriage did not constitute "hate speech," the text declared. Thomas S. Monson, who became president of the church in early 2008, warned vaguely a few months before "The Divine Institution of Marriage" came out, "The face of sin today often wears the mask of tolerance."[130] A few months later, apostle Packer spoke of the dangers of the "tolerance trap," as he termed it, explaining, "Beware of the word tolerance. It is a very unstable virtue."[131]

Already during the height of the battles about same-sex marriage, LDS leaders began to see themselves as the victims of persecution for their political involvement opposing same-sex marriage. Church leaders were especially sensitive to being called objectionable names. Dallin H. Oaks complained in 2006 about advocates who tried to "silence" opponents of same-sex marriage "by applying labels like 'homophobic.'" Worrying about this label, Oaks mused, "Ultimately it may be a test of our most basic religious freedoms to teach what we know our Father in Heaven wants us to teach."[132] This test was put even more starkly in "The Divine Institution of Marriage": "Legalizing same-sex marriage will affect a wide spectrum of government activities and policies. Once a state government declares that same-sex unions are a civil right, those governments almost certainly will enforce a wide variety of other policies intended to ensure that there is no discrimination against same-sex couples. This may well place church and state on a collision course.'"[133] Legalized discrimination against same-sex families was cast as religious freedom.

Latter-day Saint fears that a changing social landscape that accepted homosexuality would put Mormons' own acceptance in society at risk seemed, to them, confirmed in the fierce rhetoric opposing their efforts. Mormons received negative publicity for their involvement in the campaign in the months leading up to the Prop 8 election and for years afterward.[134] As the church had embraced the family as its public brand, it also earned a reputation for prejudicial heteronormativity. Supporters of same-sex marriage depicted Mormons as blurring the boundary between church and state. They believed that there was not a collision course between church and state—unless churches were acting as the aggressor by crossing the line. A few days before the vote on Prop 8, a group released an ad titled "Home Invasion" that depicted two LDS missionaries forcibly entering the home of a lesbian couple, rifling through their drawers, taking their wedding rings, and then tearing up their marriage license. "Who's going to stop us?" they gleefully asked. The narrator instructed, "Say NO to a church taking over your government."[135] Even before the election was over, the mobilization against the LDS church had already begun. Opponents did not see LDS efforts against same-sex marriage as protecting Mormons' own religious freedom but as imposing their religious values on non-Mormons in their most intimate life decisions.

After Prop 8 passed, Mormons took the brunt of the backlash with protests erupting at temples and meetinghouses across the country.[136] Though Mormons made up only a small percentage of California voters, they were seen as the primary organizers and fund-raisers for the "Yes on 8" campaign. Within days after the election, opponents of Prop 8 called its supporters bigots, launched protests at LDS temples, committed vandalism on LDS churches, and organized boycotts against companies where Prop 8 donors worked.[137] Responding to public pressure, a handful of LDS members resigned from their jobs when their financial support of Prop 8 was revealed.[138] Two LDS temples received hoax anthrax letters, and church leaders feared that these trends could become widespread.[139] They saw these reactions as based in religious bigotry, turning the charges of bigotry against their critics.[140] Reed Cowan produced the documentary *8: The Mormon Proposition* that sought to expose the level of the church's involvement and depict Mormons as hateful. The election seemed to bring upon Mormons exactly the clash between themselves and others that they feared. The belief that social sanctions would be levied against opponents of same-sex marriage had some merit, but both sides disputed who threw the first punch.

### COUNTERFEIT MARRIAGE

The passage of Prop 8 launched a major legal battle in the courts as the issue worked its way up to the Supreme Court. Throughout this period, church leaders remained committed to describing same-sex relationships as inferior to the relationships of heterosexuals. In 2013, apostle David A. Bednar warned that "the counterfeit companionship advocated by the adversary is temporary and empty."[141] Because these relationships would not exist, presumably, in the afterlife, their temporariness made them inferior. Similarly, in 2015 apostle L. Tom Perry explained, "We want our voice to be heard against all of the counterfeit and alternative lifestyles that try to replace the family organization that God Himself established. . . . We must continue to project that voice throughout the world in declaring why marriage and family are so important, why marriage and family really do matter, and why they always will."[142] This language set up heterosexual families as real families and same-sex families as illegitimate alternatives. Same-sex intercourse could at one time be dismissed as illegal in the era of anti-sodomy laws. After that, same-sex relationships could be dismissed as inferior to the monogamous, stable, and state-sanctioned bonds of heterosexual marriage. Absent distinctions by the state, this normative evaluation of families as real or counterfeit could be rooted only in religious claims to divine favor.

The California Prop 8 cases were not ultimately the ones that were ruled on in the U.S. Supreme Court. On June 26, 2015, the Court issued its 5–4 decision to legalize same-sex marriage in *Obergefell v. Hodges,* a culmination of other state lawsuits. In the case, the LDS church had signed an amicus brief with other churches. The brief invoked some of the key doctrines that had defined the "family values" movement. First, it presented a theory of civilizational decline as a fundamental religious tenet: "We believe that children, families, society, and our Nation thrive best when traditional marriage is sustained and strengthened as a primary social institution." It specifically cited the 1995 Proclamation as evidence of LDS doctrines on the subject. Second, it grounded such a belief in "rational judgments" derived from pastoral therapy "counseling and serving millions of people."[143] The document also invoked the dubious social-scientific arguments about single-parent households as evidence for these religious beliefs, noting that boys without fathers would be more likely to join gangs, be violent, and end up in prison, and girls without fathers would be more likely to be promiscuous. The brief cited the opening lines of Jesus's prohibition on divorce (Matt 19:4–5)—a prohibition that the LDS church does not follow—as evidence for Jesus's support of male-female marriage. The question of whether animus was the motivation to oppose same-sex marriage was a key issue in the brief. Since Jesus did not mention homosexuality, it argued, belief in male-female marriage could not be attributed to animus. The signers affirmed that religious objection to same-sex marriage was done out of "concern, conviction, and love."[144]

After laying out the basis for religious objection to same-sex relationships, the brief turned to the legal arguments. It stated simply that same-sex marriage would lead to inevitable clashes with "religious liberty," claiming that such conflicts would happen in two ways. First, if same-sex marriage were enshrined in law, according to the signers, "it would stigmatize us as fools or bigots, akin to racists." If religious anti-homosexuality were no longer legally acceptable, it may soon become socially unacceptable and would "impede our full participation in democratic life."[145] If religious belief were not also reflected in the law, it would "demean" their beliefs. The social and legal plausibility of a claim that opposition to same-sex relationships was based in love was at stake. Second, the brief argued that the legal protections that come with marriage would eventually prevent religious-based discrimination against such couples. However, the brief did not make a consistent case. Rather, it said that decisions about same-sex marriage should be left to the states, making the aforementioned concerns inevitable in the states where same-sex marriage was legal. Ultimately, these arguments did not compel the majority on the Supreme Court.

When *Obergefell* was decided, the two-decades-long battle against same-sex marriage was over, and LDS leaders were on the losing side. Within hours, the church issued a concise statement: "The Court's decision does not alter the Lord's doctrine that marriage is a union between a man and a woman ordained by God."[146] The church also issued a statement to its members in the United States and Canada reiterating its teachings on the family, rooted in an interpretation of Genesis 1–2 and the Proclamation.[147] A few months later, in November 2015 the church increased the ecclesiastical sanctions against married same-sex couples who were members of the church. Apostle Russell M. Nelson soon claimed the new policy was a revelation—the highest level of authoritative church teaching.[148] The new rules defined a same-sex marriage as "apostasy" and grounds for immediate excommunication from the church. Further, the policy determined that the child of any person who was in a same-sex marriage would not be allowed to receive church ordinances, including a baby blessing, baptism, or ordination to the priesthood, or to serve a mission. A child of a same-sex married couple could be eligible for these ordinances when he or she turned eighteen years old and "specifically disavow[ed] the practice of same-gender cohabitation and marriage."[149] Even under these conditions, the child of a same-sex married couple would have to receive approval from the First Presidency to join the church and serve in it. Rejecting their parents was now a precondition for such children to be in the church.

In the minds of many Latter-day Saints, these sanctions called into question the claims that there was no animus in religious objections to same-sex marriage. The announcement of the policy brought a swift public outcry from faithful members and critics alike. Some people resigned their membership and expressed disapproval over the policy shift.[150] Emeritus member of the Seventy Marlin K. Jensen acknowledged publicly that it had "damaged" many members and that "it represented a serious setback in many quarters, which is regrettable and will take some time to repair."[151] Such members of the church saw the policy change as needlessly harsh, not only because it elevated same-sex marriage to the level of apostasy (while same-sex intercourse outside of marriage was considered a lesser sin) but also because it targeted the children of such couples.[152] Many pointed to an Article of Faith of Mormonism: "We believe that men will be punished for their own sins and not for Adam's transgressions." Applying this principle, these members argued that children were not responsible for the "sins" of their parents. Others cited the well-attested saying of Jesus "Suffer little children, and forbid them not, to come unto me: for of such is the kingdom of heaven" (Matt. 19:14; see also Mark 10:14 and Luke 18:16).[153] For these members, the policy singling out the children of same-sex couples was inconsistent with such religious principles. Children of those the church considered sexual "sinners," including those who had sex before marriage, adulterers, pedophiles, or pornographers, were not subjected to the same requirements—with the exception of polygamists. On theological and doctrinal grounds, at least some members of the church found the policy out of step with key Mormon teachings.[154]

Church leaders seemed unprepared for the outcry and the many questions it raised.[155] The First Presidency had to issue a clarification almost immediately to deal with how the policy affected children of divorced parents with shared custody, same-sex couples' children who had already joined the church or were already serving missions, and the case of whether children of same-sex couples might regularly attend church but not seek to join formally.[156] Apostle D. Todd Christofferson issued a scripted interview that explained that the policy "originates from a desire to protect children in their innocence and in their minority years."[157] If a child were a member of the church and the parents were not, it might create conflicts. Christofferson also noted that it was a parallel policy for children of polygamous families; they also must wait until age eighteen to join the church, disavow polygamy, and receive approval from the First Presidency. That is, in the minds of the church's leaders, polygamy and same-sex marriage were both apostate versions of the "true" definition of heterosexual, monogamous marriage. Regardless of the claims that this new policy was designed to help children, the results of the policy isolated same-sex families from Mormon communities through the harshest sanctions available and stigmatized them as dangerous to the community.

Since the 1950s and in more muted forms in the first part of the twenty-first century, church leaders warned against the threat of homosexual contagion and predation. Among the primary reasons for opposing same-sex marriage in the 1990s and into the next two decades was the effect it would have on children's psycho-developmental acquisition of heterosexuality. Church officials warned in "The Divine Institution of Marriage" that the children of same-sex families and those exposed to such families were more vulnerable to "gender confusion." It seems likely that church leaders still believed, only seven years after this document, that same-sex couples and the children of same-sex couples posed a risk of contaminating gender confusion by their presence. As much as the policy was sold as a measure to protect the children of same-sex families from the cognitive dissonance of attending a church that rejected their family as a "counterfeit," it seems possible that the policy was also a means of protecting LDS families from association with gender-confused parents and children in ecclesiastical contexts.

---

The church's involvement in the campaigns against same-sex marriage was the culmination of decades of political activism and participation in the politicization of "the family" up until that point. The theory of gender as a fragile and liminal condition of human experience guided these decisions. When the LDS church began to mobilize against same-sex marriage in the 1990s, some observers noted that it was in continuity with anti-ERA activities. There is no doubt that there were many strategies that were repeated between the two.[158] As with the ERA, church leaders declared same-sex marriage a "moral issue" to justify the use of political power, predicted dire consequences for families without normative gender roles enshrined in law, and moderated their own teachings on gender as an effect of political engagement. Furthermore, anti-ERA teachings explicitly linked women's equality with same-sex marriage and other rights for gay and lesbian persons.

At the same time, there were significant developments in the 1990s and next decade that rendered LDS political and psychological engagement with same-sex marriage and homosexuality as distinctive from that of the 1970s. First, LDS leaders collaborated more deeply and directly with other members of the Religious Right. During the ERA issue, LDS political mobilization was mostly parallel to that of other anti-ERA campaigning, but during the battles against same-sex marriage, LDS leaders joined formal coalitions with other religious leaders to coordinate efforts and resources. Catholics, in particular, proved to be productive partners in organizing and fund-raising. These connections were not just political but extended to the realm of therapeutic treatment.

Second, there was a change in LDS approaches to gender that attenuated previous teachings. Sexual difference was now much less dependent upon hierarchy between male and female than it was in the 1970s. Church leaders emphasized gender roles in heterosexual relationships less than they had in earlier decades, especially concerning women in the labor force and patriarchal rule in the home. Same-sex relationships now moved into the spotlight as the principal site of gender instability, replacing working women and women who wanted to lead equally with their husbands in the home. Heterosexuality was not only slowly replacing patriarchy but also looming much larger as it redefined the real threats to marriage. These changes put more of the burden of preserving sexual difference on the institution of mixed-sex marriage as the other threats—like working women, interracial marriage, and egalitarian relationships—faded away.

Mormon opposition to same-sex marriage has often been framed as motivated by a theology that places mixed-sex marriage at the center of salvation.[159] This may be true, but it overlooks the stated reasons that Mormons have offered for their political motivations and the psycho-developmental theories that underpinned these teachings. These reasons have been less about providing saving rites to opposite-sex couples and more about preserving a fragile psychological and social boundary between male and female—creating an "optimal environment" in society for LDS belief. Church leaders thought that preaching alone could not uphold sexual difference; society as a whole also needed to encourage meaningful distinctions between male and female. The political coalitions the church joined (and formed) were designed to ensure that sexual difference would exist in marriage law as a supplemental form of power that could instill these values. It ultimately boiled down to a belief that social institutions such as marriage, not just private actors or parents in the home, created the sufficient norms for sexual difference. Supposedly essential differences depended on cultural production.

*Chapter Five*

# THE DEATH AND RESURRECTION OF "THE HOMOSEXUAL"

In one of several online videos produced by the church in 2012, a young woman named Suzy told of her long-standing attraction to other women. Her story was not one of being cured or healed. She came to realize, "Yeah, this is part of me, it is going to be a part of me, and I'm okay. I just need to make it a healthy part of me and opposed to the unhealthy part of me that it's been for ten plus years."[1] In another video on the site, an older man, Ted, explained, "For myself as a gay person, that [loving yourself] has been really difficult. There's nothing worse than feeling you are not okay. It's only been as I have come to know Christ even more, as I have come to allow the atonement to apply in my life, that I know that I'm okay."[2] These videos were part of an outreach program called Mormons and Gays that not only used the term "gay" but encouraged straight members to be more welcoming and accepting of nonnormative identities in their congregations. The website featured numerous stories of individual members and family members of gay and lesbian Mormons and also interviews with church leaders, including apostles. Though the church was battling same-sex marriage during this period, its teachings were also undergoing subtle yet significant transitions to the paradigms that informed their views of gender and sexuality. A new theology was emerging that could accommodate gay, lesbian, and queer identities, within strict limits of acceptable practices.

This final chapter traces the intertwined theological, linguistic, psychological, and political transitions LDS leaders instituted in the first two decades of the twenty-first century. The period overlaps somewhat with the one discussed in the previous chapter, but this chapter looks at a parallel set of materials from inside the church. Overall, in this period church leaders grew somewhat more comfortable with nonheterosexual *identities*, even while they remained committed to the ontology of sexual malleability and heteronormative prescriptions for gay, lesbian, and queer individuals. As with previous tensions between doctrines of racial lineages and universal humanity, patriarchal and egalitarian marriage, women's paid labor and domestic responsibilities, reproductive and companionate sexuality for couples, and psycho-developmental and moral etiologies of homosexuality, church leaders now began to wrestle with nonheterosexual identities in more serious ways.

What prompted these changes? The therapeutic and political approaches and theories about gender malleability created new problems as they continued to fall short of their promises to change sexual attractions. This phenomenon elicited a theological review of how church leaders defined sexuality and identity. Church leaders quietly backed away from the ideals of reparative therapy and accepted that human agency may not be entirely at work in forming and transforming human desires. With these changes, LDS leaders created new doctrines to fit the new paradigms they were bringing to homosexuality. They grew increasingly comfortable with nonheterosexual identities but transferred the "inner" heterosexuality of human beings to the pre- and post-mortal state. Sexual malleability might be less relevant to promoting deliberative changes to one's sexuality, but nonheterosexual "feelings" were also going to be transformed in the next life. The overall approach to same-sex desire in this period reflected moderating pastoral wishes, but harsh treatment was never out of the question. It was a journey to get there.

## "SAME-GENDER ATTRACTION"

The shift in attitudes about sexual identity is closely related to a set of linguistic battles that played out in Mormon circles in the 1990s. "The Family: A Proclamation to the World" arrived at the same time as another major shift in LDS approaches to homosexuality. There was now a new preferred term to challenge the psychological and sociopolitical identities of homosexual, gay, and lesbian: same-gender attraction. This new terminology was part of a larger effort to redefine how the church approached these issues in preparation for the political fight against same-sex marriage. Sexual essentialism had not abated in the popular imagination, and a clearly defined alternative needed further support. By the mid-1990s, LDS leaders had been skeptical of the notion of fixed identity implied in the label of "homosexuality" for almost two decades. However, they had not yet settled on an alternative term; they mostly insisted on a grammatical distinction between homosexual as an adjective (reflecting an anti-essentialism view) versus homosexual as a noun (reflecting essentialism). The theories of heterosexual and homosexual fixity continued to push back against notions of gender and sexual malleability.

Up until then, this debate over fixity and fluidity had occurred primarily on the turf of psychological theories. But in the 1990s, biological approaches to homosexuality were gaining stronger intellectual currency. Geneticist Dean Hamer and his colleagues made headlines in 1993 after publishing a study suggesting the possibility of having found a "gay gene."[3] These findings were discussed in the major scientific journals, including *Science* and *Nature*.[4] As presented in the popular media, the findings suggested "that sexual orientation often is at least partly inborn, rather than being solely a matter of choice."[5] It seemed a major scientific vindication for those maintaining that sexual orientation was innate and therefore morally neutral. The scientific argument for an essentialist "inborn" sexual identity seriously challenged the project of change on which Mormon therapeutics had been built. Hamer and his colleagues' research was immediately controversial, and subsequent studies have qualified its basic assumptions. But for the moment at least in the mid-1990s, it seemed that biological science may actually explain homosexuality—without moral or psychological discourse. The flagging psychological explanations needed to respond to the biological claims to retain relevance.

LDS appropriation of the psychological paradigms made it difficult to avoid this direct scientific challenge. The most important LDS answer to the 1993 study by Hamer and his colleagues came in a landmark *Ensign* article by apostle Dallin H. Oaks in 1995, just one month after President Gordon B. Hinckley presented the Proclamation. In "Same-Gender Attraction," Oaks inaugurated a discursive revolution in Mormonism by deploying "same-gender attraction" as a rival scientific label to "homosexuality," staving off the new evidence in favor of sexual fixity. Responding to Hamer and his fellow researchers, Oaks fully appropriated the language of science for his own ends. After consulting with "qualified scientists and practitioners," Oaks wrote his article "to refute the claim of some that scientific discoveries demonstrate that avowed homosexuals and lesbians were 'born that way.'"[6] Mormons had been fighting against this claim since the 1960s, but it was getting harder.

Psychological theories of human subjectivity continued to do much of the heavy lifting for Oaks in explaining and opposing homosexuality. Oaks began his 1995 article by laying out a doctrinal opposition to same-sex relationships. God created male and female, so "what we call gender was an essential characteristic of our existence prior to our birth." By appealing to both the created order and the preexistent state, Oaks sought to provide a foundation for gender essentialism in order to counter claims of sexual essentialism. If males and females were essentially so, then they could not be homosexual by nature, he reasoned. His heteronormative description of essential male and female characteristics echoed the Proclamation, underlining how that document could be used against claims of homosexual identity. At the same time, these natural and created differences were at constant risk. Oaks believed that Satan seeks to "confuse what it means to be male or female." By grounding heterosexual sexual difference in the divine creation and homosexuality in satanic confusion, Oaks objected to sexual essentialism and biological determinism by pointing to its explanatory limitations. "The current evidence is insufficient," he insisted.[7]

Oaks noted that Hamer and his colleagues' gene study was not absolutely determinative of sexual orientation. But the gaps were narrower now. Oaks hedged some bets on the possibility that the scientific evidence might still vindicate the biological determinist position. Even while insisting that "attraction between man and woman was instilled by the Creator," Oaks admitted for the first time from a church leader, "Some kinds of feelings seem to be inborn."[8] This shift qualified the possibility of sexual change as LDS leaders began to settle for a new outcome of therapeutic care—a lifetime of celibacy rather than a total cure of thoughts and feelings. The new language of "same-gender attraction" designated a new kind of person, one who might desire but was not required (or permitted) to act on those desires. Like the term "homosexuality," however, the new term "same-gender attraction" reduced same-sex relationships to sexual attractions and desires.

Oaks was not capitulating to sexual essentialism in his admission about "inborn" feelings and still expressed the possibility of change. After citing a study that suggested sexual orientation developed from genes and that hormones influence how individuals interact with their environment, Oaks was still able to interpret it as supporting the "vital element of individual choice." Mormon notions of agency required the ability of a person to affect outcomes in both thoughts and behavior, even when the scientific explanations diminished the role of the will. Still, Oaks's statement that at least for some people same-sex attraction may be inborn or have some connection to "nature" represented a revision of earlier LDS teachings. Oaks instructed members "to use our God-given agency to choose the behavior that will lead us to our divine destiny."[9] The new emphasis on changing behavior, not desires, was an easier target to hit.

Just as he had been the forward-thinking author and instigator of the church's political posture toward same-sex marriage, Oaks now laid the groundwork for shifting the goalposts for therapeutic success in treating homosexuality. He compared the idea of an inborn set of homosexual feelings to other negative and compulsive behaviors. Gambling, addiction, and a "hot temper" may be inborn or acquired characteristics, but the doctrines of agency still required moral accountability despite susceptibility to such "disorders." "All of us," he explained, "have some feelings we did not choose." He taught that it was possible to resist and reform one's feelings to ensure that they do not lead to improper thoughts. This was a new distinction. The concession that feelings may not be chosen or controlled entirely by the will had important implications. Oaks clarified, "There is no Church discipline for improper thoughts or feelings."[10] If changing thoughts and feelings could not be achieved, success could still be counted as conforming to the expectations of complete chastity.

"Same-gender attraction" provided a worthy substitute for the sociopolitical terms "homosexual," "gay," and "lesbian." Earlier official LDS manuals, including *Understanding and Helping Those Who Have Homosexual Problems* from just a few years before, did not use this term. Even LDS psychologists did not employ this language yet.[11] The first usage of this kind of language in LDS literature seems to be in the 1994 autobiographical narrative of Erin Eldridge (pen name of Laurie Campbell), *Born That Way? A True Story of Overcoming Same-Sex Attraction with Insights for Friends, Families, and Leaders*, published by the church-owned press Deseret Book.[12] The book was also significant for being the first such work to put a woman's narrative at the center. Eldridge did not invent the term "same-sex attraction," but her language does appear to have been innovative in ex-gay Christian literature.[13] Oaks seemed to latch on to this new label, explaining, "We should note that the words homosexual, lesbian, and gay are adjectives to describe particular thoughts, feelings, or behaviors. We should refrain from using these words as nouns to identify particular conditions or specific persons. Our religious doctrine dictates this usage." He put to use this clinical language of having "same-sex attraction" to describe a "condition"; those affected by it "struggled," "are troubled," and carry a "burden."[14] He also indicated that it was a doctrinal requirement to reject labels of identity and to use this new term.

Even conceding that something might be "inborn" did not make for a fixed identity.

Ambiguity over the most appropriate terminology persisted. In 1998, President Hinckley spoke about the church's position on "those who consider themselves so-called gays and lesbians." The language here indicated a double hesitancy about any claims to a sexual identity or orientation—gays and lesbians were "so-called" and "consider themselves" to be such. This language reaffirmed the battleground over terminology and a reluctant use of these labels. No consistent use of terms dominated, though Ginger Hyde and Garrick Hyde's edited volume in 1997 was subtitled "Spiritual Insights from Latter-day Saints about Same-Sex Attraction."[15] Others, however, continued to refer to "homosexual problems" as the preferred term. For instance, in the same year that the Hydes published their book, Jason Park wrote his companion guidebooks, *Resolving Homosexual Problems: A Guide for LDS Men* and *Helping LDS Men Resolve Their Homosexual Problems: A Guide For Family, Friends, and Church Leaders.*[16] Continuing into the twenty-first century, A. Dean Byrd wrote *Homosexuality and the Church of Jesus Christ: Understanding Homosexuality according to the Doctrine of the Church of Jesus Christ of Latter-day Saints* (2001) and *Mormons and Homosexuality: Setting the Record Straight* (2008).[17] The doctrine that Oaks had declared against the term never fully took hold.

## INBORN?

Not every church leader was willing to accept the possibility of an "inborn" set of homosexual feelings, even in the highly qualified form that Oaks had offered. Genetic research still held only limited value against long-standing beliefs. In the same year that Oaks published his article, another apostle argued for a different cause of homosexuality: Satan. Oaks had taught that Satan seeks to confuse male and female genders, but James E. Faust admonished, "Satan is only interested in our misery, which he promotes by trying to persuade men and women to act contrary to God's plan. One way he does this is by encouraging the inappropriate use of sacred creative powers." Faust objected to any notion that homosexuality was genetic: "How can this be? No scientific evidence demonstrates absolutely that this is so. Besides, if it were so, it would frustrate the whole plan of mortal happiness. Our designation as men or women began before this world was. In contrast to the socially accepted doctrine that homosexuality is inborn, a number of respectable authorities contend that homosexuality is not acquired by

*The Death and Resurrection of "the Homosexual"*

birth. The false belief of inborn homosexual orientation denies to repentant souls the opportunity to change and will ultimately lead to discouragement, disappointment, and despair."[18] Specifically objecting to the possibility of "inborn" homosexual attraction that Oaks had laid out, Faust dismissed it as theologically impossible by appealing to creation and to the preexistence in Mormon cosmology. Divinely designated gender roles explained why heterosexuality must be naturally occurring and homosexuality a satanic deviation.

Psycho-developmental theories of the maladaptation of gender continued to be the primary explanation for "same-sex attraction." These views were frequently pushed to LDS members not only through the trainings and information campaign by Evergreen, the semi-independent reparative therapy advocacy organization, but also in official LDS publications aimed at the general membership. In an anonymous testimonial in the *Ensign*, a man treated by LDS Social Services therapists explained, "As I learned later through study, prayer, and counseling, same-sex attraction is often a misguided feeling motivated by a longing for true brotherly love or a desire for masculine characteristics one feels he lacks. My father is a good, hardworking man, but he was seldom home while I was growing up, which in my case contributed somewhat to my emotional deficit."[19] The psycho-developmental theory that homosexuality was caused by inappropriate attachments to men, often a result of having a weak father, informed this individual's recovery: "Until someone struggling with same-gender attraction learns to relate to men in a normal way, he won't be able to overcome his problem." The ways in which homosexuality remained a male problem—with male causes and solutions—was striking, even in the late 1990s. In contrast to the notion of a "natural" homosexuality that he had heard about from the psychiatric authorities at the hospital, this man learned a counternarrative to explain his thoughts as learned behaviors. His desires could be unlearned by controlling his thoughts. He reported, "I find it helpful to say a silent prayer every time I have an inappropriate thought and to replace the thought with a Primary song or a hymn." The man advised working with a bishop and to "seek professional help through LDS Social Services," where one could work with "inspired therapists."[20] For now, reparative therapy remained the treatment.

Latter-day Saints, in a way, did not believe that "the homosexual" actually existed. The supposed modern medicalization of the homosexual as a category of person always remained tenuous. The shift from a sexual "act" to a sexual "identity" in modernity never fully settled in Mormon thought. The view of homosexuality as an identity challenged Mormonism's conception of the natural, created, divine order for sexual practices. Mormon leaders were extremely hesitant to accept anything like sexual essentialism or the idea that nonheterosexuality is natural in any way. Instead, they relied on ideas of sexual malleability—the contingency of heterosexuality and the changeability of homosexuality. As queer theorist Eve Sedgwick has argued, the notion that homosexuality is a potentially universal phenomenon undergirds the rejection that it is a problem that exclusively affects only some people.[21] Sexuality was a norm, not an essence. To be sure, LDS leaders never thought of this fluidity outside of heteronormativity. There was one right way to be sexual. But because sexuality was mutable, putting young men (and women) at special risk, gender norms needed to be very rigid. For this reason, many Mormons saw homosexuality not as a mere sexual transgression but as a much more serious transgression of gender, which must be policed and assessed. Homosexuality warranted an entire apparatus for medical, scientific, and ecclesiastical control, in addition to the political power of the state.

HEALING IN THE NEXT LIFE

In 1995, when Dallin H. Oaks conceded that "some kinds of feelings seem to be inborn," his remark introduced a theological wrinkle: the gender- and sexual-essentialist views about human identity in the preexistence may not be reflected in human reality in the mortal realm. As gay and lesbian activists had long pointed out, religious appeals to creation as the ground for deducing the divine order could easily be shifted to include homosexuality as a natural and normal human experience. But Oaks was not without a response to this problem. He explained, somewhat obliquely, "Persons who desire to do what is right but through no fault of their own are unable to have an eternal marriage in mortal life will have an opportunity to qualify for eternal life in a period following mortality, if they keep the commandments of God and are true to their baptismal and other covenants."[22] This theological loophole had often been used to comfort those who could not marry—an essential saving rite in Mormon practice—for one reason or another. Rather than relying on the creation, Oaks pointed to the fall to explain the existence of "same-gender attraction" in the mortal sphere. His solution, underdeveloped at first, sprouted into a new way to think about homosexuality in these Mormon terms. The fallen world, a state of innocent imperfection, might account for "inborn" homosexual feelings of some, "through no fault of their own." If inborn homosexuality was a result not of free agency but of a fallen condition, the solution to the fall was a future redemption when God's intention for creation would be made perfect in the resurrection. Even if "inborn" homosexuality naturally existed in the fallen world, that did not mean that it would exist in the world to come. Even if unchosen homosexual feelings prevented a heterosexual marriage in this life, heterosexual marriage was available in the next, at least to those who resisted their homosexual attractions. This was the beginning of a new Mormon doctrine about "same-gender attraction" as a condition of a fallen world.

Boyd K. Packer was among the first to develop this new doctrinal position, even though he started from a set of assumptions different from Oaks's. He never seemed fully convinced by the various etiologies of homosexuality that were emerging, especially those that could have grounded homosexual feelings in creation, but he too found the afterlife a potent solution to the intractability of same-sex desires. While Oaks sought for scientific evidence in genes, hormones, and chemistry and others pushed psycho-developmental theories about weak fathers, Packer maintained his own views. In 2000, he continued to argue that homosexuality was learned, especially in teenage years through adolescent sex play: "There is the temptation to experiment, to tamper with the sacred power of procreation. These desires can be intensified, even perverted, by pornography, improper music, or the encouragement from unworthy associations. What would have only been a more or less normal passing phase in establishing gender identity can become implanted and leave you confused, even disturbed. If you consent, the adversary can take control of your thoughts and lead you carefully toward a habit and to an addiction, convincing you that immoral, unnatural behavior is a fixed part of your nature."[23] As he did in the 1970s when he described "innocent" childhood sex play, Packer saw childhood same-sex experimentation and interests as a "normal passing phase." This was a tenuous period for acquiring gender identity that could be derailed "if you consent" to temptations, ultimately becoming an "addiction." The notion of experimentation, addiction, and the awakening of passions suggested that homosexual contagion remained a threat to anyone who was exposed to these practices.

But there was something new in his thinking now. While Packer remained optimistic about the possibility of controlling same-sex desire, he now conceded, "That may be a struggle from which you will not be free in this life." Nevertheless, he explained that God did not create these "unnatural desires" and that "He can cure and He can heal."[24] Packer's declaration that perhaps one would not be freed from same-sex desires until the next life became an increasingly important framework for reconciling the failures of some efforts to change sexual orientation. It was also a reversal of his teachings in the 1970s that those who failed to acquire heteronormative gender identity in this life would be eternally stunted.[25]

As church leaders adopted different etiologies and became more comfortable with the possible persistence of same-sex desires, LDS members found new ways of telling their stories with this theology in mind. In 2002, the church magazine *Ensign* published a different kind of story about homosexuality. First, it was from the perspective of an anonymous woman who "felt same-sex attraction and acted on it." Female voices were rare in these conversations. She described the therapeutic effects of counseling meetings with her bishop and of the spiritual practices of attending church, fasting, prayer, and scripture study. However, she did not claim to have overcome her sexual attraction to women. "Many years have passed since that first meeting with my bishop," she explained. "I wish I could say that I never again struggled or felt same-sex attraction, but that would not be true. What I have gained, however, is the strength not to act on those feelings . . . and while I do not know if my healing will be complete in this life or in the next, I do know that God is aware of my efforts, that He is actively involved in my life, and that He will bless me with a complete and total healing when the time is right."[26] This reference to the new doctrine that same-sex desires may be "healed" in the next life was becoming embedded in the rhetoric of gay and lesbian members and allowed them to describe their experiences in new ways in officially sanctioned LDS literature. The author quoted Oaks's statement that some homosexual feelings may be "inborn" and concluded with Oaks that the origins of such feelings were not relevant to whether one "acts on" the feelings or not. Sexual malleability came to mark the transition from this life to the next. If heterosexuality could not be grounded in creation, it could at least be grounded in divine order for the afterlife.

Even those involved with Evergreen were beginning to have some doubts about a cure. In 2005, member of the Seventy James O. Mason delivered the keynote address to the annual Evergreen conference. Mason was the former U.S. assistant secretary for health and acting surgeon general of the United States during the George H. W. Bush administration. His remarks overall were optimistic; for instance, he stated that "through the enabling power of the Savior's atonement some with same gender attraction will be healed." But he engaged the growing doubts about the efficacy of reparative therapy, asking, "Can individuals struggling with some same gender attraction be cured?" He continued, "'With God nothing should [*sic*] be impossible' (Luke

1:37). It really doesn't matter, however, whether or not same gender attraction can be cured. The right course of action remains the same: eliminate or diminish same sex attraction. Control thoughts and never, never participate in homosexual or lesbian behavior."[27] By declaring that "it really doesn't matter" if there is a cure but still advocating controlling thoughts and avoiding participation in sexual activity, Mason could suggest that a cure may happen for some but not for others. But more importantly, he believed, controlling thoughts and refusing to have a same-sex romantic relationship was all that was required. His ambivalence about a cure was also a repudiation of so many of the promises of earlier church leaders.

The idea that perhaps homosexuality did not have a cure, at least not for every sincere seeker, inspired new analogies for the nature of these "feelings." Church leaders supplemented their previous descriptions of same-sex attraction as an addiction with new descriptions of same-sex attraction as a disability. With the possibility of incurable desires and perhaps even a genetic cause, church leaders expanded the comparison of homosexuality to other congenital defects. In 2006, LDS Public Affairs interviewed apostle Dallin H. Oaks and Lance Wickman, an attorney member of the Seventy. In the interview, Wickman compared the condition of same-sex attraction to the mental handicap of his own daughter, who may be limited in this life but may experience the full blessings of heterosexual marriage in the next life. Both his disabled daughter and the individual who experienced same-sex attraction were innocent victims of difficulties of a fallen world beyond their agency to address, but both would be redeemed in the next life. "Same-gender attraction," Wickman explained, "did not exist in the pre-earth life and neither will it exist in the next life."[28]

Church leaders' statements were now open to the possibility that some people might never be completely cured in this life. These ideas were increasingly disseminated in LDS literature. The pastoral document *God Loveth His Children* (2007) laid out some caveats for those who could not enter into heterosexual marriages: "The perfect plan of our Father in Heaven makes provision for individuals who seek to keep His commandments but who, through no fault of their own, do not have an eternal marriage in mortal life. As we follow Heavenly Father's plan, our bodies, feelings, and desires will be perfected in the next life so that every one of God's children may find joy in a family consisting of a husband, a wife, and children."[29] The statement seemed to repeat some of Oaks's 1995 explanation, including the idea that the feelings of those attracted to others of the same sex, "through no fault of their own," would not prevent heterosexual marriage in the afterlife. When introducing this new pamphlet, apostle Jeffrey R. Holland suggested, "Perhaps there is no present attraction to the opposite gender. Whatever the reason, God's richest blessings will eventually be available to all of His children if they are clean and faithful."[30] The idea that one's nonnormative sexual desires will go away in the next life allowed church leaders to both insist upon heterosexuality as an ideal while also admitting that same-sex desires may not be curable. Those who were "tested" by same-sex desires in this life will not lose out on the blessings of heterosexual marriage, though these "blessings" will be deferred to the next life. The new doctrine secured heterosexuality in God's will for the resurrection while acknowledging sexual fluidity as a condition of the mortal world. At the same time, death was also a moment of fluid transformation from one set of sexual desires to another. Even while being open to an unchanging sexual identity in this life, church leaders still relied on the mutability of sexual identity to explain why someone's desires would be oriented differently after death.

By 2012, this new doctrine of a temporal and temporary sexual fixity was completely ingrained in official church literature. On the church's pastoral website, LDS leaders taught that the lack of a cure in this life should not be a source of discouragement:

> We believe that with an eternal perspective, a person's attraction to the same sex can be addressed and borne as a mortal test. It should not be viewed as a permanent condition. An eternal perspective beyond the immediacy of this life's challenges offers hope. Though some people, including those resisting same-sex attraction, may not have the opportunity to marry a person of the opposite sex in this life, a just God will provide them with ample opportunity to do so in the next. We can all live life in the full context of who we are, which is much broader than sexual attraction.[31]

This new doctrine was official.

Church teachings at the outset of the 1990s insisted that "such thoughts and feelings, regardless of their causes, can and should be overcome."[32] Two decades later, church teachings suggested that such thoughts and feelings be "borne as a mortal test." Both doctrines, however, continued to rely on the idea of sexual mutability and the resistance to a singular homosexual identity. Whether through the triumph of the will or through the healing of the resurrection, individuals' mortal sexual desires were not a fixed or essential

*The Death and Resurrection of "the Homosexual"*

aspect of their *eternal* nature. Even if sexuality was not malleable in this life, it remained malleable for the next life.

No longer appealing to the created order as the foundation for heterosexuality nor relying on a scientific/psychological solution, church leaders invested more in extra-mortal cosmology and anthropology, including the pre-mortal and post-mortal human being, as the foundation for their teachings. The idealized, extraterrestrial heterosexual versions of the human being represented God's will better than the created world and mortal experiences. By grounding heterosexuality in the archetypal world, church leaders could now reject both nature and mortal experience as irrelevant to discerning the divine will. Without nature or experience, heterosexuality was a norm.

The new doctrine did have its critics. LGBTQ LDS members often accepted the teachings with a great deal of ambivalence. Blogger Josh Searle commented, "If the eternal blessings promised in Mormon doctrine of being married eternally to a woman are true, then count me out. But then again, count me in? You see, I want what I don't want. As an active Mormon who is attracted to men, I battle with what I naturally want with what I believe I'm supposed to want."[33] If Mormons like Searle could not desire heterosexually, they were also unconvinced that they should desire heterosexuality as their ultimate destiny. Additionally, the idea that one would be healed from certain desires after death seemed to be a problematic message for instilling a sense of worth and hope in this life for LGBTQ-identified members.

### CONTAGIOUS LANGUAGE

Church teachings about sexuality experienced another major transition during the first decade of the twenty-first century. As with changes about women's equality during the opposition to the ERA, the changes to LDS doctrines about homosexuality in this period must be placed in the context of significant social challenges to LDS teachings. The issue of the proper label remained an outstanding question, since many had fiercely resisted the sociopolitical terms "gay," "lesbian," or other cognates that suggested a fixed nonheterosexual identity. Since 1995, church leaders used "same-gender attraction" as the preferred term. Twenty years later, the linguistic argument persisted based on theories about the contagion caused by language and labels. For instance, in an interview, Dallin H. Oaks responded to a question about what he would say to his hypothetically gay son. He answered that "homosexuality is not a noun that describes a condition. It is an adjective that describes feelings or behavior."[34]

These views continued to define official LDS discourse in the new century. The 2007 pamphlet *God Loveth His Children* spoke to those "troubled with same-gender attraction." It continued to use "homosexual" only as an adjective, such as "homosexual tendencies," "homosexual behavior," and "homosexual feelings." In the same year, apostle Holland reported a conversation he had with a man. "I'm gay," the man said. Holland replied, "And . . . ?" The man was relieved by Holland's acceptance of this self-description. However, Holland quickly shifted to "same-gender attraction" and warned, "You serve yourself poorly when you identify yourself primarily by your sexual feelings. That isn't your only characteristic, so don't give it disproportionate attention."[35] Language remained a key battleground against notions of sexual fixity.

Other church leaders continued to teach that the labels "gay," "lesbian," and "homosexual" not only were inappropriate but could actually cause the behavior. At a conference in 2009 celebrating the twentieth anniversary of the founding of Evergreen, member of the Seventy Bruce C. Hafen gave the keynote address. Hafen was a former attorney and law professor who had served as an assistant to Oaks when he was BYU president in the 1970s and later functioned in numerous high-ranking positions at church-owned schools.[36] In keeping with the perspective of Evergreen, Hafen's remarks extolled the virtues and success of reparative therapy and the ex-gay movement. In his talk, he quoted heavily from LDS reparative therapists and advocates like A. Dean Byrd, Jason Park, Jeffrey Robinson, and David Pruden. Hafen emphasized that "the Church does not endorse specific methods of treatment" but promised "well over half of those seeking treatment can be significantly helped by it."[37] (The actual "success" rates are far lower.)[38]

Adhering to the reparative therapy doctrines, Hafen strongly objected to the idea of a fixed sexual identity. Heterosexuals could even be at risk. In his address, he insisted that same-sex attraction could be encouraged "when you cultivate lustful feelings, view pornography, label yourself as gay, or associate with activists who aggressively promote gay lifestyles." Recalling accounts of homosexual predatory recruitment, Hafen saw language as a key element of that battle. He rigorously insisted that it was a satanic lie to believe that "you are hopelessly 'that way.'" Rejecting claims to sexual essentialism, he taught that this "untrue assumption tries to persuade you to label yourself." Hafen proposed an alternative "true" fixed identity of sexual difference: "You are

*The Death and Resurrection of "the Homosexual"*

not simply a child of God. You are a *son* or a *daughter* of God, with all the masculine or feminine connotations of those words. That is your true, eternal identity." While Hafen insisted that one not build an identity around (homo) sexuality, he instead taught that one's "true" identity should be built around masculinity and femininity, which he assumed to be heterosexual.

History was also an important feature of this contest. In his declension narrative, Hafen expressed nostalgia for abandoned psychological views from a previous era. He explained, "In the early 1970s, the public and most lawyers, doctors, and therapists saw homosexuality not as normal adult behavior but as a psychological disorder." What changed? He advanced a conservative revisionist history: "We have witnessed primarily an aggressive political movement more than we've witnessed substantive change in the medical or legal evidence. In 1973, in response to increasing disruptions and protests by gay activists, the American Psychiatric and Psychological Associations removed homosexuality from their official lists of disorders. Significantly, they took this action by simply putting the issue to an open vote in their professional meetings—not because of any change in actual medical findings." His view, common in ex-gay rhetoric, depicted a political hijacking of the medical community that challenged the idea of scientific progress. Science was on his side, he believed. This historical and medical view, as problematic as it was, expressed the grievances of many who saw changing attitudes about homosexuality as politically driven but did not recognize the political motivations of their own anti-homosexuality teachings or the teachings that had informed the APA to begin with.[39] Hafen's views that same-sex attraction was a "psychological disorder," that no medical (or legal?) findings could refute this position, and that the label "gay" could cause homosexual behavior were published online at the LDS Newsroom, the official source of authoritative information about the church.

Despite his appeals to a fixed sexual difference, Hafen's take on human psycho-development was remarkably open to a contingent sexuality. Hafen relied directly on the neo-Freudian theories of gender inversion promulgated by reparative therapists and gave them the authority and legitimacy of official sanction. He explained, "Before puberty, boys are typically more interested in other boys than in girls . . . but a few boys don't make this transition." He suggested that homosexuality can begin at puberty when a "fixation" on a "fear that they are 'gay'" blocks "normal emotional-sexual development." With this (male) etiology of homosexuality, Hafen explained a (male) cure: "Adult men who have had such childhood experiences can often resume their normal development by identifying and addressing the sources of their emotional blockage, which usually includes restoring healthy, appropriate male relationships."[40] Here, homosexuality was again gendered as male (in spite of the mention of women, whose homosexuality he believed was caused by sexual abuse) and the solution was in "normal" relationships between men. Still, Hafen began with the idea that before puberty, attractions are not determined by gender, and that after puberty, they must be directed into "normal" heterosexual outlets. His hypothesis of a prepubescent nonhetero-sexuality framed heterosexuality as a contingent and fluid stage of human development, not a natural given.

## THE RETURN OF "THE HOMOSEXUAL"

Even while Hafen and others were warning against the injurious effects of "labels,"[41] in other areas the church made a significant change to how it considered linguistic practices. In 2007, the LGBT-rights ministry Soul-force Equality Riders came to protest the treatment of LGBT students at BYU. A few weeks later, BYU updated its policy on homosexual identity.[42] The university denied any connection between the events, but the timing of the change seemed significant.[43] The previous version read, "Advocacy of a homosexual lifestyle (whether implied or explicit) or any behaviors that indicate homosexual conduct, including those not sexual in nature, are inappropriate and violate the Honor Code."[44] What was meant by "implied" nonsexual behavior that indicated homosexual conduct? This had been inter-preted through the lens of prior teachings of church leaders that identifying as gay or lesbian constituted a nonsexual advocacy for homosexuality and contradicted church teachings that homosexuality was not an identity. In his 1995 article on same-gender attraction, Dallin H. Oaks had declared a "doctrine" forbidding the usage of identity labels. The updated text of the BYU policy now read, "One's stated sexual orientation is not an Honor Code issue."[45] The standards for sexual conduct did not change, requiring complete abstinence from any expression of same-sex affection. However, the ability to speak openly about same-sex desires and attractions softened the "don't say gay" approach that had been enshrined in BYU policy.

Some church leaders seemed to be growing more comfortable with using these labels again. The church's 2008 official position paper opposing same-sex marriage, "The Divine Institution of Marriage," explained, "The Church's opposition to same-sex marriage neither constitutes nor condones any kind of hostility towards homosexual men and women."[46] The usage of "homo-sexual" to modify "men and women" broke with previous linguistic taboos.

*The Death and Resurrection of "the Homosexual"*

This change in official communication that used such labels continued in outward-facing messages. In 2010, church spokesman Michael Otterson came out in favor of expanding gay rights: "While the Church is strongly on the record as opposing same-sex marriage, it has openly supported other rights for gays and lesbians such as protections in housing or employment."[47]

The growing comfort with these terms was fully realized in 2012, when the church launched a new pastoral website, www.MormonsAndGays.org. The site shifted between using "gay and lesbian" to refer to people, not just to thoughts or behaviors, and "same-sex attraction." It even flirted with the idea of a natural homosexual attraction: "Individuals do not choose to have such attractions," but "they do choose how to respond to them." In a featured video, apostle D. Todd Christofferson explained, "You'll see in some of these vignettes experiences that are recounted that people have found a diminishing of that same-sex attraction, almost to the point of vanishing, and others not at all."[48] While affirming the possibility of change for some, the website conceded that this was not possible for others.

In fact, the old orthodoxy continued to exist side by side with the new changes. In October 2010, Boyd K. Packer again challenged the notion of inborn homosexuality by pointing to the doctrines of agency: "Some suppose that they were pre-set and cannot overcome what they feel are inborn tendencies toward the impure and unnatural. Not so! Why would our Heavenly Father do that to anyone? Remember he is our father."[49] A few years later, Packer generated some controversy when he stated in another meeting, "A few of you may have felt or been told that you were born with troubling feelings and that you are not guilty if you act on those temptations. Doctrinally we know that if that were true, your agency would have been erased, and that cannot happen. You always have a choice to follow the promptings of the Holy Ghost and live a morally pure and chaste life, one filled with virtue."[50] He emphasized self-discipline as the solution to temptation. Because of his strong belief in agency, Packer never accepted Oaks's concession that some feelings may be "inborn."

Others shared Packer's view. In 2014, apostle David A. Bednar responded to a question about how to welcome homosexuals in the church, retorting, "There are no homosexual members of the church."[51] The comment was widely derided, but what did he mean? Bednar was not suggesting that such people did not exist but rather that the identity "homosexual" was illegitimate as a descriptive term for people. He was drawing on the earlier teachings that the use of such terms obscured a person's "true" identity and could even cause illicit behavior. For Packer and Bednar, that meant that there was no such thing as a homosexual, either as a created identity or as a fallen identity. Even though a few years earlier official church statements and BYU had begun to use such terms again, there was an apparent internal disagreement among church leaders about the appropriateness of certain kinds of linguistic formulations.

The proper use of labels remained an open debate in the church because of the conflicting messages about etiology. Despite these objections to the impossibility of a homosexual orientation, some church leaders continued to pursue a middle road that allowed for both the persistence and the mutability of same-sex desires. In 2016, the church reaffirmed its reversal of previous doctrine that opposed identification as gay or lesbian. In an essay on same-sex attraction on the church's website, the church formally declared, "Identifying as gay, lesbian, or bisexual or experiencing same-sex attraction is not a sin and does not prohibit one from participating in the Church, holding callings, or attending the temple."[52] Officially, the church had given up the fight against labels, but it remained cautious.

The policies at BYU and the language of Christofferson, Otterson, and others made use of the labels "homosexual," "gay," and "lesbian" in part because they were more accepting of such identities. These ideas were rejected by Packer, Bednar, Hafen, and others, but the emergence of a split was significant. The new theological space to affirm a possible "inborn" set of same-sex attractions and the deferral of "healing" until the next life was an accommodation to a changing culture and a response to the weakened place of psycho-developmental approaches and solutions.

## NEW APPROACHES TO THERAPY

Reparative therapy remained a major practice through the middle of the 2010s. Surveys have shown that possibly as many as two-thirds of same-sex-attracted Mormons and former Mormons between 2005 and 2015 had undergone some kind of change effort.[53] In 2009, a book for therapists was published by the Foundation for Attraction Research, an LDS-member-run nonprofit, titled *Understanding Same-Sex Attraction: Where to Turn and How to Help*.[54] The volume's authors included A. Dean Byrd and other reparative therapists who repudiated ideas of innate homosexuality and taught that "same-sex attraction *can* be lessened or eradicated in those who desire change and are willing to try." LDS Family Services sponsored a conference based on the book in 2011.[55] The book referred readers to seek reparative therapy from LDS Family Services and Evergreen.[56]

*The Death and Resurrection of "the Homosexual"*

Evergreen's direction wavered in the 2010s. This was part of a larger trend in the ex-gay movement. Exodus International, the Christian ex-gay umbrella organization, closed its U.S. ministry in June 2013. In a stunning address, Alan Chambers, the longtime president of Exodus, apologized for having promoted sexual reorientation change efforts and for the pain he and the organization had caused individuals and their families. He was no longer convinced that change was possible or advisable.[57] Other significant defectors from this ideology came out around this time as well.[58] Though individual ministries continued to operate, Exodus's closure and repudiation of reparative therapy dealt its popularity and credibility a serious blow.

Similar shifts were happening in the LDS community, but they played out somewhat differently. On January 1, 2014, Evergreen's executive director, David Pruden, announced its closure and consolidation into North Star International to create "a single faith-based ministry organization for Latter-day Saints who experience same-sex attraction or gender identity incongruence."[59] The lumping together of same-sex attraction and gender identity issues continued to present them as related phenomena of gender fluidity. The merger was defined as combining efforts and resources and providing North Star with "an established network." Unlike in the case of Exodus, there was no apology or repudiation of reparative therapy when Evergreen closed. However, other officials associated with Evergreen were changing their approaches. Just after shuttering, former Evergreen executive director David Matheson publicly distanced himself from his mentor Joseph Nicolosi and reparative therapy. He explained, "I don't want to be known as a reparative therapist. I'm just a therapist, albeit one with a particular understanding of the semi-plasticity of human sexuality."[60] The therapeutic acceptance of gender and sexual malleability, or plasticity, was the foundation of reparative therapy, though Matheson had come to believe it was not workable for everyone.

The reasons for the collapse of Evergreen were multifaceted. North Star had sucked the membership and energy from Evergreen with a new organizational model and advertising built for the age of social media. But North Star also represented an ideological approach to homosexuality different from Evergreen's. Ty Mansfield, a visiting professor at Brigham Young University, had founded North Star just a few years before. Mansfield identified as someone challenged with same-sex attraction, but he also became a prominent spokesperson for mixed-orientation marriages.[61] He emphasized that these kinds of marriages were not a universal option for many men but suggested that for at least some, they could be fulfilling.

Mansfield's ministry included numerous books published by the church's commercial press.[62] He was also featured prominently on the church's 2012 website, www.MormonsAndGays.org.

While Evergreen's website had declared, "You don't have to be gay," North Star offered a different message. It took no position on the origin or mutability of sexual desires and emphasized that when therapy was undertaken, it should follow the principles of self-determination, not necessarily reparative therapy.[63] Many North Star leadership representatives identified as gay men—not "ex-gay"—who married straight women. They did not promise a cure, let alone suggest that one can transform their sexuality. Still, they created "options" for gay men who were interested in marrying women and living within the strictures of Mormon sexual and cultural norms. The shift in perspectives from an ex-gay organization to a gay organization that affirmed identities and desires, within limitations, and supported mixed-orientation marriages was a queerish alternative.

The shuttering of Evergreen weakened but did not eliminate reparative therapy. The practice continued to enjoy the support of many LDS therapists in private practice. Reparative therapist Michael D. Williams drew some controversy in 2015 when he advertised his services in the Sunday church meeting schedules at BYU–Idaho. After some public outcry, his proposed event was canceled, a sign that at least some officials were retreating from the reparative therapy brand.[64]

MORMON *AND* GAY

The 2016 relaunch of MormonAndGay.lds.org, with a subtle but significant name change, tried to capture the idea that one could be both Mormon and gay and to create an inclusive environment within the church. Like the earlier pastoral version www.MormonsAndGays.org, the updated site emphasized love toward all and featured short videos of high-ranking church leaders and stories of gay and lesbian church members and their families.[65] However, rather than describing "Mormons" and "gays" as two separate categories, the new title acknowledged the overlap. Member of the Seventy L. Whitney Clayton's introductory video explained, "We want you to know we love you. You are welcome. We want you to be part of our congregations. You have great talents and abilities to offer God's kingdom on earth and we recognize the many valuable contributions you make."[66] This was an explicit effort at greater inclusion. Much of this message was targeted at heterosexual members. The videos of church leaders pleaded for a change in the way gay

*The Death and Resurrection of "the Homosexual"*

members were accepted in church. "The gospel of Jesus Christ does not marginalize people," explained the First Counselor in the Young Women's General Presidency, Carol F. McConkie; "people marginalize people and we have to fix that."[67]

Though the videos did not feature stories of anyone claiming to be cured, the website still offered qualified messages that reparative therapy may still be an option. "When one seeks therapy," the site advised, "the Church recommends approaches that respect 'client self-determination.' In other words, the individual has the right to determine desired outcomes, and therapists and counselors should respect his or her wishes. . . . While shifts in sexuality can and do occur for some people, it is unethical to focus professional treatment on an assumption that a change in sexual orientation will or must occur. Again, the individual has the right to define the desired outcome."[68] There was some equivocation here, and the language of "client self-determination" was a guiding principle of reparative therapists as a way to buttress against mounting criticism of their methods.[69] This view promised that change of sexual orientation can occur and that individuals should be able to pursue this path if they want to. At the same time, it warned that it is "unethical" to expect that such changes should occur—namely, the approach the church advocated in previous decades. This did not close the door on reparative therapy, but it was a muted advocacy.

The question of labels remained a preoccupation of the updated Mormon and Gay website, even as the title of the site included the contested term. It explained the differences between same-sex attraction, gay and lesbian, gender dysphoria, and transgender.[70] Sexual fluidity was explicitly a part of this message: "Sexual desire can be fluid and changeable. If you are questioning, you should not feel pressured or rushed to reach conclusions about your sexuality."[71] It explained, "Our identity may be in flux, but there is one aspect of who we are that is eternally fixed." While sexual desires may be fluid, one's gender identity is primarily as a son or daughter of God. The site warned, "Labels can affect how we think about ourselves and how others treat us and may expand or limit our ability to follow God's plan for our happiness."[72] It also explained, "Identifying oneself as gay or lesbian is not against Church policy or doctrine; however, it may have undesired consequences in the way one is treated."[73] These cautions appealed to whether or not it was exigent to adopt nonheterosexual labels, warning that they may make life harder, but did not oppose them on any other principle.

The site's videos featuring members of the church did not reflect this same level of concern about labels. The gay and lesbian members offered familiar coming-out stories of a realization at some point about their desires, of childhood bullying by friends or family about perceived shortcomings in gender performance, and of eventual peace with recognizing and coming to terms with a nonheterosexual identity. A twenty-something named Jessyca identified as "gay" and came to this realization as a missionary but first admitted it in counseling after her mission. Her therapist "turned to me with tears in his eyes and he said, I want you to fast and pray and I want you to ask God what he thinks about you being attracted to women."[74] In response to her prayer, she felt a sense of peace that she did not "choose this" but still wanted to know how she would be able to live in the church. "I remember hearing the words, 'Just stay with me. Just a little longer, just stay with me,'" she recounted. After she came out publicly, "I am able to be myself." In this instance, the spiritual experience and therapeutic outcome was not conversion to heterosexuality but an acceptance of a gay identity along with a commitment to celibacy.

In another feature, Andy explained, "I'm gay. I hate saying that that doesn't define me because it does. It's a big part of what defines me."[75] His mother, Tonya, testified that she knew he was gay from the time he was an infant. Andy and his parents talked about the problem of reconciling his identity with church teachings, and his parents admitted that they did not have all the answers. They all learned to live with "spiritual ambiguity." His parents said that while Andy was then active in the church, they did not know where he would be in twenty years. Regardless of how things ended up, they insisted they would always love him and that would never change. This kind of story was ambivalent about the correct path for Andy and allowed Andy to express his sexual identity. Rather than challenging Andy's identity or promising change or blessings for his celibacy, the Mormon and Gay website reaffirmed the parents' choice to love him unconditionally.

Not all those interviewed for the website were comfortable with such labels. Many who were over thirty were less comfortable with the terms "gay" and "lesbian." In one case, Ricardo talked about "my SSA [same-sex attraction]," reflecting earlier teachings that this was the preferred language.[76] Laurie Campbell, who had used the pen name Erin Eldridge in her 1994 book, *Born That Way? A True Story of Overcoming Same-Sex Attraction with Insights for Friends, Families, and Leaders*, explained in her online vignette that categorizing herself by her sexual orientation was "a hindrance" and that she rejected any label.[77]

The different uses of language on the Mormon and Gay website reflected the moment of transition from the previous decade in the battle over language. The site defended the ability of people to self-define and stated, "If you're wondering what someone means when they say, 'I'm gay,' just ask them."[78] It offered some advice about coming out and suggested, "If you decide to share your experiences of feeling same-sex attraction or to openly identify as gay, you should be supported and treated with kindness and respect, both at home and in church."[79] The church invited members to be out of the closet while staying in the church. At the same time, it offered a conflicting set of ideologies about labels and identity as equally acceptable. But not all identities were acceptable. Trans issues grew increasingly fraught in this period.

## TRANS ISSUES

Notably minimized from the various pastoral efforts and even changes in terminology that were happening in this period was anything about trans identity. Since the 1970s, LDS leaders had seen trans identities as a particularly egregious form of homosexuality because of the way they conflated sexual and gender identity. By the first decade of the new century, trans theory had significantly evolved to challenge these misconceptions in public discourse. These representations moved away from the earlier views that a trans person was the soul of one gender trapped in the body of another gender. The term "transsexual" gradually fell out of favor for its reliance on an artificial sex/gender distinction, and "trans" and "transgender" replaced it, along with other terms and identities such as "genderqueer." Adopting the emergent ideas of queer theory—that gender was nonbinary and performative rather than essentialist—trans folk found new ways to talk about their experiences and to reengage with gay and lesbian activism.[80]

Though there were some instances of public attention to trans issues in the 1990s in LDS contexts, these tended to be salacious rather than salubrious.[81] It was not until the 2010s that trans issues emerged in mainstream LDS conversations about gender. This may have reflected the broader context of a renewed focus on trans issues in popular culture.[82] Trans characters and actors were appearing in popular television and Internet programming. Even in religious communities, trans issues were increasingly in the spotlight. Pope Francis had recently made news by inviting a trans man to the Vatican, embracing him, and reassuring him that there is a "corner in the house of God" for him.[83] There were major debates about transgender use of bathrooms in 2016 and 2017, when North Carolina passed (and later repealed) a bill to restrict bathroom use to the gender assigned at birth. Other Republican-controlled states introduced similar legislation.[84] The LDS church filed a brief in support of the so-called bathroom bills.[85]

At the same time, the number of advocates for trans issues was growing in the 2010s in progressive circles, including in Mormon communities. In 2013, the flagship gay and lesbian Mormon organization, Affirmation, changed its name to be more inclusive. Originally called "Affirmation: Gay Mormons United," and soon after "Affirmation: Gay and Lesbian Mormons," the new name in 2013, "Affirmation: LGBT Mormons, Families, and Friends" now explicitly included bisexual and transgender people and LGBT allies. In 2014, *Transmormon,* a fifteen-minute documentary film, told the story of a young Mormon's gender transition and of her supportive family. The film won numerous awards, was featured in dozens of media outlets, and went viral on social media. Equality Utah, an LGBT advocacy group, sponsored a Transgender Awareness Project that featured transgender Mormons.[86]

LDS leaders seemed to be willing to rethink trans issues and began to decouple it from sexual immorality but made no formal changes. In a rare interactive interview held at the end of January 2015, high-ranking church leaders fielded public questions on LGBT issues. Church members flooded the moderator with queries about how to navigate the tension between supporting family members and friends and following one's conscience on LGBT issues when it was at variance with current church teachings. A mother said, "I have a transgender son who came out to us about a year ago. . . . I hate having to fear what retaliation [from church leaders] I might have for supporting him. . . . I think we as members need that assurance that we can indeed have our own opinions, support our children, and still follow our beliefs." Apostle Dallin H. Oaks responded to the mother's request with a rare admission: "This question concerns transgender, and I think we need to acknowledge that while we have been acquainted with lesbians and homosexuals for some time, being acquainted with the unique problems of a transgender situation is something we have not had so much experience with, and we have some unfinished business in teaching on that."[87] Despite the church's policy since the 1970s that required excommunication for trans individuals, Oaks's tone was conciliatory and optimistic. He expressed some reservations about current church teachings on transgender issues, anticipating that more experience might lead to changes. These experiences appear to be what motivated Oaks's acknowledgment that church teaching was not yet up to the task of dealing with transgender individuals.

Some seized on this admission. In the Mormon context, the chance to rethink some fundamental teachings about gender in light of transgender

*The Death and Resurrection of "the Homosexual"*

experiences represented a huge opportunity. John Gustav-Wrathall, then an Affirmation board member who was active in the LDS church even after being excommunicated, said of Oaks's statement, "Given the background and the history, it is actually an astonishing statement to me. I think it is really the first time that I've seen a church leader with that high of a rank even using the term *transgender* at all." What's more, it is "significant to have church leaders acknowledge that they don't know about an issue." For some, Oaks's statement represented a responsiveness to the conversations that had been occurring in recent years and an acknowledgment of the work that was still to be done.[88]

There were other signs that LDS leaders were disentangling sexuality from gender. On the updated Mormon and Gay website, there was a clarification for why the site did not address "gender dysphoria," the term that had come to replace "gender identity disorder" in psychological discourse.[89] The site explained, "Many of the general principles shared on this website (for example, the importance of inclusion and kindness) apply to Latter-day Saints who experience gender dysphoria or identify as transgender. However, same-sex attraction and gender dysphoria are very different. For example, those who experience gender dysphoria may or may not also experience same-sex attraction, and the majority of those who experience same-sex attraction do not desire to change their gender. From a psychological and ministerial perspective, the two are different."[90] A decade before, in "The Divine Institution of Marriage," Latter-day Saint leaders had been arguing that same-sex relationships would cause "gender confusion" in children. On this relaunched website, they were careful to distinguish gender from sexuality and insist that they be treated as separate issues.

Part of the difficulty trans Mormons faced is that some church meetings and rituals and priesthood ordination are strictly separated along gender lines. Therefore, the perception of ambiguity of gender identity had important practical implications for participation in the faith. According to church policy, members who had undergone an "elective transsexual operation" were not eligible to worship in gender-separated special temple rites or to receive the priesthood. Any LDS member considering surgery was warned that it may result in formal church discipline. A trans prospective member of the church could be baptized only with approval from the highest governing body in the church, but anyone even considering transition-related surgery was barred from joining the faith.[91]

But new precedents made it clear that even nonsurgical transitions may be prohibited. In 2012, Laurie Lee Hall was quietly released from her calling as stake president after revealing her female identity to a select few. In 2016, she came out during Sunday church testimony meeting to the members of her congregation in Tooele, Utah, and resigned a few months later from her employment. At fifty-six years old, Hall's case was particularly interesting because not only had she been serving as a stake president at the time that she acknowledged her identity, but she had been an employee at the church's headquarters as chief architect over temple design. After coming out to her ward, Hall's local church leaders offered her the choice to either return to living as a man or face excommunication. She refused to detransition and was excommunicated in 2017.[92]

Hall's case raised difficult questions. What of those who identified and lived trans lives but did not undergo surgery? What about those who took hormones? What about those who elected facial reconstruction, mastectomies or breast implants, or other surgeries that non-trans individuals might also undertake?[93] Hall had not undergone any surgical changes and expressed that she had no plans to do so. Her case made it clear that bodily integrity was not the issue but that performed gender remained central to LDS orthopraxis. Heteronormative gender roles were not about bodies or about one's body of birth but about performing masculine or feminine roles, dress, and comportment.

## FROM FAMILY VALUES TO RELIGIOUS FREEDOM

The actions on trans bathroom rights were representative of a major shift in legal concerns that drove political action. Since 2009, LDS leaders have given dozens of speeches on religious freedom in General Conference and at LDS and non-LDS universities around the country, created public campaign social media videos and images, and launched a website to train LDS members on how to have "conversations" to advocate for religious freedom. Church leaders cautioned that religious freedom was under attack in the era of same-sex marriage and that churches and religious people could be disenfranchised because of their dissent from the law. Concerns about religious freedom were not new to the fight against same-sex marriage; as discussed in the previous chapter, LDS leaders had expressed their worries about religious freedom as far back as their efforts in Hawaii. The courts, however, had disagreed, arguing that LDS and Catholic interventions not only were based on unfounded fears about religious freedom but also were a violation of the establishment clause prohibiting religious preference in the law.

*The Death and Resurrection of "the Homosexual"*

For LDS leaders, the rhetoric of religious freedom was a familiar retreat in hard times. They had often fallen back on appeals to religious freedom when they were out of step with national norms. Church leaders had invoked religious freedom to defend the practice of men marrying multiple women in the nineteenth century and the practice of racial exclusion from the priesthood and temple in the twentieth century. In the case of polygamy, the church had faced actual legal restrictions that prohibited the free exercise of religion—the right to perform marriages they believed were ordained by God.[94] Mormonism had a real history of legal persecution, and the images and memory of church leaders jailed for polygamy remained a crucial aspect of Mormon distrust of government interference with religion—especially when it came to marriage. In the case of its teachings on race, the church never faced any legal restrictions but did confront negative cultural opinions and social consequences for those beliefs and practices. Church leaders defended themselves, at least in the short run, by claiming that religious beliefs that others saw as socially harmful should be respected. As religious freedom arguments had been used to justify patriarchal and racial hierarchy and privilege, now they were used to emphasize heterosexual hierarchy and privilege as matters of religious conscience.

Just what religious freedom meant was something of a moving target. In their opposition to same-sex marriage, LDS church leaders had used religious freedom rhetoric to oppose any recognition of same-sex marriage as a right. On October 13, 2009, Dallin H. Oaks delivered a speech at BYU–Idaho that focused on the coming court battles over Prop 8 and that also laid the foundations for a new pivot to politicizing the relationship between LGBT rights and religion. He directly addressed the reputation that the LDS church had earned in the wake of Prop 8 for seeking to take away the right to marry from Californian gay and lesbian couples. Oaks did not see anything wrong with the religious motivation to define civil marriage and denied that marriage was an issue of civil rights at all: "The Proposition 8 battle was not about civil rights, but about what equal rights demand and what religious rights protect." He warned, "Those who seek to change the foundation of marriage should not be allowed to pretend that those who defend the ancient order are trampling on civil rights. . . . Religious freedom needs defending against the claims of newly asserted human rights."[95] Religious freedom, he believed, was dependent on heterosexual-only marriage.

Oaks's strong statement that same-sex marriage proponents "should not be allowed to pretend" that this was a matter of civil rights revealed how much LDS officials resented their stigmatization as anti-gay. In response, LDS leaders sought to show good faith by looking for respectful compromises and areas where they might agree with gay rights activists. In 2009, church leaders surprised many by publicly supporting LGBT antidiscrimination legislation for housing and employment in Salt Lake City because these protections "do no violence to the institution of marriage."[96] On the issue of nondiscrimination laws in the nonreligious marketplace, the church broke with other conservatives in supporting what it saw as "reasonable" accommodations for LGBT individuals and families. The church repeatedly advertised its support and advocacy of rights in medical, housing, employment, and probate spheres.[97] In exchange, church leaders asked for protections for the exemption of church-run institutions from these laws.

Even while LDS leaders were seeking to cooperate with new LGBT allies in carving out a compromise between LGBT rights and religious freedom, they continued to build on the friendly cooperative relationships they had forged with other conservatives to oppose same-sex marriage. After 2009, Prop 8 was being challenged in the courts and faced a possible judicial overruling on U.S. constitutional grounds. Oaks delivered a cri de coeur on religious freedom in an address to Chapman University School of Law, a private school in California affiliated with the Disciples of Christ church, on February 4, 2011. The backdrop of the ongoing legal battle over Prop 8 loomed large in his remarks. In this speech, Oaks argued religion and freedom were linked. He challenged the secularist idea that religion impeded freedom and drew upon conservative historiography that saw religion as an unqualified force for good in society. He noted that religion contributed a great deal to the United Sates and reasoned that this meant that citizens needed the "influence of religion in our public life."[98] Oaks worried about trends that would "brand religious beliefs as an unacceptable basis for citizen action or even for argument in the public square," casting any who disagreed with religious influence on public policy as engaged in "anti-religious bigotry" and "intimidation," which is "anti-democratic." While Oaks championed the free exercise clause of the First Amendment of the U.S. constitution, he avoided the limits set out in the establishment clause.

LDS calls for religious freedom were increasingly acute. In this same speech, Oaks proposed a new coalition modeled on the Religious Right that would be more broadly based and more narrowly focused. "The religious community must unite," he explained. "It is imperative that those of us who believe in God and in the reality of right and wrong unite more effectively to protect our religious freedom to preach and practice our faith in God and the principles of right and wrong He has established." Oaks contrasted this proposed coalition with Jerry Falwell's Moral Majority, which was mostly evangelical and Republican. Instead, Oaks wanted to create a religious political movement with a narrower agenda that was not tied to a particular party or particular religious tradition: "I speak for a broader principle, non-partisan and, in its own focused objective, ecumenical. . . . This proposal that we unite more effectively does not require any examination of the doctrinal differences among Christians, Jews, and Muslims, or even an identification of the many common elements of our beliefs. All that is necessary for unity and a broad coalition along the lines I am suggesting is a common belief that there is a right and wrong in human behavior that has been established by a Supreme Being."[99] This ecumenical goal of religious freedom replaced the ecumenical goal of family values, which was also meant to unite disparate people in common beliefs about a shared, neutral principle. Oaks saw the organization of a new political movement as an extension of his ecclesiastical duties in the same way that previous leaders of the Religious Right had— religious and legal norms were joint projects.

The first test for this new coalition on religious freedom arose in the 2012 election—and Mormons largely sat out of it. Conservatives claimed that President Barack Obama's signature health care access legislation, "Obamacare," was an attack on religious freedom, especially for Catholics, because it required employers to offer insurance that included birth control options for women. Catholics and evangelicals led the charge against this requirement in court and in the media. A relatively low-ranking LDS General Authority was a signatory to a letter in 2012, "Standing Together for Religious Freedom: An Open Letter to All Americans."[100] The letter acknowledged that not all its signatories held religious objections themselves against contraception but that as a matter of principle they united together to defend the religious freedom of those who did hold such objections. Otherwise, the LDS church was uninvolved in the birth control battles of 2012. This may have been because in the contemporary LDS church, birth control was largely uncontroversial, or perhaps because any political action from the church in 2012 may have negatively affected Republican presidential candidate Mitt Romney.[101] But even in the years since 2012, church leaders have only rarely mentioned birth control as an issue of religious freedom. The church's own training materials to educate people about religious freedom made no clear mention of it.[102]

After Romney's failed bid for the U.S. presidency, in 2013 LDS leaders again began to invite several prominent evangelicals to join them in a coalition for religious freedom.[103] The 2012 election season had been rocky as evangelicals expressed tepid support at best for Romney because of his Mormonism, while other evangelicals openly criticized him because of it.[104] However, undeterred by these setbacks, LDS leaders forged ahead in an effort to build greater relationships of trust. Evangelicals seemingly embraced these overtures. Speaking of the Evangelical-Mormon coalition, Richard Land, president of the Southern Evangelical Seminary, explained, "We are common targets in this. The secularists are out to circumscribe our constitutional rights."[105] Others were supportive but expressed some reservations about cooperation with Latter-day Saints. Albert Mohler, president of Southern Baptist Theological Seminary, gave a speech at BYU on October 21, 2013. He warned, "The moral revolution revolving around marriage, the family, and human sexuality is now clearly becoming a religious liberty issue." Dramatically, he declared, "I do not believe that we are going to heaven together, but I do believe we may go to jail together."[106] Like the old coalition of the Religious Right, the new coalition for religious freedom eschewed doctrinal differences for collaboration against a common enemy—same-sex marriage. Religious freedom was the new family values for evangelicals as well.

Church leaders were proud of their political organizing. In a 2014 training meeting, apostle L. Tom Perry reportedly boasted, "You would be amazed at the network we have among other religious organizations to protect religious freedom." Still, he worried about the coming changes if same-sex marriage were to be legalized. For Perry, these were still strictly partisan concerns, and he communicated his own partisan preferences to local leaders. He mused, "Unfortunately the Supreme Court is listening to the voice of the people through the [Obama] administration that is currently in place." He laid out a solution for the local leaders:

> The individual members of the Church must step up and
> get involved. It must come from the people, not the General
> Authorities. As local leaders you have a fine line to walk between
> dictating and teaching the doctrine so that there will be a revival
> of lay members stepping up to fight for God's cause. So that people
> in important positions and courts will see that the majority voice
> of the people will always be in favor of the Lord. If we do not
> follow Him you can expect calamities to come. He will not let this
> go forward to destroy the basic family unit He has created for the
> progression of His children. We have a great responsibility on us
> and I hope you take it seriously.[107]

*The Death and Resurrection of "the Homosexual"*

Church leaders like Perry used local training meetings to politically mobilize a "revival" among church members. They hoped that "teaching the doctrine" would lead straight to mass political action without having to directly connect the dots.

Despite the network connections, LDS leaders positioned themselves as a more reasonable alternative to other members of the Religious Right. For instance, Oaks was critical of Kim Davis, the Kentucky county clerk who achieved some notoriety for refusing to issue marriage licenses to same-sex couples.[108] Furthermore, LDS leaders wanted to model a productive and realistic strategy that was based on compromise with LGBT groups, not a zero-sum war. On January 27, 2015, church leaders released a series of proposals for "laws that protect religious freedom" to be adopted across the United States. The proposals framed the need for both religious freedom and LGBT rights. Adopting the slogan "Fairness for All," the church advocated an "approach that balances religious freedom protections with reasonable safeguards for LGBT people—specifically in areas of housing, employment and public transportation, which are not available in many parts of the country."[109] This effort launched what came to be known as the "Utah Compromise," which would provide the greatest set of legal protections for LGBT individuals in any majority Republican state in exchange for robust exemptions for religious institutions and their affiliated organizations, including universities. The Utah Compromise became an important strategy in LDS public relations, and LDS leaders sought to export the model to other states.[110] However, the efforts were unfruitful. No other state adopted the proposal.

As the conversation continued to develop, LDS leaders accepted relatively moderate notions of religious freedom, taking into consideration public accommodations and a pluralistic society. One issue that had made its way into the national conversation on the topic was whether Christians working in the wedding industry who objected to same-sex marriage might refuse services to gay couples. In 2012, Jack Phillips, owner of Masterpiece Cakeshop in Colorado, refused to bake a wedding cake for a gay couple, citing his religious objections as a Catholic to participation in such a ceremony.[111] Cake makers, florists, photographers, and others were objecting to selling their services for same-sex marriages and were losing in court.[112]

At first, church leaders were not necessarily in support of these commercial cases. Member of the Seventy Lance Wickman, who was also the church's general counsel, set out a clear vision of a compromise in July 2016. In it, he described three concentric rings of interest in religious freedom—individual and church, church-affiliated organizations, and for-profit businesses. He suggested that believers should set priorities to protect the first two but not worry so much about the arena of business. He explained, "The ability of secular businesses to deny employment or services to those whose lifestyles they consider immoral will often be limited." Arguing for "fairness for all," he suggested that the church would publicly defend religious freedoms only for the "core" activities of individuals, churches, and church-affiliated organizations and that in the commercial setting one must be "willing to make prudential compromises." He called for "reasonable" accommodations for religious practitioners for religious dress, Sabbath observance, and others but also for "greater pragmatism and compromise" in commercial and government settings.[113]

Wickman and Oaks were central figures in the turn to religious freedom. On September 10, 2016, church leaders launched ReligiousFreedom.lds.org, a new website to train its membership on how to "defend religious liberty." The website was announced at a Regional Religious Freedom Conference in Dallas–Fort Worth for LDS members. Oaks explained, "A paramount motive for this Regional Religious Freedom Conference is to get our members involved in a constructive way in the vital contest for religious freedom."[114] The website urged members to "focus on seeking to understand one another's perspective and finding common ground that unites you."[115] It also outlined what was at stake in losing religious freedom. In the workplace, one might be fired for religious beliefs, religious doctors might be "forced" to perform abortions, business owners might face penalties if they refuse to perform services that contradict their religious beliefs, or one may be "forced" to work on religious holidays. Children could be required to learn information about sex and gender that "contradict basic Church teaching," or religious people could be barred from adoption. The risk to churches might be that they lose tax exemption, are "forced" to employ people who reject the beliefs or practices of the faith, or cannot operate universities according to their "moral standards."[116] At the training conference, Wickman emphasized the mobilization of church members on the issue of religious freedom. "Tonight," he said, "we have heard a clarion call from an apostle of the Lord to also be citizens in defense of our most basic civil rights—the freedom to practice our faith, the freedom to trumpet our beliefs in the public square and the freedom to live according to our core principles in every aspect of our lives."[117]

The campaign for religious freedom built on the "Fairness for All" accommodation to gay rights. One of the church's training videos for its members depicted an atheist critic and a faithful Mormon getting into a heated exchange. When the Mormon returned to approach the conversation again from a more cooperative standpoint, she explained that she just wanted fairness for her beliefs to be respected. The atheist critic skeptically commented, "You would never stand up for gay rights." In response, the faithful Mormon exclaimed, "Of course I would! For example, I think it is wrong when someone gets turned down for a job or even is fired because they're gay. It isn't fair when they can't get an apartment because of a prejudiced landlord. I will stand up for you in those rights." She concluded dramatically, "All I'm asking is that you recognize that the same rights that you want for gays be granted to those who think differently than you." Later, she lamented, "Gay bigotry toward reasonable religious people isn't the answer. . . . I think we can stand up for each other by protecting everyone's rights."[118] Stopping short of supporting same-sex marriage, the Mormon explained that she did support some gay rights.

In other areas, church leaders were still trying to find their footing in a more accommodationist stance toward gay rights. When the case of Jack Phillips's Masterpiece Cakeshop advanced to the Supreme Court in 2017, LDS church leaders decided that "prudential compromises" in businesses did not include all public accommodations for same-sex couples. LDS leaders signed onto an amicus brief in support of Masterpiece Cakeshop. The church believed that in this case, "fairness for all" supported "pluralism rather than dominance by either side."[119] The brief argued that religious "conscientious objectors" to same-sex weddings should be protected from having to participate in an event that they believed to be ordained by God. While the brief made it clear that this would not grant a blanket right of discrimination against same-sex couples or gay and lesbian individuals, it did not explain why the wedding ceremony was uniquely burdensome over other ways that one might participate in support of a same-sex marriage, including celebratory occasions within the relationship, anniversaries, or funerals. The brief also declined to make a distinction between these cases and religious objectors to interracial marriages—a religious view that LDS leaders once held themselves. Further, it did not explain why cake makers alone were protected while hotel owners, caterers, makeup artists, or photographers might not be. In a rival amicus brief, other religious leaders from Christian, Jewish, Muslim, and Unitarian Universalist backgrounds vigorously disagreed with the defense of the cake maker, arguing that religious belief was not a license to discriminate.[120]

The transition to religious freedom from family values then marked a shift away from protecting society itself from the dangers of homosexual contagion and gender fluidity and toward protecting individual and institutional actors from personally having to support such relationships. It signaled a serious weakening, if not the end, of civilization decline narratives about social acceptance of homosexuality. The church was at risk more than society itself. Religious freedom functioned as a boundary against such contagion.

Though the continuities in LDS thought continued to reveal a concern about gender fluidity and emphasis on performativity as the constitutive feature of gender, this period was nevertheless marked by a number of transitions, both subtle and significant, in LDS approaches to gender and sexuality. Mormon officials introduced new doctrines that affirmed gay and lesbian identities as a theological possibility, reversing multiple decades of uncompromising linguistic warfare against sociopolitical terms that implied sexual essentialism. Church leaders began to limit the use of therapy as the sole method of treatment and qualify its successes as something less than a cure. They expressed some ambivalence about trans identities as well, hinting at a gap in LDS knowledge on the issue, even as some trans individuals faced punitive treatment that went beyond stated church policies. Finally, church leaders abandoned the fight against legalized same-sex marriage once the Supreme Court made its decision and shifted to ask for legal protection of religious freedom. These retreats displayed some moderation of LDS objections to sexual essentialism and of heteronormative theories of nature. But these changes did not represent a complete abandonment of a theory of sexual and gender fluidity or heterosexual norms. Church leaders continued to hold onto ideas of unstable gender fluidity even as they shifted toward greater accommodation to LGBTQ identities.

These changes were not unidirectional toward liberalization. Church leaders also introduced new doctrines that made same-sex kinship one of the most serious sins for LDS members. The battle over language of individual identity shifted to a new terrain over "real" and "counterfeit" relationships. Church leaders continued to excommunicate trans individuals. Their approach to religious freedom at times offered support for same-sex families and LGBTQ legal protections while also backing efforts that would curtail LGBTQ access to public accommodations like bathrooms and business services. While open to accepting gay and lesbian identities as real features of the human condition, LDS teachings reframed these identities as temporary features of a mortal sphere. The afterlife would take on a new role in grounding heterosexuality and gender binary that was no longer credibly based in creation and nature. For LDS leaders, these accommodations did not represent a fundamental change in ontological truths. For modern Mormonism, gender had always been open to vulnerability and change, and the ideal was still heteronormative.

*Concluding Thoughts*

# MORMONISM IN THE
# HISTORY OF SEXUALITY

At the beginning of 2018, Russell M. Nelson became the seventeenth president of the Church of Jesus Christ of Latter-day Saints. The ninety-three-year-old's first year in office was a torrent of significant changes. He called the first Asian American and the first South American to the Quorum of the Twelve Apostles, greatly expanding the diversity of that body in unprecedented ways.[1] He replaced the half-century-old Home and Visiting Teaching programs with a new program called Ministering and reorganized the male priesthood quorums in local congregations.[2] He announced the end of the century-old partnership with the Boy Scouts of America.[3] He changed the decades-old Sunday meeting schedule from three hours to just two, introducing a program for more "gospel instruction" in people's homes.[4] He changed the age at which young men may be ordained to the Aaronic Priesthood to just eleven years old and advanced girls to the Young Women program at the same age.[5] The dress code for female missionaries was relaxed from skirts and dresses at all times to pants in some circumstances.[6] He even instituted significant changes to the sacred covenants Latter-day Saints make in the temples, eliminating hierarchical teachings about men and women to reflect a more egalitarian perspective.[7] A few months later, he established a policy that allowed for civil marriages outside of the temple to take place before the temple sealing ceremony.[8] Most controversially, he declared that the long-standing practice of using the name "Mormon" to refer to the church and its members had been "a victory of Satan" and encouraged the use of the full name of the church instead.[9]

It is difficult to overstate the scope and pace of these changes, some of which had long been in the works and others that appeared to happen rather quickly. His wife explained, "It is as though he's been unleashed. He's free to finally do what he came to earth to do. . . . And also, he's free to follow through with things he's been concerned about but could never do. Now that he's president of [the church], he can do those things."[10] Nelson was exercising his authority in quite remarkable ways, even when it undermined the institutions and teachings of his predecessors. Addressing long-standing grievances and upending traditions, including consensus leadership, Nelson redefined the traditional position of LDS presidents.

Nelson was not expected to make progressive changes on gender and sexuality issues. He promoted Dallin H. Oaks, his immediate successor, to a position alongside him in the First Presidency, downgrading the popular apostle Dieter F. Uchtdorf in a rare shake-up of norms that would typically retain the counselors of the First Presidency.[11] At his first press conference, when asked about LGBT members, Nelson expressed "love" and a place for all in the church "regardless of challenges" but added (at the suggestion of Oaks) that one must balance the "love of the Lord" with the "law of the Lord." And even the progress for women seemed dim at the outset. When asked about gender equity in the church, he responded with a lengthy discussion about his daughters and their role as mothers and grandmothers. He encouraged women to participate more in the councils in the church. His counselor Henry B. Eyring praised the "influence" that women have, especially as mothers, despite the lack of position and recognition. Nelson explained, "Before the foundation of the world, women were created to bear and care for the sons and daughters of God and in doing so they glorify God." The citation was a paraphrase of Doctrine and Covenants 132:63, a passage in the revelation announcing the legitimacy of polygamy that repeatedly expresses how "ten virgins" are "given unto" a man to "multiply and replenish the earth."[12] The citation and emphasis on women's roles to care for children did little to comfort women concerned about their place in the church beyond motherhood.[13]

At the same time, Nelson surprised many when he reversed the November 2015 policy that declared same-sex married couples "apostates" and prohibited their children from joining the church or receiving blessings in it.[14] Nelson had been one of the most vocal defenders of the original policy when it was rolled out three and half years before, declaring it a "revelation," the highest level of authority in LDS teachings.[15] The reversal of the policy was also announced as part of "revelation upon revelation" the new prophet had received during the previous year. While the initial policy was designed to "protect children," the reversal was announced as "very positive policies" that would "help affected families," adding, "We want to reduce the hate and contention so common today."[16]

The combination of progressive changes for women's dress and egalitarian teachings in the temple and the willingness to walk back unpopular policies underscored an interesting feature of modern Mormonism. Latter-day Saints have been able to see both continuity and change as evidence of divine inspiration. Change would serve as evidence of "continuing revelation," the gradual unfolding of God's will and the adaptation of the church to changing circumstances. But not everything was supposed to be subject to change. What Nelson once called "unchanging constants" were the foundational principles that were immutable.[17] As historian David Holland has noted, "Mainstream Mormons have historically remained open to new inspirations that cross past doctrines or personal revelations or traditional practice, but one that ran counter *to all* of those would likely be resisted as the work of an uninspired hand."[18] What is remarkable about the Mormon tolerance for change (and its limits) is how resistant Latter-day Saints can be to acknowledging that there is really any change at all. Even the reversal of the 2015 policy emphasized continuity: "These changes do not represent a shift in Church doctrine related to marriage or the commandments of God in regard to chastity and morality."[19]

This book has explored one example of a set of teachings that are widely believed to be quite stable in Mormonism but have actually been open to dramatic changes. LDS teachings about marriage, gender roles, sexual difference, and sexuality have undergone remarkable transformation since World War II. The teachings and practices of the LDS church in the early twenty-first century would already be unrecognizable to Mormon leaders in the mid-twentieth century. On marriage, Mormons once opposed interracial marriage as a weakening of divinely designed racial boundaries that would transmit a curse to the offspring of any individual of African descent. Too much mixing, socially and reproductively, was a special threat to whiteness and hence to the Mormon priesthood. Church leaders also discouraged marriage between any of the races, with special concern about the budding relationships from white integration with Native Americans and Pacific Islanders. Racial difference was hierarchal difference, and LDS leaders treated the mythology of race and lineage as essential to Mormonism's self-understanding, tracing back to its nineteenth-century worldview and heritage. They gradually downgraded this from official doctrine to advice before eventually repudiating the worst expressions of these teachings.

Similarly, Mormon leaders once strongly emphasized that the patriarchal order of marriage was an unchangeable divine decree, warning against grave dangers to individuals and society if it were not followed. This established the father as the head of the home responsible for making decisions, providing financially, and teaching his family. The mother was responsible for bearing children and attending to the duties of the household. Gradually, these teachings gave way to more egalitarian forms of marriage. This soft egalitarianism reconsidered women's duties to bear numerous children and to avoid paid labor, instead encouraging education and personal fulfillment as acceptable values. It also encouraged men to participate more in child care and household responsibilities. While the older forms of racial and patriarchal hierarchy continue to haunt contemporary Mormonism, their dominance was fractured and replaced.

Mormon leaders also changed their views about what kinds of sexual practices may be enjoyed within these marriages. Generally, the restrictions also became more relaxed over time. Church leaders once condemned non-reproductive sexual exchange between couples, warning against the use of birth control as a jeopardy to one's eternal salvation. For a period, Mormon leaders prohibited "unholy and impure" sexual practices like oral sex between married couples. The puritanical and procreationist framework for sexual exchange gave way to new ideas about companionate sexuality. Sexual contact was no longer reducible to reproductive ends but could also be engaged in to strengthen the bonds between couples and for their mutual enjoyment. As the range of acceptable sexual practices broadened and reproductive pressure diminished, sex took on new meanings.

Mormon teachings about sexual difference similarly underwent dramatic changes as church leaders experimented with different doctrines. While there was considerable variation in these teachings, church officials often taught that there was a great deal of contingency in sexual difference. Influential leaders justified patriarchal hierarchy by teaching that individuals made a choice long before they were born on earth about whether they would live as male or female. Further, church leaders repeatedly taught that the choices one made in this life would determine whether one might continue as male or female in the next life or be demoted once again to a genderless condition. Sexual difference was salvation. The possibility of being without sexual difference not only extended to the conditions before birth and after death but also was a significant threat to human beings in this life. Church leaders launched preaching and political campaigns against a "unisex" and genderless society. To prevent this state of affairs, sexual difference had to

*Concluding Thoughts*

be socially and legally reinforced. In this context, Mormons began to drift rhetorically toward gender essentialism in order to give the rigid distinctions between men and women some foundation. They abandoned the idea that sexual difference was either chosen before birth or would be eliminated after death. Instead, they taught that sexual difference was an eternal characteristic of one's identity and was not chosen nor subject to being lost. But the fears about fluidity still defined how Mormons talked about sexual difference in this life. Though it was supposed to be eternal and essential, sexual difference could still be weakened or lost if not practiced and reinforced.

Teachings on marriage, sexual practices within marriage, and gender roles all trended toward greater liberalization during the period of modern Mormonism, even if they lagged behind broader cultural changes. But this progress had its trade-offs. Latter-day Saints could accommodate liberalizing trends on race, marriage, sexual contacts, birth control, and gender roles in part because their attention focused on homosexuality as a particularly egregious problem. The construction of a more threatening outsider rendered accommodation to these other changes benign. Church leaders marshaled significant attention and developed new resources for combating homosexuality—a concern that at times both strengthened their resolve for patriarchy and at times enabled its relaxation. But the newness of these efforts must be emphasized in the context of the newness of the category of homosexuality itself. Mormons borrowed this category from the psychological approaches developing in the twentieth century. Mingling psychotherapeutic philosophy with Victorian sexual morality, Mormons developed a new subject of censure, but also one deserving of therapeutic care. In this framework, Mormons came to believe that homosexuality was a result of either a deficit of masculinity or femininity or an overabundance of it. Either way, sexuality was tied to heteronormative gender roles.

Two new forms of power were developed to confront the concept of homosexuality. Church leaders had long been engaged in sexual purity campaigns and preaching about the household, though these too became more acute in this period. In order to buttress these efforts, the church invested significant capital into psychological treatment and political influence. Complementing their use of counter-psychological frameworks, LDS leaders developed new institutions staffed with trained counselors who promised a "total cure" to the individual who tried hard enough. At the same time, LDS leaders pursued a political strategy to socially stigmatize and marginalize gay and lesbian individuals, first by opposing the Equal Rights Amendment and supporting anti-sodomy laws and later by objecting to same-sex marriage. These efforts were similarly rooted in a theory of gender and sexual instability—without strong social and legal frameworks to enforce sexual difference, gender would become "confused" and a unisex society might result. Some church leaders were so nervous about these outcomes that they believed that within a single generation after destigmatizing same-sex relationships, these sexual practices might be universally adopted.

It is a truism in the history of sexuality to say that the concept of heterosexuality can come into existence only jointly with the concept of homosexuality. What allowed Mormons to adapt to these changes was their acceptance of the concept of heterosexuality as the alternative theory of human relations to those of racial difference and patriarchy. Once homosexuality was constructed in Mormon thought in the second half of the twentieth century, heterosexual subjectivity also came into existence. But the heterosexual subject was a new kind of category that need not rely on race (though it sometimes did) or on patriarchal hierarchy (though it sometimes did). Instead, heterosexuality as a concept was more able to accept new and different kinds of relationships between men and women than previously allowed. The binary between heterosexual and homosexual delegitimized same-sex relationships but also created the possibility of new kinds of relationships between men and women that were once considered highly suspect, if not outright forbidden.

Though I am arguing that the concept of homosexuality and heterosexuality came to dominate the structure of Mormon teachings about gender and sexuality in the period since World War II—eventually eclipsing racial and patriarchal teachings—I also want to underscore the dramatic changes that these categories themselves have undergone. Church leaders were comfortable with the concept of "the homosexual" as a distinctive type of individual, but they were deeply wary of attempts to ground this category in nature, creation, or any type of fixed essence. Instead, they saw same-sex attraction as a pathological and temporary condition that could be cured through self-help and therapeutic and pastoral assistance. This approach also saw gender and sexuality as inseparably intertwined so much that they were basically the same thing—gender failure was the cause of same-sex attraction, and successful gender performance was its cure. Gender and sexual malleability better explained not only how the homosexual might be cured but also how the presumed priority of an inner heterosexual could have faltered to begin with. At first, moral theories like masturbation and a lack of manly character seemed good explanations. As "the homosexual" moved from a freely chosen moral condition to one established in psycho-developmental stages, church leaders pushed for new etiologies and treatments.

Among these was a fierce battle over the language of identity. Church leaders once objected to the sociopolitical labels of "homosexual," "gay," and "lesbian" because they implied fixity instead of fluidity. As moral theories gave way to psycho-developmental theories, church leaders even tried to accommodate genetic theories, accepting that some feelings might be "inborn." After decades of resistance to such labels, even declaring such rejection to be a doctrine, in recent years church leaders reversed course on this approach and accepted and adopted these identity categories in new pastoral outreach efforts and reduced their expectations for any "cure" at all.

---

Such changes may be explained, at least in part, by tracking broader changes to religion in American culture. Mormon developments in this period indeed look very similar to what was happening among conservative Christian movements and American Christianity in general. As part of this "restructuring," sociologist Robert Wuthnow has noted, "American religion actively put itself on the line, making itself vulnerable to social influences of all kinds."[20] Conservative American religion in this period pushed to expand its influence in the public sphere, gaining some success but also acting as a polarizing force in American society. Latter-day Saints were no exception. While Mormonism often expressed itself in its own unique idioms, it largely turned to external influences—therapeutic and political—to define its teachings. Sexuality and the family were especially active nodes for both rapid changes and the illusion of stability.

This history then makes one skeptical of claims about Mormon exceptionalism, which sees a stable Mormon counterculture maintaining a traditional distinctiveness over and against "the world." While that is indeed a powerful myth of Mormon self-identity, Mormonism actually has followed a number of broad evolutionary trends on key social and theological issues. Mormons tracked closely conservative teachings on patriarchal marriage and later accommodations to soften those views and also conservative opposition to interracial marriage and later indifference. They opposed and later accepted birth control in similar ways to other conservatives. They started speaking about homosexuality at the same time as other conservatives and in the same ways. They established a ministry service at the same time that other conservatives founded ex-gay ministries and used the same treatment methodologies. Mormons deliberately partnered with other conservatives to oppose the Equal Rights Amendment, to develop counter-knowledge to the psychological and medical establishment about homosexuality, and to resist same-sex marriage. Mormons even backed away from reparative therapy just as other conservatives began to do so. Mormon teachings about gender and sexuality in this period reflected the conservative culture around them and serve as one more example of how these denominations adapted their teachings in response to liberalizing trends in American culture. Though Mormons have a distinctive set of ecclesiastical leaders, scriptures, and theological resources, all of these were molded to the cultural lens provided by conservative Christian American culture through direct and indirect ties and influence. Mormons sometimes acted as leaders in this culture—organizing against same-sex marriage and developing a coalition for religious freedom—but just as often conformed to the expectations of the agenda of the Religious Right, broadly construed. Starting in the second half of the twentieth century, Mormonism accommodated to American culture by steeping itself in the language of religious conservatism.

At the same time, Mormons need to be separated out from these broader trends in order for us to better understand how they shaped their identity and distinctiveness among their conservative peers. Mormons weren't just reacting to and opposing these cultural trends; they were also adapting them into a Mormon idiom. Theologically, Latter-day Saints merged their own distinctive teachings about pre-mortal and post-mortal bodies, identity, and character to define an essential self and to ground gender and sexual norms in something other than biblical authority, creation, or nature. The idea of an "eternal identity" was meant to indicate an underlying permanence and fixity to heterogender that was the substratum for mutability and fluidity in the world as it is. Further, the distinctive theology that Mormons have about marriage as an "eternal covenant" holds that when people are joined by the LDS priesthood in the ritual of "sealing," that relationship forms a bond that lasts eternally in the afterlife—a soteriological necessity for entrance into the highest "kingdom" of heaven. Such a belief raises the stakes of marrying the right person and of protecting the social acceptance of marriage, let alone preserving the legal right of Mormons to practice this sealing ritual unimpeded. Furthermore, in the modern period Mormons believed that sealing is what unites a Heavenly Father with a Heavenly Mother as the model of human relationships. By connecting mixed-sex marriage to salvation, Latter-day Saints held a distinctive attachment to heterosexuality.

Mixed-sex relationships were not simply the absence of sin but the imitation of a divine archetype.

The institutions of the church also contributed to a distinctive approach to gender and sexuality in this period. The structure and organization of the church at the congregational level provided for incomparable levels of supervision and oversight. Standards of "worthiness" were periodically checked through regular interviews, where church leaders would inquire about adherence to "the law of chastity." Such interviews were required for a member's full participation in church assignments and in special rituals at temples and as a prerequisite to attend one of the church's universities, serve a mission, get married in the temple, or perform various ordinances in the church like baptism. The centralized church and the concentration of its resources also gave it massive influence over its universities as mechanisms to produce and disseminate knowledge, control access to education through ecclesiastical oversight, and support a cadre of intellectuals to defend and define church teachings. It further allowed for the creation and support of para-ecclesial organizations like LDS Social Services that could supplement pastoral counseling with therapeutic techniques, including reparative therapy, and create a market for those seeking such services in private practice. Finally, the centralization of the church also meant that it could very efficiently mobilize and persuade its membership on political matters, from opposing the ERA to opposing same-sex marriage ballot initiatives.[21] Among the other institutions that made up the Religious Right for the past three decades, Mormons have spent and mobilized with incredible influence.

Internally, Mormonism was also beset by familiar tensions between religious liberals and conservatives in this period. Such tensions certainly trace their lineage to at least the modernist-fundamentalist split in the early twentieth century and have not fully resolved themselves to this day. But after World War II, the return of Mormon feminism and the rise of LGBT activists and allies brought gender and sexuality squarely into these debates. Despite strong opposition, these liberal groups actually have seen a number of successes over time as the leadership and membership sought to adjust around the edges. However, the central issues of ecclesiastical equality for both groups remain unachieved. But Mormonism did not fracture and is unlikely to fracture over these issues, as so many other American churches have done. The strong centralization of financial and real estate resources and the total monopoly on theological and priesthood authority in church leadership make a liberal offshoot of Mormonism today improbable. Only conservatives and fundamentalist Mormons who wish to continue or revive early Mormon polygamy have any success in forming schismatic groups with some semblance of replicating a coherent Mormon structure of authority. Liberals are more likely to wait patiently, actively resist, or simply leave Mormonism altogether.

---

One can expect further pressures on LDS institutions and culture as they continue to swim within a broader environment that is still moving away from so-called traditional values. Resisting these trends, church leaders have expressed dim prospects for any considered change on teachings regarding same-sex marriage.[22] At the same time, these teachings are producing an increasing strain on church members, especially younger members who have grown up in a world that is more open and accepting of nonnormative identities and relationships. When recently surveyed, 60 percent of regularly attending millennial Mormons (eighteen to twenty-six years old) and 53 percent of older millennial Mormons (twenty-seven to thirty-nine years old) believe that homosexuality should be accepted by society. Latter-day Saint support is growing rapidly in all age groups. In 2016, overall Mormon support for this statement was at 48 percent, double what it was just ten years before. Among Mormon millennials who have left the church, they cite "LGBT issues" as the third most important reason they disaffiliated. The generation gap is massive on this issue and has only grown, despite persistent LDS messaging from the top.[23]

Besides same-sex marriage, the male-only priesthood also seems particularly burdensome in the contemporary LDS church. The exclusion of women from ordination to the priesthood remains one of the most powerful ways that Mormons mark sexual difference in embodied practices. Once, this sharp division of roles would have mimicked broader social divisions of labor between public and domestic, leaders and followers, and the rational and emotional. Today, the church's policy looks increasingly anachronistic and is more easily recognized as a product of a particular time in American culture in which gender hierarchy defined gender roles. A recent survey shows that 61 percent of Mormon millennials agree that "women do not have enough say in the LDS church" and that 59 percent are "troubled that women don't hold the priesthood."[24] The gendered division of responsibilities between men and women in the church no longer reflects the time in which such divisions were created but is a social anomaly that must justify itself to many younger members in the face of its strangeness. Today, modern Mormons have become accustomed to women professors and male elementary school teachers, female doctors and male nurses, women heads of state, and women business executives. There is no doubt that there remain barriers, prejudices, and setbacks in these various fields, and there are still significant inequities that drive some skewed outcomes in labor and wealth. But the notion that men and women can share power in the market, education, and government is the new norm and has been for decades. The fact that a woman may be a chief financial officer for a company but may not be entrusted to count LDS tithing donations in her local congregation on the basis of not being ordained to the priesthood highlights the strangeness in Mormon practice for many younger generations.

The burden of the tradition here is particularly weighty. As the broader social barriers separating male and female roles dissipate, the reasons for such divisions are increasingly opaque. Even church leaders have a hard time articulating them. Amid the 2014 controversy between an activist organization called "Ordain Women" and LDS church headquarters, LDS Public Affairs director Michael Otterson wrote a letter to a handful of Mormon-themed blogs. These influential blogs had been hubs for engaged, vociferous debates about the merits of women's ordination at the time. Otterson wrote by way of justification, "I suppose we do not know all the reasons why Christ did not ordain women as apostles, either in the New Testament or the Book of Mormon, or when the Church was restored in modern times. We only know that he did not, that his leaders today regard this as a doctrinal issue that cannot be compromised, and that agitation from a few Church members is hindering the broader and more productive conversation about the voice, value and visibility of women in the Church that has been going on for years."[25] The comment was revealing in that it not only emphasized that women can never be ordained, grounding that decision in questionable precedent, but also expressed a lack of understanding of whether there were any reasons for the precedent at all.[26] Is tradition the evidence of an unchanging "doctrine," or a reflection of the cultures in which these traditions were developed? Otterson's articulation looked familiar when compared to the discourse surrounding the exclusion of black men from the priesthood. At that time, a similar debate raged over whether the doctrine was a product of its cultural milieu or a reflection of an unchangeable divine order, and church leaders had regularly claimed ignorance before and after it was changed about why the policy and doctrines had been instituted in the first place.

For Mormonism to accommodate same-sex marriage or include women in the priesthood, the tradition would need to change its stance on norms that define gender and sexual difference—norms that have already proven to be historically contingent. While anti-homosexuality and gender divisions seemed normal to a generation of church leaders who by and large took them for granted, to younger generations who are raised in a new cultural context, those ideas appear anachronistic at best and immoral at worst.

—————————————————————————————

The present study is not, however, simply an exploration of Mormonism's historical transformations or its relationship to conservative American cultural values. Rather, I hope that it might also contribute to a fuller history of sexual difference and history of sexuality. Conflicting sets of ideas about gender have defined the cultural shifts of modernity itself. Michel Foucault's *History of Sexuality: An Introduction* identified a grand paradigm shift in which the category of sexuality appeared in modernity. This category, he argued, took the form of various discourses and new regulations on sexual activity, reproduction, and interrogation of desires. At the same time that he recognized this paradigm shift, he noted its continuities with the past—the psychiatrist's couch being a significant point of continuity with the acts of Christian confession. But Foucault argued that the modern era is defined by the notion that sexuality appears as a fixed and essential feature of one's identity.

Similarly, Thomas Laqueur's influential treatment of a history of "sex" and "gender" relied on a notion of a grand paradigm shift in modernity. Laqueur argued that prior to the modern era, Western thought relied on a "one-sex" model of human beings, wherein males and females reflected a difference in degree, not in kind. Males were warmer, dryer, and harder, and females were cooler, wetter, and softer. These were simply different versions of the same underlying thing, though the differences also established a natural hierarchy. Laqueur proposed that in the modern era, a new theory emerged and took precedence—that there are two sexes that are fundamentally and essentially distinct in kind from one another. Even with moments of greater complexity, the thrust of his account relied on a largely singular conception of "sex as we know it" in modernity.[27]

The Mormon case shows that these narratives of modernity are oversimplified. Mormons did not adopt notions of sexual essentialism or a "two-sex" ontology but advocated an ontology of malleability and fluidity to explain the world as they experienced it. As this example has shown, even in Mormonism there is no "being" to gender, only its "becoming" through regulated norms. The possibility for the transgression of the boundaries between male and female—at the juncture of roles, sexuality, or identity itself—suggests a theory of gender that does not rest on an essential foundation. The notions of gender failures, confusions, transgressions, transitions, excesses, and incompletions expose the limits of a theory of sexual difference as an essentialist feature of identity. As Mormonism has embraced a norm of enforced sexual differences, it has done so by being rooted in compulsory heterosexuality. For this reason, Mormonism has been unable to assimilate identities that fall outside these norms, including "the homosexual," at times the feminist who exceeds her prescribed sphere, or the father who does not take his place at the head of the home.

Mormonism resisted and subverted the notions of the essential sexual subject and relied on a model of sexual difference that held that the barrier between male and female was fragile and permeable. The difference between male and female, heterosexuality and homosexuality, was socially contingent. While Laqueur would argue that this feature is an echo of premodern ideas, it may be more accurate to say that modernity (like premodernity) is conflicted between multiple theories of sexual difference. Indeed, Mormons relied not on premodern thinkers to express their views but on twentieth-century sociological and psychoanalytical accounts of a malleable human subject. Mormon resistance to essentialism in favor of fluidity pushed back against dominant norms of modernity but did so in the language of modernity. Mormonism's complex engagement with sexual and gender essentialism does not mark it as premodern or anti-modern but rather reveals the queer contours of modern notions of gender and sexuality as persistently marked by ambiguity, fluidity, contradiction, and paradox. Mormonism produces and is produced by these modern conflicts about the nature of gender and sexuality.

# Notes

## INTRODUCTION

1. Ludger H. Viefhues-Bailey, *Between a Man and a Woman? Why Conservatives Oppose Same-Sex Marriage* (New York: Columbia University Press, 2010); Seth Dowland, *Family Values and the Rise of the Christian Right* (Philadelphia: University of Pennsylvania Press, 2015); R. Marie Griffith, *Moral Combat: How Sex Divided American Christians and Fractured American Politics* (New York: Basic Books, 2017); Amy DeRogatis, *Saving Sex: Sexuality and Salvation in American Evangelicalism* (New York: Oxford University Press, 2014); Robert O. Self, *All in the Family: The Realignment of American Democracy since 1960* (repr.; New York City: Hill and Wang, 2013); Mark D. Jordan, *Recruiting Young Love: How Christians Talk about Homosexuality* (Chicago: University of Chicago Press, 2011); Heather White, *Reforming Sodom: Protestants and the Rise of Gay Rights* (Chapel Hill: University of North Carolina Press, 2015).

2. Sally K. Gallagher, *Evangelical Identity and Gendered Family Life* (New Brunswick, NJ: Rutgers University Press, 2003). For LDS hermeneutical approaches, see Philip Barlow, *Mormons and the Bible* (New York: Oxford University Press, 1991); and Laurie Maffly-Kipp, "Mormons and the Bible," in *Oxford Handbook of Mormonism*, ed. Terryl L. Givens and Philip L. Barlow (New York: Oxford University Press, 2015), 121–33.

3. "Approaching Mormon Doctrine," LDS Newsroom, May 4, 2007, http://www.mormonnewsroom.org/article/approaching-mormon-doctrine.

4. Kathleen Flake, *The Politics of American Religious Identity: The Seating of Senator Reed Smoot, Mormon Apostle* (Chapel Hill: University of North Carolina Press, 2004); Thomas W. Simpson, *American Universities and the Birth of Modern Mormonism, 1867–1940* (Chapel Hill: University of North Carolina Press, 2016); Ethan Yorgason, *Transformation of the Mormon Culture Region* (Champaign: University of Illinois Press, 2010).

5. Thomas Alexander, *Mormonism in Transition: A History of the Latter-day Saints, 1890–1930* (Champaign: University of Illinois Press, 1986).

6. See, for instance, George L. Mosse, *Nationalism and Sexuality: Respectability and Abnormal Sexuality in Modern Europe* (New York: Howard Fertig, 1997).

7. Patrick Mason and John Turner, eds., *Out of Obscurity: Mormonism since 1945* (New York: Oxford University Press, 2016).

8. Gregory A. Prince and W. M. Robert Wright, *David O. McKay: The Rise of Modern Mormonism* (Salt Lake City: University of Utah Press, 2005).

9. There is imprecision in the use of this term, as one might expect. See, for instance, Matthew J. Grow, "The Modern Mormon Church," in Givens and Barlow, *Oxford Handbook of Mormonism*, 55–69. Grow covers the twentieth century in its entirety as modern Mormonism.

10. "Prophet, Seer, and Innovator," *Time*, February 2, 1970, 50.

11. Harold B. Lee, "Meeting the Needs of a Growing Church," *Improvement Era*, January 1968, 29.

12. John D'Emilio and Estelle B. Freedman, *Intimate Matters: A History of Sexuality in America*, 2nd ed. (Chicago: University of Chicago Press, 1997), 239–360.

13. Frances FitzGerald, *The Evangelicals: The Struggle to Shape America* (New York: Simon and Schuster, 2017); Grant Wacker, *America's Pastor: Billy Graham and the Shaping of a Nation* (Cambridge, Mass.: Harvard University Press, 2014); Jon R. Stone, *On the Boundaries of American Evangelicalism: The Postwar Evangelical Coalition* (New York: Palgrave Macmillan, 1997).

14. Stephanie Coontz, *The Way We Never Were: American Families and the Nostalgia Trap*, revised ed. (New York: Basic Books, 2016).

15. Elaine Tyler May, *Homeward Bound: American Families in the Cold War Era*, revised ed. (New York: Basic Books, 2008).

16. Nancy Cott, *Public Vows: A History of Marriage and the Nation* (Cambridge, Mass.: Harvard University Press, 2002), 185–97.

17. Sara Moslener, *Virgin Nation: Sexual Purity and American Adolescence* (New York: Oxford University Press, 2015).

18. David O. McKay, "Marriage and Divorce," *Conference Report*, April 1945, 140–45.

19. Matthew Bowman, "Zion: The Progressive Roots of Mormon Correlation," in *Directions for Mormon Studies in the Twenty-First Century*, ed. Patrick Q. Mason (Salt Lake City: University of Utah Press, 2016), 15–34.

20. Lawrence Foster, "Between Heaven and Earth: Mormon Theology of the Family in Comparative Perspective," in *Multiply and Replenish: Mormon Essays on Sex and Family*, ed. Brent Corcoran (Salt Lake City: Signature Books, 1994), 12.

21. The First Presidency and Council of the Twelve Apostles of the Church of Jesus Christ of Latter-day Saints, "The Family: A Proclamation to the World," *Ensign*, November 1995; Terryl L. Givens, *Feeding the Flock: The Foundations of Mormon Thought: Church and Praxis* (New York: Oxford University Press, 2017), 190.

22. Armand Mauss, *The Angel and the Beehive: The Mormon Struggle with Assimilation* (Champaign: University of Illinois Press, 1994); Gordon Shepherd and Gary Shepherd, *A Kingdom Transformed: Early Mormonism and the Modern LDS Church*, 2nd ed. (Salt Lake City: University of Utah Press, 2015).

23. In a more recent article, Mauss offers an argument for a moderation of retrenchment in the past few decades. Armand Mauss, "Rethinking Retrenchment: Course Corrections in the Ongoing Campaign for Respectability," *Dialogue: A Journal of Mormon Thought* 44, no. 3 (Winter 2011): 1–42.

24. O. Kendall White Jr., "Swimming Up the Mainstream," *Sunstone*, June 1996, 62–65. Mauss rejects this argument, saying, "To the extent that Mormonism identifies itself with other relatively high-cost religions, it is still resisting and rejecting assimilation with the secular culture of the society in general." Mauss, "Rethinking Retrenchment," 3. This view identifies secular culture as the mainstream and conservative religious culture as atypical.

25. Shepherd and Shepherd, *Kingdom Transformed*, 225.

26. Shepherd and Shepherd, 225, 210–14.

27. Maxine Hanks, ed., *Women and Authority: Re-emerging Mormon Feminism* (Salt Lake City: Signature Books, 1992).

28. Claudia Bushman, "Women in Mormonism," in Givens and Barlow, *Oxford Handbook of Mormonism*, 69–80, esp. 75–78.

29. Dave Hall, *A Faded Legacy: Amy Brown Lyman and Mormon Women's Activism, 1872–1959* (Salt Lake City: University of Utah Press, 2015), 7, 170–82.

30. Kate Holbrook, "Housework: The Problem That Does Have a Name," in Mason and Turner, *Out of Obscurity*, 198–213.

31. Caroline Kline, "Saying Goodbye to the Final Say: The Softening and Reimagining of Mormon Male Headship Ideologies," in Mason and Turner, *Out of Obscurity*, 214–33.

32. See especially Colleen McDannell, *Sister Saints: Mormon Women since the End of Polygamy* (New York: Oxford University Press, 2018); and Kate Holbrook and Matthew Bowman, eds., *Women in Mormonism: Historical and Contemporary Perspectives* (Salt Lake City: University of Utah Press, 2016).

33. D. Michael Quinn, *Same-Sex Dynamics among Nineteenth-Century Americans: A Mormon Example* (Urbana: University of Illinois Press, 1996); Rocky O'Donovan, "'The Abominable and Detestable Crime against Nature': A Brief History of Homosexuality and Mormonism, 1840–1980," in Corcoran, *Multiply and Replenish*, 123–70. In 2004, O'Donovan privately published a greatly expanded version of this history; future references are to the online edition. Connell O'Donovan, "'The Abominable and Detestable Crime against Nature': A Revised History of Homosexuality and Mormonism, 1840–1980," http://www.connellodonovan.com/abom.html. See also Rick Phillips, *Conservative Christian Identity and Same-Sex Orientation: The Case of Gay Mormons* (New York: Peter Lang, 2005), 30–47; Ron Schow, Wayne Schow, and Marybeth Raynes, eds., *Peculiar People: Mormons and Same-Sex Orientation* (Salt Lake City: Signature Books, 1991), esp. xxii–xxviii; and Douglas A. Winkler, "Lavender Sons of Zion: A History of Gay Men in Salt Lake City, 1950–79" (PhD diss., University of Utah, 2008).

34. Ryan T. Cragun, J. E. Sumerau, and Emily Williams, "From Sodomy to Sympathy: LDS Elites' Discursive Construction of Homosexuality over Time," *Journal of the Scientific Study of Religion* 54, no. 2 (May 2015): 291–310.

35. Gregory A. Prince, *Gay Rights and the Mormon Church: Intended Actions, Unintended Consequences* (Salt Lake City: University of Utah Press, 2019).

36. Prince, 4, 20–24.

37. Alan Michael Williams, "Mormon and Queer at the Crossroads," *Dialogue: A Journal of Mormon Thought* 44, no. 1 (Spring 2011): 67.

38. Annamarie Jagose, *Queer Theory: An Introduction* (New York: New York University Press, 1996).

39. John D'Emilio, "Religion Is Calling," *Out History*, November 12, 2004, http://outhistory.org/blog/religion-is-calling. See also Rebecca Davis, Gillian Frank, Bethany Moreton, and Heather White, "Believe It: Finding Religion in the History of U.S. Sexuality," *Notches Blog*, November 24, 2014, http://notchesblog.com/2014/11/24/believe-it-finding-religion-in-the-history-of-u-s-sexuality/; and Gillian Frank, Bethany Moreton, and Heather White, "Introduction: More Than Missionary: Doing the Histories of Religion and Sexuality Together," in *Devotions and Desires: Histories of Sexuality and Religion in the Twentieth-Century United States*, ed. Gillian Frank, Bethany Moreton, and Heather R. White (Chapel Hill: University of North Carolina Press, 2018), 1–16.

40. Viefues-Bailey, *Between a Man and a Woman?*, 96.

41. Viefues-Bailey, 100–115.

42. Lynne Gerber, "The Opposite of Gay: Nature, Creation, and Queerish Ex-gay Experiments," *Nova Religio: The Journal of Alternative and Emergent Religions* 11, no. 4 (May 2008): 8–30.

43. Tanya Erzen, *Straight to Jesus: Sexual and Christian Conversion in the Ex-gay Movement* (Berkeley: University of California Press, 2006), 14–15.

44. Lisa Diamond, *Sexual Fluidity: Understanding Women's Love and Desire* (Cambridge, Mass.: Harvard University Press, 2008).

45. Brian Maffly, "U. Psychologist Says Sex Research Distorted," *Salt Lake Tribune*, November 11, 2008, http://www.sltrib.com/ci10958958.

46. Douglas A. Abbot and A. Dean Byrd, *Encouraging Heterosexuality: Helping Children Develop a Traditional Sexual Orientation* (Orem: Millennial Press, 2009).

47. Jagose, *Queer Theory*, 101–26.

48. Michel Foucault, *History of Sexuality, Volume 1: An Introduction* (New York: Vintage, 1990), 43.

49. Thomas Laqueur, *Making Sex: Body and Gender from Greeks to Freud* (Cambridge, Mass.: Harvard University Press, 1992), 149.

50. Laqueur, 193.

51. Jennifer Terry, *An American Obsession: Science, Medicine, and Homosexuality in Modern Society* (Chicago: University of Chicago Press, 1999), 159–77.

52. Eve Kosofsky Sedgwick, *Epistemology of the Closet* (Berkeley: University of California Press, 1990), 82–86.

53. Sedgwick, 47.

54. Judith Butler, *Gender Trouble: Feminism and the Subversion of Identity*, 2nd ed. (New York: Routledge, 1999), 180.

55. Butler, 176.

56. Frank, Moreton, and White, *Devotions and Desires*, 4.

57. Siobhan B. Somerville, *Queering the Color Lines: Race and the Invention of Homosexuality in American Culture* (Durham: Duke University Press, 2000).

58. Julian B. Carter, *The Heart of Whiteness: Normal Sexuality and Race in America, 1880–1940* (Durham: Duke University Press, 2007).

CHAPTER 1

1. Francis M. Gibbons, *Spencer W. Kimball: Resolute Disciple, Prophet of God* (Salt Lake City: Deseret Book, 1995), 160–61.

2. Spencer W. Kimball Journal, January 27, 1947, Church History Library, Church of Jesus Christ of Latter-day Saints, Salt Lake City.

3. Edward Kimball and Andrew E. Kimball Jr., *Spencer W. Kimball: Twelfth President of the Church of Jesus Christ of Latter-day Saints* (Salt Lake City: Bookcraft, 1977), 271.

4. Siobhan B. Somerville, *Queering the Color Lines: Race and the Invention of Homosexuality in American Culture* (Durham: Duke University Press, 2000), 5.

5. Nancy Cott, *Public Vows: A History of Marriage and the Nation* (Cambridge, Mass.: Harvard University Press, 2002), 184–85.

6. Fay Botham, *Almighty God Created the Races: Christianity, Interracial Marriage, and American Law* (Chapel Hill: University of North Carolina Press, 2013), 91–129.

7. Quoted in Botham, 108.

8. Quoted in Botham, 109.

9. Quoted in Botham, 2.

10. David Goldberg, *The Curse of Ham: Race and Slavery in Early Judaism, Christianity, and Islam* (Princeton: Princeton University Press, 2003); Sylvester Johnson, *The Myth of Ham in Nineteenth-Century American Christianity: Race, Heathens, and the People of God* (New York: Palgrave, 2004). All subsequent quotes from the Bible are from the King James Version.

11. Max Perry Mueller, *Race and the Making of the Mormon People* (Chapel Hill: University of North Carolina Press, 2017), chaps. 1–3; Joseph R. Stuart, "'A More Powerful Effect upon the Body': Early Mormonism's Theory of Racial Redemption and American Religious Theories of Race," *Church History* 87, no. 3 (September 2018): 769–96.

12. 2 Nephi 5:21.

13. 1 Nephi 13:15.

14. Abraham 1:27.

15. Brigham Young, Speech, February 5, 1852, Papers of George D. Watt, MS 4534, box 1, folder 3, Church History Library; John J. Stewart, *Mormonism and the Negro: An Explanation and Defense of the Church of Jesus Christ of Latter-day Saints in Regard to Negroes and Others of Negroid Blood* (n.p.: Bookmark Division of Community Press, 1960). For excellent secondary sources, see W. Paul Reeve, *Religion of a Different Color: Race and the Mormon Struggle for Whiteness* (New York: Oxford University Press, 2015); and Armand L. Mauss, *All Abraham's Children: Changing Mormon Conceptions of Race and Lineage* (Champaign: University of Illinois Press, 2003).

16. Brigham Young, March 8, 1863, in Franklin D. Richards and Stephen W. Richards, eds., *Journal of Discourses*, 26 vols. (London: LDS Booksellers Depot, 1854–86), 10:110–11.

17. Reeve, *Religion of a Different Color*, 107–11.

18. Armand Mauss traces the history of these racial teachings through Joseph Fielding Smith in the 1930s but notes, "Whatever the extent of Joseph Fielding Smith's doctrinal influence by mid-century, his teachings could hardly be regarded as heterodox, for nearly all of his colleagues in the church leadership and most of the general membership embraced similar ideas." Mauss, *All Abraham's Children*, 31.

19. J. Reuben Clark Jr., *Improvement Era*, August 1946, 492, quoted in Matthew L. Harris and Newell G. Bringhurst, *Mormon Church and Blacks: A Documentary History* (Champaign: University of Illinois Press, 2015), 110.

20. Harris and Bringhurst, *Mormon Church and Blacks*, 65–66.

21. Quoted in Gregory A. Prince and W. M. Robert Wright, *David O. McKay: The Rise of Modern Mormonism* (Salt Lake City: University of Utah Press, 2005), 62–68, quote on 62.

22. Quoted in Prince and Wright, 63.

23. Quoted in Prince and Wright, 65.

24. Mark E. Petersen, "Race Problems—as They Affect the Church," address at the Convention of Teachers of Religion on the College Level, BYU, Provo, August 27, 1954.

25. Petersen, "Race Problems."

26. Petersen.

27. Joseph Anderson to Chauncey D. Harris, May 4, 1954, cited in Connell O'Donovan, "'I Would Confine Them to Their Own Species': LDS Historical Rhetoric and Praxis Regarding Marriage between Whites and Blacks," March 28, 2009, http://www .connellodonovan.com/black_white_marriage.html#30.

28. Joseph Fielding Smith, *Answers to Gospel Questions* (Salt Lake City: Deseret Book, 1958), 2:184–88.

29. Matthew Bowman, *The Mormon People: The Making of an American Faith* (New York: Random House, 2012), 200.

30. J. Smith, *Answers to Gospel Questions*, 1:169–71.

31. J. Smith, 2:184–88.

32. Bruce R. McConkie, *Mormon Doctrine* (Salt Lake City: Bookcraft, 1958), 107–8.

33. Bowman, *Mormon People*, 198–200.

34. Alvin R. Dyer, "For What Purpose?" Mission Conference, Oslo, Norway, March 18, 1962, Church History Library.

35. Patrick Q. Mason, "The Prohibition of Interracial Marriage in Utah: 1888–1963," *Utah Historical Quarterly* 76, no. 2 (Spring 2008): 108–31.

36. First Presidency minutes in David O. McKay Journal, September 26, 1961, box 48, folder 5, David O. McKay Papers, Marriott Library Special Collections, University of Utah, quoted in Harris and Bringhurst, *Mormon Church and Blacks*, 110.

37. Amanda Hendrix-Komoto, "Mahana, You Naked! Modesty, Sexuality, and Race in the Mormon Pacific," in *Out of Obscurity: Mormonism since 1945*, ed. Patrick Mason and John Turner (New York: Oxford University Press, 2016), 173–97, esp. 175.

38. Mueller, *Race and the Making of the Mormon People*, 153–211.

39. 2 Nephi 30:6 (1830 ed.); Royal Skousen, *Analysis of Textual Variants of the Book of Mormon: Part Two, 2 Nephi 11–Mosiah 16* (Provo: FARMS, 2005), 895. Cf. 2 Nephi 5:21; Alma 3:6–7.

40. Matthew Garrett, *Making Lamanites: Mormons, Native Americans, and the Indian Student Placement Program, 1947–2000* (Salt Lake City: University of Utah Press, 2016); James B. Allen, "The Rise and Decline of the LDS Indian Student Placement Program, 1947–1996," in *Mormons, Scripture, and the Ancient World: Studies in Honor of John L. Sorenson*, ed. John L. Sorenson and Davis Bitton (Provo: FARMS, 1998), 85–119.

41. Edward K. Kimball, *Lengthen Your Stride: The Presidency of Spencer W. Kimball* (Salt Lake City: Deseret Book, 2005), 288–95.

42. Spencer W. Kimball, "The Lamanite," address to BYU student body, April 15, 1953, in *Speeches of the Year, 1952–53* (n.p., n.d.), 10–11.

43. E. Kimball, *Lengthen Your Stride*, 288–95.

44. Mauss, *All Abraham's Children*, 119–20.

45. Spencer W. Kimball, *Conference Report*, October 1960, 32–37.

46. Indian Committee Minutes, January 9, 1959, quoted in Garrett, *Making Lamanites*, 143–44.

47. Edward L. Kimball, *The Teachings of Spencer W. Kimball* (Salt Lake City: Deseret Book, 1982), 302.

48. Undated letter [1959?], quoted in E. Kimball, 302–3.

49. Hendrix-Komoto, "Mahana, You Naked!," 182–86.

50. Quoted in Hendrix-Komoto, 186.

51. For an account of this episode, see Prince and Wright, *David O. McKay*, 69–70.

52. For an excellent recent treatment, see the essays in Matthew L. Harris, ed., *Thunder from the Right: Ezra Taft Benson in Mormonism and Politics* (Urbana: University of Illinois Press, 2019), especially Harris's chapter "Martin Luther King, Civil Rights, and Perceptions of a 'Communist Conspiracy,'" 124–56.

53. "Reed A. Benson Takes Post in Birch Society," *Deseret News*, October 27, 1962, B-5; "Reed Benson Takes Post with John Birch Group," *Salt Lake Tribune*, October 27, 1962, 24; "Benson-Birch Tie Disturbs Utahans," *New York Times*, November 4, 1962, 65; "Benson's

Praise of the Birchers," *San Francisco Chronicle*, March 14, 1963, 16; "Elder Benson Makes Statement," *Deseret News, Church News* supplement, March 16, 1963; "Socialism Warning Sounded: Elder Benson Hits Liberals," *Deseret News*, February 12, 1966, B-l; and "LDS Apostle Backs Up Birch Group," *Salt Lake Tribune*, January 16, 1966, B-14.

54. Robert A. Goldberg, "From New Deal to New Right," in Harris, *Thunder from the Right*, 76–91; D. Michael Quinn, "Ezra Taft Benson and Mormon Political Conflicts," *Dialogue: A Journal of Mormon Thought* 26, no. 2 (Summer 1992): 1–87.

55. Quinn, "Ezra Taft Benson," 58–64.

56. Quinn, 32, 41. Some of his comments were deleted by the time the talks were published.

57. Prince and Wright, *David O. McKay*, 71–72.

58. Ezra Taft Benson, "Trust Not in the Arm of Flesh," *Conference Report*, October 1967, 34–39. In addition to his 1967 speech, in 1968 Benson delivered an incendiary anti–civil rights speech at BYU. Benson, "The Book of Mormon Warns America," in *An Enemy Hath Done This*, comp. Jerreld L. Newquist (Salt Lake City: Parliament Publishers, 1969), 328–42. The speech prompted a rebuttal from Brown just ten days later. Quinn, "Ezra Taft Benson," 66.

59. Ezra Taft Benson, *Conference Report*, October 1963, 15–19; R. Goldberg, "From New Deal to New Right," 82–89.

60. Max Perry Mueller, "The Pageantry of Protest in Temple Square," in Mason and Turner, *Out of Obscurity*, 136.

61. J. B. Haws, *The Mormon Image in the American Mind: Fifty Years of Public Perception* (New York: Oxford University Press, 2013), 47–73.

62. Harris and Bringhurst, *Mormon Church and Blacks*, 81–83.

63. P. Mason, "Prohibition of Interracial Marriage in Utah," 129.

64. Gordon Shepherd and Gary Shepherd, *A Kingdom Transformed: Early Mormonism and the Modern LDS Church*, 2nd ed. (Salt Lake City: University of Utah Press, 2015), 83–86.

65. Cott, *Public Vows*, 185–97; Elaine Tyler May, *Homeward Bound: American Families in the Cold War Era*, revised ed. (New York: Basic Books, 2008).

66. Sara Moslener, *Virgin Nation: Sexual Purity and American Adolescence* (New York: Oxford University Press, 2015), 48–77.

67. Margaret Lamberts Bendroth, *Fundamentalism and Gender: 1875 to the Present* (New Haven: Yale University Press, 1996).

68. Charles Ryrie, "Is Your Home Scriptural?," *Biblioteca Sacra* 109 (October–December 1952): 346–52.

69. Carmon Hardy, "Lords of Creation: Polygamy, the Abrahamic Household, and Mormon Patriarchy," *Journal of Mormon History* 20, no. 1 (1994): 119–52.

70. For an account of the history of Short Creek and the implications of the raid, see Martha Sontag Bradley, *Kidnapped from That Land: The Government Raids on the Short Creek Polygamists* (Salt Lake City: University of Utah Press, 1993).

71. *Deseret News*, July 27, 1953.

72. Bradley, *Kidnapped*, 152.

73. Bradley, 193.

74. Richard Kimball, "Muscular Mormonism," *International Journal of the History of Sport* 25, no. 5 (2008): 549–78.

75. David O. McKay, *Conference Report*, April 1945, 119–24.

76. Stephen L. Richards, "Be 'Not Ashamed of the Gospel of Christ,'" *Conference Report*, April 1954, 31–35.

77. LeGrand Richards, *A Marvelous Work and a Wonder* (repr.; Salt Lake City: Deseret Book, 1968), 200; Ephesians 5:23.

78. S. Richards, "Be 'Not Ashamed,'" 33.

79. For examples of quotations of Ephesians 5:22–23, see Joseph L. Wirthlin, *Conference Report*, April 1946, 160–67; Wirthlin, *Conference Report*, October 1953, 12–16; Hugh B. Brown, *Conference Report*, October 1954, 14–17; Stephen L. Richards, *Conference Report*, April 1958, 93–97; Spencer W. Kimball, *Conference Report*, October 1962, 55–60; William J. Critchlow Jr., *Conference Report*, October 1963, 26–30; Spencer W. Kimball, *Conference Report*, April 1965, 60–65; William J. Critchlow Jr., *Conference Report*, October 1965, 36–40; Harold B. Lee, *Conference Report*, April 1966, 64–68; and Alvin R. Dyer, *Conference Report*, October 1966, 133–35. For citations of Colossians 3:18, see A. Theodore Tuttle, *Conference Report*, October 1969, 130–32.

80. McConkie, *Mormon Doctrine*, 844.

81. Spencer W. Kimball, "Keep Mothers in the Home," *Conference Report*, October 1963, 34–40.

82. Stephen L. Richards, "The Father and the Home," *Conference Report*, April 1958, 93–97.

83. S. Richards, 93–97.

84. Hugh B. Brown, "To Your Tents, O Israel!," *Conference Report*, October 1954, 14–17.

85. The cover of the 1990 Bantam "updated edition" announces that over two million copies were already in print.

86. Colleen McDannell, *Sister Saints: Mormon Women since the End of Polygamy* (New York: Oxford University Press, 2018), 95–98.

87. Helen B. Andelin, *Fascinating Womanhood* (1964; repr., Santa Barbara: Pacific Press, 1965), 218–19.

88. For a rich discussion of competing LDS theologies of housework in this period, see Kate Holbrook, "Housework: The Problem That Does Have a Name," in Mason and Turner, *Out of Obscurity*, 198–213.

89. Holbrook, 206.

90. Garth Mangum and Bruce Blumell, *The Mormons' War on Poverty: A History of LDS Welfare, 1830–1990* (Salt Lake City: University of Utah Press, 1993).

91. Michael A. Goodman, "Correlation: The Turning Point (1960s)," in *Salt Lake City: The Place Which God Prepared*, ed. Scott C. Esplin and Kenneth L. Alford (Salt Lake City: Deseret Book, 2011), 259–84; Matthew Bowman, "Zion: The Progressive Roots of Mormon Correlation," in *Directions for Mormon Studies in the Twenty-First Century*, ed. Patrick Q. Mason (Salt Lake City: University of Utah Press, 2016).

92. Harold B. Lee, "Priesthood Correlation and the Home Evening," *Conference Report*, October 1964, 80–87.

93. Dale Mouritsen, "The Historical and Prophetic Significance of Priesthood Correlation" (master's thesis, Brigham Young University, 1967), 7.

94. Goodman, "Correlation," 259–84. See also *General Handbook of Instructions* (Salt Lake City: Church of Jesus Christ of Latter-day Saints, 1968), 121–22: "Bishops are directed to investigate and handle all cases of serious transgression. Home Teachers holding the Melchizedek Priesthood may be appointed to make the investigations."

95. Harold B. Lee, "Meeting the Needs of a Growing Church," *Improvement Era*, January 1968, 27.

96. H. Lee, "Priesthood Correlation and the Home Evening," 80–87. Lee's teachings repeatedly sought to downplay the novelty of the program, giving Family Home Evening a long heritage despite its near total absence from official teachings.

97. Harold B. Lee, "Search Diligently, Pray Always, and Be Believing," *Conference Report*, October 1964, 137–39.

98. James P. Mitchell and Terri Tanner Mitchell, "Family Home Evening," in *Encyclopedia of Mormonism*, ed. Daniel H. Ludlow (New York: Macmillan, 1992), 495–97.

99. *Melchizedek Priesthood Lessons* (Salt Lake City: Church of Jesus Christ of Latter-day Saints, 1965), 1.

100. In the 1950s and 1960s, the manuals covered such topics as Christian history and theology but also produced and treated many classics of LDS scriptural teachings, such as Hugh Nibley, *An Approach to the Book of Mormon* (1957), and James E. Talmage, *Jesus, the Christ* (1963).

101. "Magnifying Priesthood in the Home," in *Melchizedek Priesthood Lessons*, 73, 77, 80.

102. Spencer W. Kimball, "Home Training—the Cure for Evil," *Conference Report*, April 1965, 60–65.

103. Irwin Phelps, *A Blue Ribbon Affair*, MIA Parent and Youth Night Program, 1969–70, Church History Library.

104. "Magnifying Priesthood in the Home," 74–75.

105. Holbrook, "Housework," 208.

106. "Homemaking Discussions: Education for Living: A Lovelier You," *Relief Society Magazine*, June 1970, 468.

107. Charles R. Harrell, "The Development of the Doctrine of Preexistence, 1830–1844," *BYU Studies* 28, no. 2 (Spring 1998): 75–96. See also Terryl L. Givens, *Wrestling the Angel: The Foundations of Mormon Thought: Cosmos, God, Humanity* (New York: Oxford University Press, 2015), 147–63.

108. Moses 2:27; Abraham 4:27; Genesis 1:27.

109. Hyrum L. Andrus, *Doctrinal Commentary on the Pearl of Great Price* (Salt Lake City: Deseret Book, 1967), 116.

110. Rodney Turner, *Woman and the Priesthood* (Salt Lake City: Deseret Book, 1972), 17.

111. Bushman, "Women: One Man's Opinion," *Dialogue: A Journal of Mormon Thought* 7, no. 4 (1974): 85–87.

112. William J. Critchlow, "Women and the Priesthood," *Conference Report*, October 1965, 38–39.

113. Critchlow, 39.

114. Bushman, "Women," 86.

115. McConkie, *Mormon Doctrine*, 354.

116. James E. Talmage, "The Eternity of Sex," *Young Woman's Journal* 25 (October 1914): 600–604.

117. Gordon B. Hinckley, "Live Up to Your Inheritance," *Conference Report*, October 1983.

118. This teaching is primarily found in Doctrine and Covenants 76 and 131.

119. J. Smith, *Answers to Gospel Questions*, 4:64–67.

120. Joseph Fielding Smith, *Doctrines of Salvation* (Salt Lake City: Bookcraft, 1954), 2:396.

121. Haws, *Mormon Image*, 62–71.

122. Spencer W. Kimball, "Marriage and Divorce," in *1976 Devotional Speeches of the Year* (Provo: Brigham Young University Press, 1977), 144.

123. Boyd K. Packer, "Follow the Rule," January 14, 1977, *BYU Devotional Speeches of the Year* (Provo: Brigham Young University Press, 1978).

124. "Smooth Succession," *Time*, January 14, 1974, 41.

125. Prince and Wright, *David O. McKay*, 60–105.

126. Edward L. Kimball, "Spencer W. Kimball and the Revelation on Priesthood," *BYU Studies* 47, no. 2 (2008): 5–78.

127. Official Declaration 2, Doctrine and Covenants.

128. Bruce R. McConkie, "All Are Alike unto God," A Symposium on the Book of Mormon, the Second Annual Church Educational System Religious Educator's Symposium, BYU, August 18, 1978.

129. There were a few exceptions, such as a First Presidency letter in 1992 that condemned "the abhorrent theory of racial or cultural superiority." See Statement of the First Presidency and Quorum of the Twelve, October 18, 1992, quoted in *Church News*, October 24, 1992, 4. Part of the text was cited by Russell M. Nelson, "Teach Us Tolerance and Love," *Ensign*, May 1994.

130. Margaret Young and Darius Gray, "Mormons and Race," in *Oxford Handbook of Mormonism*, ed. Terryl L. Givens and Philip L. Barlow (New York: Oxford University Press, 2015), 378.

131. "Interview with Jeffrey Holland," *The Mormons*, PBS.org, March 4, 2006, http://www.pbs.org/mormons/interviews/holland.html.

132. Gordon B. Hinckley, "The Need for Greater Kindness," *Ensign*, May 2006.

133. Peggy Fletcher Stack, "Mormon and Black," *Salt Lake Tribune*, June 8, 2008.

134. Jason Horowitz, "The Genesis of a Church's Stand on Race," *Washington Post*, February 22, 2012.

135. "Racial Remarks in *Washington Post* Article," LDS Newsroom, February 29, 2012, http://www.mormonnewsroom.org/article/racial-remarks-in-washington-post-article.

136. Mario Ruiz, "BYU Religion Prof Bott Retiring in June," *Daily Herald*, March 22, 2012.

137. "The Church and Race: All Are Alike Unto God," LDS Public Affairs Department, February 29, 2012, https://newsroom.churchofjesuschrist.org/article/race-church; "Race and the Priesthood," Gospel Topics, December 6, 2013, https://www.lds.org/topics/race-and-the-priesthood?lang=eng&old=true.

138. "Race and the Priesthood."

139. Keith Coffman, "Latter-day Saints Launch 'I'm a Mormon' Ad Campaign," *Reuters*, October 3, 2011, http://www.reuters.com/article/us-mormons-media-idUSTRE7911CM20111003.

140. For example, "Nnamdi," Mormon.org, October 30, 2011, https://youtu.be/C3NaOSNSBGA; https://www.mormon.org/nnamdi. See also W. Paul Reeve, "From Not White Enough, to Too White: Rethinking the Mormon Racial Story," FAIR Conference 2015, http://www.fairmormon.org/fair-conferences/2015-fairmormon-conference/rethinking-the-mormon-racial-story.

141. Laurie Goodstein, "Mormon Ad Campaign," *New York Times*, November 18, 2011.

142. Doug Robinson, "Mr. Mia Love: The Man behind the Congresswoman," *Deseret News*, January 3, 2015. It should be noted that there are several aspects of this story that reinforce patriarchal marriage. Mr. Love explains that he does not want to be financially dependent on her career and that if he didn't feel that she could contribute to the state and country, "I'd keep her home to myself."

143. Jason Swenson, "'All Are Equal,' Prophet Proclaims at 'Be One' Celebration," LDS Newsroom, June 1, 2018, https://www.lds.org/church/news/all-are-equal-prophet -proclaims-at-be-one-celebration?lang=eng.

144. "Church Releases Statement Condemning White Supremacist Attitudes," LDS Newsroom, August 15, 2017, https://www.lds.org/church/news/church-releases -statement-condemning-white-supremacist-attitudes?lang=eng.

## CHAPTER 2

1. Victor Brown Jr., "The Critical Influence of the Father in Social and Emotional Problems. Report Number Two for the First Presidency," May 18, 1976, 6, hosted at http://www.ldspapers.faithweb.com.

2. Brown, 7.

3. Connell O'Donovan, "The Etiology of Homosexuality from Authoritative Latter-day Saint Perspective, 1879–2006," November 2006, http://www.connellodonovan.com /etiology.htm.

4. Jennifer Terry, *An American Obsession: Science, Medicine, and Homosexuality in Modern Society* (Chicago: University of Chicago Press, 1999), 307–10, 365–67.

5. William B. Turner, *A Genealogy of Queer Theory* (Philadelphia: Temple University Press, 2000), 106–38.

6. Terry, *American Obsession*, 297–328.

7. D. Michael Quinn, *Same-Sex Dynamics among Nineteenth-Century Americans: A Mormon Example* (Urbana: University of Illinois Press, 1996), 366–75.

8. Heather White, *Reforming Sodom: Protestants and the Rise of Gay Rights* (Chapel Hill: University of North Carolina Press, 2015), 1–4.

9. Quinn documents the different approaches church leaders took to punishing same-sex "crimes" as well as the increasingly strict attention in the early twentieth century. Quinn, *Same-Sex Dynamics*, 265–313, 366–400.

10. Connell O'Donovan, "'The Abominable and Detestable Crime against Nature': A Revised History of Homosexuality and Mormonism, 1840–1980," http://www .connellodonovan.com/abom.html.

11. In part, these statements against sodomy might also be understood in the context of Mormon polygamy, considered to be the height of immorality by outsiders. Anti-sodomite discourse and practice were a way of both normalizing Mormonism by uniting with shared prejudices about sodomy and deflecting criticism from polygamy. O'Donovan, "'Abominable and Detestable.'" Yet even this is difficult to demonstrate because of how infrequently Mormon leaders spoke about the issue.

12. George Q. Cannon, April 6, 1879, *Journal of Discourses*, 26 vols. (London: LDS Booksellers Depot, 1854–86), 20:200.

13. George Q. Cannon, *Report of the 68th Semiannual General Conference of the Church of Jesus Christ of Latter-day Saints* (Salt Lake City: Deseret News Publication Company, October 1897), 65–66.

14. Quinn, *Same-Sex Dynamics*; O'Donovan, "'Abominable and Detestable.'"

15. Michael Bronski, *A Queer History of the United States* (Boston: Beacon Press, 2011), 152–75; John D'Emilio, *Sexual Politics, Sexual Communities: The Making of a Homosexual Minority in the United States, 1940–1970*, 2nd ed. (Chicago: University of Chicago, 1998).

16. Allan Berube, *Coming Out under Fire* (New York: Free Press, 2000).

17. John D'Emilio and Estelle B. Freedman, *Intimate Matters: A History of Sexuality in America*, 2nd ed. (Chicago: University of Chicago Press, 1997), 288.

18. U.S. Senate, 81st Cong., 2nd sess., Committee on Expenditures in Executive Departments, *Employment of Homosexuals and Other Sex Perverts in Government* (Washington, D.C.: Government Printing Office, 1950), 3–4.

19. D'Emilio, *Sexual Politics*.

20. Douglas A. Winkler, "Lavender Sons of Zion: A History of Gay Men in Salt Lake City, 1950–79" (PhD diss., University of Utah, 2008), 49–86.

21. Fred Fejes, *Gay Rights and Moral Panic: The Origins of America's Debate on Homosexuality* (New York: Palgrave Macmillan, 2011).

22. Mark D. Jordan, *Recruiting Young Love: How Christians Talk about Homosexuality* (Chicago: University of Chicago Press, 2011), 1–27.

23. American Psychiatric Association, *Diagnostic and Statistical Manual of Mental Disorders* (Washington, D.C., American Psychiatric Association Mental Health Service, 1952).

24. Mark D. Jordan, *The Invention of Sodomy in Christian Theology* (Chicago: University of Chicago Press, 1997), 163–64.

25. Annamarie Jagose, *Queer Theory: An Introduction* (New York: New York University Press, 1996), 22–71.

26. Terry, *American Obsession*, 329–52.

27. Quoted in Sara Moslener, *Virgin Nation: Sexual Purity and American Adolescence* (New York: Oxford University Press, 2015), 62.

28. Moslener, 48–65.

29. Marion G. Romney, "Home Teaching and Family Home Evening," *Improvement Era*, June 1969.

30. Moslener, *Virgin Nation*, 66–76.

31. David O. McKay, "Only One Standard of Morality," *Conference Report*, April 1966.

32. David O. McKay, *Conference Report*, April 1959, 74.

33. Moslener, *Virgin Nation*, 105–6.

34. David O. McKay, *Conference Report*, April 1966, 105.

35. Ezra Taft Benson, "Responsibilities of the Latter-day Saint Home," *Conference Report*, October 1947. Cf. Benson, "Strengthening the American Home," *Conference Report*, October 1953.

36. Ezra Taft Benson, "America—What of the Future," *Conference Report*, April 1952.

37. Ezra Taft Benson, "Americans Are Destroying America," *Conference Report*, April 1968.

38. E. Brooks Holifield, *A History of Pastoral Care in America: From Salvation to Self-Realization* (Nashville: Abingdon Press, 1983).

39. Beryl Satter, *Each Mind a Kingdom: American Women, Sexual Purity, and the New Thought Movement, 1875–1920* (Berkeley: University of California Press, 1999).

40. White, *Reforming Sodom*, 15–23.

41. White, 17.

42. Eric Swedin, *Healing Souls: Psychotherapy in the Latter-day Saint Community* (Champaign: University of Illinois Press, 2003), 42.

43. David O. McKay, *Conference Report*, April 1927, 104; Joseph Fielding Smith, *Conference Report*, April 1927, 108; Charles A. Hart, *Conference Report*, April 1927, 139; David O. McKay, *Conference Report*, April 1929, 100; James H. Moyle, *Conference Report*, October 1929, 125; Richard R. Lyman, *Conference Report*, October 1930, 33–35; James H. Moyle, *Conference Report*, April 1933, 88. LeGrand Richards, *Conference Report*, April 1955, 122, introduced Fosdick as "one of our great spiritual leaders in the United States." At times, speakers simply referred to him as "Fosdick" since he was so well known; a full introduction was unnecessary. See, for instance, Abel S. Rich, *Conference Report*, April 1936, 113. In the 1960s, he was cited the most times; see, for instance, Sterling W. Sill, *Conference Report*, October 1962, 37 (specifically mentions *On Being a Real Person*); John H. Vandenberg, *Conference Report*, April 1967, 14; Spencer W. Kimball, *Conference Report*, October 1967, 30; Marion D. Hanks, *Conference Report*, October 1967, 59; David O. McKay, *Conference Report*, October 1967, 150; David O. McKay, *Conference Report*, April 1968, 92; and Richard L. Evans, *Conference Report*, October 1968, 52. The citations became less frequent but occur every decade through 2010.

44. N. Eldon Tanner, *Conference Report*, April 1965, 20; Bernard B. Brockbank, *Conference Report*, April 1966, 17; David O. McKay, *Conference Report*, April 1966, 105.

45. Edward K. Kimball, *Lengthen Your Stride: The Presidency of Spencer W. Kimball* (Salt Lake City: Deseret Book, 2005), 43.

46. Edward K. Kimball, "Confession in LDS Doctrine and Practice," *BYU Studies* 36, no. 2 (1996–97): 54–62. The manual *Handling the Transgressor* (Salt Lake City: Church of Jesus Christ of Latter-day Saints, 1956) indicated that public confession was not required for "young unmarried couples involved in sin" or "married couples involved in sin" so long as the sin was otherwise secret and voluntarily confessed. When the sin was publicly known, the man had to stand before the Melchizedek Priesthood meeting and confess to having violated the rules of the church, without divulging the details. Women confessed to the bishop, who then made explanation to the Melchizedek Priesthood meeting as necessary (3–4). The 1963 edition of the *General Handbook of Instructions* still discussed the conditions under which public confession of sexual sins was expected and when it could be avoided. *General Handbook of Instructions* (Salt Lake City: Church of Jesus Christ of Latter-day Saints, 1963), 106.

47. E. Kimball, "Confession in LDS Doctrine and Practice," 54–62.

48. Jordan, *Recruiting Young Love*, 1–27.

49. Winkler, "Lavender Sons of Zion," 14–48.

50. Quinn, *Same-Sex Dynamics*, 371–72.

51. Gary James Bergera, "Transgressions in the Latter-day Saint Community: The Cases of Albert Carrington, Richard R. Lyman, and Joseph F. Smith—Part 2: Richard R. Lyman," *Journal of Mormon History* 37, no. 4 (Fall 2011): 173–207. For more on Lyman's relationship, see Dave Hall, *A Faded Legacy: Amy Brown Lyman and Mormon Women's Activism, 1872–1959* (Salt Lake City: University of Utah Press, 2015), 162–65.

52. Quinn, *Same-Sex Dynamics*, 375–83. Other histories of Mormonism and homosexuality have situated the church in broader conservative Christian rhetoric. Ryan T. Cragun, J. E. Sumerau, and Emily Williams have argued that in spite of Mormonism's distinctive theological anthropology and primacy of place of heterosexuality, "the LDS Church also provides an example of responses to homosexuality found within a wide

variety of contemporary Christian traditions and engages with politics and the public sphere in ways that are largely identical to those employed by other conservative Christian groups." Cragun, Sumerau, and Williams, "From Sodomy to Sympathy: LDS Elites' Discursive Construction of Homosexuality over Time," *Journal of the Scientific Study of Religion* 54, no. 2 (May 2015): 292.

53. Edward Kimball and Andrew E. Kimball Jr., *Spencer W. Kimball: Twelfth President of the Church of Jesus Christ of Latter-day Saints* (Salt Lake City: Bookcraft, 1977), 271.

54. J. Reuben Clark, "Home, and the Building of Home Life," *Relief Society Magazine*, December 1952, 793–94.

55. Clark, *Conference Report*, October 1954, 78–79.

56. *Handling the Transgressor.*

57. McConkie, *Mormon Doctrine*, 639.

58. Allen Drury, *Advise and Consent: A Novel of Washington Politics* (New York: Doubleday, 1959).

59. Kimball and Kimball, *Spencer W. Kimball*, 381.

60. Ernest Wilkinson Diary, September 12, 1962, quoted in Quinn, *Same-Sex Dynamics*, 379.

61. Primary source documents quoted in Connell O'Donovan, "Private Pain, Public Purges: A History of Homosexuality at Brigham Young University," Recovery from Mormonism, April 28, 1997, https://exmormon.org/d6/drupal/byuhis.

62. Quoted in D. Michael Quinn, *Elder Statesman: A Biography of J. Reuben Clark* (Salt Lake City: Signature Books, 2002), 191.

63. Spencer W. Kimball, "Love vs. Lust," January 5, 1965, https://speeches.byu.edu /wp-content/uploads/mp3/Kimball65.mp3. I transcribed the audio. This speech exists in three forms. There is an audio version of the talk as it was originally delivered at Brigham Young University. Shortly afterward, the talk was published as a pamphlet in 1965 with expanded sections, clearer language, and in some cases a softer tone emphasizing the possibility of forgiveness. In 1974, Kimball delivered the speech again to the Young Adults in the Central Utah Stakes in Manti, Utah, which was published as a pamphlet in 1975.

64. Ernest L. Wilkinson, "Make Honor Your Standard," *Deseret News, Church News* supplement, November 13, 1965, 11.

65. O'Donovan, "Private Pain."

66. O'Donovan, "Private Pain."

67. Spencer W. Kimball, "A Counselling Problem in the Church," Brigham Young University, July 10, 1964, 17, Church History Library, Church of Jesus Christ of Latter-day Saints, Salt Lake City.

68. In 1968, "homosexual acts" were added to the list of sexual sins in the *General Handbook of Instructions*, the guidebook for church leaders. *General Handbook of Instructions*, no. 20 (1968): 122. In 1976, "lesbianism" was added to clarify that not just male homosexuality was subject to discipline. *General Handbook Supplement* (Salt Lake City: Church of Jesus Christ of Latter-day Saints, 1976).

69. The entire eighth chapter of his 1969 book, *The Miracle of Forgiveness*, is based on Allen's book, which he explicitly recommends. It is the only non-Mormon source cited besides news reports and a quotation from Dante. Spencer W. Kimball, *The Miracle of Forgiveness* (Salt Lake City: Bookcraft, 1969).

70. Terryl L. Givens, *Wrestling the Angel: The Foundations of Mormon Thought: Cosmos, God, Humanity* (New York: Oxford University Press, 2015), 14–16.

71. McConkie, *Mormon Doctrine*, 548.

72. McConkie, 549.

73. Swedin, *Healing Souls*, 48.

74. The subtitle of the official transcript reads, "Based upon a similar discourse to a group of L.D.S. Psychiatrists." S. Kimball, "Counselling Problem in the Church," 13.

75. S. Kimball, 13.

76. Irving Bieber, *Homosexuality: A Psychoanalytic Study of Male Homosexuals* (New York: Basic Books, 1962).

77. "Homosexuality Can Be Cured," *Time*, February 12, 1965.

78. S. Kimball, "Counselling Problem in the Church," 13.

79. S. Kimball, 14.

80. S. Kimball, 14.

81. S. Kimball, 20.

82. S. Kimball, 12.

83. S. Kimball, 12.

84. S. Kimball, 16.

85. S. Kimball, 17.

86. E. Kimball, *Lengthen Your Stride*, 86.

87. Kimball and Kimball, *Spencer W. Kimball*, 382–83.

88. Swedin, *Healing Souls*, 37–47.

89. S. Kimball, "Love vs. Lust" (audio; see n. 63 above); S. Kimball, "Counselling Problem in the Church," 17.

90. S. Kimball, "Love vs. Lust" (audio).

91. Mark Kim Malan and Vern Bullough, "Historical Development of New Masturbation Attitudes in Mormon Culture: Silence, Secular Conformity, Counterrevolution, and Emerging Reform," *Sexuality and Culture* 9, no. 4 (Fall 2005): 80–127.

92. S. Kimball, "Love vs. Lust" (audio).

93. S. Kimball, "Love vs. Lust" (audio); S. Kimball, *Conference Report*, April 1967, 67.

94. Francis M. Gibbons, *Spencer W. Kimball: Resolute Disciple, Prophet of God* (Salt Lake City: Deseret Book, 1995), 253.

95. S. Kimball, *Miracle of Forgiveness*, 77–85.

96. S. Kimball, 77–78.

97. S. Kimball, 79.

98. Terry, *American Obsession*, 43–45. See also the early ex-gay book by Kent Philpott, *The Third Sex? Six Homosexuals Tell Their Stories* (Plainfield, NJ: Logos Publishers, 1975).

99. S. Kimball, *Miracle of Forgiveness*, 78.

100. S. Kimball, 79.

101. S. Kimball, 367–68.

102. S. Kimball, 82.

103. First Presidency of the Church of Jesus Christ of Latter-day Saints to All Stake Presidents and Mission Presidents, March 19, 1970, Lester E. Bush Papers, box 12, folder 1, Marriott Library Special Collections, University of Utah (hereafter Bush Papers).

104. Spencer W. Kimball and Mark E. Petersen, *Hope for Transgressors* (Salt Lake City: Church of Jesus Christ of Latter-day Saints, 1970), 1.

105. Kimball and Petersen, 2.

106. Kimball and Petersen, 7.

107. Kimball and Petersen, 6.

108. Kimball and Petersen, 4.

109. Kimball and Petersen, 5.

110. Kimball and Petersen, 5–6.

111. Spencer W. Kimball, *New Horizons for Homosexuals* (Salt Lake City: Deseret News Press, 1971), 28.

112. S. Kimball, 33.

113. S. Kimball, 10–11.

114. Andrew M. Boxer and Joseph M. Carrier, "Evelyn Hooker: A Life Remembered," *Journal of Homosexuality* 36, no. 1 (1998): 1–17.

115. Tanya Erzen, *Straight to Jesus: Sexual and Christian Conversion in the Ex-gay Movement* (Berkeley: University of California Press, 2006), 139–42.

116. Mary McIntosh, "The Homosexual Role" (1968), in *Sociological Perspectives in Lesbian and Gay Studies: A Reader*, ed. Peter M. Nardi and Beth E. Schneider (London: Routledge, 1998), 68–76; William Simon and John H. Gagnon, "Homosexuality: The Formulation of a Sociological Perspective" (1967), in Nardi and Schneider, 59–67; John H. Gagnon and William Simon, *Sexual Conduct: The Social Sources of Human Sexuality* (London: Routledge, 1973), 176–216.

117. Bieber, *Homosexuality*; Charles Socarides, "Psychoanalytic Therapy of a Male Homosexual," *Psychoanalytic Quarterly* 38 (April 1969): 173–90.

118. Terry, *American Obsession*, 365–67.

119. Seth Dowland, *Family Values and the Rise of the Christian Right* (Philadelphia: University of Pennsylvania Press, 2015), 87–91.

120. James Dobson, *Dr. Dobson Answers Your Questions* (Wheaton, Ill.: Tyndale House, 1982), 451–52.

121. For an oral history with audio excerpts, see "Dr. Davidson and the Gay Cure," *UnErased: The History of Conversion Therapy in America* (podcast), November 16, 2018, https://art19.com/shows/unerased.

122. Erzen, *Straight to Jesus*, 22–51.

123. The letter is described in V. Brown, "Critical Influence of the Father," 4.

124. John P. Livingstone, "Historical Highlights of LDS Family Services," in *Salt Lake City: The Place Which God Prepared*, ed. Scott C. Esplin and Kenneth L. Alford (Salt Lake City: Deseret Book, 2011), 285–304.

125. Victor L. Brown [Sr.], "The Meaning of Morality," *Ensign*, April 1971.

126. *Homosexuality: Welfare Services Packet 1* (Salt Lake City: Church of Jesus Christ of Latter-day Saints, 1973), in Lester E. Bush Papers, box 12, folder 1. This was the first training manual produced for local LDS church leaders on this topic and the first in a series of specialized manuals for specialized problems. Elders Victor L. Brown Sr., H. Burke Peterson, and Vaughn J. Featherstone were behind the project.

127. *Homosexuality* in Bush Papers.

128. *Homosexuality* in Bush Papers.

129. *Homosexuality* in Bush Papers.

130. *Homosexuality* in Bush Papers.

131. *Homosexuality* in Bush Papers.

132. First Presidency of the Church of Jesus Christ of Latter-day Saints to Stake Presidents, Bishops, and Branch Presidents, December 23, 1970; First Presidency of the Church of Jesus Christ of Latter-day Saints to All Stake, Mission, and District Presidents,

Bishops, and Branch Presidents, May 30, 1975; First Presidency of the Church of Jesus Christ of Latter-day Saints to All Stake, Mission, and District Presidents, Bishops, and Branch Presidents, May 8, 1978, all in Bush Papers, box 12, folder 1.

133. *Homosexuality* in Bush Papers, 16.

134. *Homosexuality* in Bush Papers, 16, 17.

135. David A. Albrecht, "Seminar on Homosexuality," Washington D.C. Stake, December 1, 1979, p. 7, Bush Papers, box 12, folder 1. See also *Homosexuality* in Bush Papers.

136. *Homosexuality* in Bush Papers.

137. *Homosexuality* in Bush Papers.

138. *Homosexuality* in Bush Papers.

139. *Homosexuality* in Bush Papers.

140. *Homosexuality* in Bush Papers.

141. *Homosexuality* in Bush Papers.

142. Quoted in J. Richard Clarke, "Ministering to Needs through LDS Social Services," *Ensign*, May 1977, 85.

143. Livingstone, "Historical Highlights of LDS Family Services," 285–304.

144. *Homosexuality* in Bush Papers.

145. Swedin, *Healing Souls*, 52–62.

146. "Part II: AMCAP," *AMCAP Journal* 4, no. 2 (Fall 1978): 11–30.

147. Robert L. Blattner, "Counseling the Homosexual in a Church Setting," *AMCAP Journal* 1, no. 1 (October 1975): 6–9.

148. Don Lankford, "Editorial Comments," *AMCAP Journal* 1, no. 1 (October 1975): 2.

149. "Part II: AMCAP."

150. Carlfred Broderick, "New Wine in New Bottles," *AMCAP Journal* 1, no. 1 (October 1975): 30–35.

151. Victor Brown Jr., "Two Views of Sexuality," *Ensign*, July 1975, 50.

152. Clarke, "Ministering to Needs through LDS Social Services," 85.

153. The quote is not cited, but in a 1976 article Bieber makes specific mention of his treatment of 850 individuals and the importance of the father-son relationship in causing homosexuality. Irving Bieber, "A Discussion of 'Homosexuality: The Ethical Challenge,'" *Journal of Consulting and Clinical Psychology* 44, no. 2 (1976): 163–66. Further, this article is cited in Victor Brown's report to General Authorities, "Critical Influence of the Father," 17–18.

154. V. Brown, "Critical Influence of the Father," 9.

155. Brown, 9.

156. Brown, 12.

157. This theme was common in the 1970s and 1980s, but it does not appear that the advice was directly taken up in any noticeable way. However, in 1977, at least someone took the advice. Brown himself delivered a speech at BYU in 1977 titled "The Patriarchal Order."

158. Dallin H. Oaks to Elder Thomas S. Monson, September 13, 1979, private collection, http://www.connellodonovan.com/oaksmonson.html.

159. FAIR Examination 8: "Aversion Therapy at BYU—Dr. Eugene Thorne (Interview)," Fair Mormon, February 1, 2012, http://blog.fairmormon.org/2012/02/01/fair-examination-8-aversion-therapy-at-byu-dr-eugene-thorne. See also Gregory A. Prince, *Gay Rights and the Mormon Church: Intended Actions, Unintended Consequences* (Salt Lake City: University of Utah Press, 2019), 89–94.

160. Terry, *American Obsession*, 294–96, 470n31.

161. O'Donovan, "Private Pain." See also, *Legacies: A Documentary by Sean Weakland* (1996), D. Michael Quinn Papers, Beinecke Library, Yale University. Available online at https://www.youtube.com/watch?v=F8Ihx2tBris.

162. Blattner, "Counseling the Homosexual in a Church Setting," 9.

163. G. Terence Wilson and Gerald C. Davison, "Behavior Therapy and Homosexuality: A Critical Perspective," *Behavior Therapy* 5, no. 1 (January 1974): 16–28; Gerald C. Davison, "Homosexuality: The Ethical Challenge," *Journal of Consulting and Clinical Psychology* 44, no. 2 (1976): 157–62.

164. Prince, *Gay Rights and the Mormon Church*, 92–94.

165. Oaks to Monson.

166. Victor L. Brown Jr., *Human Intimacy: Illusion and Reality* (Salt Lake City: Parliament Publishers, 1981).

167. Eric G. Swedin, "'One Flesh': A Historical Overview of Latter-day Saint Sexuality and Psychology," *Dialogue: A Journal of Mormon Thought* 31, no. 4 (1998): 6–7.

168. Swedin, *Healing Souls*, 158–60.

169. Marvin Rytting, "Review of *Human Intimacy: Illusion and Reality*, by Victor L. Brown Jr.," *Sunstone Review*, July 1982, 25.

170. [Cloy Jenkins], *Prologue: An Examination of the Mormon Attitude toward Homosexuality* [pamphlet] (Provo: Prometheus Enterprises, 1978). See also O'Donovan, "Abominable and Detestable.'"

171. [Jenkins], *Prologue*, 56.

172. O'Donovan, "Abominable and Detestable.'"

173. O'Donovan.

174. BYU Executive Committee Minutes, September 15, 1977, quoted in O'Donovan, "Abominable and Detestable.'"

175. O'Donovan.

176. Derrick Sherwin Bailey, *Homosexuality and the Western Christian Tradition* (London: Longmans, Green, 1955).

177. John Boswell, *Christianity, Social Tolerance, and Homosexuality: Gay People in Western Europe from the Beginning of the Christian Era to the Fourteenth Century* (Chicago: University of Chicago Press, 1980).

178. Connell O'Donovan, "Affirmation: Singing the Songs of Our Redemption, 1977 to 2007," May 27, 2007, http://www.connellodonovan.com/redemption.html.

179. "Our History," Affirmation: LGBTQ Mormons, Families and Friends, https://affirmation.org/who-we-are/our-history.

180. "National Charter Affirmation: Gay and Lesbian Mormons," March 13, 1982, 1. Copy in author's possession.

181. Boyd K. Packer, *To Young Men Only* (Salt Lake City: Church of Jesus Christ of Latter-day Saints, 1976). This pamphlet was "retired" from publication in November 2016 after forty years in circulation. Peggy Fletcher Stack, "LDS Church 'Retires' Mormon Apostle's 'Little Factory' Pamphlet," *Salt Lake Tribune*, November 21, 2016.

182. Packer, *To Young Men Only*, 13–14.

183. Packer, 16.

184. Packer, 16.

185. [Jenkins], *Prologue*; O'Donovan, "Abominable and Detestable.'"

186. At the end of 1977, Val D. MacMurray had argued in the LDS publication *Dialogue* that the term "homosexual" "may be hazardous to your health," expressing discomfort with the way the label had come to imply a fixity of identity. MacMurray, "Warning: Labels Can Be Hazardous to Your Health," *Dialogue: A Journal of Mormon Thought* 10, no. 4 (Winter 1977): 130–31.

187. Boyd K. Packer, *To the One* [pamphlet] (Salt Lake City: Church of Jesus Christ of Latter-day Saints, 1978), 2.

188. First Presidency of the Church of Jesus Christ of Latter-day Saints to All Stake, Mission, and District Presidents, Bishops, and Branch Presidents, May 30, 1975, Bush Papers.

189. Judith Butler, *Excitable Speech: A Politics of the Performative* (New York: Routledge, 1997), 108.

190. Packer, *To the One*, 8.

191. Packer, 6.

192. Packer, 7–8.

193. Packer, 8.

194. Packer, 8.

195. Packer, 3.

196. Packer, 8–9.

197. Packer, 9–10.

198. Packer, 10.

199. Packer, 15–16.

200. Packer, 16.

201. LDS Social Services, *Understanding and Changing Homosexual Orientation Problems* (Salt Lake City: Church of Jesus Christ of Latter-day Saints, 1981).

202. LDS Social Services, 6–9.

203. LDS Social Services, 12.

204. LDS Social Services, 6.

205. LDS Social Services, 11.

206. *Homosexuality* (Salt Lake City: Church of Jesus Christ of Latter-day Saints, 1981), 2.

207. *Homosexuality*, 4–7.

208. For instance, Hartman J. Rector, "Turning the Hearts," *Ensign*, April 1981: "If children have a happy family experience they will not want to be homosexuals, which I am sure is an acquired addiction, just as drugs, alcohol, and pornography are. The promoters of homosexuality say they were born that way, but I do not believe this is true" (transcription from audio). The *New York Times* reported on these controversial remarks. "Mormon Church Elder Calls Homosexuality Addiction," *New York Times*, April 6, 1981. The video of Rector's speech and a redacted transcript are available at lds.org under the General Conference section, April 1981. The *Ensign* report (also redacted) is in May 1981.

209. "Talking with Your Children about Moral Purity," *Ensign*, December 1986.

210. "Talking with Your Children about Moral Purity."

211. Church of Jesus Christ of Latter-day Saints, *A Parent's Guide* (Salt Lake City: Church of Jesus Christ of Latter-day Saints, 1985), 1.

212. Church of Jesus Christ of Latter-day Saints, 8.

213. Church of Jesus Christ of Latter-day Saints, 19.

214. Church of Jesus Christ of Latter-day Saints, 20.

215. Church of Jesus Christ of Latter-day Saints, 25.

216. Church of Jesus Christ of Latter-day Saints, 26.

217. Church of Jesus Christ of Latter-day Saints, 26.

218. Church of Jesus Christ of Latter-day Saints, 29.

219. Church of Jesus Christ of Latter-day Saints, 20.

220. Elizabeth Moberly, *Homosexuality: A New Christian Ethic* (Cambridge: James Clarke, 1983).

221. Thomas E. Pritt and Ann F. Pritt, "Homosexuality: Getting beyond the Therapeutic Impasse," *AMCAP Journal* 13, no. 1 (1987): 37–66, 49.

222. Pritt and Pritt, 50.

223. Pritt and Pritt, 59–61.

224. Pritt and Pritt, 63.

225. Pritt and Pritt, 55.

226. S. Kimball, *Miracle of Forgiveness*, 86; Kimball and Petersen, *Hope for Transgressors*, 6.

227. Ron Schow, "Homosexual Attraction and LDS Marriage Decisions," *Dialogue: A Journal of Mormon Thought* 38, no. 3 (2005): 133–42. See also Ted's story at the officially produced Mormons and Gays website from 2012, which recounts, "One of the solutions that I was counseled that would help me with this same-gender attraction when I returned home from my mission was to get married. Well, I did get married and it didn't solve the problem. In fact, it actually made me feel worse. The Church no longer counsels that as the option." https://web.archive.org/web/20121208042918; http://www.mormonsandgays.org.

228. "An Interview with Elder Dallin H. Oaks on Homosexuality and AIDS," CBS News, December 30, 1986, https://web.archive.org/web/20101119165902/https://affirmation.org/rhetoric_on_homosexuality/oaks_interview.shtml.

229. Gordon B. Hinckley, "Reverence and Morality," *Ensign*, April 1987.

230. Rick Phillips, *Conservative Christian Identity and Same-Sex Orientation: The Case of Gay Mormons* (New York: Peter Lang, 2005), 39–41.

231. Pritt and Pritt, "Homosexuality," 64.

232. Swedin, "'One Flesh,'" 18–20.

233. Susan Stryker, *Transgender History: The Roots of Today's Revolution*, 2nd ed. (New York: Seal Press, 2017), 66.

234. George Chauncey, *Gay New York: Gender, Urban Culture, and the Making of the Gay World, 1890–1940* (New York: Basic Books, 1994), 15–28, 48–49.

235. Stryker, *Transgender History*, 118.

236. Prince, *Gay Rights and the Mormon Church*, 271–73.

237. Packer, *To Young Men Only*, 16.

238. Spencer W. Kimball, "God Will Not Be Mocked," *Ensign*, November 1974, 8.

239. Rector, "Turning the Hearts."

240. Stryker, *Transgender History*, 116–38.

241. Stryker, 138–41.

242. "The Church Judicial System," revision to the *General Handbook of Instructions* (1980), 2.

243. "Church Judicial System," 2.

244. *General Handbook of Instructions* (1983), 52–53.

245. *General Handbook of Instructions* (1989), 10–13.

246. Swedin, *Healing Souls*, 205.

1. Barbara B. Smith, interviewed by Jessie L. Embry, July 8, 1977, the James Moyle Oral History Program, Church History Library, Church of Jesus Christ of Latter-day Saints, Salt Lake City.

2. Sara Moslener, *Virgin Nation: Sexual Purity and American Adolescence* (New York: Oxford University Press, 2015), 87–108.

3. Quoted in Stephanie Coontz, *Marriage, a History: How Love Conquered Marriage* (New York: Penguin, 2005), 256.

4. Randall Balmer, "The Real Origins of the Religious Right," *Politico*, May 27, 2014, https://www.politico.com/magazine/story/2014/05/religious-right-real-origins-107133.

5. Seth Dowland, *Family Values and the Rise of the Christian Right* (Philadelphia: University of Pennsylvania Press, 2015), 25–30.

6. Dowland, 25–30; R. Marie Griffith, *Moral Combat: How Sex Divided American Christians and Fractured American Politics* (New York: Basic Books, 2017); Neil Young, *We Gather Together: The Religious Right and the Problem of Interfaith Politics* (New York: Oxford University Press, 2015).

7. Stephanie Coontz, *The Way We Never Were: American Families and the Nostalgia Trap* (New York: Basic Books, 1993).

8. Ludger H. Viefhues-Bailey, *Between a Man and a Woman? Why Conservatives Oppose Same-Sex Marriage* (New York: Columbia University Press, 2010), 122.

9. Janice Irvine, *Talk about Sex: The Battles over Sex Education in the United States* (Berkeley: University of California Press, 2004), 35.

10. Mary Frances Berry, *Why the ERA Failed: Politics, Women's Rights, and the Amending Process of the Constitution* (Bloomington: Indiana University Press, 1986); Stacie Taranto, *Kitchen Table Politics: Conservative Women and Family Values in New York* (Philadelphia: University of Pennsylvania Press, 2017); Michelle M. Nickerson, *Mothers of Conservatism: Women and the Postwar Right* (New York: Oxford University Press, 2012).

11. Phyllis Schlafly, *A Choice, Not an Echo* (Alton, Ill.: Pere Marquette Press, 1964).

12. Phyllis Schlafly, "What's Wrong with 'Equal Rights' for Women?," *Phyllis Schlafly Report* 5, no. 7 (February 1972): 1–4, https://eagleforum.org/publications/psr /feb1972.html.

13. Donald G. Matthews and Jane Sherron de Hart, *Sex, Gender, and the Politics of the ERA: A State and the Nation* (New York: Oxford University Press, 1990), 152–80.

14. Schlafly, "What's Wrong with 'Equal Rights' for Women?," 4.

15. Schlafly, 1.

16. Neil Young, "Fascinating and Happy: Mormon Women, the LDS Church, and the Politics of Sexual Conservatism," in *Devotions and Desires: Histories of Sexuality and Religion in the Twentieth-Century United States*, ed. Gillian Frank, Bethany Moreton, and Heather R. White (Chapel Hill: University of North Carolina Press, 2018), 193–213.

17. Harold B. Lee, "Maintain Your Place as a Woman," *Ensign*, February 1972.

18. Thomas S. Monson, "The Women's Liberation Movement: Liberation or Deception?," *Ensign*, January 1971, 17, 19.

19. H. Burke Peterson, "Mother, Catch the Vision of Your Call," *Ensign*, May 1974, 31.

20. N. Eldon Tanner, "No Greater Calling: The Woman's Role," *Ensign*, January 1974, 7.

21. Coontz, *Marriage*, 249.

22. Rodney Turner, *Woman and the Priesthood* (Salt Lake City: Deseret Book, 1972), 69.

23. Turner, 23.

24. Turner, 25.

25. John H. Vandenberg, *Conference Report*, October 1967, 75–78.

26. Turner, *Woman and the Priesthood*, 45.

27. Turner, 46. This view of culpability of Eve was common among BYU religious education professors at the time. See also Hyrum L. Andrus, *Doctrinal Commentary on the Pearl of Great Price* (Salt Lake City: Deseret Book, 1967), 187–90.

28. Turner, *Woman and the Priesthood*, 52–53.

29. Turner, 96–97.

30. Turner, 51.

31. Turner, 98.

32. Turner, 48.

33. See also Brent A. Barlow, "Strengthening the Patriarchal Order of the Home," *Ensign*, February 1973.

34. Belle S. Spafford, "The American Women's Movement," address delivered at the Lochinvar Club, New York City, July 12, 1974. An excerpt of her talk was printed in *Exponent II* 2 (October 1974): 1. The full text is reprinted in Gayle Morby Chandler, "Belle S. Spafford: Leader of Women" (master's thesis, Brigham Young University, 1983), 129–40.

35. B. Smith interview, 65.

36. *San Jose Mercury News*, January 5, 1975, quoted in Martha Sontag Bradley, *Pedestals and Podiums: Utah Woman, Religious Authority, and Equal Rights* (Salt Lake City: Signature Books, 2005), 146.

37. B. Smith interview, 66.

38. Jane Cartwright, "Relief Society President Assails ERA: Proposal Tabbed 'Step Backward,'" *Salt Lake Tribune*, December 14, 1974, B1.

39. Colleen McDannell, *Sister Saints: Mormon Women since the End of Polygamy* (New York: Oxford University Press, 2018), 101–8.

40. Bradley, *Pedestals and Podiums*, 94–97.

41. B. Smith interview, 67.

42. "Boycott over ERA," *Church News*, January 11, 1975, 16.

43. Bradley, *Pedestals and Podiums*, 97–99, 147–48.

44. The statement first appeared as "First Presidency Statement," *Church News*, October 30, 1976, 2. It was then republished for the global church as "First Presidency Issues Statement Opposing Equal Rights Amendment," *Ensign*, December 1976, 79.

45. Bradley, *Pedestals and Podiums*, 99.

46. Lawrence Foster, "From Frontier Activism to Neo-Victorian Domesticity: Mormon Women in the Nineteenth and Twentieth Centuries," *Journal of Mormon History* 6 (1979): 4.

47. Bradley, *Pedestals and Podiums*, 189–222.

48. D. Michael Quinn, "The LDS Church's Campaign against the Equal Rights Amendment," *Journal of Mormon History* 20, no. 2 (Fall 1994): 85–155.

49. Neil Young, "Mormons and Same-Sex Marriage: From ERA to Prop 8," in *Out of Obscurity: Mormonism since 1945*, ed. Patrick Q. Mason and John G. Turner (New York: Oxford University Press, 2016), 149–53.

50. Mark D. Jordan, *Recruiting Young Love: How Christians Talk about Homosexuality* (Chicago: University of Chicago Press, 2011), 129–49.

51. Spencer W. Kimball and Mark E. Petersen, *Hope for Transgressors* (Salt Lake City: Church of Jesus Christ of Latter-day Saints, 1970), 3.

52. Spencer W. Kimball, *New Horizons for Homosexuals* (Salt Lake City: Deseret News Press, 1971), 12.

53. N. Young, "Mormons and Same-Sex Marriage," 150.

54. Spencer W. Kimball, "God Will Not Be Mocked," *Ensign*, November 1974.

55. Thomas Laqueur, *Making Sex: Body and Gender from Greeks to Freud* (Cambridge, Mass.: Harvard University Press, 1992), 148.

56. "First Presidency Reaffirms Opposition to ERA," *Ensign*, October 1978.

57. "The Church and the Proposed Equal Rights Amendment: A Moral Issue," *Ensign*, March 1980.

58. Spencer W. Kimball, "Love vs. Lust," January 5, 1965, https://speeches.byu.edu /wp-content/uploads/mp3/Kimball65.mp3. I transcribed the audio. (See chap. 2, n. 63.)

59. Kimball, "Love vs. Lust" (1965 pamphlet), 21. This phrase is left out of the 1975 published version of this talk. However, Kimball repeated the section about civilizations going extinct because of homosexuality in his address, "President Kimball Speaks Out on Morality," *Ensign*, November 1980.

60. Kimball, "Love vs. Lust" (audio).

61. Kimball, "Love vs. Lust," July 10, 1974 (speech published as pamphlet), 17.

62. The First Presidency to All Stake Presidents in California, July 3, 1975, Salt Lake Public Communications Council Files, 1976–77, Church History Library, quoted in N. Young, "Mormons and Same-Sex Marriage," 153.

63. Spencer W. Kimball, "The Foundations of Righteousness," *Conference Report*, October 1977.

64. "Is It a Menace?," *Church News*, July 28, 1978.

65. "Unnatural, without Excuse," *Church News*, July 9, 1977.

66. According to the note after his death on January 11, 1984, Mark E. Petersen "had written the editorials in the Church News since the beginning of the publication in 1931." *Church News*, January 15, 1984.

67. "Relief Society Leader Hails Anita Bryant's Homosexual Stand," *Salt Lake Tribune*, June 11, 1977; "LDS Leader Hails Anti-gay Stand," *Salt Lake Tribune*, November 5, 1977; "Relief Society Commends Anita," *Deseret News*, June 11, 1977, B1; "Unnatural, without Excuse."

68. "House Opposes Marriage of Gays," *Deseret News*, June 29, 1977, A7.

69. N. Young, "Mormons and Same-Sex Marriage," 153.

70. "First Presidency Statement," 2.

71. "A Conversation with Sister Barbara B. Smith, Relief Society General President," *Ensign*, March 1976.

72. Spencer W. Kimball, "The Blessings and Responsibilities of Womanhood," *Ensign*, March 1976. Italics and capitalization in the original. See also Kimball, "The Lord's Plan for Men and Women," *Ensign*, October 1975.

73. Nadine Hansen, "Women and the Priesthood," *Dialogue: A Journal of Mormon Thought* 14, no. 4 (Winter 1981): 50–59, 51.

74. Boyd K. Packer, "The Equal Rights Amendment," *Ensign*, March 1977.

75. Packer.

76. Packer.

77. Andrea G. Radke-Moss, "Women and Gender," in *Thunder from the Right: Ezra Taft Benson in Mormonism and Politics*, ed. Matthew L. Harris (Urbana: University of Illinois Press, 2019), 178–207.

78. Ezra Taft Benson, *God, Family, Country: Our Three Great Loyalties* (Salt Lake City: Deseret Book, 1974).

79. Ezra Taft Benson, "In His Steps," Devotional, BYU Speeches, March 4, 1979, https://speeches.byu.edu/talks/ezra-taft-benson_in-christs-steps.

80. Radke-Moss, "Women and Gender," 196–98.

81. Ezra Taft Benson, "The Honored Place of Woman," *Ensign*, November 1981.

82. Rex E. Lee, *A Lawyer Looks at the Equal Rights Amendment* (Provo: Brigham Young University Press, 1980).

83. Maurine Ward, *From Adam's Rib to Women's Lib: A Mormon Looks at the Women's Movement* (Salt Lake City: Bookcraft, 1981), 66–78.

84. Ward, 137.

85. Ward, 138.

86. Gordon B. Hinckley, "If I Were You, What Would I Do?," Devotional, BYU Speeches, September 20, 1983, https://speeches.byu.edu/talks/gordon-b-hinckley_if-i-were-you-what-would-i-do.

87. Joan S. Iversen, "Feminist Implications of Mormon Polygyny," *Feminist Studies* 10, no. 3 (1984): 505–22.

88. Claudia Lauper Bushman, "Women in *Dialogue*: An Introduction," *Dialogue: A Journal of Mormon Thought* 6, no. 2 (1971): 5–8.

89. Caroline Kline, "Saying Goodbye to the Final Say: The Softening and Reimagining of Mormon Male Headship Ideologies," in Mason and Turner, *Out of Obscurity*, 218–19.

90. McDannell, *Sister Saints*, 87–91.

91. Dowland, *Family Values*, 129–56.

92. See, for instance, the famous "Pink Issue" of *Dialogue: A Journal of Mormon Thought* 6, no. 2 (1971). This issue was dedicated to exploring the relevance of the "women's movement" on Mormonism.

93. Claudia Bushman, "Women: One Man's Opinion," *Dialogue: A Journal of Mormon Thought* 7, no. 4 (1974): 87.

94. McDannell, *Sister Saints*, 98–100.

95. Joanna Brooks, Rachel Hunt Steenblik, and Hannah Wheelwright, *Mormon Feminism: Essential Writings* (New York: Oxford University Press, 2015), 33–40.

96. William J. Critchlow, "Women and the Priesthood," *Conference Report*, October 1965, 39.

97. Sonja Farnsworth, "Mormonism's Odd Couple: The Motherhood-Priesthood Connection," in *Women and Authority: Re-emerging Mormon Feminism*, ed. Maxine Hanks (Salt Lake City: Signature Books, 1992), 299–314.

98. "Mormonism Enters a New Era," *Time*, August 7, 1978, 56.

99. Brooks, Steenblik, and Wheelwright, *Mormon Feminism*, 33–116.

100. Sonia Johnson, "Patriarchal Panic: Sexual Politics in the Mormon Church," in Brooks, Steenblik, and Wheelwright, *Mormon Feminism*, 73–74, 78.

101. Brooks, Steenblik, and Wheelwright, *Mormon Feminism*, 73.

102. Hansen, "Women and the Priesthood," 48–57.

103. Jennifer Rycenga and Linda Barufaldi, eds., *The Mary Daly Reader* (New York: New York University Press, 2017), 65.

104. Merlin Stone, *When God Was a Woman* (New York: Harcourt, 1976).

105. Luce Irigaray, "Divine Women," in *Sexes and Genealogies* (New York: Columbia University Press, 1987), 63.

106. David L. Paulsen and Martin Pulido, "'A Mother There': A Survey of Historical Teachings about Mother in Heaven," *BYU Studies* 50, no. 1 (2011): 1–28; Jill Mulvay Derr, "The Significance of 'O My Father' in the Personal Journey of Eliza R. Snow," *BYU Studies* 36, no. 1 (1996): 98; Jill Mulvay Derr, Janath Russell Cannon, and Maureen Ursenbach Beecher, *Women of Covenant: The Story of Relief Society* (Salt Lake City: Deseret Book, 1992), 57–58; Susanna Morrill, "Mormon Women's Agency and Changing Conceptions of the Mother in Heaven," in *Women in Mormonism: Historical and Contemporary Perspectives*, ed. Kate Holbrook and Matthew Bowman (Salt Lake City: University of Utah Press, 2016), 121–35.

107. Margaret Munk, "First Grief," *Exponent II* 5, no. 1 (Fall 1978): 17.

108. Spencer W. Kimball, "The True Way of Life and Salvation," *Conference Report*, April 1978.

109. Linda Wilcox, "The Mormon Concept of a Mother in Heaven," *Sunstone*, September/October 1980, 9–15, 9.

110. Wilcox, 13.

111. Wilcox, 14.

112. Melissa Proctor, "Bodies, Babies and Birth Control," *Dialogue: A Journal of Mormon Thought* 36, no. 3 (2003): 159–75.

113. David O. McKay, "Birth Control," *Relief Society Magazine*, July 1916, 366–67.

114. B. H. Roberts, *Improvement Era*, January 1928, 184.

115. "Message of the First Presidency: Parenthood," *Conference Report*, October 1942, 12–13.

116. Samira Mehta, "Family Planning Is a Christian Duty: Religion, Population Control, and the Pill in the 1960s," in Frank, Moreton, and White, *Devotions and Desires*, 152–69.

117. Linda Gordon, *The Moral Property of Women: A History of Birth Control Politics in America* (Urbana: University of Illinois Press, 2007), 321–56.

118. Joseph Fielding Smith, *Conference Report*, October 1965, 29.

119. Letter of First Presidency (David O. McKay, Hugh B. Brown, N. Eldon Tanner) to Mission, Stake, and Ward Leaders, April 14, 1969, quoted in *Statements of the LDS First Presidency: A Topical Compendium*, comp. Gary James Bergera (Salt Lake City: Signature Books, 2007), 41.

120. Joseph Fielding Smith, *Doctrines of Salvation* (Salt Lake City: Bookcraft, 1954), 2:88. See also Smith, *Conference Report*, October 1965, 29.

121. Turner, *Woman and the Priesthood*, 236–39.

122. Phyllis Ann Roundy, "An Analysis of BYU Women Graduates' Present Status as Mothers in the Church of Jesus Christ of Latter-day Saints" (master's Thesis, Brigham Young University, 1970). Mormon birth rates generally outpaced their non-Mormon peers but rose and fell with national trends. Lester E. Bush Jr., "Birth Control among the Mormons: Introduction to an Insistent Question," *Dialogue: A Journal of Mormon Thought* 10, no. 2 (1977): 12–44.

123. Gordon B. Hinckley, *Cornerstones of a Happy Home* (Salt Lake City: Church of Jesus Christ of Latter-day Saints, 1984), 6. The official statement he refers to is from the *General Handbook of Instructions* (Salt Lake City: Church of Jesus Christ of Latter-day Saints, 1983), 77. This was an adaptation of the 1969 First Presidency letter, which had acknowledged the need to limit childbearing in some cases but advised "self-control."

124. "Birth Control," Gospel Topics, lds.org, https://www.lds.org/topics/birth -control?lang=eng&old=true. Though apostle Hugh B. Brown was opposed by the more conservative voices of Joseph Fielding Smith and his allies, Brown had laid the foundations for this doctrinal prioritization of the mother's health in 1960. Hugh B. Brown, *You and Your Marriage* (Salt Lake City: Bookcraft, 1960), 135–36.

125. Edward L. Kimball, "The History of LDS Temple Admission Standards," *Journal of Mormon History* 24, no. 1 (Spring 1998): 135–75, 149; *General Handbook of Instructions* (1978), supp. 3, p. 4.

126. First Presidency of the Church of Jesus Christ of Latter-day Saints, Letter to All Stake, Mission, and District Presidents; Bishops; and Branch Presidents, January 5, 1982, 1. Copy in author's possession.

127. First Presidency of the Church of Jesus Christ of Latter-day Saints, Letter to All Stake, Mission, and District Presidents; Bishops; and Branch Presidents, 2.

128. Kimball explicitly made this interpretation in "The Gospel Perspective on Morality," in Edward L. Kimball, *The Teachings of Spencer W. Kimball* (Salt Lake City: Deseret Book, 1982), 312.

129. Romel W. Mackelprang, "'And They Shall Be One Flesh': Sexuality and Contemporary Mormonism," *Dialogue: A Journal of Mormon Thought* 25, no. 1 (1992): 61.

130. First Presidency of the Church of Jesus Christ of Latter-day Saints, Letter to All Stake, Mission, and District Presidents; Bishops; and Branch Presidents, October 15, 1982, 1, http://rationalfaiths.com/wp-content/uploads/2015/11/Oct-15-1982.pdf.

131. E. Kimball, "History of LDS Temple Admission Standards," 149. This language of "unnatural, unholy, and impure practices" defining moral "cleanness" was eliminated in the 1991 *General Handbook of Instructions*.

132. Gordon B. Hinckley, "Keeping the Temple Holy," *Ensign*, May 1990, 52.

133. Lecia Parks Langston, *Hard at Work: Women in the Utah Labor Force*, February 2010, 16, Utah.gov, https://jobs.utah.gov/wi/pubs/hardatwork/womenspub.pdf.

134. Langston, 10.

135. Ezra Taft Benson, "To the Mothers in Zion," ScottWoodward.org, February 22, 1987, http://scottwoodward.org/Talks/html/Benson,%20Ezra%20Taft/BensonET _ToTheMothersInZion.html.

136. Benson, "To the Mothers in Zion."

137. Ezra Taft Benson, *Teachings of Ezra Taft Benson* (Salt Lake City: Bookcraft, 1988), 547–48.

138. Ezra Taft Benson, "To the Fathers in Israel," *Ensign*, November 1987.

139. Benson, "To the Fathers in Israel."

140. "I Have a Question," *Ensign*, April 1988.

141. H. Burke Peterson, "Unrighteous Dominion," *Ensign*, July 1989.

142. Kline, "Saying Goodbye to the Final Say," 219–22.

143. Gordon B. Hinckley, "Our Responsibility to Our Young Women," *Ensign*, September 1988.


CHAPTER 4

1. The First Presidency and Council of the Twelve Apostles of the Church of Jesus Christ of Latter-day Saints, "The Family: A Proclamation to the World," *Ensign*, November 1995. The Proclamation is also quoted in the next paragraph.

2. Robert J. Matthews, "Proclamations of the First Presidency and Quorum of the Twelve Apostles," in *Encyclopedia of Mormonism*, ed. Daniel H. Ludlow (New York: Macmillan, 1992), 1151–57.

3. James E. Talmage, "The Eternity of Sex," *Young Woman's Journal* 25 (October 1914): 600–604.

4. Boyd K. Packer, "For Time and All Eternity," *Ensign*, November 1993, 27–32.

5. Packer, 27–32.

6. Boyd K. Packer, "The Relief Society," *Ensign*, May 1998, 96.

7. Gordon B. Hinckley, "Women of the Church," *Ensign*, May 1996, 69.

8. Gordon B. Hinckley, "Stand True and Faithful," *Ensign*, May 1996.

9. Hinckley, "Stand True and Faithful."

10. L. Tom Perry, "Fatherhood an Eternal Calling," *Ensign*, May 2004.

11. Caroline Kline, "Saying Goodbye to the Final Say: The Softening and Reimagining of Mormon Male Headship Ideologies," in *Out of Obscurity: Mormonism since 1945*, ed. Patrick Mason and John Turner (New York: Oxford University Press, 2016), 215.

12. Dallin H. Oaks, "Principles to Govern Possible Public Statement on Legislation Affecting Rights of Homosexuals," memorandum, August 7, 1984, E. Jay Bell Papers, box 48, folder 9, Marriott Library Special Collections, University of Utah.

13. Dallin H. Oaks, "The Popular Myth of the Victimless Crime" (1974), reprinted in *Law Alumni Journal*, Summer 1975, 3–14.

14. "Archdiocese Seeks New York Accord," *New York Times*, June 18, 1984, cited by Oaks, "Principles to Govern," 7. Oaks admired the "skillful way the Catholic spokesmen have communicated this critical distinction between tendency on the one hand and practice or advocacy on the other" (7). The antidiscrimination ordinance finally passed in 1986.

15. Oaks, "Principles to Govern," 10.

16. Oaks, 15.

17. Oaks, 16–17.

18. Oaks, 18.

19. Oaks, 19.

20. "Family Manifesto," Liberty University Digital Collections, MOR 1-3-1 folder 1, MOR 1:1–4 box 1, http://cdm17184.contentdm.oclc.org/cdm/ref/collection/p17184coll1 /id/436.

21. Seth Dowland, *Family Values and the Rise of the Christian Right* (Philadelphia: University of Pennsylvania Press, 2015), 149.

22. "Danvers Statement," CBMW.org, June 26, 2007, https://cbmw.org/uncategorized /the-danvers-statement.

23. Ronald Brownstein, "GOP Leaders Embrace Christian Coalition Plan: Congress: Conservative Group's 10-Point Agenda Includes Abortion Restrictions, Elimination of Education Department," *LA Times*, May 18, 1995.

24. Thomas W. Waldron, "Christian Coalition Unveils Social 'Contract with the American Family,'" *Baltimore Sun*, May 18, 1995.

25. "Commentary on Article XVIII—The Family," Baptist Faith and Message (1998), Southern Baptist Convention, http://www.sbc.net/bfm2000/articleXVIII.asp.

26. "Church Opposes Same-Sex Marriages," *Church News*, March 4, 1995.

27. Boyd K. Packer, "Talk to the All-Church Coordinating Council," Zion's Best, May 18, 1993, http://www.zionsbest.com/face.html.

28. Russell M. Nelson, "Combatting Spiritual Drift—Our Global Pandemic," address to the 1993 Parliament of World Religions, Chicago, September 2, 1993.

29. "First Presidency Opposes Efforts to Legalize Same-Gender Marriage," *Church News*, February 19, 1994.

30. "Utah Won't Accept Same-Sex Marriages," *New York Times*, March 3, 1995.

31. David W. Dunlap, "Some States Trying to Stop Gay Marriages before They Start," *New York Times*, March 15, 1995.

32. Clinton later denounced the law. Richard Socarides, "Why Bill Clinton Signed the Defense of Marriage Act," *New Yorker*, March 8, 2013.

33. Mike Carter, "Same Sex Marriage: Are LDS Gearing Up for a Holy War?," *Salt Lake Tribune*, March 26, 1994.

34. Gregory A. Prince, *Gay Rights and the Mormon Church: Intended Actions, Unintended Consequences* (Salt Lake City: University of Utah Press, 2019), 46–66.

35. "Church Opposes Same-Sex Marriages"; Douglas Palmer, "3 LDS Officials Seek to Join Hawaii Suit," *Deseret News*, April 14, 1995.

36. "Hawaii Court Rejects LDS Request," *Deseret News*, January 25, 1996.

37. David L. Chambers, "Couples: Marriage, Civil Unions, and Domestic Partnerships," in *Creating Change: Sexuality, Public Policy, and Civil Rights*, ed. John D'Emilio, William B. Turner, and Urvashi Vaid (New York: St. Martin's Press, 2000), 281–304.

38. David W. Dunlap, "Panel in Hawaii Recommends Legalizing Same-Sex Marriage," *New York Times*, December 11, 1995.

39. James E. Faust, "Serving the Lord and Resisting the Devil," *Ensign*, September 1995.

40. "President Hinckley Meets with Catholic Leaders," *Church News*, February 24, 1996.

41. Stephanie Mencimer, "Of Mormons and (Gay) Marriage," *Mother Jones*, March/April 2010, https://www.motherjones.com/politics/2010/04/fred-karger-save-gay-marriage.

42. Elder Loren C. Dunn to Elder Henry B. Eyring, November 19, 1996, http://www.rightsequalrights.com/mormongate/church-documents.

43. Elder Loren C. Dunn to Elder Neal A. Maxwell, December 20, 1995, 2, http://www.rightsequalrights.com/mormongate/church-documents.

44. Elder Loren C. Dunn to Elder Neal A. Maxwell, March 6, 1996, http://www.rightsequalrights.com/mormongate/church-documents.

45. Elder Loren C. Dunn to Elder Neal A. Maxwell, June 5, 1996, http://www.rightsequalrights.com/mormongate/church-documents.

46. Elder Loren C. Dunn to Elder Neal A. Maxwell, March 21, 1996, http://www.rightsequalrights.com/mormongate/church-documents.

47. Elder Loren C. Dunn to Elder M. Russell Ballard, March 4, 1997, http://www.rightsequalrights.com/mormongate/church-documents.

48. Elder Loren C. Dunn, Report to the Public Affairs Committee on Same-Gender Marriage Issue in Hawaii, November 21, 1995, http://www.rightsequalrights.com/mormongate/church-documents.

49. Elder Loren C. Dunn to Henry B. Eyring, November 19, 1996, http://www.rightsequalrights.com/mormongate/church-documents.

50. Elder Loren C. Dunn and Richard B. Wirthlin to Elder Marlin K. Jensen, January 8, 1998, http://www.rightsequalrights.com/mormongate/church-documents.

51. Bob Mins, "Gay-Marriage Foes Thank LDS Church for Financial Aid," *Salt Lake Tribune*, November 5, 1998.

52. Mins.

53. "New Voice for 416: Original Backers Reject Funds from Out of State," *Lincoln Journal-Star*, October 1, 2000.

54. Prince, *Gay Rights and the Mormon Church*, 72–75.

55. Elder Loren C. Dunn to President Gordon B. Hinckley, February 11, 1997.

56. Elder Loren C. Dunn to Elder M. Russell Ballard, March 4, 1997.

57. Prince, *Gay Rights and the Mormon Church*, 76–79.

58. Robert Salladay, "Prop. 8 Lawyer Vetted First Gay Marriage Initiative with Mormon Leaders," *California Watch*, January 29, 2010. The report includes PDF files of the original letters between Andy Pugno (working for Pete Knight) and Lynn Wardle, and Lynn Wardle's communications with Elder Loren C. Dunn and other General Authorities, http://californiawatch.org/dailyreport/prop-8-lawyer-vetted-first-gay-marriage -initiative-mormon-leaders-926.

59. North America West Area of the Church of Jesus Christ of Latter-day Saints, "Letter to Stake Presidents," May 20, 1999, reprinted in "Proposition 22 Dominates California Wards' Attention, Divides Members," *Sunstone*, April 2001, 88.

60. "Proposition 22 Dominates California Wards' Attention," 88.

61. "Proposition 22 Dominates California Wards' Attention," 88.

62. BYU spokespeople explained that students would have to petition and pay for the credits. Jeffrey P. Haney, "California Group seeks Y. Interns," *Deseret News*, December 16, 1999.

63. "Proposition 22 Dominates California Wards' Attention," 90–91.

64. Gordon B. Hinckley, "Why We Do Some of the Things We Do," *Ensign*, November 1999.

65. Prince, *Gay Rights and the Mormon Church*, 77–78.

66. M. Russell Ballard, "Beware of False Prophets and False Teachers," *Ensign*, November 1999.

67. "Gay Mormon Hoped Suicide Would Help Change Church," *San Francisco Examiner*, March 2, 2000; "Gay Mormon Kills Self on Church Steps: California Man Had Expressed Anguish over Anti-Gay-Marriage Proposition 22," *Salt Lake Tribune*, March 3, 2000. Suicide has long been a recognized problem for gay Mormons. See Christopher J. Alexander, "Suicidal Behavior in Gay and Lesbian Mormons," in *Peculiar People: Mormons and Same-Sex Orientation*, ed. Ron Schow, Wayne Schow, and Marybeth Raynes (Salt Lake City: Signature Books, 1991), 257–63. This remains a central issue for many LDS who discuss this issue. See Carol Lynn Pearson, *No More Goodbyes: Circling the Wagons around Our Gay Loved Ones* (n.p.: Pivot Point Books, 2007); and Michael Barker, Daniel Parkinson, and Benjamin Knoll, "The LGBTQ Mormon Crisis: Responding to the Empirical Research on Suicide," *Dialogue: A Journal of Mormon Thought* 49, no. 2 (2016): 1–24. See also Stephen Cranney, "The LGB Mormon Paradox: Mental, Physical, and Self-Rated Health among Mormon and Non-Mormon LGB Individuals in the Utah Behavioral Risk Factor Surveillance System," *Journal of Homosexuality* 64, no. 6 (2017): 731–44.

68. "Henry Stuart Matis," Affirmation.org, https://web.archive.org/web /20060430195539/http://affirmation.org:80/suicides/stuart_matis.shtml.

69. "Brian DJ Hyer Thompson," Affirmation.org, https://web.archive.org/web/20060621060602/http://www.affirmation.org/suicides/dj_thompson.shtml.

70. "Clay Douglas Whitmer," Affirmation.org, https://web.archive.org/web/20060621043411/http://www.affirmation.org:80/suicides/clay_whitmer.shtml; "Gay Mormon Suicides Mourned in Prop's Wake," *Sunstone*, April 2001, 90–91.

71. Tanya Erzen, *Straight to Jesus: Sexual and Christian Conversion in the Ex-gay Movement* (Berkeley: University of California Press, 2006), 142–48.

72. "Frequently Asked Questions," NARTH.com, http://www.narth.com/faq.

73. *Report of the American Psychological Association Task Force on Appropriate Therapeutic Responses to Sexual Orientation* (Washington, D.C.: American Psychological Association, 2009).

74. "First Presidency Statement on Standards of Morality and Fidelity," November 14, 1991, reprinted in *Preparing for an Eternal Marriage Student Manual* (Salt Lake City: Church of Jesus Christ of Latter-day Saints, 2003), 230.

75. *Understanding and Helping Those Who Have Homosexual Problems: Suggestions for Ecclesiastical Leaders* (Salt Lake City: Church of Jesus Christ of Latter-day Saints, 1992).

76. *Understanding and Helping*, 2, 3.

77. *Understanding and Helping*, 5.

78. *Understanding and Helping*, 6.

79. Boyd K. Packer, "Our Moral Environment," *Ensign*, May 1992.

80. *Understanding and Helping*, 3.

81. Packer, "Talk to the All-Church Coordinating Council."

82. Boyd K. Packer, "Covenants," *Ensign*, November 1990.

83. Boyd K. Packer, "Ye Are the Temple of God," *Ensign*, November 2000.

84. Dallin H. Oaks, "Same-Gender Attraction," *Ensign*, October 1995.

85. Ronald D. Bingham and Richard W. Potts, "Homosexuality: An LDS Perspective," *AMCAP Journal* 19, no. 1 (1993): 14.

86. A. Dean Byrd and Mark D. Chamberlain, "Dealing with Issues of Homosexuality: A Qualitative Study of Six Mormons," *AMCAP Journal* 19, no. 1 (1993): 47–89.

87. Jeff Konrad, *You Don't Have to Be Gay: Hope and Freedom for Males Struggling with Homosexuality or for Those who Know Someone Who Is* (Newport Beach, Calif.: Pacific Publishing House, 1987); Elizabeth Moberly, *Homosexuality: A New Christian Ethic* (Cambridge: James Clarke, 1983).

88. Byrd and Chamberlain, "Dealing with Issues of Homosexuality," 49.

89. Christine M. Robinson and Sue E. Spivey, "The Politics of Masculinity and the Ex-gay Movement," *Gender and Society* 21, no. 5 (October 2007): 650–75.

90. Evergreen, "You Don't Have to Be Gay: Developing a Healthy Male Identity," conference flyer, Salt Lake City, May 4, 1990.

91. Evergreen International, *20th Anniversary History* (Salt Lake City: Evergreen International, 2009), 10.

92. Evergreen International, 10.

93. "About Us," GenderWholeness.com, http://genderwholeness.com/becomingwhole/about-us.

94. Vince Horiuchi, "LGBT Mormons Share Their Struggles," *Salt Lake Tribune*, February 25, 2014.

95. Evergreen International, *20th Anniversary History*.

96. Evergreen International, *20th Anniversary History*.

97. Steve Densley Jr., "FAIR Examination 7: Therapy and Same-Sex Attraction, David Matheson," Fair Mormon, January 11, 2012, https://www.fairmormon.org/blog/2012 /01/11/fair-examination-7-therapy-and-same-sex-attraction-david-matheson.

98. Ted Cox, "My Journey into Manhood: Undercover at a Gay Conversion Camp," *Stinque*, April 22, 2010.

99. Jeffrey Robinson, "Understanding Unwanted Same-Sex Attraction," Guard Rail, http://www.theguardrail.com/files/Understanding_Unwanted_Same-Sex%20 Attraction.pdf.

100. Evergreen International, *20th Anniversary History*.

101. Carrie A. Moore, "Christmas Spirit Celebrated," *Deseret News*, December 8, 2003.

102. Sherrie L. Dew, "Defenders of the Faith (Family)," *Meridian Magazine*, March 10, 2004. The speech was originally published in *Meridian Magazine* but was pulled because of the controversy it generated. A copy may be found at http://www.freerepublic.com /focus/f-religion/1095244/posts.

103. William H. Munk, "Disgusting, Hate-Mongering Statement," *Salt Lake Metro*, April 29, 2004, 11.

104. Mates Gold and Melanie Mason, "As Governor, Romney Faced Challenge on Gay Marriage," *LA Times*, April 29, 2012.

105. "First Presidency Statement on Same-Gender Marriage," LDS Newsroom, October 20, 2004, https://www.mormonnewsroom.org/article/first-presidency -statement-on-same-gender-marriage.

106. *2004 Republican Party Platform: A Safer World and a More Hopeful America*, 83, The American Presidency Project, August 30, 2004, https://www.presidency.ucsb.edu /documents/2004-republican-party-platform.

107. Stephanie Spackman, "LDS Church Signs Letter on Traditional Marriage," *Deseret News*, April 25, 2006.

108. "A Letter from America's Religious Leaders in Defense of Marriage," Religious Coalition for Marriage, https://web.archive.org/web/20061005024309/http://www .religiouscoalitionformarriage.org.

109. "Family Code, 297.5," California Legislative Information, http://leginfo.legislature .ca.gov/faces/codes_displaySection.xhtml?sectionNum=297.5.&lawCode=FAM.

110. Catholic activist Maggie Gallagher, the president of National Organization for Marriage in 2008, and the Knights of Columbus organized initial funding for the signature gathering to get Prop 8. William C. Duncan, "Golden Moment: California Moves to Protect Marriage," *National Review Online*, May 2, 2008.

111. Prince, *Gay Rights and the Mormon Church*, 128–29.

112. Archbishop George H. Niederauer had previously served as bishop of Salt Lake City for eleven years prior to moving to San Francisco in 2006. Matthai Kuruvila, "Catholics, Mormons Allied to Pass Prop. 8," *San Francisco Chronicle*, November 10, 2008; Jesse McKinley and Kirk Johnson, "Mormons Tipped Scale in Ban on Gay Marriage," *New York Times*, November 14, 2008. Niederauer confirmed this chain of events later in 2008 but added that he learned that LDS leaders "were already considering an involvement in connection with Proposition 8." Niederauer, "Moving Forward Together," Archdiocese of San Francisco.org, December 5, 2008. https://web.archive.org/web/20081207222650 /http://www.sfarchdiocese.org/about-us/news/?i=1505.

113. Prince, *Gay Rights and the Mormon Church*, 128–29.

114. Holland was replaced by Orson Scott Card, LDS novelist and anti-homosexual activist. See "National Organization for Marriage," Wikipedia, http://en.wikipedia.org /wiki/NationalOrganizationforMarriage.

115. First Presidency, "Preserving Traditional Marriage and Strengthening Families," June 20, 2008, LDS Newsroom, https://newsroom.churchofjesuschrist.org /ldsnewsroom/eng/commentary/california-and-same-sex-marriage. The letter instructed that it be read in sacrament meeting on June 29, 2008.

116. Mark Schoofs, "Mormons Boost Anti-gay Marriage Effort," *Wall Street Journal*, September 20, 2008.

117. The filings are publicly available at the California Secretary of State website, http://dbsearch.ss.ca.gov/ContributorSearch.aspx.

118. Bob Packer, "Letter to Stake Presidents," ChinoBlanco.com, July 28, 2008, http://www.chinoblanco.com/2008/08/in-american-defense-of-your-religious.html.

119. McKinley and Johnson, "Mormons Tipped Scale in Ban on Gay Marriage."

120. The Knights of Columbus were the main organizers of the organization Catholics for ProtectMarriage.com, which provided volunteering information and networking. See Catholics for the Common Good, http://ccgaction.org/protectmarriage/announcement.

121. The full text of "Six Consequences If Prop 8 Fails" is quoted in the response by Morris A. Thurston, "A Commentary on the Document 'Six Consequences . . . If Proposition 8 Fails'" (2008), http://www.connellodonovan.com/thurston_response.pdf.

122. "The Divine Institution of Marriage," LDS Newsroom, August 13, 2008, https://web.archive.org/web/20120324032650/http://www.mormonnewsroom.org /article/the-divine-institution-of-marriage. The document appeared only in online format on the church's Newsroom site. At some later point, this document was edited and the changes were unannounced. The edited version greatly softened the language opposing same-sex marriage as a political outcome.

123. "Divine Institution of Marriage."

124. "Divine Institution of Marriage."

125. "Divine Institution of Marriage."

126. "Divine Institution of Marriage."

127. "Divine Institution of Marriage."

128. The cited evidence included the works in this note. David Blankenhorn's *Fatherless America: Confronting Our Most Urgent Social Problem* (New York: Basic Books, 1995) is about single-parent families. Barbara Schneider, Allison Atteberry, and Ann Owens's *Family Matters: Family Structure and Child Outcomes* (Birmingham: Alabama Policy Institute, June 2005) is a policy report for the state of Alabama that compared married couples to single parents, stepfamilies, and cohabiting adults. All samples looked at opposite-sex couples. David Popenoe, *Life without Father* (New York: Martin Kessler Books, 1996), reports on single-parent families. David Popenoe and Barbara Defoe Whitehead's *The State of Our Unions 2007: The Social Health of Marriage in America* (Piscataway, NJ [Rutgers University]: The National Marriage Project, 2007), 21–25, looks at divorce and cohabitation among opposite-sex couples only, especially the impacts of fatherless families. Maggie Gallagher and Joshua K. Baker's "Do Moms and Dads Matter? Evidence from the Social Sciences on Family Structure and the Best Interests of the Child," *Margins Law Journal* 4 (2004), is the only citation that directly addresses same-sex families, and the article actually concludes that the studies are inconclusive. It states,

"Credible new research needs to be done comparing outcomes of children of same-sex couples and children of married mothers and fathers," 179–80.

129. "Divine Institution of Marriage."

130. Thomas S. Monson, "Examples of Righteousness," *Ensign*, May 2008.

131. Boyd K. Packer, "Be Not Afraid," address at the Ogden Institute of Religion, November 16, 2008, 5, quoted in Dallin H. Oaks, "Truth and Tolerance," CES Devotional for Young Adults, September 11, 2011, https://www.lds.org/broadcasts/ces-devotionals/2011-09-truth-and-tolerance?lang=eng.

132. "Interview with Elder Dallin H. Oaks and Elder Lance B. Wickman: 'Same-Gender Attraction,'" LDS Newsroom, 2006, http://www.mormonnewsroom.org/article/interview-oaks-wickman-same-gender-attraction.

133. "Divine Institution of Marriage."

134. Prince, *Gay Rights and the Mormon Church*, 161–74.

135. "Home Invasion," November 1, 2008, https://youtu.be/q28UwAyzUkE.

136. "Proposition 8 Passes, Triggers Massive Protests against LDS Church," *Sunstone*, December 2008, 76–79.

137. Mary Ann Ostrom, "Protests, Boycotts, Erupt in Wake of Prop. 8's Passage," *Mercury News* (San Jose), November 13, 2008; Steve Gehrke, "More Than Mischief: Are Recent Acts of Church Vandalism Tied to Bigotry?," *Salt Lake Tribune*, November 24, 2008.

138. Jesse McKinley, "Theater Director Resigns amid Gay Rights Ire," *New York Times*, November 12, 2008; Rachel Abramowitz, "Film Fest Director Resigns," *LA Times*, November 26, 2008.

139. "White Powder Sent to Mormon Temples in Utah, LA," *USA Today*, November 13, 2008; "First Presidency Urges Respect, Civility in Public Discourse," LDS Newsroom, November 14, 2008.

140. "Measured Voices Provide Reason, Support amid Proposition 8 Reaction," LDS Newsroom, November 21, 2008.

141. David Bednar, "We Believe in Being Chaste," *Ensign*, May 2013.

142. L. Tom Perry, "Why Marriage and Family Matter—Everywhere in the World," *Ensign*, May 2015.

143. Brief of Major Religious Organizations as Amici Curiae in Support of Respondents, Obergefell v. Hodges, Nos. 14-556, 14-562, 14-571, 14-574 (2015), 5–6, The Alliance, http://www.cmalliance.org/resources/church/Amicus-Curiae-Brief.pdf.

144. Brief of Major Religious Organizations, 2.

145. Brief of Major Religious Organizations, 3.

146. "Supreme Court Decision Will Not Alter Doctrine on Marriage," LDS Newsroom, June 26, 2015.

147. First Presidency Letter to General Authorities et al., June 29, 2015, LDS Newsroom, http://www.mormonnewsroom.org/multimedia/file/1st-Pres.-Letter-SSM.pdf.

148. Peggy Fletcher Stack, "Mormon Gay Policy Is 'Will of the Lord' through His Prophet, Senior Apostle Says," *Salt Lake Tribune*, February 3, 2016.

149. Jennifer Dobner, "New Mormon Policy Makes Apostates of Married Same-Sex Couples, Bars Children from Rites," *Salt Lake Tribune*, November 6, 2015.

150. Laurie Goldstein, "New Policy on Gay Couples and Their Children Roils Mormon Church," *New York Times*, November=14, 2015.

151. Peggy Fletcher Stack, "'Sucker Punch to My Gut'—Mormon Policy on Gay Couples Is a Year Old, but Some Wounds Are Fresh," *Salt Lake Tribune*, November 10, 2016.

152. Prince, *Gay Rights and the Mormon Church*, 260–66.

153. For example, RJH, "Behold the Broken Camel," ByCommonConsent.com, November 8, 2015.

154. The policy did not cause a "mass exodus" but was a "last straw" for many. Jana Reiss, "Did the 2015 Mormon LGBT Exclusion Policy Drive a Mass Exodus Out of the Church?," Religion News Service, May 29, 2019, https://janariess.religionnews.com/2019/05/29/did-the-2015-mormon-lgbt-exclusion-policy-drive-a-mass-exodus-out-of-the-church.

155. Prince, *Gay Rights and the Mormon Church*, 257–68.

156. "First Presidency Clarifies Church Handbook Changes," First Presidency Letter to General Authorities et al., LDS.org, November 13, 2015, https://www.lds.org/pages/church-handbook-changes?lang=eng.

157. "Church Provides Context on Handbook Changes Affecting Same-Sex Marriages," LDS Newsroom, November 6, 2015, http://www.mormonnewsroom.org/article/handbook-changes-same-sex-marriages-elder-christofferson.

158. N. Young, "Mormons and Same-Sex Marriage," 144–69.

159. Young, 148.


CHAPTER 5

1. "Suzanne's Story," Mormonsandgays.org, December 8, 2012, https://web.archive.org/web/20121208042918/http://www.mormonsandgays.org.

2. "Ted's Story," Mormonsandgays.org, December 8, 2012, https://web.archive.org/web/20121208042918/http://www.mormonsandgays.org.

3. D. Hamer, S. Hu, V. Magnuson, N. Hu, and A. Pattatucci, "A Linkage between DNA Markers on the X Chromosome and Male Sexual Orientation," *Science*, July 1993, 321–27.

4. "Evidence for Homosexuality Gene," *Science*, July 1993, 291–92; M. C. King, "Human Genetics: Sexual Orientation and the X," *Nature*, July 1993, 288–89.

5. Natalie Angier, "Report Suggests Homosexuality Is Linked to Genes," *New York Times*, July 16, 1993.

6. Dallin H. Oaks, "Same-Gender Attraction," *Ensign*, October 1995.

7. Oaks.

8. Oaks.

9. Oaks.

10. Oaks.

11. The 1993 issue of the *AMCAP Journal* was devoted entirely to homosexuality but did not use the term "same-sex attraction" at all.

12. Erin Eldridge, *Born That Way? A True Story of Overcoming Same-Sex Attraction with Insights for Friends, Families, and Leaders* (Salt Lake City: Deseret Book, 1994).

13. Google Ngram searches of "same-sex attraction" and "same-gender attraction" show that both terms appeared in the late 1970s and rose in usage dramatically until the early 2000s, when they both started to taper off. In the early clinical literature, the terms describe the kinds of attractions and do not describe a condition that one has. The dominant book titles from the 1980s and 1990s in Christian ex-gay literature all used "homosexuality" and "gay" in the titles. See Gerard Van Den Aardweg, *Homosexuality and Hope: A Psychologist Talks about Treatment and Change* (Ann Arbor, Mich.: Servant Publications, 1985); Jeff Konrad, *You Don't Have to Be Gay: Hope and Freedom for Males*

*Struggling with Homosexuality or for Those who Know Someone Who Is* (Newport Beach, Calif.: Pacific Publishing House, 1987); Andrew Comiskey, *Pursuing Sexual Wholeness: Real Help for Christians Who Struggle with Homosexuality and for Those Who Minister to Them* (Santa Monica, Calif.: Desert Stream Ministries, 1988); Frank Worthen, *Helping People Step Out of Homosexuality* (Baltimore: Regeneration Books, 1991); Joseph Nicolosi, *Reparative Therapy of Male Homosexuality: A New Clinical Approach* (Northvale, N.J.: J. Aronson, 1991); William Consiglo, *Homosexual No More: Practical Strategies for Christians Overcoming Homosexuality* (Wheaton, Ill.: Victor Books, 1991); Bob Davies and Lori Rentzel, *Coming Out of Homosexuality: New Freedom for Men and Women* (Downers Grove, Ill.: InterVarsity Press, 1994); and Leanne Payne, *The Broken Image: Restoring Personal Wholeness through Healing Prayer* (Grand Rapids, Mich.: Baker Books, 1996). Today, the terms "same-sex attraction" and "same-gender attraction" are ubiquitous in Christian ex-gay literature.

14. Oaks, "Same-Gender Attraction."

15. Ginger Hyde and Garrick Hyde, eds., *A Place in the Kingdom: Spiritual Insights from Latter-day Saints about Same-Sex Attraction* (n.p.: Century Publishing, 1997).

16. Jason Park, *Resolving Homosexual Problems: A Guide for LDS Men* (n.p.: Century Publishing, 1997); and Park, *Helping LDS Men Resolve Their Homosexual Problems: A Guide for Family, Friends, and Church Leaders* (n.p.: Century Publishing, 1997).

17. A. Dean Byrd, *Homosexuality and the Church of Jesus Christ: Understanding Homosexuality according to the Doctrine of the Church of Jesus Christ of Latter-day Saints* (Orem: Cedar Fort, 2001); Byrd, *Mormons and Homosexuality: Setting the Record Straight* (Orem: Millennial Press, 2008).

18. James E. Faust, "Serving the Lord and Resisting the Devil," *Ensign*, September 1995.

19. Name withheld, "Becoming Whole Again," *Ensign*, January 1997.

20. Name withheld, "Becoming Whole Again."

21. Eve Kosofsky Sedgwick, *Epistemology of the Closet* (Berkeley: University of California Press, 1990), 82–86. See also Alan Michael Williams, "Mormon and Queer at the Crossroads," *Dialogue: A Journal of Mormon Thought* 44, no. 1 (Spring 2011): 53–84.

22. Oaks, "Same-Gender Attraction."

23. Boyd K. Packer, "Ye Are the Temple of God," *Ensign*, November 2000.

24. Packer, "Ye Are the Temple of God."

25. Boyd K. Packer, *To the One* [pamphlet] (Salt Lake City: Church of Jesus Christ of Latter-day Saints, 1978).

26. Name withheld, "My Battle with Same-Sex Attraction," *Ensign*, August 2002.

27. James O. Mason, "The Worth of a Soul Is Great," Evergreen International 15th Annual Conference, September 17, 2005. EvergreenInternational.org, https://web.archive .org/web/20120724194231/http://www.evergreeninternational.org/2005%20Mason.pdf.

28. "Official Statement: Same-Gender Attraction," LDS Newsroom, 2006, https://newsroom.churchofjesuschrist.org/article/interview-oaks-wickman-same -gender-attraction.

29. *God Loveth His Children* (Salt Lake City: Church of Jesus Christ of Latter-day Saints, 2007). For some history behind the pamphlet, see Gregory A. Prince, *Gay Rights and the Mormon Church: Intended Actions, Unintended Consequences* (Salt Lake City: University of Utah Press, 2019), 114–17.

30. Jeffrey R. Holland, "Helping Those Who Struggle with Same-Gender Attraction," *Ensign*, October 2007.

31. See www.MormonsandGays.org.

32. "First Presidency Statement on Standards of Morality and Fidelity," November 14, 1991, reprinted in *Preparing for an Eternal Marriage Student Manual* (Salt Lake City: Church of Jesus Christ of Latter-day Saints, 2003), 230.

33. Josh Searle, "I Want What I Don't Want," *Bravely Botching Life* (blog), March 14, 2015, https://web.archive.org/web/20160806092731/http://www.bravelybotchinglife .com/blog/2015/3/14/i-want-what-i-dont-want-eternal-blessings.

34. "Official Statement: Same-Gender Attraction."

35. Holland, "Helping Those Who Struggle."

36. "News of the Church," *Ensign*, May 1996.

37. Bruce C. Hafen, "Elder Bruce C. Hafen Speaks on Same-Sex Attraction," LDS Newsroom, September 19, 2009, http://www.mormonnewsroom.org/article/elder-bruce -c-hafen-speaks-on-same-sex-attraction. This is the source of several of the quotes in the next few paragraphs.

38. Hafen cited Jason Park's self-help guide for the statistic, but Park was not a trained counselor or researcher. Ariel Shidlo and Michael Schroeder, "Changing Sexual Orientation: A Consumers' Report," *Professional Psychology: Research and Practice* 33, no. 3 (2002): 249–59.

39. For a detailed discussion, see Ronald Bayer, *Homosexuality and American Psychiatry: The Politics of Diagnosis* (Princeton: Princeton University Press, 1987).

40. Hafen, "Elder Bruce C. Hafen Speaks."

41. "Remarks by Bishop Keith B. McMullin to Evergreen International," LDS Newsroom, September 21, 2010, https://www.mormonnewsroom.org/article/remarks -by-bishop-keith-b.-mcmullin-to-evergreen-international.

42. Tad Walch, "BYU Clarifies Honor Code about Gay Orientation," *Deseret News*, April 18, 2007.

43. "Brigham Young University Revises Policy on Sexuality; Discriminatory Policy Revisited after Soulforce Equality Riders Visit," *SoulForce*, April 17, 2007, http://www .archives.soulforce.org/2007/04/17/brigham-young-university-revises-policy-on -sexuality-discriminatory-policy-revisted-after-soulforce-equality-riders-visit.

44. Julia Lyon, "BYU Changes Honor Code Text about Gay Students," *Salt Lake Tribune*, April 17, 2007.

45. "Homosexual Behavior," Church Educational System Honor Code, November 9, 2015, https://policy.byu.edu/view/index.php?p=26.

46. "The Divine Institution of Marriage," LDS Newsroom, August 13, 2008, https://web.archive.org/web/20120324032650/http://www.mormonnewsroom.org /article/the-divine-institution-of-marriage. The document later uses the term again: "We can express genuine love and friendship for the homosexual family member or friend without accepting the practice of homosexuality."

47. "Church Responds to HRC Petition: Statement on Same-Sex Attraction," LDS Newsroom, October 12, 2010, https://newsroom.churchofjesuschrist.org/article /church-mormon-responds-to-human-rights-campaign-petition-same-sex-attraction.

48. D. Todd Christofferson, "Purpose," Mormonsandgays.org, https://web.archive.org /web/20121208042918/http://www.mormonsandgays.org.

49. Boyd K. Packer, "Cleansing the Inner Vessel," *Ensign*, November 2010. The printed version of the talk changed "tendencies" to "temptations," and the question about God's

motives was struck from the text. Peggy Fletcher Stack, "Packer Talk Jibes With LDS Teachings After Tweak," *Salt Lake Tribune*, October 25, 2010.

50. Boyd K. Packer, "How to Survive in Enemy Territory," *New Era*, April 2012.

51. Curtis M. Wong, "Mormon Leader: 'There Are No Homosexual Members of the Church,'" *Huffington Post*, March 1, 2016, http://www.huffingtonpost.com/entry /mormon-leader-homosexuality_us_56d5c8a3e4b03260bf782ee5.

52. "Same-Gender Attraction," LDS.org (new update), October 25, 2016, https://web .archive.org/web/20161025204633/https://www.lds.org/topics/same-gender -attraction?lang=eng.

53. John P. Dehlin, "Sexual Orientation Change Efforts, Identity, Conflict, and Psychosocial Health among Same-Sex Attracted Mormons" (PhD diss., Utah State University, 2015), 11–42.

54. Dennis V. Dahle et al., *Understanding Same-Sex Attraction: Where to Turn and How to Help* (Salt Lake City: Foundation for Attraction Research, Millennial Press, 2009).

55. "Attraction Research Foundation Conference (Church Sponsored Conference on Homosexuality)," *Mormon Chronicles*, October 20, 2011, http://mormon-chronicles .blogspot.com/2011/10/attraction-research-foundation.html.

56. Kimberley Webb Reid, "Review of *Understanding Same-Sex Attraction: Where to Turn and How to Help*," *BYU Studies* 49, no. 1 (2010): 189–90.

57. Alan Manning Chambers, "Exodus International President to Gay Community: We're Sorry," AlanChambers.org, June 21, 2013, http://alanchambers.org/exodus-intl -president-to-the-gay-community-were-sorry/; Ian Lovett, "After 37 Years of Trying to Change People's Sexual Orientation, Group Is to Disband," *New York Times*, June 20, 2013.

58. Wayne Besen, "Former 'Ex-Gay' Activist Admits Gay People Don't Change," *Falls Church News-Press*, October 12, 2011.

59. *North Star Newsletter*, email dated March 1, 2014.

60. David Matheson, "How Do We Handle Ambiguity, Diversity, and the Unknown?," Circling the Wagons Conference, February 22, 2014, http://conferences .circlingthewagons.org/how-do-we-handle-ambiguity-diversity-and-the-unknown.

61. Ty Mansfield and Danielle Mansfield, "Living with Same-Sex Attraction: Our Story," *LDS Living*, May 22, 2012.

62. Ty Mansfield, *In Quiet Desperation: Understanding the Challenge of Same-Gender Attraction* (Salt Lake City: Deseret Book, 2004); Ty Mansfield, comp., *Voices of Hope: Latter-day Saint Perspectives on Same-Gender Attraction—An Anthology of Gospel Teachings and Personal Essays* (Salt Lake City: Deseret Book, 2011).

63. "Frequently Asked Questions," North Star, April 23, 2015, http://northstarlds .org/faq.

64. Samantha Allen, "Conversion at BYU-I Axed," *Daily Beast*, November 16, 2015.

65. Highlights of the 2012 "Love One Another" site are incorporated into the new version. See the Mormon and Gay website, https://mormonandgay.lds.org/articles /love-one-another-a-discussion-on-same-sex-attraction.

66. See the Mormon and Gay website at https://mormonandgay.lds.org.

67. "Church Teachings," Mormon and Gay, October 25, 2016, https://mormonandgay .lds.org/articles/church-teachings.

68. "Seeking Professional Help," Mormon and Gay, October 25, 2016, https:// mormonandgay.lds.org/articles/seeking-professional-help.

69. Tanya Erzen, *Straight to Jesus: Sexual and Christian Conversion in the Ex-gay Movement* (Berkeley: University of California Press, 2006), 126–48. "Therapeutic choice" is the driving principle of the Alliance for Therapeutic Choice and Scientific Integrity, a research and advocacy nonprofit similar to NARTH, with many LDS leaders, including Executive Director David Pruden, former executive director of Evergreen. See the Alliance's website at https://www.therapeuticchoice.com.

70. "Frequently Asked Questions," Mormon and Gay, October 25, 2016, https://mormonandgay.lds.org/articles/frequently-asked-questions.

71. "Frequently Asked Questions."

72. "Who Am I?," Mormon and Gay, October 25, 2016, https://mormonandgay.lds.org/articles/who-am-i.

73. "Who Am I?"

74. "Jessyca's Story," Mormon and Gay, October 25, 2016 https://mormonandgay.lds.org/articles/jessycas-story.

75. "Tonya's Story," Mormon and Gay, October 25, 2016, https://mormonandgay.lds.org/articles/tonyas-story (video clip).

76. "Ricardo's Story," Mormon and Gay, October 25, 2016, https://mormonandgay.lds.org/articles/ricardos-story.

77. "Laurie's Story," Mormon and Gay, October 25, 2016, https://mormonandgay.lds.org/articles/lauries-story.

78. "Frequently Asked Questions," Mormon and Gay.

79. "Frequently Asked Questions."

80. Susan Stryker, *Transgender History: The Roots of Today's Revolution*, 2nd ed. (New York: Seal Press, 2017), 153–64.

81. In 1995, a Utah man discovered that the woman he married in an LDS temple three years prior was a trans woman on hormones who had her testicles surgically removed. As reported, the wife was frequently represented in transphobic terms describing her transition of twenty years as "posing" and "masquerade." See "Marital Masquerade: Man Posing as Wife Is Jailed for Fraud," *Salt Lake Tribune*, July 14, 1995; and Mark L. Reece, "'Husband Knew I Was a Man,' Urioste Tells Tabloid TV," *Deseret News*, November 7, 1995.

82. J. Bryan Lowder, "The Uses of Trans in Art," *Slate*, December 18, 2014.

83. Terrence McCoy, "Pope Francis Reportedly Met With a Transgender Man at the Vatican," *Washington Post*, January 27, 2015.

84. "'Bathroom Bill' Legislative Tracking," National Conference of State Legislatures, July 28, 2017, http://www.ncsl.org/research/education/-bathroom-bill-legislative-tracking635951130.aspx.

85. Taylor W. Anderson, "Mormon Church Joins Fight against Feds' Transgender Restroom Directive," *Salt Lake Tribune*, February 17, 2017.

86. "Equality Utah Launches Video Series to Shine Light on Trans Utahns," Equality Utah, November 4, 2014, https://www.equalityutah.org/state-of-the-movement-report/item/168-equality-utah-launches-video-series-to-shine-light-on-trans-utahns.

87. Jennifer Napier-Pearce, "Trib Talk: LDS Leaders Oaks, Christofferson on Religious Freedom, LGBT rights," *Salt Lake Tribune*, January 30, 2015, https://archive.sltrib.com/article.php?id=2112602&itype=CMSID.

88. Taylor G. Petrey, "A Mormon Leader Signals New Openness on Transgender Issues. This Could Be Huge," *Slate*, February 13, 2015.

89. The 2013 edition of the *DSM* changed this terminology. Stryker, *Transgender History*, 17–20.

90. "Frequently Asked Questions," Mormon and Gay.

91. *Church Handbook of Instructions*, book 1 (Salt Lake City: Church of Jesus Christ of Latter-day Saints, 2017), 16.3.16.

92. Peggy Fletcher Stack, "After Leading LDS Congregations and Designing Mormon Temples, This Utah Dad Is Building a New Life—as a Woman," *Salt Lake Tribune*, July 30, 2017.

93. Isaac Stanley-Becker, "'He Made Me Transgender on Purpose': Breast Removal Surgery Could Boot Mormon Student from Brigham Young," *Washington Post*, August 24, 2018.

94. Sarah Barringer Gordon, *The Mormon Question: Polygamy and Constitutional Conflict in Nineteenth-Century America* (Chapel Hill: University of North Carolina Press, 2002).

95. "Transcript of Elder Dallin H. Oaks Speech on Religious Freedom," LDS Newsroom, October 13, 2009, https://newsroom.churchofjesuschrist.org/article /oaks-religious-freedom.

96. Matt Canham, Derek P. Jensen, and Rosemary Winters, "Salt Lake City Adopts Pro-gay Measures, with LDS Support," *Salt Lake Tribune*, November 10, 2009.

97. "Same-Gender Attraction," LDS.org, May 11, 2013, https://web.archive.org/web /20130511151212/https://www.lds.org/topics/same-gender-attraction?lang=eng.

98. "Transcript of Elder Dallin H. Oaks' Speech Given at Chapman University School of Law," LDS Newsroom, February 4, 2011, http://www.mormonnewsroom.org/article /elder-oaks-religious-freedom-Chapman-University.

99. "Transcript of Elder Dallin H. Oaks' Speech."

100. "Standing Together for Religious Freedom: An Open Letter to All Americans." Among the signatories is Presiding Bishop Gary L. Stevenson. United States Conference of Catholic Bishops, July 17, 2013. See http://www.usccb.org/issues-and-action/religious -liberty/upload/standing-together-for-religious-freedom.pdf.

101. Neil Young, *We Gather Together: The Religious Right and the Problem of Interfaith Politics* (New York: Oxford University Press, 2015), 284–86.

102. "Why Religious Freedom Matters: What's at Risk," LDS.org, https://www.lds.org /religious-freedom/understand/why-it-matters-whats-at-stake.

103. N. Young, *We Gather Together*, 295–96.

104. Abe Levy, "Dallas Pastor: 'Romney Lesser of Evils,'" *My San Antonio*, September 17, 2012; David E. Campbell, John C. Green, and J. Quin Monson, *Seeking the Promised Land: Mormons and American Politics* (New York: Cambridge University Press, 2014), 194–252.

105. Matthew Brown, "Q&A: Evangelical Leader Richard Land Shares Views on LDS Church, Threats to Religious Liberty, Other Issues," *Deseret News*, September 6, 2013.

106. Albert Mohler, "A Clear and Present Danger," AlbertMohler.com, October 21, 2013, http://www.albertmohler.com/2013/10/21/a-clear-and-present-danger-religious-liberty -marriage-and-the-family-in-the-late-modern-age-an-address-at-brigham-young-university.

107. "Utah Layton Priesthood Leadership Conference," Mormon Leaks, February 15, 2014, 4–5, https://mormonleaks.io/wiki/documents/0/01/Utah_Layton_Priesthood _Leadership_Conference-2014-02-15.pdf.

108. "Mormon Apostle Calls for Balance and Accommodation, Not Culture Wars," LDS Newsroom, October 20, 2015, https://newsroom.churchofjesuschrist.org/article/elder -oaks-balance-accommodation-not-culture-wars; Michelle Boorstein, "Mormon Leader

Speaks Out against Kim Davis, Urges Balance in Religious Freedom Disputes," *Washington Post*, October 20, 2015.

109. "Mormon Leaders Call for Laws that Protect Religious Freedom," LDS Newsroom, January 27, 2015.

110. "How Utah's Compromise Could Serve as a Model for Other States," NPR.org, June 1, 2016.

111. Nicholas Riccardi, "Religious Freedom and Same-Sex Marriage: How a Wedding Cake in Colorado Became a Cause," *Deseret News*, April 5, 2014.

112. Fernanda Santos, "Studio Has No Right to Bias, Court Rules," *New York Times*, August 22, 2013; Erik Eckholm, "Colorado Court Rules against Baker Who Refused to Serve Same-Sex Couples," *New York Times*, August 13, 2015.

113. Lance B. Wickman, "Promoting Religious Freedom in a Secular Age: Fundamental Principles, Practical Priorities, and Fairness for All," LDS Newsroom, July 7–8, 2016, https://newsroom.churchofjesuschrist.org/article/promoting-religious-freedom-secular -age-fundamental-principles-practical-priorities-fairness-for-all.

114. Tad Walch, "Elder Oaks Leads Special Mormon Regional Conference on 'Defining Issue' of Religious Freedom," *Deseret News*, September 10, 2016.

115. "Religious Freedom," LDS.org, September 19, 2016, https://www.lds.org /religious-freedom.

116. "Why It Matters," LDS.org, September 19, 2016, https://www.lds.org/religious -freedom/understand/why-it-matters-whats-at-stake.

117. Walch, "Elder Oaks Leads Special Mormon Regional Conference."

118. "Religious Freedom."

119. Thomas C. Berg and Douglas Laycock, "Brief of Christian Legal Society, Center for Public Justice, The Church of Jesus Christ of Latter-day Saints, The Lutheran Church– Missouri Synod, [et al.]"; Appendix: Individual Statements of Interest, A2–A3; Brief of Christian Legal Society, Center for Public Justice, The Church of Jesus Christ of Latter-Day Saints, The Lutheran Church–Missouri Synod, National Association of Evangelicals, Queens Federation of Churches, Rabbinical Council of America, and Union of Orthodox Jewish Congregations of America as Amici Curiae in Support of Petitioners, Masterpiece Cake Shop, Ltd. v. Colorado Civil Rights Commission, et al. No. 16–111 (2017), Scotusblog, https://www.scotusblog.com/wp-content/uploads/2017/09/16-111_tsac_christian_legal _socy.pdf.

120. Kelsey Dallas, "Faith Leaders Raise Their Voices in Opposing Rights of Christian Baker in Supreme Court Case," *Deseret News*, October 31, 2017; Brief for the General Synod of The United Church of Christ, The Baptist Joint Committee for Religious Liberty, The Presiding Bishop of the Episcopal Church, The Evangelical Lutheran Church in America, and The Chicago Theological Seminary as Amici Curiae in Support of Respondents, Masterpiece Cake Shop, Ltd. v. Colorado Civil Rights Commission, et al. No. 16–111 (2017), Scotusblog, https://www.scotusblog.com/wp-content/uploads /2017/11/16-111_bsac_general-synod-of-the-unitedchurchofchrist.pdf.

### CONCLUDING THOUGHTS

1. Peggy Fletcher Stack, "The Mormon Church's Newest—and Most Diverse— Apostles Say They're Just Regular People Humbled by the Calling," *Salt Lake Tribune*, June 28, 2018.

2. "'Ministering' to Replace Home and Visiting Teaching," LDS Newsroom, April 1, 2018.

3. Laurie Goodstein and Christine Hauser, "Mormon Church Ends Century-Old Partnership with Boy Scouts of America," *New York Times*, May 9, 2018.

4. "Church Announces New Balance between Gospel Instruction in the Home and Church," LDS Newsroom, October 6, 2018.

5. "Age Changes for Youth Progression and Ordination Announced," LDS Newsroom, December 14, 2018.

6. "Dress Standards Updated for Sister Missionaries," LDS Newsroom, December 20, 2018.

7. Peggy Fletcher Stack and David Noyce, "LDS Church Changes Temple Ceremony; Faithful Feminists Will See Revisions and Additions as a 'Leap Forward,'" *Salt Lake Tribune*, January 2, 2019.

8. "Couples Married Civilly Now Authorized for Immediate Temple Marriage," LDS Newsroom, May 6, 2019.

9. Deanna Paul, "Using the Term 'Mormon' Is a 'Victory for Satan,' Says President of 'The Church of Jesus Christ,'" *Washington Post*, October 8, 2018.

10. "Latter-day Saint Prophet, Wife and Apostle Share Insights of Global Ministry," LDS Newsroom, October 30, 2018.

11. Sarah Jane Weaver, "Elder Dieter F. Uchtdorf Responds to Questions, Comments, 'I'm Just Fine,' He Writes," *Deseret News*, January 17, 2018.

12. "Mormon President Russell M. Nelson's First Press Conference 1/16/18." Full video at Jeramy Richter, January 16, 2018, https://www.youtube.com/watch?v=keqbSQtqyOk.

13. Ardis Parshall, "Verse 63," *Keepapitchinin*, January 17, 2018, http://www.keepapitchinin.org/2018/01/17/verse-63.

14. "First Presidency Shares Messages from General Conference Leadership Session," LDS Newsroom, April 4, 2019.

15. "President Nelson Explains Origins of the Handbook Change," LDS Newsroom, January 10, 2016.

16. "First Presidency Shares Messages from General Conference Leadership Session."

17. Russell M. Nelson, "Constancy Amid Change," *Ensign*, November 1993.

18. David F. Holland, "Revelation and the Open Canon in Mormonism," in *Oxford Handbook of Mormonism*, ed. Terryl L. Givens and Philip L. Barlow (New York: Oxford University Press, 2015), 159.

19. "First Presidency Shares Messages from General Conference Leadership Session."

20. Robert Wuthnow, *The Restructuring of American Religion* (Princeton: Princeton University Press, 1988), 11.

21. David E. Campbell, John C. Green, and J. Quin Monson, *Seeking the Promised Land: Mormons and American Politics* (New York: Cambridge University Press, 2014), 132–64.

22. "Same-Sex Marriage," LDS.org, March 2014, https://www.lds.org/topics/same-sex-marriage?lang=eng. The above text is drawn from a letter prepared by the Council of the First Presidency and Quorum of the Twelve Apostles to church leaders in March 2014.

23. Jana Riess, *The Next Mormons: The Rising Generation of Latter-day Saints* (New York: Oxford University Press, 2019), 131.

24. Riess, 98–99.

25. Michael Otterson, "Context Missing from Discussion about Women," ByCommonConsent.com, May 29, 2014, https://bycommonconsent.com/2014/05/29/an-open-letter-from-otterson-context-missing-from-discussion-about-women.

26. Cory Crawford, "The Struggle for Female Authority in Biblical and Mormon Theology," *Dialogue: A Journal of Mormon Thought* 48, no. 2 (2015): 1–66.

27. Thomas Laqueur, *Making Sex: Body and Gender from Greeks to Freud* (Cambridge, Mass.: Harvard University Press, 1992), 149.

# Index

Chambers, Alan, 159, 193. *See also* ex-gay movement; Exodus International

Christofferson, D. Todd, 172, 191

civil rights, 3, 23–24, 29–32, 106–7, 153, 161. *See also* Equal Rights Amendment; race and LDS

Clark, J. Reuben, 19, 23–24, 63, 83

Clinton, Bill, 146, 148

Cold War, 9, 33, 58

communism, 30–31, 34, 58, 107, 116

companionate patriarchy, 119–25, 132. *See also* domestic hierarchy; gender hierarchy; marriage; patriarchal hierarchy; soft egalitarianism; submission of wives

confession, 3, 62, 73–74, 79, 222, 237n46

Correlation. *See* Priesthood Correlation Committee

cosmology, Mormon. *See* afterlife; preexistence/pre-mortal state

creation, 25, 39–43, 115, 147, 178, 181–84, 209, 216, 218. *See also* sexual difference

Critchlow, William J., Jr., 41–43, 126

"cure" for homosexuality. *See* homosexuality: "cure" for; marriage: as "cure" for homosexuality

Defense of Marriage Act, 148, 151–52, 161–62; Bill Clinton and, 149. *See also* gay rights movement; same-sex marriage

Deseret Book, 162, 179

deviant sexual activity. *See* sexual deviance

"Divine Institution of Marriage, The," 166–68, 172, 190–91, 199

divorce, 6, 29, 33, 95, 170, 172

Dobson, James, 76, 163. *See also* Focus on the Family

domestic hierarchy, 35–39, 82–84, 122–23, 140. *See also* companionate patriarchy; gender hierarchy; marriage; motherhood; patriarchal hierarchy; sexual difference; soft egalitarianism; submission of wives

Dunn, Loren, 150–52

Durant, Will, 59–60

Dyer, Alvin, 26–27

Ecclesiastical interviews. *See* worthiness interviews

Eldridge, Erin: *Born That Way? A True Story of Overcoming Same-Sex Attraction with Insights for Friends Families, and Leaders,* 179, 196

ERA (Equal Rights Amendment), 3, 16, 104, 107, 114, 119, 123, 215–16, 218

essentialism. *See* gender essentialism; sexual essentialism

Eve (biblical figure), 111–12, 120–21. *See also* Adam; fall, the; gender hierarchy

Evergreen, 158–61, 181, 184, 188, 192–94. *See also* homosexuality, "cure" for; reparative therapy

excommunication, 34, 62–63, 65, 100, 127, 171, 198–200, 208

ex-gay movement, 10–11, 16, 76–78, 80, 95, 155–56, 158–61, 179, 188–89, 193–94; and aversion therapy, 84. *See also* Exodus International; queer theory; reparative therapy; sexual fluidity

Exodus International, 10–11, 77, 155, 159, 193. *See also* ex-gay movement; reparative therapy

exogamy. *See* marriage: interracial

fall, the, 111–12, 120, 182–83. *See also* gender hierarchy

Falwell, Jerry, 107, 145, 203. *See also* Religious Right

"Family: A Proclamation to the World, The." *See* Proclamation, the

Family Home Evening, 7, 37–38, 58, 123. *See also* domestic hierarchy

family planning. *See* birth control

family values, 17, 83, 106–7, 151, 169, 203–4, 208. *See also* Religious Right

Faust, James E., 149–50, 180–81

female deity, concept of. *See* Heavenly Mother

femininity, 10, 32, 36, 82, 90, 117, 122, 135, 139–40. *See also* gender, performance of; masculinity

feminism, 1, 32, 36, 109, 114, 123, 125, 137; and homosexuality, 16, 76, 99, 105, 110, 146;

Mormon feminism, 125–29, 219. *See also* antifeminism

fluidity. *See* gender fluidity; sexual fluidity

Focus on the Family, 76–77, 159

fornication, 19, 67, 101, 153

Fosdick, Harry Emerson: *On Being a Real Person*, 60–61

Foucault, Michel, 12–13, 15, 57, 222; *History of Sexuality*, 13, 222

Freud, Sigmund, 13, 54, 59, 75–76, 79, 95, 189–90

gay (term), 156–57, 175–80, 187–92, 195–96. *See also* homosexual/homosexuality (term); lesbian (term)

gay marriage. *See* same-sex marriage

gay rights movement, 75–76, 117–18, 143–44. *See also* LGBT movement; same-sex marriage

gender, binary, 7–8, 14–15, 36, 44, 95, 99, 145

gender, performance of, 13–14, 54, 93–95, 139–40, 156. *See also* masculinity; femininity; Butler, Judith

gender confusion, 13, 90–91, 166–67, 172, 199

gender dysphoria, 95–96, 195, 199. *See also* gender identity disorder; trans issues

gender essentialism, ix, 2, 7–8, 11, 13–14, 97, 178, 215, 223

gender failure, 16, 95, 103, 155, 216, 223. *See also* homosexuality

gender fluidity, 12, 15, 40, 105, 165–66, 172–73. *See also* unisex theory

gender hierarchy, 20, 25, 41–42, 111–12, 122, 140, 173, 220. *See also* domestic hierarchy; patriarchal hierarchy; Proclamation, the

gender identity, 12–14, 41, 90, 94, 97–99, 135, 158–60, 183–84, 193–95, 197

gender identity disorder, 100, 199. *See also* gender dysphoria; trans issues

gender instability, 54, 78, 110, 173. *See also* gender inversion; homosexuality

gender inversion, 90, 97–99, 189. *See also* gender instability; homosexuality

gender purity, 22, 32, 35, 112, 123, 127, 135, 141–42

gender segregation, 109, 122, 126–27. *See also* domestic hierarchy

God Loveth His Children, 185–86, 188

Graham, Billy, 58, 107. *See also* Religious Right

Hafen, Bruce C., 188–90

Hansen, Nadine, 127–28

Hawaii, same-sex marriage in, 147–51, 153, 162–64, 200. *See also* gay rights movement; same-sex marriage

Heavenly Mother, 128–29, 218

heteronormativity, 1, 8, 73–74, 95, 98–99, 103, 155, 168, 176, 178, 182, 184, 200, 208–9, 215. *See also* heterosexual order

heterosexual order: as defining norm in LDS, 13, 17, 103, 137, 141–42, 187, 218–19. *See also* heteronormativity; patriarchal order

Hinckley, Gordon B., 43, 48–49, 124, 131, 134, 136–42, 149–50, 177; on homosexuality, 96–97, 149–50, 152–53, 161–62, 180. *See also* Proclamation, the

Holland, Jeffrey R., 48–49, 164, 186, 188

homophobia, 9, 63, 166–68

homosexual/homosexuality (terms), 3, 57, 63, 60–66, 89, 156–57, 176–81, 187–92, 195, 216–17. *See also* gay (term); homosexuality; lesbian (term)

homosexuality: and aversion therapy, 78, 84; as contagion, 55–56, 65–66, 71, 73–75, 149–50, 172, 188–89; "cure" for, 54–55, 66–68, 79, 91, 96–97, 155, 158, 184–86, 215–17; as inborn, 177–78, 180, 182–84; invention of, 12, 15, 54, 61, 62–66; moral theories of, 16, 53–54, 62, 65, 78, 87–92, 101–2; pathologizing of, 57, 66–68, 71, 75, 82, 154–55, 189. *See also* American Psychiatric Association; gay (term); gender instability; gender inversion; homosexual/homosexuality (terms); lesbian (term); reparative therapy; same-gender attraction/same-sex attraction; sodomy; third sex

homosexual predatory recruitment, 116, 144, 157, 166–67, 188–89

NARTH (National Association for Research and Therapy of Homosexuals), 11, 154–55, 158–59. *See also* Exodus International; reparative therapy

Native Americans, 19, 22, 27–28, 46, 213. *See also* marriage: interracial; race and LDS

Nelson, Russell M., 52, 147–48, 163, 171, 211–12

New Testament, 39, 221

New Thought movements, 60, 66, 156

Nicolosi, Joseph, 154–55, 159–60, 193. *See also* NARTH

Oaks, Dallin H., on homosexuality, 84–85, 96–97, 143–50, 157, 167–68, 177–85, 187–91, 212; on religious freedom and LGBT rights, 201–6; on transgender issues, 198,

Obama, Barack, 203–4

*Obergefell v. Hodges*, 169–71. *See also* same-sex marriage

one-sex model, 12–13, 117, 222.

oral sex, 133–34, 214. *See also* marriage: sexual relations within

ordination, 9, 22, 27, 41, 126–29, 171, 199, 220–21. *See also* priesthood

Otterson, Michael, 191, 221

Pacific Islanders, 29, 213. *See also* Polynesians

Packer, Boyd K.: on homosexuality, 87–92, 97, 99, 147, 156–57, 167, 183–84, 191–92; on gender roles, 140, on Equal Rights Amendment, 121–22; on transgender, 97, 99

parenting, 37, 76, 139–40; and homosexuality, 53–54, 82–83, 88, 91, 92–96, 101–2

Park, Jason, 180, 188

pastoral counseling, 16, 19, 60–62, 64, 69–72, 78, 80–81, 89, 91–92, 96, 156, 158

pastoral therapy. *See* pastoral counseling

patriarchal hierarchy, 2–3, 33, 35, 38, 53, 58, 83–84, 106, 201, 214. *See also* companionate patriarchy; domestic hierarchy; gender hierarchy

patriarchal order of marriage, 2, 7, 17, 35, 37–39, 83, 103, 105–6, 109–12, 124, 131, 137, 139–42, 214. *See also* heterosexual order

patriarchy. *See* companionate patriarchy; patriarchal hierarchy; patriarchal order of marriage

Peale, Norman Vincent, 61, 66

Perry, L. Tom, 142, 169, 204–5

Petersen, Mark E., and homosexuality, 64, 69, 72–73, 116, 118–19, 144; and polygamy, 34; and race, 24–26, 28

petting, 67, 101

Phillips, Jack, 205, 207

plural marriage. *See* polygamy

polygamy, 5–7, 33–34, 105, 130, 201, 212. *See also* monogamy

Polynesians, 27–28. *See also* marriage: interracial; Pacific Islanders

preexistence/pre-mortal state, 23, 25–27, 39–43, 45, 47–48, 126, 139–40, 181–82, 187, 218. *See also* intelligences

priesthood: and race, 29–30, 32–33, 46–49; and women, 37, 41, 126, 128, 199, 221. *See also* ordination

Priesthood Correlation Committee, 37–39, 78, 106, 109, 127

Prince, Gregory A., 5, 9

Pritt, Ann and Thomas, 95–97

Proclamation, the, 7, 138–40, 142, 145–47, 149, 154, 162, 170–71, 176, 177, 178. *See also* Hinckley, Gordon B.

procreation, 44, 130–32, 144–45, 166, 183, 214. *See also* birth control; marriage: sexual relations within

Proctor, Maurine. *See* Ward, Maurine

Proposition 8, 3, 161–65, 168–69, 201–2. *See also* California, same-sex marriage in; gay rights movement

Proposition 22, 151–55, 161, 163. *See also* California, same-sex marriage in; gay rights movement

Pruden, David, 188, 193. *See also* Evergreen

psychology: and homosexuality, 1, 3, 53–57, 60–63, 75–77, 85–87; and Mormonism, 7, 16–17, 60–63, 66–74, 77–85. *See also*

companionate patriarchy; domestic hierarchy; patriarchal order of marriage
suicide: individual, 153–54; national/ civilizational, 144, 150. *See also* socio-sexual myth of civilizational decline

Talmage, James E., 42, 66, 139
therapy. *See* aversion therapy; pastoral counseling; reparative therapy
third sex, 45, 71, 98. *See also* homosexuality
transgender (term), 195, 197–99
trans issues, 1, 97–101, 197–200, 208; and bathroom bills, 197–98, 200, 208–9. *See also* gender dysphoria; gender identity disorder; LGBT movement; transgender (term); transsexual (term)
transsexual (term), 97–101, 197
Turner, Rodney, 41–42, 110–12, 120, 125, 128; *Woman and the Priesthood*, 111, 125–26

*Understanding and Changing Homosexual Orientation Problems*, 92, 93. *See also* reparative therapy

*Understanding and Helping Those Who Have Homosexual Problems*, 155–57. *See also* reparative therapy
unisex theory, 16, 112, 115, 117, 121–22, 137, 214–16. *See also* gender fluidity

Values Institute, 84–86, 143
Victorian sexual morality, 7, 33, 70, 79, 215
Viefues-Bailey, Ludger H., 10, 106

Ward, Maurine: *From Adam's Rib to Women's Lib: A Mormon Looks at the Women's Movement*, 123–24
Welfare Services. *See* LDS Social Services
white supremacy, 20–27, 52
Wickman, Lance, 185, 205–6
Wilkinson, Ernest, 46, 64–66
World War II, impact of, on gender roles, 6, 32–33, 140
Worthen, Frank, 77–78, 159
worthiness interviews, 19, 64–65, 72, 79, 132–34, 219. *See also* Brigham Young University

www.ingramcontent.com/pod-product-compliance
Lightning Source LLC
Chambersburg PA
CBHW030343270326
41926CB00009B/942